Aerial view of the pyramids at Gizeh

The Author

JOHN ARTHUR THOMPSON has for long made a special study of Biblical archaeology. For a number of years he was Director of the Australian Institute of Archaeology in Melbourne. While in Melbourne he also lectured in the School of Semitic Studies at the University, and in Old Testament and Hebrew in two of the Theological Colleges at various times. He has had practical experience of archaeological field-work with the American Schools of Oriental Research at the sites of Roman Jericho and Dibon. And as Lecturer in Old Testament Studies in the Baptist Theological College of New South Wales he knows how to relate the findings of archaeology to the wider interests of Biblical study. Mr. Thompson holds degrees from the University of Queensland and the University of Melbourne in science, the arts, and theology. During 1961 and 1962 he undertook additional study in theology at Cambridge University.

THE BIBLE AND ARCHAEOLOGY

THE BIBLE AND
ARCHAEOLOGY

by J. A. Thompson

Lecturer in Biblical Archaeology
University of Melbourne

Wm. B. Eerdmans Publishing Co., Grand Rapids, Michigan

THE BIBLE AND ARCHAEOLOGY

Reprinted, November 1968

PHOTOLITHOPRINTED BY GRAND RAPIDS BOOK MANUFACTURERS, INC.
GRAND RAPIDS, MICHIGAN, UNITED STATES OF AMERICA
1968

To Marion, my Parents, and my
past and present Students

PREFACE

The present volume contains the material which formerly appeared in the three smaller Pathway Books *Archaeology and the Old Testament* (1957, 2nd. ed., 1959), *Archaeology and the Pre-Christian Centuries* (1958, 2nd ed., 1959), and *Archaeology and the New Testament* (1960). These smaller volumes have now been brought together into one volume with some rearrangement, and with the addition of more recent information, new maps and numerous relevant and excellent photographs. Reference to more recent works is made in footnotes, and additional quotations from the ancient records of the Near East have been woven into the text.

The aim of the volume is to provide a concise resumé of the information that is now available for the study of the Biblical records as a result of many years of excavation in Bible lands. In so short a compass there can be no pretense of being exhaustive. Indeed many important items have been mentioned only in passing, and significant books in French and German with their wealth of detail have been given very scant mention. Many have not even been cited. This results from the fact that this volume is intended in the first place for English-speaking readers who are not familiar with other languages. In a few cases the footnotes will point to some of these works. But the Bibliography at the end of this volume will provide a list of larger works in many of which the diligent reader will find comprehensive reading lists.

It is some gratification to the author to discover that the material of the three Pathway Books, which originally comprised courses of lecture given in theological college, Bible college, and university classes in Australia in the past decade, should prove of value to similar classes in America.

Special acknowledgment should again be made of the help given by the author's wife in the preparation of this composite volume and also of the encouragement of the Publishers.

The author's hope is that this larger volume will continue to prove useful to students who are learning their first lessons in Biblical Archaeology.

—J.A.T.

Book layout and picture editing by Cornelius Lambregtse
Maps by Macy Schwarz
Jacket and symbol designs by Jack Wells

TABLE OF CONTENTS

Contents

Contents

Contents

Contents

LIST OF ILLUSTRATIONS

xvii

Illustrations

xviii

Illustrations

Illustrations

exaggerated claims for archaeology or try to make it fill a role for which it is unsuited. For all the light that archaeology throws upon the text, language and narrative of the Bible, it is improper, and in any case unnecessary, to appeal to it to "prove" the Bible. Archaeology has indeed corroborated the substantial historicity of the biblical record from the patriarchal period to the apostolic age, but it is not by archaeology that the essential message of the Bible can be verified.

Sometimes, indeed, archaeology has made the interpretation of the biblical narrative more difficult rather than less so. It has happened at times that an earlier phase of research has appeared to solve one particular problem satisfactorily, whereas later study has thrown the whole question into the melting-pot again. This has happened, for example, with Professor Garstang's interpretation of the Joshua story in the light of his Jericho excavations, and with Sir William Ramsay's solution of the Quirinius problem in St. Luke's Gospel.

There is no finality in biblical archaeology. As more pieces of the jigsaw puzzle come to light, we see that we have sometimes put previously discovered pieces into the wrong place and produced a distorted pattern. Archaeological surveys for the Bible student must therefore be subjected to repeated revision in the light of new knowledge. Such a revision now lies before us, and it is to be hoped that Mr. Thompson's survey will have many readers, and will guide them to a better understanding of the Bible story.

— F. F. BRUCE

University of Manchester

FOREWORD

The three shorter studies which have been brought together in this volume were first published in a series called Pathway Books. As I was one of the consulting editors of that series, I have a prior interest in introducing this work; but that is not my principal reason for doing so. My principal reason is that I believe this work, now revised, brought up to date, and so lavishly illustrated, to be a very useful handbook for Bible readers.

Mr. Thompson has for long made a special study of biblical archaeology. For a number of years he was Director of the Australian Institute of Archaeology in Melbourne. He has had practical experience of archaeological field-work with the American Schools of Oriental Research at the sites of Roman Jericho and Dibon. And as lecturer in Old Testament Studies in a theological school he knows how to relate the findings of archaeology to the wider interests of biblical study.

Archaeology certainly makes an important contribution to the study of the Bible. Large areas, especially of the Old Testament, have been so greatly illuminated by it that it is not easy to imagine what readers made of them before the days of biblical archaeology. Yet the scale of its contribution can be exaggerated, and it is one of the merits of Mr. Thompson's book that it does not make

Illustrations

xxi

Illustrations

LIST OF MAPS

LIST OF CHARTS

LIST OF ABBREVIATIONS

AASOR: *Annual of the American Schools of Oriental Research*
AJA: *American Journal of Archaeology*
ANET: *Ancient Near Eastern Texts*
BA: *Biblical Archaeologist*
BASOR: *Bulletin of the American Schools of Oriental Research*
BJRL: *Bulletin of the John Rylands Library*
ICC: *International Critical Commentary*
IEJ: *Israel Exploration Journal*
JBL: *Journal of Biblical Literature*
JNES: *Journal of Near Eastern Studies*
QDAP: *Quarterly of the Department of Antiquities of Palestine*
RB: *Revue Biblique*
VT: *Vetus Testamentum*

THE BIBLE AND ARCHAEOLOGY

INTRODUCTION

One:

BIBLICAL ARCHAEOLOGY TODAY

I N THE PAST QUARTER OF A CENTURY A NEW SUBJECT HAS ENTERED the curriculum of Bible colleges and theological colleges. It is Biblical Archaeology. Its importance is beyond dispute. It is a vital branch of general Biblical research, which has made tremendous progress in recent years. One outstanding worker in the field of Biblical archaeology and general Biblical research has recently written:

> There are few fields of human knowledge where the progress of discovery makes constant revision of handbooks and other aids to study more necessary than in biblical research.[1]

Biblical archaeology has all the fascination of the science of archaeology, which seeks to unravel the story of past ages by digging up their material remains. But it has the added interest that through this study we are better able to understand and interpret the textbook of our faith. Not the least fascinating part of these modern

---

1. G. E. Wright and F. V. Filson, *Westminster Historical Atlas* (London, 1953), opening article by W. F. Albright, p. 9.

3

studies is that they go far towards authenticating the history of the written records which are the basis of our faith. Of course, it is impossible to authenticate archaeologically all that is in the Bible. Many of its statements lie beyond the sphere of archaeological investigation. No excavator can comment, in terms of his science, on the simple statement: "Abraham believed God, and it was counted unto him for righteousness." But in its own sphere this science does much for the student of the sacred record.

THE VALUE OF BIBLICAL ARCHAEOLOGY

When we extract from the field of general archaeology all the material that is relevant to the Bible, and then organize our material into a formal study, we have the substance of a course in Biblical archaeology. Such material has significance for the Bible student in at least four ways.

In the first place, it provides the general background of the history of the Bible. It is not sufficient merely to read the Bible if we wish to appreciate the significance of its narratives. The men of Bible history lived in an environment. Abraham, for example, moved in a world that had its own peculiar customs. It is necessary for us to learn from non-Biblical information what this world of his was like if we would understand more clearly the significance of the things he said and did. We realize that the picture we get of Abraham is not artificial, for the archaeologist shows that he was typical of tens of thousands long ago. The same kind of thing could be said of Joseph, Moses, Joshua, David, and the whole family of Bible personalities.

Secondly, the Bible is by no means a complete record. It would take a whole library to recount all the events necessary to give a complete account of the experiences of God's people. But there is now a vast amount of non-Biblical material available to supplement our Bible story. The Bible historians selected only certain aspects of the life of a man. They did not aim to give us a complete picture. They simply wrote about what was important for their purpose and passed over other things in silence. The archaeologist helps us to fill out the picture. We learn, for example, that King Omri, dismissed in six verses in the book of Kings, was known to the Assyrians and was the conqueror of Moab. We discover that King Ahab sent a large contingent of troops to a great battle against the Assyrians. Neither of these facts is mentioned in the Bible. These

4

and many other items of information are made available to us by the archaeologist.

Then, thirdly, Biblical archaeology helps us in the translation and explanation of many passages in the Bible that are hard to understand. Sometimes we find a word in a kindred language that gives an alternative meaning which will suit the Bible context better. Sometimes we learn that the Bible has preserved valuable geographical information which we have missed because we did not understand. At other times we gain a completely new impression of a passage in the light of fuller historical knowledge.

Finally, it is perfectly true to say that Biblical archaeology has done a great deal to correct the impression that was abroad at the close of the last century and in the early part of this century, that Biblical history was of doubtful trustworthiness in many places. If one impression stands out more clearly than any other today, it is that on all hands the over-all historicity of the Old Testament tradition is admitted. In this connection the words of W. F. Albright may be quoted: "There can be no doubt that archaeology has confirmed the substantial historicity of Old Testament tradition."[2]

Even if some writers want to speak of divergences from the historical picture, they do so with caution and admit that there is no serious modification of that picture.

THE SOURCES OF INFORMATION

The archaeologist obtains his information from material objects left behind by the people of those far-off days. They are to be found in the ruined towns, graves, and inscriptions of the people. The objects now investigated by the excavator may be either quite exposed to human view even today, or covered up completely or partially by earth.

There are numerous structures that are still quite exposed. We need only refer to the pyramids and temples of Egypt, the Parthenon and other structures on the Acropolis in Athens, the great ziggurat at Ur of the Chaldees, various Roman temples, aqueducts, roads, and the like, scattered all over the East as well as in Europe, and the massive Crusader castles still to be seen in many lands. These buildings are more or less completely exposed and their inscriptions, art work,

2. W. F. Albright, *Archaeology and the Religion of Israel* (Baltimore, 1955), p 176.

and general architectural features are readily available to the archaeologist.

Some buildings are partly covered and need to be cleaned up. Perhaps debris has gathered about their lower portions. This has to be cleared away before the complete structure is visible. Some of the buildings already referred to required a certain amount of clearing before they could be made to tell their story.

The completely covered remains, however, are the ones that require the skill of the trained excavator. How did they become covered? By a variety of means. Perhaps the buildings lay in the lower part of a town in early times. Once the town was deserted, the rains brought silt down from the hills around, which, in the course of centuries, covered the town. The market place at Athens and the forum at Rome were covered in this way.

Perhaps a town would be overwhelmed by such means as volcanic ash. This was the fate of Pompeii and Herculaneum near to modern Naples, in A. D. 79. Today the archaeologist can clear away the ash and view a Roman town of the first century A. D.

Some of the covered remains are in tombs and graves. These are very important because when people in the ancient world buried

Ruins of an early Christian church in Faras East, Sudan. (Courtesy, UNESCO/Keating/1960)

their dead, they placed in the grave objects that they believed would be needed by their departed friends in the afterlife. It is from graves that we obtain many of our fine museum pieces. There was no reason for them to be broken since they were protected by the walls of the tomb.

The most important type of covered ruin is that in which we find the remains of several towns one on top of the other. To us moderns this is strange. But in the ancient world, when a walled town was burned, or beaten down by battering rams, or destroyed by an earthquake, the newcomers who rebuilt the town did not remove the debris and the foundations of the old city. They selected the best material for re-use, leveled off the remains, and rebuilt on top of them. Some feet of debris from the previous town would thus be sealed off. The general pattern of houses and streets would remain, and a great many small items would be left in the rubbish.

Most of the towns in Palestine known to us in the Bible are of this type — Bethel, Jericho, Samaria, Jerusalem, Megiddo, Bethshan, Bethshemesh, Debir, Gezer, and so on. Some of these towns had ten or twelve or even twenty strata of destroyed towns. Each recounts its own story. When the whole is excavated by cutting large trenches across the mound and comparing the finds, the story of the town slowly emerges. These sites are known to the archaeologist as "tells" or "mounds."

These, then, are the sources from which the excavator reconstructs his story. The items that speak are the ruined buildings with their walls and rooms and floors, the pottery, the metal implements and tools, the weapons, the ivory work, the glass, coins, jewelry, the inscribed and written material, whether it be on stone, bone, or baked clay. Indeed, any item at all contributes to the final picture.

Among the most significant of the finds in an excavation are the written records, letters, receipts, census lists, contracts, and literary pieces, written on stone, broken pottery, leather, or papyrus. Material like this has been found in caves, wrapped around mummies, lying about in ruined buildings, or cast out on a rubbish heap. Such perishable material as leather and papyrus requires a dry climate, so that it is normally found only in Egypt above the level of the Nile floods, or in the dry parts of Palestine. Inscriptions in stone are likely to be found anywhere. Often inscriptions were filled with lead, but sometimes they were little more than scratches on the rock (*graffiti*). Occasionally written information was painted on the wall of a tomb, or marked in carbon on a coffin or a wall. Although this written material lacks popular appeal, it is possibly the most important of all the information that can be recovered from an ancient civilization, for it records the names of people and places and gives detailed information of events, laws, and customs.

Coins fall into a special class, for they are of value, not only in dating remains, but they also contain in themselves valuable historical material. They were important instruments of the propaganda machine in the ancient world, and a study of them gives us a good deal of information about the appearance of kings and emperors, as well as about events. There are several references to coins in the New Testament as, for example, the one where Jesus was questioned about the payment of taxes and He asked to see a coin. This was the occasion for an important lesson in loyalty: "Render therefore unto Caesar the things which are Caesar's; and unto God the things that are God's" (Matt. 22:21).

Finally, after several seasons of work, the story is told. The Biblical archaeologist hastens to discover whether there are important items in the report of the excavator that bear on Bible history, and that will be of use in one of the ways we have suggested above.

Biblical Archaeology and the New Testament

The average Bible reader sometimes gains the impression that the spectacular discoveries of the archaeologist apply only to the Old Testament. This is a serious misunderstanding. The New Testament, too, has benefited greatly from archaeological discovery. There lies to the credit of the modern excavator an impressive array of material that has not only thrown light on the history of the New Testament period but that has also had important repercussions in the field of New Testament study generally. It is not too much to claim that there have been important modifications brought about in scholarly theories about the New Testament, almost entirely as a result of archaeological discovery. We shall notice some of these in this volume.

There is probably a good reason for the development of the idea that archaeology has little to say about the New Testament. The really significant discoveries that bear upon it are not nearly so striking as those that refer to the Old Testament. Many people who know very little about Bible history would nevertheless have heard of Sir Leonard Woolley and his excavations at Ur, the home of Abraham, or of Professor Garstang and his work at Jericho. Again, the excavations of Professor Koldewey at Babylon, the capital of the famous Nebuchadnezzar, seem to be commonplace in history books. The achievements of the great Assyrians have been known for over a century now since Sir Henry Layard, H. Rassam, and George Smith carried out their remarkable researches in the ruins of Nineveh and Nimrud. But all of these are of interest chiefly to the Old Testament scholar. Even the casual visitor to Egypt, Palestine, Syria, Lebanon, Iraq, and other countries in the East sees before his eyes massive structures like the pyramids of Egypt, the great ziggurat of Ur, the widespread ruins of Babylon, the Assyrian palaces of Nineveh, Khorsabad, and Nimrud, and the palaces of the Persians, all of which are of specific interest to the Old Testament reader. Moreover, all of these are so old and carry with them so much of the mystery connected with those long-past days that, in comparison, Roman remains seem to come from yesterday and to lack the fascination of the more ancient past. Without this glamor, the antiquities of New Testament times have made less appeal to the public and so the impression has grown that there is little of value to be found in the excavation of remains of New Testament times.

Despite the absence of popular appeal, archaeological finds relating to the New Testament are by no means lacking. The most important of them are written records, inscriptions, and papyri. But there are some building remains and a considerable variety of other items which have their own special interest.

For many of the towns mentioned in the New Testament there are still considerable remains above the ground. For others there is a great deal that has become covered through the ages and needs to be excavated. The important town of Jerusalem, which we shall discuss in detail later, is rich in archaeological material, but this has not been excavated because the city is at present inhabited by people whose houses stand above the ruins of earlier centuries.[3] However, when these towns are laid bare by the archaeologist, there is much to be discovered, both about the life that was lived in these towns and about some of the buildings that are mentioned in the New Testament. We need only call to mind the great temple of Diana at Ephesus, or the market place at Athens. There are other towns unearthed by the archaeologist which, though not mentioned in the

---

3. The British School of Archaeology under Dr. Kathleen Kenyon, and in co-operation with other bodies, will commence some excavation in the old Jewish quarter inside the walls at an early date.

Bible, nevertheless tell us much about the life of the times. Such a town is Pompeii, which was overwhelmed by Mount Vesuvius in A.D. 79. Here we have a typical town of Paul's day, and a study of its remains will give us a clear idea of the sort of towns in which Paul delivered his message.

Babylonian clay tablets inscribed with linear characters that are directly derived from pictographs. They contain accounts of fields, crops, and commodities, and date from c. 3100 B.C. (Courtesy, The British Museum)

10

PART ONE:

ARCHAEOLOGY AND THE OLD TESTAMENT STORY UP TO 587 B.C.

Two:

ABRAHAM THE MIGRANT

I T WOULD APPEAR THAT THE WRITER OF THE BOOK OF GENESIS was concerned merely to lay down some general statements about mankind in his first ten chapters and to move as quickly as possible to the story of Abraham. Those general statements concern the creating hand of God behind all things material and living, the universality of human rebellion and of divine judgment, the fact of God's desire to save men, and the fact that men may be saved by faith in God and in obedience to Him.

The author of Genesis took from the information available to him certain data to illustrate his general principles. Unfortunately his sketches are so summary and so carefully selected that it is difficult to provide archaeological support for them. But some useful material is available for comparison along at least three lines.

(a) Creation. There are other ancient stories of creation, the best known being *Enuma Elish*, a Babylonian-Sumerian epic which tells of the origin of the gods from the primeval chaos in which two strange entities, Apsu and Tiamat, were commingled in a single body. From these came the gods. One of the younger gods, Marduk,

13

Illustration on page 12: Part of a marble slab with late cuneiform text and huge images of Assyrian king and priests, found at Nimrud, near Mosul. (Courtesy, Consulate General of the Republic of Iraq)

Two of the seven tablets in the Assyrian series containing the Creation Epic. They are copies of the older Babylonian text, and were made for the Assyrian royal library at Nineveh. The text may be traced to Sumerian originals of the third millennium B.C. (Courtesy, The British Museum)

finally overthrew Tiamat, cut her in two, and formed heaven and earth from her body. He then created man, as well as the rest of the universe. In comparison with this strange story recorded today on seven clay tablets, the majestic narrative of Genesis 1 and 2 stands out above the weird polytheism of the Babylonian legend as a masterpiece. The one true God created all things in a series of divine utterances.[1]

(b) The Flood. The Babylonian tablets also have a flood story.[2] The hero Ut-napishtim was saved in a ship with people and animals from a great flood. There are interesting parallels with the Biblical story — the sending forth of birds to discover dry land, the building of an altar, and the offering of a sacrifice. But again, whereas the Bible story of the flood is monotheistic, the Babylonian story is set in a strange polytheistic framework. There are, in fact, many differences between the two stories despite the resemblances, and it

1. J. B. Pritchard, *ANET* (Princeton, 1955), pp. 60ff., translation of E. A. Speiser, A. Heidel, *The Babylonian Genesis* (Chicago, 1942).
2. J. B. Pritchard, *op. cit.*, pp. 42ff., translation of S. N. Kramer, A. Heidel, *The Gilgamesh Epic and Old Testament Parallels* (Chicago, 1946).

is more likely that both stories reach back to an original event than that the Hebrew story is a modification of the ancient myth.

That there were great floods in Mesopotamia in early times is shown by considerable deposits of silt in several excavated sites like Ur, Erech, Shuruppak. The deposits vary in thickness and in age and none can be identified with the Bible flood. But both the ancient literature and these flood deposits point to the fact of a great flood, although the date and the extent are uncertain.

(c) Early people, kings, and towns. Ancient Mesopotamian king lists mention "kings before the flood" and "kings after the flood." These kings had lengthy years of reign. Whatever the interpretation of this may be, the fact is to be compared with the great ages of the patriarchs (Gen. 11:10ff.). Again, the list of peoples and towns in Genesis 10, though compiled at a later date, has gathered data about early towns and people, and this material is open to archaeological investigation. Thus a place like Erech (Gen. 10:10), the former Uruk, was in fact a very ancient town, one of the earliest in lower Mesopotamia. Further excavations in lower Mesopotamia are likely to provide valuable evidence on such a list as that in Genesis 10.

After his introductory chapters, the author of Genesis moves into the story of Abraham, for which he provides a great deal more information.

The Original Home of Abraham

The Bible places the home of Abraham in lower Mesopotamia, in the region of Ur. The date is not easy to determine with accuracy because we do not always understand the chronological methods of the ancients. It is generally agreed, however, that we must place the days of the patriarchs in the period 2000-1700 B.C., perhaps rather earlier than later. During these centuries Ur was an important town in Mesopotamia. It had once been the center of a strong state. The excavations of Sir Leonard Woolley during the years 1922 to 1934 showed something of the splendor of the centuries before Abraham.[3] The royal tombs of Ur, dating to about 2500 B.C., produced a collection of magnificent golden vessels which are still the delight and wonderment of the students of the ancient world. Ur was a town with a complex system of government and a well-developed system of commerce, one with writing in common use for

3. L. Woolley, *Ur of the Chaldees* (Pelican).

the issue of receipts, the making of contracts, and many other purposes. There were town drains, streets, two-storied houses, a great temple tower (ziggurat), trade routes joining the town with other great towns to the north and the south, and various other evidences of a highly developed civilization.

This area of southern Mesopotamia had formerly been occupied mainly by the Sumerians who were the first settlers on the plains of Shinar. At an early date Semitic people began to infiltrate into these areas. These became known as the Akkadians. They lived peacefully among the Sumerians and took over their culture. Eventually they became the dominant group and replaced the Sumerians as the rulers of these lands. In later centuries yet other Semites came to dwell here, such as the Amorites and the Aramaeans. There is good evidence that the area was occupied by Semites at an early date. It is not at all unlikely, therefore, that a Semite like Abraham should come from southern Mesopotamia although we may not be able to tell the precise Semitic group from which he came.

Statue of a he-goat, sometimes erroneously called "the ram caught in a thicket," but probably a holder for burning incense or an offering bowl. The legs and face are made of gold, the belly of silver, the horns, eyes, and upper fleece of lapis, while the lower fleece is made of white shell on a wooden core. The statue was found in Ur and dates from c. 2500 B.C. (Courtesy, The British Museum)

PEOPLES IN THE EAST IN THE DAYS OF ABRAHAM

It is important to realize that the world in which Abraham lived was a very busy world indeed. We may say that the centuries following 2000 B.C. were centuries of great change all over the East. In addition to the older Sumerians and the Semitic Akkadians who were scattered all over Mesopotamia, we find other important groups of people coming into prominence in these lands, such as the Amorites, the Hurrians, and the Hittites.

We hear of the *Amorites* in the Bible where they are included among the inhabitants of Palestine and particularly of Transjordan. They were to be found, however, in many lands in the Near East at this time. Just before 2000 B.C. they began to move into lower Mesopotamia and by 1800 B.C. they were in possession of most of this region. At the same time they were active in the general area northeast of Galilee as we learn from a valuable collection of execration (cursing) texts from Egypt. It was precisely in this area of Transjordan that the Amorites were found by the Israelites in the days of the Exodus, although they had moved further south by then. The kingdoms of Sihon and of Og, kings of the Amorites, were taken by the people of Israel.

It was the Amorites who gave to the world the great lawgiver Hammurabi, who lived during the years around 1700 B. C. A study of his code of laws shows a number of interesting parallels with the law code of Moses. This is not really surprising since the Israelite patriarchs came from these lands, and Abraham must have known and lived under similar laws before the days of Hammurabi.

The second group of people that calls for brief mention are the *Hurrians.* They began to enter the lands around the Tigris about 2000 B.C. Some clay tablets of this period introduce a new type of name, different from the other names of the area. These new names are now known to have belonged to the Hurrians who, during the next couple of centuries, spread across central Mesopotamia and formed the main population in a number of very important kingdoms like the Mitanni kingdom which occupied the area between the Tigris and Euphrates rivers about 1500 B.C. In recent years the important town of Nuzi to the east of the Tigris has yielded an amazing collection of clay documents which have given insight into the customs of these lands. These customs are strongly reminiscent of many of the patriarchal customs. We shall make reference to

BIBLE LANDS
in the days of the
PATRIARCHS

CASPIAN SEA

PERSIAN GULF

HITTITES

HURRIANS

ASSYRIA

Nuzi

Haran

Mari

AMORITES

Babylon

Ur

Shechem

Jerusalem

NEGEB

MEDITERRANEAN SEA

RED

Thebes

Two typical portraits of Hammurabi, king of Babylon, c. 1792-1750 B.C., surrounded by the well-known Code of Laws. The portrait to the left is cut in limestone (Courtesy, The British Museum); *the diorite stele to the right is eighty inches high and depicts Hammurabi receiving the symbols of authority from the god Marduk. The stele is inscribed with 282 laws* (Courtesy, Consulate General of the Republic of Iraq)

these Nuzi documents in due course. For the present it should be noticed that in the Bible the Hurrians are known as Horites.

The *Hittites* were the third group which became active about the time when the Israelite patriarchs were moving about in the East. This was a group of peoples which originated somewhere in Europe and formed part of the great Indo-European migration that reached as far as India. The group that is of special interest to the Bible student settled in Asia Minor. Here they found a more ancient people known as the Hatti people. The newcomers took over their name. It is not always clear whether the early records in the Bible refer to the original Hittites or to the newer Hittites. Abraham bought a field in Machpelah from Ephron the Hittite. It is possible that we have here one of the earlier Hittites. It is known that they were a people that did in fact travel around the East. They traded

19

with the people in Assyria as early as about 2000 B.C. according to baked clay documents found in Asia Minor and now known as the Cappadocian Documents.[4] It would have been possible for Abraham to have had dealings with Hittites of one kind or another in the period 2000-1700 B.C., which is almost certainly the period in which he lived. In the days of the Israelite exodus the Hittites of the Bible were, of course, the Indo-European Hittites.

When we add to these three main groups several other smaller groups which were to be found in the lands where Abraham moved, we see that it was a busy world indeed. In Palestine there was already a mixed population comprising such peoples as Canaanites and other related groups. The Canaanites had already been in the land for perhaps a thousand years.

ABRAHAM'S JOURNEYINGS

The Bible describes the journeys of Abraham in some detail. Leaving Ur, he first traveled north to the town of Haran where he lived for a number of years before setting out again to journey to Palestine (Gen. 12). A later writer in the Bible described this first journey of Abraham as one in which "he went out, not knowing whither he went" (Heb. 11:8b). Recent research suggests quite strongly that it is not in a physical sense that this verse must be applied. There were well-trodden trade routes throughout these lands and we have no reason to think that Abraham left the usual roads when he made his journey. We should rather interpret this verse in a spiritual sense, namely, that having set out at the call of God, he did not quite know where this response was likely to lead him in the end.

Not only were there great roads from Ur to Haran, but other roads connected northern Mesopotamia with the Mediterranean coast and with Palestine. Still others connected Palestine with Egypt. There was a good deal of traffic between these latter two lands. This is shown by the numerous Egyptian items found in the tombs of Palestine dating to the years 2000-1800 B. C. It was the period of the great Twelfth Dynasty which seems to have exercised some sort of control over Syria and Palestine. The Execration Texts, already referred to, come from this period, as does a valuable set of paintings from tombs found at Beni Hasan, 250 miles down the Nile, in which the artist has portrayed for us a group of semi-nomads who

4. O. R. Gurney, *The Hittites* (Pelican), pp. 18f.

A masterpiece of early Sumerian art, this mosaic standard is made of lapis lazuli and shell set in bitumen on wood. The upper row depicts the prince (the large figure), the royal family, chariot, and prisoners; the middle row, soldiers and prisoners; and the lower row, Sumerian chariots. It was found in Ur and dates from c. 2500 B.C. (Courtesy, The British Museum)

visited Egypt about 1900 B. C.[5] There were thirty-seven of these people who were led by a man with a perfectly good Semitic name, Absha. The dress and the equipment of these people probably give us a good idea of the dress and equipment of the patriarchal family which moved into Egypt about the same time.

It is interesting to discover that the towns visited by Abraham according to the Bible records lie today in the zone where the rainfall is between ten and twenty inches annually. This is the zone where sheep can live. We have no serious reason to think that the general rainfall pattern has changed through the centuries. Another important fact made clear by modern archaeology is that towns like Shechem, Bethel, Haran, Gerar were in existence at this time. A string of ancient sites throughout this area provides evidence of early occupation.

PATRIARCHAL TOWNS, NAMES, AND BEASTS OF BURDEN

It may be asked whether we have any contemporary evidence about towns mentioned in the Bible records. There is, of course, good evidence for Ur. Some excavation has been undertaken at Haran in recent years although only in the upper, later levels of the mound. It was known in the important Cappadocian texts of 1900 B. C.

5. Photo in *Westminster Historical Atlas* (London, 1953), p. 23.

A sketch of what the ziggurat of Ur-Nammu may have looked like. In this drawing the temple buildings in the angles of the stairs have been omitted. (Courtesy, The University Museum of the University of Pennsylvania)

These were left by the forerunners of the Hittites in Asia Minor. The name was still referred to in important texts from Mari on the middle Euphrates coming from about 1700 B.C. The site has never been lost. The name Nahor, as a town, is also attested in these northern areas in the Cappadocian texts, the Mari texts, and late Assyrian texts. It belonged to the district of Haran. Many other towns in this area are known from documents, and sometimes the same name is used for a person in the Bible record. The names Serug and Terah are cases in point.[6]

It is precisely in these northern Mesopotamian lands where Biblical records place the home of the patriarchs that we find these names. We may conjecture that a good deal of contact took place between Palestine and these lands to ensure a continuity of culture. For this reason we look to northern Mesopotamia for the cultural background of the patriarchs.

6. A discussion of place names, as well as of the whole range of modern knowledge now available, has been undertaken by R. de Vaux, "Les patriarches Hébreux et les découvertes modernes," *RB*, LIII (1946), LV (1948), LVI (1949). See also H. H. Rowley, "Recent Discoveries and the Patriarchal Age," *BJRL* (1949), pp. 3-38.

As to personal names like Abraham, Isaac, Jacob, we are able to say today that these were current names in the areas referred to in the Bible. The details have been collected by a variety of writers in recent years. The Amorites in particular were fond of names of the type of Jacob and Isaac, names which are really verbal forms.

An analysis of the beasts of burden of Abraham and the other patriarchs shows that these were camels and asses. The asses seem to have been used more widely than the camels. It has been argued that camels were not used in the East at this time. This cannot be maintained any longer. It is probably true that camels had not come into very general use at the time. It was more like 1300 B.C. before this beast of burden became popular. However, there is clear evidence that the camel was used somewhat in earlier times. Small clay figures, some carvings, and some pieces of camel bone and camel hair are known from graves in both Egypt and Mesopotamia before 2000 B.C. There is no need to regard these references in the patriarchal narratives, therefore, as being anachronisms.[7]

7. J. P. Free, *JNES,* III (1944), pp. 187-193.

The remains of the actual ziggurat of Ur, seen from the southwest side. (Courtesy, The University Museum of the University of Pennsylvania)

Professor Nelson Glueck examining a piece of pottery that dates from the time of Abraham. (Courtesy, Israel Office of Information)

THE CUSTOMS PORTRAYED IN THE PATRIARCHAL NARRATIVES

One of the most important contributions of modern archaeology to our understanding of the Bible is the information which is given about the laws and customs of the people. This material comes either from the formal law codes or from the many incidental references to the customs of the people to be found on the documents of everyday life such as receipts, letters, contracts, licenses, and the like.

From patriarchal times in particular we now have a great deal of this kind of material. In the first place, we know of at least three Amorite law codes, one of which is complete, namely, the code of the great Hammurabi. But this code was but the later expression of the earlier codes of the town of Eshunna and of the king Lipit Ishtar.[8] In the second place, we have a great variety of

8. J. B. Pritchard, *op. cit.,* pp. 159-163.

A beautiful example of Akkadian craftman-ship, dating from c. 2400 B.C. This bronze head of Sargon the Great is rather stylized and nearly perfectly symmetrical, yet note the realism of the combed waves of the beard. (Courtesy, Consulate General of the Republic of Iraq)

baked-clay tablets which give us remarkable glimpses into the customs of the ordinary people of the day.

Perhaps the most important of these written records are those of the ancient Hurrian town of Nuzi which lay to the east of the Tigris River. Its modern name is Yorghan Tepe. Here, in the years 1925 to 1931, Professor Chiera and his colleagues of the American Schools of Oriental Research found some 20,000 clay documents in the family archives of several of the villas of the town.[9] The date of these documents is actually somewhat later than the time of the patriarchs, being placed by the excavators in the fifteenth century B. C. This may be as much as four or five hundred years after the traditional date of the patriarchs, but because customs persist, the tablets give important evidence about the legal and social structure of society in these lands in previous centuries.

9. R. H. Pfeiffer and E. A. Spelser, *One Hundred New Selected Nuzi Texts* (New Haven, 1936).

When the Nuzi tablets were translated it became apparent at once that there were many very close parallels between the customs in this town and those to be found in the society of the patriarchs. In other cases the parallels were not so close, but the same general pattern could be observed with modifications in details. At last it was possible for the Bible student to look into an ancient form of society closely resembling the society of the days of Abraham, Isaac, and Jacob. What was particularly significant was that the town of Nuzi lay in the general area of northern Mesopotamia which was the home of Abraham for a considerable time. The Bible records indicate that Abraham's descendants kept their contact with this area for quite a time. Isaac found a wife here, and Jacob actually lived here for twenty years. Perhaps there were other contacts between the family living in Palestine and their relatives living in northern Mesopotamia as well as those mentioned in the Bible. It would not be surprising, therefore, if laws and customs found in the northern areas were paralleled in Palestine, for the simple reason that they were brought to the new land by the patriarchs and preserved there through regular contact with the former homeland. The result of this discovery has been that, whereas it was commonly held at the close of the last century and at the beginning of this one that these stories in Genesis were artificial stories composed in the days of the kings, it is now clear that we are here dealing with genuine society of the early part of the second millennium B.C. The comment of W. F. Albright in this connection is typical of many now being made:

An example of a private cylinder seal with which Babylonians signed their documents by rolling it across the surface of a clay tablet while the clay was still wet.
(Courtesy, Consulate General of the Republic of Iraq)

So many corroborations of details have been discovered in recent years that most competent scholars have given up the old critical theory according to which the stories of the patriarchs are mostly retrojections from the time of the dual monarchy, 9th-8th centuries B.C.[10]

Let us turn then to a discussion of some of the more important of these customs. It will be our method to refer to the Nuzi custom first and then to draw out some Biblical parallels. For convenience we shall deal first with such major items as inheritance and marriage, and then refer briefly to one or two miscellaneous customs.

In Nuzi, inheritance was of major importance. Property was, theoretically at least, inalienable and could not pass from the family. In order to overcome this difficulty a fictitious system of adoption was used. By this device it was possible for a man to adopt any

10. W. F. Albright, *From Stone Age to Christianity* (Baltimore, 1940), p. 183.

Various types of daggers and a sheath found in Ur, dating from c. 2600 B.C. The handles are made of lapis lazuli studded with gold, while the smooth blades, as well as the filigreed sheath, are of gold. Note the mark of the craftsman or owner on some of the bades. (Courtesy, Consulate General of the Republic of Iraq)

These copper miniatures, dating from c. 3000 B.C., are fine examples of Sumerian art. Although it is very likely that they had some religious significance, they also portray daily-life activities. The chariot is the earliest representation we have of this vehicle. The statuette of the wrestlers was found at Khafaje, east of Baghdad. The large jars may have been carried as a test of skill. (Courtesy, Consulate General of the Republic of Iraq)

number of "sons" or "brothers," and then to pass over the property rights quite legally to the adopted party. Cases are known where there was a regular traffic in this kind of adoption.

A property owner who had no son would normally adopt an heir. The adopted "son" might be a freeborn man, a slave, or a relative. The tablet of adoption was written on clay after proclamation at the gate of the city. When party A adopted party B, he willed to B the major portion of his lands, buildings, and other items, in consideration of the fact that B promised to serve A during A's lifetime and then undertook to give him a decent burial on his death. There was generally a proviso that if A had no son, B would inherit the property outright. If, however, A had a son subsequent to the signing of the adoption document, then the natural son would become the heir and take the father's "gods," which were generally small clay figures used in family worship, but which seem to have become in time something like our modern title deeds. At any rate, the man who owned the property possessed the gods, and he passed these over when the property came into the possession of another.

There was another possibility that could arise in the case of a man who had no son. It was quite common for the man's wife

28

to take a slave woman and present her to her husband in order to raise up a child for herself. In this case the son of the slave woman became the heir if there were no other sons. But here, too, should there be in due course a son born to the first wife, then the son of the slave woman took second place and had to surrender the inheritance to the true son. It was, however, provided that in that case the son of the slave woman should not be cast out but should have some share in the inheritance.

Here is a typical tablet of adoption whereby a man called Zike allowed his son Shennima to be adopted by a certain Shuriha-ilu:

> The tablet of adoption belonging to Zike, the son of Akkuya: he gave his son Shennima in adoption to Shuriha-ilu, and Shuriha-ilu, with reference to Shennima, from all the lands . . . and his earnings of every sort gave to Shennima one portion of his property. If Shuriha-ilu should have a son of his own, as the principal son he shall take a double share; Shennima shall then be next in order and take his proper share. As long as Shuriha-ilu is alive, Shennima shall revere him. When Shuriha-ilu dies, Shennima shall become the heir. Furthermore, Kelim-ninu has been given in marriage to Shennima. If Kelim-ninu bears children, Shennima shall not take another wife; but if Kelim-ninu does not bear, Kelim-ninu shall acquire a woman of the land of Lullu as wife for Shennima, and Kelim-ninu may not send the

Painting in the tomb of Khnemhotep (1920-1900 B.C.) at Beni Hassan of a Semite and his donkey, and of Semite women bringing kohl *(eye paint) to Prince Khnemhotep.* (Courtesy, The Oriental Institute, The University of Chicago)

offspring away. Any sons that may be born to Shennima from the womb of Kelim-ninu, to these sons shall be given all the lands and buildings of every sort. However, if she does not bear a son, then the daughter of Kelim-ninu from the lands and buildings shall take one portion of the property. Furthermore, Shuriha-ilu shall not adopt another son in addition to Shennima.[11]

There is more on the tablet as well. There is provision that a handmaiden should be given as a gift on the occasion of the marriage of Shennima to Kelim-ninu, and a proviso that if Shennima takes another wife beside Kelim-ninu after Kelim-ninu has borne children, then Kelim-ninu may take certain action against him.

With these illustrations of Nuzi law before us we may draw a number of comparisons between the customs of the patriarchs and those of the people of northern Mesopotamia as depicted here.

It would seem that in the first attempt of Abraham to secure an heir he resorted to the current practice of adopting a slave as his heir. It was "Eliezer of Damascus" who was chosen as heir and he was to Abraham "one born in my house" (Gen. 15:2, 3). At a later stage Abraham resorted to the method of taking a subsidiary wife. Actually the Bible makes the point quite clearly that it was Sarah the wife of Abraham who invited Abraham to take this woman. "It may be that I may obtain children by her" was Sarah's hope (Gen. 16:2).

When Ishmael was born, he presumably was regarded as the heir of Abraham. However, in due course Sarah herself gave birth to a son Isaac, who quite naturally took the place of Ishmael. Sarah wanted to cast out the bondwoman and her son but this thing was very grievous in the eyes of Abraham (Gen. 21:10, 11). While Sarah does not seem to have had a great deal of compunction about this suggestion, it was, of course, quite out of keeping with the customs of the land, and Abraham revolted at the thought. Only a divine injunction led Abraham to allow the child and his mother to depart (Gen. 21:12).

The case of Jacob and Laban has been interpreted by some writers in terms of an adoption arrangement between these two. When we first meet Laban he does not appear to have had any sons. Only later do sons receive a mention. It is interesting to note that after the reference to sons (Gen 31:1), trouble started between

11. J. B. Pritchard, *op. cit.,* p. 220.

Left: *Bronze statuette of the god Ba'al, found at Tyre, dating from c. 1400 B.C.* (Courtesy, The British Museum). Right: Limestone *statue of the god Abu, a Sumerian deity, found in his temple at Esh-nunna, Central Iraq.* (Courtesy, Consulate General of the Republic of Iraq)

the two men. Jacob was urged on by his wives, who said that their father had treated them as "strangers" (Gen. 31:14, 15). Jacob decided to leave Laban and take his two wives, the daughters of Laban, away with him. Rachel, as shrewd as her father, stole the father's "gods" (Gen. 31:30, 32, 34, etc.). Was it that Rachel thought that by possessing these gods she could thus secure for her husband the rights to the property of the father that Jacob had now lost through the birth of sons to Laban? There is some reason to interpret this story in this way.

Our discussion has already touched briefly on marriage. A study of some of the ways of Nuzi is instructive here, too, because there

31

are interesting parallels between the Nuzi customs and the Biblical customs found in the stories of the patriarchs.

It was quite common for a man who adopted a son to give his daughter as a wife to the adopted son. In many cases the Nuzi documents show also that a man worked a period of time before the wife was given to him. In Nuzi it seems to have been more usual, however, in the case of slaves than of free men. A slave was often required to do this period of service before he was given a girl in marriage, so that the case is not exactly parallel to the examples which we see in the Bible. Again, in quite a number of cases, in Nuzi a man was forbidden to take a second wife. Penalties ensued if a man broke this injunction. As an illustration of these marriage customs we quote here another of the more famous documents of Nuzi. It is the adoption tablet of a certain Nashwi who adopted a certain Wullu:

> The adoption tablet of Nashwi son of Arshenni. He adopted Wullu son of Puhishenni. As long as Nashwi lives, Wullu shall give him food and clothing. When Nashwi dies, Wullu shall be the heir. Should Nashwi beget a son, the latter shall divide equally with Wullu, but only Nashwi's son shall take Nashwi's gods. But if there be no son of Nashwi, then Wullu shall take Nashwi's gods. And Nashwi had given his daughter Nuhuya as a wife to Wullu. And if Wullu takes another wife, he forfeits Nashwi's land and buildings. Whoever breaks the contract shall pay one mina of silver, and one mina of gold.[12]

12. *Ibid.,* pp. 219f., Tablet 2.

Another example of a cylinder seal and its impression, dating from c. 2000 B.C. Because of the objects in the representation — two human figures, a tree and a snake — it has been thought that the scene depicts a Babylonian version of the temptation of Eve, but no proof has been found in cuneiform texts. (Courtesy, **The British Museum**)

We recall the marriage of Jacob to the daughters of Laban (Gen. 29:16-30). In each case Jacob was required to work a period of seven years for his wife. In each case also, the daughter was given a handmaiden by the father Laban, the names of the handmaidens being quite clearly stated in the Biblical narrative as Bilhah and Zilpah (Gen. 29:24, 29). This incident is one of the cases in the Bible where we have a prohibition of other marriages on pain of penalties. Laban's words to Jacob are quite telling.

> *If thou shalt afflict my daughters, or if thou shalt take other wives beside my daughters, no man is with us; see, God is witness betwixt me and thee* (Gen. 31:50).

In this case the penalty may be regarded as divine disapproval.

The practice of levirate (*levir*, brother-in-law) marriage was known in Nuzi. Indeed it was widely practiced all over the ancient East. One case is well known in Nuzi where a father in obtaining a bride for his son specified that if the son died, the girl was to be married to another of the sons. This practice is also known in the Bible, and provision for it was made in later Israelite law (Deut. 25:5-10). The story of Judah and Tamar in the days of the patriarchs shows us that the principle was in use in those earlier days.

There was peculiar significance attached to the words of a dying father in Nuzi. If it could be shown that a father had made certain pronouncements on his deathbed, these were held to be binding on his sons after death. A case is known where two brothers entered into a lawsuit with a younger brother, seeking a court injunction that would forbid his marriage to a certain girl. We have only the judges' finding on the document from Nuzi. It appears, however, that when the case came before the judges the younger brother, Tarmiya by name, pleaded that at the time of his father's death the old man had seized his hand, saying:

> The other sons of mine are older, and wives they have taken. But you have not taken a wife. So Zulul-Ishtar as your wife to you herewith I am giving.[13]

The young man was able to produce several witness to testify to the truth of his statement, whereupon the judges gave a decision in his favor. This incident may throw some light on the importance

13. *Ibid.*, p. 220, Tablet 4.

33

of the last words of some of the patriarchs. Once a decision had been made and the blessing had been given, there could be no change (Gen. 27 and 49). The parallel is not exact but there is a very suggestive resemblance between the two Bible incidents and the Nuzi custom.

Another strange custom at Nuzi was associated with the passing of a pair of boots or shoes from one party to another in certain transactions. Several tablets are known in which there seems to have been some kind of agreement between parties in which a transaction was being undertaken that was not quite above board. In one case a dowry was involved and it seems that property, which was inalienable in Nuzi, was being transferred. This and other cases appear to have in them elements that are actually outside the normal legal framework. However, by a special transaction, involving the passing of a pair of shoes and some other articles of quite inadequate economic worth when compared with the value of the item being transferred, the whole thing was given a legal cloak.

We are reminded of later incidents in the Bible where shoes were transferred between parties to cover up the avoidance of certain moral obligations. When Ruth was redeemed by Boaz, the kinsman took off his shoe and gave it to Boaz. This was according to *"the manner* in former time in Israel concerning redeeming and concerning changing, for to confirm all things" (Ruth 4:7, 8). There are two references in the prophet Amos (2:6, 8:6) in which we learn that the rich sold the poor for a pair of shoes. It is evident that the poor were being deprived of certain legal rights, so an old symbolism was used to describe the incident.

There are numbers of other parallels that can be drawn between the customs of the patriarchs and those of the citizens of northern Mesopotamia during these early centuries of the second millennium B.C.[14] If there was ever any doubt that a society similar to that portrayed in the patriarchal records did actually exist at the time, the reasons for the doubt are now largely removed. The narratives of Genesis in the stories of Abraham and his immediate successors now find a well-authenticated background in contemporary non-Biblical sources. The following words of H. H. Rowley, former Professor of Hebrew at the University of Manchester, are significant:

> In all of these cases we have customs which do not recur in the Old Testament in later periods, and which therefore are not

---

14. C. H. Gordon, "Biblical Customs and the Nuzi Tablets," *BA* (Feb., 1940).

likely to reflect contemporary society in the age when the documents were written. Their accurate reflection of social conditions in the patriarchal age in some parts of Mesopotamia from which the patriarchs are said to have come, many centuries before the present documents were composed, is striking. Speiser conjectures that the true significance of these incidents had probably been lost even before the time of David. It is in any case significant that if these stories had been carried in oral tradition they correctly reflect obsolete customs, and it is not surprising that today there is a disposition to treat them with more respect than some of the earlier scholars accorded them.[15]

It is evident that archaeology has revealed to us in recent years a great number of facts about the days of the patriarchs. We must go further and say that there is a growing number of facts becoming available for the student of patriarchal times. We now know the names of many of the gods of the peoples of the East at that time. The names Abraham, Isaac, and Jacob are quite in place in the Amorite world of the day. Our knowledge of the codes of Hammurabi and others gives us the laws, manners, and customs of Mesopotamia before 1700 B.C. This picture is enriched by other insights into the laws of the Sumerians, Hittites, Assyrians, and Babylonians. In particular the Nuzi documents of about 1500 B.C. tell of the habits of the Hurrians.

The Biblical patriarchs fit admirably into such a cultural setting. There are many resemblances to patriarchal society. It is particularly noticeable that a great many of these customs were not known in later times, say in the tenth or in the ninth century B.C. The fact that there are so many links with the world of the first part of the second millennium B.C. is inexplicable if the stories of the patriarchs are only the inventions of later days. It would have been impossible for the Israelites of those centuries to have access to such information as we now find beneath the earth on thousands of baked-clay tablets. The fact that the Bible customs are so close to the contemporary customs is a strong argument either for written records, or for reliable oral traditions. We are compelled to conclude that the narratives of Genesis 12-50 have a solid historical basis.

15. H. H. Rowley, "Recent Discovery and the Patriarchal Age," *BJRL* (Sept., 1949), p. 76.

It is not an overstatement to suggest that there cannot be a true appreciation of the significance of Abraham if we attempt to understand him without the important background material we have outlined in this chapter. As we grasp this setting more firmly we understand more clearly the character of Abraham the migrant, and the citizen of many lands.

Three:

IN THE LAND OF THE PHARAOHS

T HERE MUST BE FEW PEOPLE WHO HAVE NEVER HEARD OF THE noble Joseph who was sold by his brothers into Egypt and rose to a place of prominence in that land. In due course he was able to have his whole family, numbering seventy people, brought to this new land. If we ask whether there is Egyptian evidence for the rise of this very Joseph to fame, the answer is that up to the present we have no formal evidence for the Bible stories about Joseph and his family. However, students of the history of Egypt have brought to light in recent years a considerable number of important facts which furnish a background into which the Biblical narratives fit very naturally. This is the sort of thing we have seen in the case of the patriarchs. We shall see it again and again in this book.

THE COMING OF THE HYKSOS RULERS TO EGYPT

We must digress just here for a brief reference to some facts of Egyptian history. Historians recognize some thirty more or less well-defined dynasties covering the period of Egyptian history

*Scenes from the so-called Ani Papyrus, one of the p̶a̶
governor of the granaries. In the left scene the h̶
The Ani Papyrus is a roll seventy-six feet long*
The British Museum)

from about 3000 B.C. to Roman times. In patriarchal times it was
probably the Twelfth Dynasty that ruled Egypt. This line of rulers
came to an end about 1786 B.C., to be succeeded by Dynasties
Thirteen and Fourteen, which ruled from Thebes in southern Egypt.
However, before Dynasty Thirteen had run its course, northern
Egypt was invaded by a group of people who were to become known
to the later historians as the Hyksos rulers. They were to give to
Egypt, while they were established there, two ruling families, namely,
Dynasties Fifteen and Sixteen. There must have been contemporary
Egyptian rulers at Thebes but these were subject to the Hyksos rulers
until finally the Egyptians were able to rise and throw out the
foreigners. The date of the Hyksos rule in Egypt was from about
1720 to 1570 B.C.

The word *hyksos* seems to be a degenerate form of an Egyptian
word meaning "rulers of foreign countries." The term is known
in the form *hekau khasut* in the so-called Execration (cursing) Texts
as early as 1960 B.C.[1] The picture of the traveling Semites referred
to in our last chapter and found in a tomb at Beni Hasan in Egypt
carries this very word above the horns of the small animal that the
chief Absha is offering to the Egyptian governor of the town.

1. J. B. Pritchard, *ANET* (Princeton, 1955), pp. 328-329.

...e Book of the Dead. Ani was a royal scribe and ...soul is being weighed in the judgment hall of Osiris. ...n inches wide, dating from c. 1300 B.C. (Courtesy,

Numerous documents and archaeological discoveries lead us to think that about 1700 B.C. or a little earlier Egypt was inundated by a wave of invaders at the time of the feeble kings of the Thirteenth Dynasty. These invaders came from Palestine and installed themselves at first in the region of the Delta.[2] Later they were able to control the whole of the land. The precise origin of this movement is not known, but it is known that in composition the invaders were largely Semitic. Possibly the movement is to be related to the movement of other peoples further to the north, brought about by the great Indo-European migration which began early in the second millennium and gathered momentum as the years went by. It could be that under the influence of these pressures the population of Palestine, already well mixed, was set in movement. In any case, wherever we have names preserved on scarabs of the Hyksos period, the Semitic element is predominant.

We have a special interest in such a group because in the latter chapters of Genesis we find the patriarchal family settling into their new home in Egypt, apparently with the goodwill of the rulers of the land. At a later day, when a "king arose who knew not Joseph," we find that the Israelite group was ill-treated. We conclude that at

2. R. M. Engberg, *The Hyksos Reconsidered* (Chicago, 1939); A. Alt, *Die Herkunft der Hyksos in neuer Sicht* (Berlin, 1954), pp. 26ff.

an earlier date the rulers were not Egyptians but people who were sympathetic to the patriarchal family itself and perhaps related to it in a broad ethnical sense. The Hyksos rulers would fit into this category very well.

What the Hyksos Rulers Gave to Egypt

Let us outline some facts about these people. Despite the fact that the Egyptians did all in their power to destroy all record of them once they had cast them out, they brought a great deal to Egypt that was to be for the benefit of the Egyptians themselves.[3] We now know that the rulers of the Eighteenth Dynasty went to great lengths to erase all traces of these Hyksos rulers. Their names were cut out of the monuments and every written record that could be found was destroyed. Only the keen eyes of the modern archaeologist have been able to discover clear evidence of the Hyksos invaders and to give us a picture of their achievements. These Hyksos rulers were, for the most part, of western Semitic stock, that is to say, they were largely Canaanite in origin. They evidently had a widespread empire in their time, for objects such as scarabs, which belong specifically to their culture, have been found in many lands in the East. Their most famous king was Khayan, whose name has been found on inscribed material in Egypt, Palestine, Mesopotamia, and even in

3. J. A. Wilson, *The Burden of Egypt* (Chicago, 1951), Chap. 7.

Tomb model of an Egyptian death ship carrying mummified body to the underworld and the "fields of peace." (Courtesy, The British Museum)

A partly deteriorated wooden tomb model of brickmakers, found at Beni Hassan, dating from c. 2000 B.C. The central figure is digging mud that is to be placed in a basket the figure to the right once held. The third figure is pressing mud into a form. Three rows of finished bricks lie in front of him. (Courtesy, The British Museum)

Crete. This suggests that they had wide trade connections all over the East.

Many new features were introduced into Egypt at this time. We think today that the Hyksos people brought to Egypt such items as the horse and chariot, new types of daggers and swords, the strong compound Asiatic bow, and new types of fortification. Of special interest were the huge earth ramparts which enclosed fortified areas where chariots were housed. These have been found in several places in Palestine and Syria, as well as in Egypt. At places like Jericho and Shechem in Palestine great fortifications of this age were found during excavations there. It seems that Palestine itself was organized in a feudal manner at this time and consisted of numerous little states which owed allegiance to the Hyksos king.

PALESTINE IN THE SIXTEENTH AND SEVENTEENTH CENTURIES B. C.

In Palestine there was evidently great prosperity if we are to judge from the wealth of the graves of the Canaanites of this period. These are among the richest of the tombs of all time in Palestine. During these years numerous new towns were built in the hill areas.

Despite the picture of over-all prosperity and of great urban development, there was evidently no public security, for there were many occasions when the towns were destroyed with violence. Excavation shows layers of burning in several towns dating back to this period. At no time in the history of Palestine were there so many walled towns in the land. We are quite naturally reminded of the report of the spies of Moses who visited the land and reported "cities are walled, *and* very great" (Num. 13:28).

Joseph came from Palestine and was later able to arrange for the migration of his aged father Jacob and his brothers from his homeland to Egypt. There are many lines of evidence to suggest that it was during the Hyksos period that the events of Genesis 40-50 took place. We may suggest that Joseph came to prominence in Egypt about 1700 B. C.

THE HYKSOS CAPITAL AT AVARIS

The Hyksos rulers conquered northern Egypt and placed their capital in the Delta area, calling it Avaris. It seems that they allowed the Egyptians to continue to exercise some sort of governing power from a local capital at Thebes some four hundred miles up the Nile, although this authority was naturally supervised by the Hyksos rulers. Once the Hyksos conquerors were expelled, the town of Thebes again became the capital of Egypt.

The town of Avaris has been the subject of some discussion among the experts in recent years. Its location is now known with practical certainty. The land of Goshen, referred to as the area to which Jacob and his sons came, was in all probability the area around the Wadi Tumilat, which lay quite close to the capital of the Hyksos kings but a little to the southeast.

We have some reason to think that the new rulers, while they brought a good deal to Egypt, learned a great deal from Egypt. They soon adopted all sorts of ways and customs that were current in the land. For example, they copied Egyptian methods of writing and imitated the religious zeal of the Egyptians by building many new temples. An ancient god of Egypt, Seth by name, was honored in Avaris as Seth-Sutekh. This god bore a close resemblance to some of the Asiatic gods like Ba'al. His garments, headdress, and horns of divinity were Asiatic in type. Other gods were honored in addition to Seth.

In matters of court procedure we think that the Hyksos rulers took over a great deal from the local rulers. In the ordinary matters of every day the newcomers soon took advantage of the experience of the Egyptians.

Because the Hyksos kings were Semites like the sons of Jacob, and in view of the Bible evidence that this family was made welcome in Egypt, we conclude that it was during the time of Hyksos rule that the small family, which was later to become Israel, came to Egypt. There is a further reason to associate the two groups. The Bible states that the time the children of Israel spent in Egypt was four hundred years. If we take the date of the Exodus as shortly after 1300 B.C.[4] and count back this period of time, we arrive at a date of about 1700 B. C., which is approximately the date of the Hyksos kings. These and other lines of evidence make the most likely time for Jacob's entry into Egypt as that during which Egypt was ruled by Semitic foreigners.

THE EGYPTIAN LOCAL COLOR IN THE JOSEPH STORY

A study of the local color of the Joseph story will soon lead the student to the conclusion that it is strongly Egyptian in character. This fact has been recognized for a long time and some scholars have made a special study of resemblances between the customs of Egypt and those of Genesis 40-50. The ordinary reader will profit greatly from the works of Professor Yahuda, even though some scholars think that he has seen too many resemblances.[5] The fact remains, however, that the Joseph narratives must have been written by someone who was well acquainted with the customs of Egypt.[6]

In the first place, it is clear that Joseph was by no means the only Asiatic Semite sold into Egypt about 1700 B. C. (Gen. 37:36, 39:1ff.), and also that Egyptian prisons were highly organized (Gen. 39, 40). An ancient papyrus in the Brooklyn Museum, once part of the register of criminals at Thebes, lists each offender under name, sex, crime, sentence, etc. This papyrus was reused later on, and on

---

4. See next chapter, pp. 55-63.
5. A. S. Yahuda, *The Language of the Pentateuch in Its Relation to Egyptian* (London, 1933), or his more popular work, *The Accuracy of the Bible* (London, 1934).
6. J. Vergote, *Joseph en Egypte, Génèse* 37-50 *à la lumiere des études égyptologiques récentes* (1959).

Wooden statue of an Egyptian nobleman of high rank. He wears a tight-fitting pleated linen garment with wide skirt. The statuette dates from c. 1400 B.C. (Courtesy, The British Museum)

the back was written a list of seventy-nine servants of a big Egyptian household, of which forty were Asiatics bearing good Semitic names.

Then, there are numerous titles that are well known in Egypt. Such titles as we find in Genesis 40:2, "the chief of the butlers" and "the chief of the bakers," are well known as the titles of certain palace officials in Egyptian writings. Joseph's designation as "overseer over his house" (Gen. 39:4) is also a title often used of officers in Egyptian noble houses. After Joseph's elevation to a place of real prominence in Pharaoh's court, the titles ascribed to him in the Bible are thoroughly Egyptian. Among these we may note "lord over my [Pharaoh's] house" (Gen. 41:40), "ruler throughout all the land of Egypt" (Gen. 45:8), "father to Pharaoh" (Gen. 45:8). The office of Joseph may have corresponded with that of a vizier of Egypt, though it could have been that a special high office, second only to the Pharaoh, was taken up by Joseph in the times of emergency. One other office not specifically mentioned in the Bible is that of "superintendent of the granaries." In a land like Egypt this was an important office, since so much depended on the storage and distribution of grain for the welfare of the country. Joseph probably had this title as well, for he certainly held the office.[7]

Various items of court procedure give us further evidence of an intimate knowledge of the Egyptian background. Joseph's elevation to an honored position in Egypt as we have it in the Bible follows the pattern of procedure in the Egyptian court. The Bible reference describes the manner in which the Pharaoh honored Joseph in these words:

> *And Pharaoh took off his ring from his hand, and put it upon Joseph's hand, and arrayed him in vestures of fine linen, and put a gold chain about his neck; and he made him to ride in the second chariot which he had; and they cried before him, Bow the knee: and he made him ruler over all the land of Egypt* (Gen. 41:42, 43).

The investiture of an Egyptian vizier with a gold chain is depicted by the artists of Egypt. One famous picture from the days of Seti I (1308-1290 B. C.) shows this Pharaoh honoring a man in this way. It is acknowledged by most scholars that we have here in the Bible a description that is quite in keeping with Egyptian procedure. Incidentally, some writers have seen in this reference to "riding in a chariot" an important piece of local color for the time of the Hyksos rulers, for it was they who seem to have used the chariot for public occasions for the first time in Egypt. In any case, artistic productions as well as literary evidence point in the same direction. The Bible has faithfully represented the Egyptian way of honoring an important man in the land.

The dream of the Pharaoh at the time of the famine provides another group of interesting Egyptianisms. In the first place, dreams were regarded as of great significance in Egypt, as they were in many lands in Bible times (Gen. 41). There is meaning in the number of cows that feature in the dream. One of the chief deities of Egypt was a goddess, Hathor by name, who was regularly repre-

7. K. A. Kitchen, *Tyndale Bulletin,* No. 2 (Cambridge, 1957) ; W. C. Hayes, *A Papyrus of the Late Middle Kingdom in the Brooklyn Museum* (1955) .

sented in the shape of a cow. Further, the male ox was used at times to symbolize the Nile. He was sacred to the god Osiris, the inventor of agriculture. In many of the pictures of ancient Egypt the Osiris bull was depicted accompanied by seven cows. There is a further possible symbolism here in that there were seven zones of the goddess Hathor in Egypt. It would seem to be entirely possible that a Pharaoh had been one day to one of the temples to worship and had seen a picture of the seven sacred cows. These had troubled him in his dream that same night.

We have a great deal of information about the famines of Egypt. Years of drought and bad harvests are well attested in Pharaoh's domain. There is even evidence of a seven-year famine. The famous King Zoser (about 2700 B.C.) once sent a message to the governor of one region down the Nile. Here are his words:

> I am very much concerned about the people in the palace. My heart is heavy over the calamitous failure of the Nile floods for the past seven years. There is little fruit; vegetables are in short supply; there is a shortage of food generally.[8]

That great granaries were built and that steps were taken to appoint officers to control the storing and the issue of food for this great land is now well established. The message of the Pharaoh Zoser tells of the storehouses. However, in that case he sadly reported that

> . . . the storehouses have been opened, but everything that was in them has been consumed.[9]

The instructions outlined in the Bible in Genesis 41:33-36 and 47-49 are therefore quite in keeping with what we now know of Egyptian practice.

Naturally, people outside Egypt sometimes visited the land in a time of famine to look for food. One papyrus (in a very fragmentary condition), is a report from a frontier official in the days of Seti II (about 1210 B. C.). Certain Bedu from the land of Edom had been allowed to pass the frontier, it seems, in a time of famine:

> We have permitted the transit of the Bedouin of Edom through the fortress of Merneptah . . . in Theku to the pools

---

8. Quoted in W. Keller, *The Bible as History* (New York, 1956), p. 105.
9. *Ibid.*

This wall painting from the tomb of Sebek-hetep shows Semites from Retenu in Syria bringing a young child and gifts of Phoenician craftmanship in gold, silver, and bronze. The painting dates from c. 1400 B.C. (Courtesy, The British Museum)

of Pithom of Merneptah . . . in order to sustain them and their herds in the domain of Pharaoh, the good sun of every land . . . .[10]

We may suspect that this went on at other times, and that the events of Genesis 42-44, in the days of Joseph, were only typical of what happened many times through the centuries.

The practice of magic was widespread in Egypt. The Bible makes several references to magic and magicians in Egypt at the time of the Israelite sojourn there. The magicians of the land failed to interpret the dream of Pharaoh (Gen. 41:8). Later, Moses had dealings with these men (Exod. 8:7, 18; 9:11; etc.). It was the practice of magic that enabled the people of Egypt to hope for a continuance of the pleasures of this life in the next world. One needed

10. "The Papyrus Anastasi VI," quoted by J. B. Pritchard in *ANET* (Princeton, 1955), p. 259.

only to represent the item hoped for in picture form on the walls of the tomb, and to add the necessary magic words, and all would be fulfilled in the next life. Even the picture was sufficient in some cases. By the use of magic one could even escape the terrors of the judgment day and achieve a safe passage through all the intricate pathways of the underworld. The Book of the Dead with its elaborate pictures gives us a good idea of the extent to which magic was practiced in Egypt.

The custom of embalming the dead referred to in Genesis 50:3 and 26 is quite typical of this land. The multiplicity of butlers

The Egyptians believed strongly in a life after death and considered it their religious duty to preserve the body for the soul's use in the realm beyond. Not only human beings were embalmed but also certain animals and birds that were representative of their deities. The illustration above shows a casket and mummy of a falcon and a mummified cat. Note the artistic pattern of the linen bandages in which the cat is swathed. (Courtesy, The British Museum)

and bakers, of which some were designated "chief" (Gen. 40:1, 2), the use of slaves of the state (Exod. 1:14), the festivities of the Pharaoh's birthday (Gen. 40:20), and the release of certain prisoners on this day are all well attested items in the general background of the life of Egypt.

These items will suffice for our purpose. There are many pieces of Egyptian coloring in the Joseph narratives that have been beautifully illustrated by Egyptological discoveries of the type we have referred to in this section. W. F. Albright has written in this connection:

The Egyptian sojourn of Israel is a vital part of early Israelite historical tradition, and cannot be eliminated without leaving an inexplicable gap. Moreover, we know from the Egyptian names of Moses and a number of the Aaronids that part of Israel must have lived in Egypt for a long time. Then there are a great many correct local and antiquarian details which would be inexplicable as later invention. Most striking is the obvious relation in which the Joseph story and the later history of Israel in Egypt stand to the Hyksos movement. The "king who knew not Joseph" and who oppressed the Israelites should be a pharaoh of the New Empire, after the expulsion of the hated Asiatics from Egypt.[11]

11. W. F. Albright, *From the Stone Age to Christianity* (Baltimore, 1946), p. 184.

An example of the embalming of a human body. It is the mummy of the woman Katebet. Her face is covered with a mask and jewelry is placed above the parts of the body that normally wore such items. Note the scarabaeus which is prominently displayed. It was the symbol of the sun-god Khepera as well as of resurrection. (Courtesy, The British Museum)

49

SILENT YEARS IN THE LAND OF GOSHEN

According to the Bible it was to the land of Goshen that Jacob and the brothers of Joseph came when they finally settled in Egypt (Gen. 46:26ff.). This name is actually not known outside the Bible. Some scholars have tried to see in the word a sort of Semitism and have related it to a place in Palestine.[12] The name occurs elsewhere in the Bible as, for example, in Joshua 15:51 where it is a town in southern Judah, or in Joshua 10:41 where it is a "country." In Joshua it is known as the country of "the Goshen" (literal Hebrew). M. Z. Mayani has recently suggested that the word was originally not a proper name but a common noun, referring to something that could be found in both Egypt and southern Palestine, the two strong areas of the Hyksos people. He notes the occurrence of the word in Genesis 47:4 where parallelism of thought suggests that the meaning is "pasturage."[13] Further, he finds interesting parallels to this word in the Indo-Iranian group of languages of which there are many living representatives in India today, most of them coming from the older Sanscrit. These words all have the sense of something to do with pastures and cattle. This discussion is of particular value to the linguists, but for the ordinary Bible reader it is of some interest to know that there were groups of these same Indo-Iranian peoples in Palestine in the time of Joseph and Jacob. Indeed, they were a type of ruling class. They may well have left some elements of their language in the land, and the Hyksos conquerors may have taken this term with them to Egypt.

We may be fairly certain that this area was where the Wadi Tumilat is to be found today, in the eastern part of the Nile Delta. It is a narrow valley between thirty and forty miles long, connecting the Nile with Lake Timsah. It is a very rich area and is well described in the Bible as the "best of the land" (Gen. 47:1, 6, 11). We can think of the sons of Jacob carrying on their life here much the same as formerly, with perhaps more and more tendency to live a settled life, but depending on their flocks for their main sustenance.

All Semites were to become objects of scorn and contempt to the Egyptians in later years, as they remembered the humiliating experiences of the Hyksos rule. In particular, however, those who were shepherds were "an abomination unto the Egyptians" (Gen.

---

12. *Ibid.,* p. 326.
13. *Revue d'histoire et de philosophie réligieuses* (1955), No. 1. Note by M. Z. Mayani, pp. 58-60.

43:32, 46:34). The reason for this may not be clear to us now but it was a fact. It may have been because the flocks of the Egyptians were tended by men of a lower class. If these men were foreigners as well, the contempt would be still greater.

It is to be noted that there had been a continual stream of Semites into the delta zone for centuries. The Israelite element was only one of the groups. We have a great deal of evidence to show that Semites from the general area of Palestine were drifting into Egypt as early as 2000 B. C. or even earlier.[14] The pasture land of the delta area was the place where these peoples settled. When the Hyksos irruption took place it was really a military invasion. But the invaders were of the same general stock as the people of Palestine. They were the Canaanites and Amorites of Palestine and they spoke roughly the same language as did the family of Jacob. For example, one of the Hyksos princes had the name Jacob-hur, and one of the Hyksos viziers had the name Hur.

There was, then, a considerable collection of Semitic peoples in the delta area of Egypt, especially at the time of the Hyksos rulers. When the native Egyptians rose in revolt, energetic leaders from Thebes expelled the foreigners a little over a century after their invasion. The armies of the Hyksos rulers were chased out of the land and were pursued into Palestine. The large Semitic population of Egypt, however, still remained in the delta area. We can suppose that the little group of Israelites lived there quite unnoticed, among a mixed collection of Semites. The reaction of the Egyptians was now to place these peoples under some sort of supervision lest the same sad fate should befall Egypt again.

The book of Exodus opens with a picture of oppression for God's people. We must imagine that other people, too, shared in this general oppression. It was a "king who knew not Joseph" that now arose to oppress the people of God. This must have been a king of the new Eighteenth Dynasty which took over the government of Egypt after the expulsion of the Hyksos rulers.

It is impossible to say precisely how long a period is represented by the story we have in the first chapter of Exodus. It must occupy some four hundred years in all. If we have been right in making a strong link between the Hyksos conquerors of Egypt and the Israelites, we must think of the days of Joseph as being somewhere

14. See Beni Hasan Tableau, referred to in Chapter 2, pp. 20f.

in the vicinity of 1700 B.C. It is evident that the court of the ruler at the time was not far from the land of Goshen, for the narrative in Genesis 46 and 47 suggests an easy passage from the Pharaoh and Joseph to the land of Goshen. This would mean that the capital was in the delta area, a circumstance which would suit the times of the Hyksos rulers. Both before and after these times the capital was at Thebes, well down the Nile. The sojourn in Egypt thus lasted for some four hundred years. This lapse of time is referred to more than once in the Bible. Thus Exodus 12:40 states that

> *the sojourning of the children of Israel, who dwelt in Egypt, was four hundred and thirty years.*

It is interesting to notice that the story of these years is practically a closed one. The only details about them are given in Exodus 1. This chapter opens with a summary of the original migration to Egypt (vv. 1 to 6). Then there is a vivid description of the great increase in the numbers of these people, couched in the typical language of the Semite. The rise of "the king who knew not Joseph" is given in verse 8. We must think of this king as the first king of the Eighteenth Dynasty who began to rule about 1546 B. C. From verses 9 to 14 the narrative is concerned only with the fact that these people had lost their freedom and had become servants of the Pharaoh. This period in Exodus 1 must represent about three hundred years in all. There is only one item of interest in all these years and it is probably to be placed towards the end of the time. It is the reference to the use of the Israelites in the building of the store cities of Pithom and Raamses. We shall return to these facts later, as they have an important bearing on the date of the Exodus. Finally, in this chapter we learn of the special means of oppression that were introduced just before the Exodus took place.

There is thus a considerable gap in the story of the Israelites from the days of Joseph till the days of the Exodus. We know a good deal about the general history of Egypt during these years and can picture the sort of environment in which the people of Israel lived. But we lack any specific detail about their fortunes. Although the presence of Semitic peoples in Egypt is attested in a variety of ways, Egyptian records do not know of this little group as such. We have to be content to remain ignorant of the story of Israel for those years when they were struggling on towards independence and nationhood, not as a recognizable group in the annals of the Egyptians, but as a most significant group in the mind of God. We have to move on to the days of the Exodus before we find more tangible evidence.

The mummy prop-er of the falcon depicted on page 48 taken out of its form-fitting cof-fin. (Courtesy, The British Museum)

Four:

FROM EGYPT TO CANAAN

T HE BIBLE SPEAKS IN SEVERAL PLACES OF THE WILDERNESS WANDER-
ing of the Israelites. It was a memory that was never forgotten. God's
people had experienced a divine deliverance from Egypt and the
strange period of wandering in the general area of southern Palestine
and in Transjordan provided the liberated Israelites with opportunities
to learn much about the ways of God and the ways of men. It was
in these years that they were welded into a nation under the leadership of Moses. Here they received the law of God. Here, too, they
revealed some of the inherent national weaknesses that were to be
their sorrow in the centuries that followed.

There has been a good deal of discussion about these events
in recent years, and it seems that we may be much nearer a solution
to many of our questions as a result of recent archaeological discovery.

When Did the Exodus Take Place?

It has been widely held that the Exodus took place about 1440 B. C.
One reason for this has been found in I Kings 6:1, where we have
the statement:

ustration on page 54: *An imposing aerial view of the pyramids at Gizeh, Egypt. The
ree large ones are, from left to right, the Third Pyramid, the Second Pyramid, and
e Great Pyramid.* (Courtesy, The Oriental Institute, University of Chicago)

> *And it came to pass in the four hundred and eightieth year after the children of Israel were come out of the land of Egypt, in the fourth year of Solomon's reign over Israel . . . that he began to build the house of the Lord.*

We have good reason to believe that Solomon began to reign about the middle of the tenth century B.C., that is, about 950 B.C. It would follow from this that the Exodus took place about 1430 B.C., in the time of the Eighteenth Dynasty which ruled Egypt from about 1570 to 1310 B.C.

Scholars have been very ready to point out that there are many features about such a date that appear to be impossible to reconcile with certain facts both of history and of archaeology.

In the first place, if we are to take the Bible narrative seriously (and there is every reason that we should), we are bound to notice that the picture in the Bible is easiest to interpret if we regard the residence of the Pharaoh as being in the region of the delta at the time of the Exodus. The frequent going to and fro in the days of Moses, and the easy access to the ruler in the days of Joseph seem to require that the capital of Egypt was in the north of the land. There were two periods in Egyptian history when this was so — one under the Hyksos rulers, and the other under the Pharaohs of the Nineteenth

Statue of Rameses II, who may be the pharaoh of the Exodus. Here he wears the double crown of Upper and Lower Egypt and holds the symbols of his authority, the flail and scepter. This granite statue dates from c. 1350 B.C. (Courtesy, The British Museum)

Dynasty. All other evidence suggests that the period of the Hyksos was too early for the Exodus. The days of Joseph fit in there. It seems evident, therefore, that we must set these events at the time of the Nineteenth Dynasty (about 1319 B. C. to 1200 B. C.). The rulers of the Eighteenth Dynasty did not build in the north and had their capital in the south, at Thebes. Modern excavation has demonstrated by contrast that there was intense building activity in the north in the years following 1310 B.C.

The capital of Egypt during these years was called "House of Raamses." It was built on the site of the old Hyksos capital Avaris (later Tanis), and its foundation was commemorated by a monument which we now know as the "Year 400" stele. This monument was erected in honor of the god Seth, who appears in Asiatic dress. It was a naive device for recognizing that the original foundation of this city was laid in the days of the Hyksos kings, for the god Seth was honored by these foreigners. The new city was begun by Seti I and continued by his son Rameses II (1290 to 1224). We cannot help recalling at this stage that the Bible states that Israelites were used to build Pharaoh's "treasure cities, Pithom and Raamses" (Exod. 1:11; 12:37; Num. 33:3, 5). It is to be noted also that "the land of Raamses" is the same district as "the field of Zoan" (cf. Gen. 47:11 and Ps. 78:12, 43). This city was described in glowing terms

This huge sandstone head is from the statue of Amenophis (Amen-hetep III) who ruled Egypt c. 1413-1377. At one time he was thought to have been the pharaoh of the Exodus. (Courtesy, The British Museum)

Pharaoh Sheshonq I, known in the Bible as King Shishak who looted the Temple in Jerusalem (I Kings 14:25), made this pair of bracelets for his son Nemareth. They were made of gold and lapis lazuli. The image is that of the infant god Harpocrates emerging from a lotus bloom. Date, c. 940 B.C. (Courtesy, The British Museum)

by the scribes of Egypt. It was a seaport, a military base, and the center of government for the Pharaohs of the Nineteenth Dynasty.[1] So, if the Israelites did indeed help in building Raamses, they must have been still in Egypt in 1310 B.C. This seems to rule out an early date for the Exodus.

There has been some debate about the exact position of these two towns mentioned in the Bible. We are now able to give a reasonable identification of the two.[2] Pithom can be identified with an ancient site in the valley which connects the Nile with Lake Timsah. This site has a fine temple built by the great Rameses II. There is no earlier building here. Raamses, as we have seen, is built on the same site as Tanis. The excavations of the French archaeologist P. Montet have at last established this identification.[3]

Our general conclusion is that a date of shortly after 1300 B.C. for the Exodus would suit the facts disclosed by the archaeologists working in Egypt.

There is important evidence also from Transjordan to which we shall refer in some detail below. The Bible indicates a considerable degree of organization in these areas at the time of the Exodus. There were organized kingdoms with towns and walled cities which had to be taken by the Israelites. We may ask whether there were walled towns in this area at all times, or whether they were here only

1. W. F. Albright, *The Biblical Period* (1950), p. 8.
2. G. E. Wright and F. V. Filson, *Westminster Historical Atlas* (London, 1953), p. 37.
3. P. Montet, *Le drame d'Avaris* (Paris, 1940).

An Egyptian brick made of chopped straw and mud from the Nile. It bears the name and title of Rameses II, and may very well be one of the bricks made by the oppressed Israelites. It dates from c. 1330 B.C. (Courtesy, The British Museum)

at a particular period. The answer is that during the period from about 1850 B.C. till just before 1300 B.C. practically the whole of Transjordan was given over to semi-nomads who did not build walled cities. There had been walled cities here before 1850 B. C., but after that date the land reverted to the nomads, and no serious attempt to settle in towns and to wall these around was made again till about 1300 B.C. This state of affairs suggests that the Exodus did not take place till after 1300 B.C.

Evidence from Palestine is not so clear, but it can be correlated with the material from Egypt and Transjordan. There is a fairly general picture of destruction to be found in Palestine about the middle of the thirteenth century, that is, about 1250 B. C. Such towns as Bethel, Debir, Lachish, and Hazor all show serious burning at this time.[4] It is interesting to learn that excavations at the old Moabite town of Dibon have revealed in an actual excavation that there is a gap in the occupation of this town corresponding to the period of nomadic occupation of the land. We could very well fit the story of the invasion under Joshua into the picture we have given here.

The excavation of Professor John Garstang at the important site of Jericho was once used as a strong argument for an early date of the Exodus. After his work here in the years 1929 to 1935

4. J. Bright, *History of Israel* (London, 1960), pp. 118-120; G. E. Wright, *Biblical Archaeology* (London, 1957), Chap. 5.

he expressed the opinion that the last city of Jericho was destroyed about 1400 B. C. Various important correlations between the story in the Bible and the discoveries which were made were pointed out in his popular account of the excavations.[5] Such items as the fallen walls, the burning, the king's palace, the city gate, the proximity of the mountains, the smallness of the town, and so on seemed to correlate so closely with the Bible narrative that it was understandably concluded that the city captured by the Israelites had been excavated. By making reference to I Kings 6:1, Garstang made out a case for the fall of Jericho in 1400 B. C. and for an exodus in about 1440 B. C. More recent work carried out by the British archaeologist Dr. Kathleen Kenyon has shown that the wall of Jericho fell at various times

5. J. and J. B. E. Garstang, *The Story of Jericho* (London, 1940), pp. 157-173.

Some parts of the walls of Jericho still stand, as shown in this excavation scene. It was around this six-acre site that Joshua led the marching Israelites. In the background is the Mount of Temptation, presumably the place where Christ was tempted by Satan for forty days. (Religious News Service Photo)

in its history.[6] The town was burned several times, and the features mentioned by Garstang could have been discovered for a number of the cities of Jericho. Moreover, pottery found in the graves showed that there was occupation in this area rather later than 1400 B.C. There were, in fact, traces of a still later city to be found on the top of the ruins that Garstang had found. He had observed this but had interpreted these as belonging to the city of Hiel referred to in I Kings 16:34.[7] The net result of Miss Kenyon's work is that we cannot accept the excavation of Garstang as proving beyond all doubt that the Exodus took place as early as 1440 B. C. It is entirely possible that Jericho fell to the Israelites in the thirteenth century, about the same time as the towns we have referred to already. Unfortunately, most of this last city has disappeared due to natural

6. Kathleen M. Kenyon, *Digging Up Jericho* (1957).
7. J. and J. B. E. Garstang, *op. cit.,* pp. 149f.

Another view of the walls of Jericho. ". . . the wall fell down flat. . . . And they utterly destroyed all that was in the city. . . . And they burnt the city with fire" (Josh. 6:20, 21, 24). (Courtesy, Trans World Airlines)

erosion, or through its remains being used by the local inhabitants to fertilize their farms.

One important Egyptian monument prevents our speculation beyond a date of 1220 B. C. for the final entry of Israel into the land. It is the stele of Merneptah who ruled Egypt from 1224 to 1216 B. C. In the fifth year of his reign he had a long poem prepared that celebrates his victories over the Libyans. The conclusion of the poem describes the results of this victory. The peoples of Asia were duly impressed and submitted to Egypt without trouble. In the list of Asiatic lands and peoples we have for the first time the occurrence of the name Israel. The relevant passage reads:

> The princes are prostrate, saying, "Mercy,"
> Not one raises his head among the Nine Bows.
> Desolation is for Tehenu; Hatti is pacified;
> Plundered is Canaan with every evil;
> Carried off is Askelon; seized upon is Gezer;
> Yanoam is made as that which does not exist;
> Israel is laid waste, his seed is not;
> Hurru is become a widow for Egypt:
> All lands together, they are pacified.[8]

This stele is dated about 1220 B. C. The reference to Israel shows that by this date there was already a recognizable people of this name in Palestine.

It is clear on this evidence that we cannot come any further down in time than 1220 B. C. for the time of the conquest, although this stele does not really tell us how much before this date the Exodus took place.

Most scholars today feel that the weight of evidence is for an Exodus from Egypt about 1280 B. C. What, then, are we to say of the date implied by the statement in I Kings 6:1? A comparison with the Greek Septuagint shows that there was a difference of opinion in the minds of the translators in the time when this text was prepared, say in the period between 300 and 100 B. C. The Septuagint gives a period of four hundred and forty years as the time lapse between the Exodus and Solomon. It has been suggested that there may be a sort of symbolic usage of the numbers. Some scholars have pointed out that the list of high priests in I Chronicles 6:3-8 has eleven priests inclusive between Aaron and Zadok, the priest of Solomon's time.

8. J. B. Pritchard, *ANET* (Princeton, 1955), pp. 376-378.

If we think of a generation as forty years, we can see how the four hundred and forty years of the Septuagint was deduced. If, however, this is only a round number for a generation and if in fact the generations were something less than forty years, we may arrive at a date for the Exodus closer to the date suggested by the above evidence. The real answer to these problems is not yet available.

THE JOURNEY FROM EGYPT TO THE WILDERNESS

If our suggestion that Israel left Egypt about 1280 B. C. is correct, then the Pharaoh of those days must have been Rameses II. He was a great man in many ways, although he was also a great boaster. He sought desperately to recover the lost power of Egypt in Asia and had a good deal of trouble with the Hittites of Asia Minor, who naturally opposed him as he sought to extend his influence in Pales-

Another aerial view of the pyramids at Gizeh, Egypt, taken from the opposite direction. From left to right are the Great Pyramid, the Second Pyramid, and the Third Pyramid. Note the encroaching sands of the desert. (Courtesy, Trans World Airlines)

tine and further north. It was really after he was compelled to recognize that the Hittites were a power to be reckoned with that he formed a non-aggression pact with them and returned with zeal to building. The Israelites became involved in this program, for the Pharaoh used the subject Semitic peoples of the delta area to construct his buildings there. So Israel was oppressed. At this time a deliverer in the person of Moses arose to lead God's people out of their bondage.

We have no opportunity here to comment on the plagues which preceded the final departure from the land apart from saying that they are neither improbable nor unusual. They are part of the local color of Egypt. No doubt they were more serious than usual, and the last plague, namely, the death of the firstborn (Exod. 12), was one without parallel. It has been pointed out by various writers that there is some hint in these plagues of an exposure of the weakness of the gods of Egypt, for most of them, if not all, were produced by creatures that were held to be gods in the land. While there is a good deal of information available in modern times bearing on these plagues, we shall concern ourselves rather with the journeyings of the Israelites, for which we now have valuable evidence.

According to the Bible, the Israelites departed from Rameses (Exod. 12:37) and traveled to Succoth. Thence they journeyed to Etham (Exod. 13:20), and Pi-hahiroth (Exod. 14:2) "between Migdol and the sea, over against Baal-zephon." It was here that the Egyptians caught up with them. They were able to cross the sea by a wonderful intervention of God.

Thanks to modern research we have gone a long way towards discovering at least some of the path taken by the fleeing Israelites. Avoiding the "way of the land of the Philistines" (Exod. 13:17), which was traveled by the armies of Egypt, they turned to the south and moved from Rameses-Tanis to Succoth, about thirty-two miles away. This site is to be identified with the modern village called Tell-el-Maskhutah. The road then led by "the way of the wilderness of the Red Sea" (Exod. 13:18). Scholars are fairly generally agreed on the actual identification of Etham, Migdol, and Baal-zephon today. Baal-zephon can be identified in the light of an important Phoenician papyrus found in Egypt referring to the god "Baal-zephon and all the gods of Tahpanhes." This Tahpanhes is the Greek town of Daphne whose position has never been lost. The town, according to this papyrus, was the site of a temple of the god Baal-zephon.

THE PATH of the EXODUS

MEDITERRANEAN SEA

Tahpanhes

LAND OF GOSHEN

Raamses
Pithom
Succoth

Bitter
Lakes

Migdol

WAY OF THE LAND OF THE

PHILISTINES

Beersheba

Hormah

Serabit
el Khadem

Sinai

Kadesh-
barnea

Punon

Ezion Geber

KING'S HIGHWAY

EDOM

MOAB

Dibon

Arnon River

Wadi el Hesa

A recent French writer, H. Cazelles, commenting on this identification, says that archaeological evidence for this town is very strong.[9] In passing he draws attention to a comment of S. R. Driver in his commentary of 1911, in which he said that the place was absolutely unknown. But knowledge moves on. Today the place can be identified.

The site of Migdol may be a little harder to identify because there were many migdols (towers). Several are known in the records of Egypt. We are probably correct in identifying this site with the Migdol referred to in Jeremiah 44:1 and 46:14 and in Ezekiel 29:10 and 30:6. The position of Pihahiroth was evidently not far away. W. F. Albright claims that the Hebrew word here is an attempt to transcribe the Egyptian word Pi-H-r-t which means "Temple of the goddess H-r-t," a Syrian deity known elsewhere.[10]

The term Red Sea can generally be translated Sea of Reeds. The translators of the Old Testament have been responsible for a misunderstanding here. The reference is evidently not to the Red Sea proper, but rather to some of its marshy extensions to the north in the region of Succoth. The name is too general for us to be able to identify the place today, but it was evidently well known, for the same name occurs in several Egyptian records.[11]

Attempts have been made to trace the path of the Exodus from the other side of the sea, across into the Sinai peninsula. These are not entirely successful although the general path was almost certainly along the western edge of the peninsula. One of the best attempts to outline the journey is set out in the *Westminster Historical Atlas*. We shall not attempt to pursue our exposition any further, but proceed to some observations about the journey up to the point where the Israelites made their first contact with the kings of Transjordan.

After a stay of twelve months at Sinai and a further period of wandering in the areas to the south of Palestine, the Bible seems to indicate that they were ready to attempt an entry into the promised land from the south, moving in from the general area of Kadesh. At this point Moses sent twelve spies into the land to seek out information that would help the invaders. The instructions given to the spies and the report they brought back are set out in Numbers

9. "Donneés géographiques sur l'exode," *Revue d'histoire et de philosophie réligieuses* (Paris, 1955).

10. "Exploring in Sinai," *BASOR* (Feb., 1948), p. 16.

11. H. Cazelles, *op. cit.*, p. 55.

Figures of Pharaoh Akh-en-Aton and Queen Nefert-iti standing with offerings for the sun-god Aton, cut into a balustrade at Tell el Amarna. The sun-god is represented by the solar disc whose rays stream in benediction upon the worshippers. Note that each ray ends in a hand, and that the hands just above the faces hold a hieroglyph that means "life." (Courtesy, The Metropolitan Museum of Art)

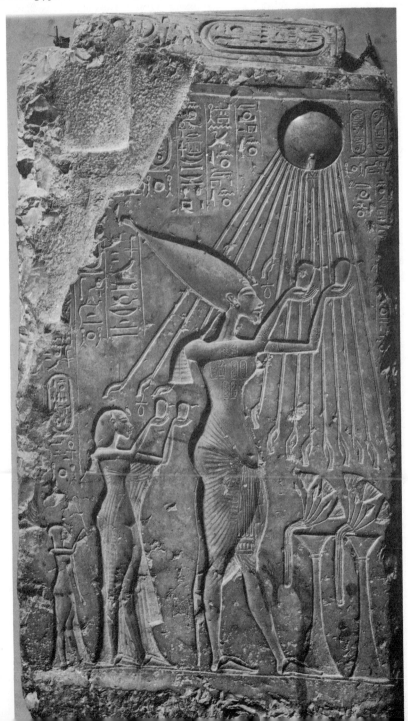

13. Three features of this report are of interest to us just here. The spies reported walled cities, a mixed population, and a fertile land. Each of these takes on a new meaning in the light of modern research. It is a fact that Palestine was studded with walled fortresses at the time. The feudal system under which the land was ruled made for small fortified centers. It was necessary for the local rulers to pay their annual dues to the Egyptian overlord or to his representative and to remain loyal to the Pharaoh. Apart from this they were allowed a good deal of independence, and they seem to have engaged in frequent petty wars among themselves. If ever the Pharaoh showed signs of weakness, there was immediate revolt. This happened in the days of the Pharaoh Akhenaton (about 1370-1353 B. C. or a little later), one of the Eighteenth Dynasty. This ruler was more interested in religious reform than in the maintenance of his Asiatic empire. As a result of his neglect there were inroads into his domains on all sides. The local governors and princes who remained loyal to Egypt wrote letters to Akhenaton pleading for help from the Pharaoh who had removed his capital to Amarna some distance up the Nile. Late in the nineteenth century a peasant woman, rummaging in the ruins of Amarna, discovered some of these letters written on baked clay. Others were found later. They are now known as the Amarna letters. They give a very good insight into the state of Palestine about a century before the Israelites came there. In particular they tell us of several of these walled towns and of how they were being taken over by the invaders. At one time it was thought that the picture given in these letters was a portrayal of the Israelite invasion, but further information now available has shown that the event was quite a different one. The Israelites invaded violently and destroyed towns, whereas in the Amarna letters we see the local inhabitants selling out to the invading peoples, the Aramaeans, the Habiru (not to be confused with the Israelites), and so on.

A second aspect of the report of the spies is their reference to the mixed races of the land (Num. 13:29). Documents from the Palestine of that period have preserved many names which give a general idea of the elements in the population, in much the same way as names like Mackenzie, O'Reilly, Le Page, Schmidt, Kwei-Lian, Ramamurthi in an American town give some indication of racial origins.

And finally the description of the land as one that "flowed with milk and honey" had been given to the same land by Egyptian

In Tell el Amarna were found a number of letters from city governors who appealed to the Egyptian pharaoh for help against incoming Habiru. In the smaller of these two letters the governor of Gubbu informs the king that everything is now well and that he, with his men and chariots, is ready to join Pharaoh's army wherever needed. (Courtesy, The British Museum)

writers of an earlier day. There are extant today at least two accounts of the land in the general area of Palestine, and both give a glowing picture of at least some of its territory. We refer to the tale of Sinuhe the traveler,[12] dated to about 1900 B. C., and to the account of the campaigns of Pharaoh Pepi I,[13] about 2350 B. C.

The story of Israel's fear at the report of the spies and of her failure to proceed with the conquest at that time is well known. The people turned back and remained in the wilderness for many years. When they finally decided to move, they proceeded at once to the east and, skirting Edom and Moab, were able to launch their attack from the east.

SOME ARCHAEOLOGICAL NOTES ON THE WILDERNESS PERIOD

Some reference should be made to the contact of the Israelites with the Kenites. Moses had fled to their land in an earlier day and had married a Kenite woman, daughter of the priest of Midian

12. J. B. Pritchard, *op. cit.*, pp. 18-22.
13. *Ibid.*, p. 227.

69

(Exod. 2:16ff.). The name Kenite suggests the Hebrew word *qain* which means "smith." That there may be significance in this name is shown by the fact that the area below the Dead Sea was, and still is, an area rich in minerals, an area "whose stones *are* iron, and out of whose hills thou mayest dig brass" (Deut. 8:9). The researches of archaeologists like Nelson Glueck have shown that copper was mined in this area at a very early date. The great Solomon had wonderful smelting works here at Ezion Geber, as we shall see. These have now been excavated. It becomes a point of great interest to find that it was precisely in this region that Moses had the serpent of brass prepared (Num. 21:9). Moreover, one of the towns passed on the way to the land of Edom was Punon (Num. 33:42). This is the modern Feinan, an area rich in copper ores, where mining has been carried on at various times in the past.

Another point of interest on which modern discovery has shed light is the reference to Israel's success over some of the foes they met on the way. The Bible states that the people of Israel smote the enemy "with the edge of the sword" (Exod. 17:13, Deut. 13:15, 20:13, Num. 21:24). In Hebrew this phrase is literally "to the mouth of the sword." This now turns out to be a most precise description. Archaeological work has brought to light a great variety of swords, daggers, battle axes, and the like. Many of these have the representation of an animal mouth at the top of the blade, so that the blade appears to issue from the jaws of a wild beast.[14] The phrase "to devour to the mouth of the sword" is a very vivid one indeed.

It was during the wilderness period that the Israelites began to learn the significance of the laws that Moses had drawn up for them. It used to be the opinion of some scholars in the last century that not only were these laws largely the invention of a later day but that even the figure of Moses was largely legendary. Few would hold either of these positions today.[15] It has become increasingly evident that in the thirteenth century B. C. legal and religious codes were well developed. The discovery of the ancient site of Ugarit (modern Ras Shamra) opposite modern Cyprus on the coast of Syria has given to the world a great insight into the religious practices of the Canaanites. Baked clay documents found here have shown that even before the days of Moses the Canaanites had a most complex

14. T. J. Meek, "Archaeology and a Point of Hebrew Syntax," *BASOR* (April, 1951).

15. M. Noth, *The History of Israel* (Engl. transl., 2nd ed.), pp. 135f.

*e back of the throne chair of Tut-ankh-Amon (c. 1358 B.C.) found in an antechamber of
 tomb which was discovered in 1922 in the Valley of the Kings, near Luxor. This panel,
ich is made mostly of gold, shows the young king and his wife in ornate royal attire, and
tes from the period when he still worshipped Aton. This is evident from the symbol of
e sun-god above them. Queen Ankhesenpa-Aton holds a small vase of perfume while she
vingly puts a drop of its contents on her husband's broad collar. (Courtesy, The Metro-
litan Museum of Art)*

system of prayers and rituals, many of them bearing at least some
resemblance to those of the Israelites. We may argue that if the
people of Canaan had such development at the time, there is no
serious reason why the people of Israel should not have had their
own system also.

The same thing applies to the law codes of the ancient East.
It was once thought that the earliest law code was that of the great
Hammurabi, who was supposed to live about 2100 B. C. We know that
he lived nearer to 1700 B.C. and that there were law codes before
his time in Mesopotamia. In very recent years at least two codes
have been discovered in excavations, namely, the codes of the town

71

of Eshnunna and of King Lipit Ishtar.[16] Both of these precede the code of Hammurabi in time, and both show remarkable resemblances to it. There is no serious reason, therefore, why the Israelites should not have had a code of their own. There are, of course, a number of very remarkable resemblances between the code of Moses and that of Hammurabi. This is not to be wondered at since the patriarchal family came from Mesopotamia and would naturally bring with them something of the legal structure of the society which had been theirs until the time of their migration. Many of these laws would be necessary in any system, and we can understand that it would have divine approval.

Perhaps a few words about the Tabernacle in the wilderness would be in order here.[17] The idea of a traveling sacred ark was not peculiar to Israel. Tent shrines are depicted in the third century B. C. and the writer Diodorus tells of Phoenicians taking tent shrines into battle in the seventh century B. C. These are, of course, later than the Israelite period, but they provide a hint that this sort of thing was not unknown in the ancient world.

The shape and structure of the Tabernacle were both familiar to other peoples at the time, particularly to the Canaanites. The materials used were all such as could be obtained in the areas where the Israelites were wandering. Recent discussion has inclined scholars in general to take the Biblical accounts of the Tabernacle in the wilderness more seriously than they have for the past century.

THE LAST STAGE OF THE JOURNEY TO THE PROMISED LAND

Then came a day when Moses and the children of Israel decided to move on. But the decision was to go by an indirect way. There was a well-known trade road that wound its way through Transjordan, the King's Highway (Num. 20:17, 21:22, Deut. 2:27, etc.). It is now established that this road existed from early times. It was used much earlier than the days of the Exodus. A string of Bronze Age fortresses, scattered here and there fairly close to the modern bitumen highway, shows that the road was in use even before 2000 B. C.[18] It was probably the conquest of this road that lay behind the invasion of the four kings of the east mentioned in Genesis 14. In

16. J. B. Pritchard, *op. cit.,* pp. 159-163.
17. F. M. Cross, "The Tabernacle," *BA,* X (1947), pp. 45-68; W. F. Albright, *BASOR,* No. 91 (1943), pp. 39-44, and No. 93, pp. 23-25.
18. N. Glueck, *AASOR,* Vol. XV, p. 104; etc.

the days when the Israelites were passing by, this road was again protected by small walled fortresses which stood at strategic points such as at the descent into the wadis and at the edges of the plateaux where the road came up again from the deep valleys. It is interesting to learn that the Romans used the same path for their great road through Transjordan in the days of Trajan.

Having made the decision to proceed to the promised land, a message was sent to the king of Edom asking permission to pass along the King's Highway. The promise was made that all food and water used would be paid for. The king of Edom refused passage to Israel (Num. 20:14-22). It may be asked why Israel did not attack the Edomites at once since, in any case, they did attack the Amorites a little later on. They had no intention of settling there because they were forbidden by an injunction from God to abhor Edom, who was their brother (Deut. 23:7). There was one strong physical reason why Edom was not attacked at this time. This has become clear only in recent years, largely owing to the work of Professor Nelson Glueck, who has made a thorough surface survey of the whole of Transjordan.[19] He has been able to show that Edom was a small, well-defined and self-contained kingdom surrounded on the west, the east, and the north by fortresses strategically placed. There was no need to have them on the south for there was no danger of invasion from this direction. Israel would have been foolish indeed to attempt to scale the heights of the Edomite plateau which rose two or three thousand feet above the beds of the valleys that surrounded the land. So Israel had to move north up the valley of the Arabah to the west of Edom, then enter the Wadi Zered which formed the northern boundary of Edom, and proceed in an easterly direction, skirting Edom to the north (Num. 21:4; 11-13; Judg. 11:17, 18). The king of Edom would not worry unduly about the passage of Israel to the east, away down there in the valley. There was a good deal of room for the people and their flocks and herds to pass through. Incidentally, it was about this time that the incidents of the brazen serpent and the death of Aaron took place (Num. 20:23-29, 21:5-9).

If Edom refused Israel the right to pass along the King's Highway, perhaps Moab would allow her to pass. Messengers sent to Moab were met by the same refusal. Israel did not attempt to force a passage for much the same reasons. The land of Moab

19. Nelson Glueck, *AASOR*, Vols. 4, 15, 16-19, 25-28; *"The Other Side of Jordan"* (New Haven, 1940).

had been given to the Moabites by God and was not for the possession of Israel at this stage (Deut. 2:9). Moab, like Edom, was surrounded by fortresses and stood securely on her own plateau. So Israel moved along the Wadi Zered to the east.

> *Then they went along through the wilderness, and compassed the land of Edom, and the land of Moab, and came by the east side of the land of Moab, and pitched on the other side of Arnon, but came not within the border of Moab: for Arnon was the border of Moab* (Judg. 11:18).

Next a message was sent to the Amorite king Sihon. He, too, refused to allow Israel to pass along the King's Highway, but he made one foolish mistake. He left the shelter of his fortresses and came out to the plains in front of his kingdom. This gave Israel the chance she wanted. Sihon was defeated in battle and the way was open for the Israelites to move up to the highlands of the Transjordan plateau. Very soon the whole of Transjordan was in the hands of Israel. The two kingdoms of Sihon and Og were subdued and their lands given to the tribes of Reuben, Gad, and half the tribe of Manasseh (Num. 21:21-35; 32).

THE CONQUEST OF THE LAND

Little will be said about the period of Israel's settlement in western Palestine. The Bible pictures two main phases of the operations carried out by Joshua during the conquest. There was one campaign in the south and one in the north.

In the south such towns as Jericho, Ai, Lachish, Debir, Eglon, and Libnah were taken and destroyed. Archaeological work has been done in nearly all of these, and insofar as there is a consistent picture anywhere, it would seem that there was considerable destruction in these towns about 1250 B.C. There are, of course, some problems yet to be solved. The town of Ai poses its own peculiar problem because it seems that the site that has been identified with Ai was destroyed about 2350 B.C. and lay in ruins at the time of the Israelite conquest.[20] Its very name means "ruin." Various suggestions have been offered to account for the fact that Ai is mentioned as being taken by Joshua. One is that it was merely an outpost of Bethel under the control of a military captain. He is styled "king," but this need occasion no difficulty as the Hebrew root simply means

---

20. W. F. Albright, *Archaeology of Palestine* (London, 1954), p. 76.

"ruler." If Ai was only a military outpost there may not have been any substantial buildings there and so nothing tangible would remain. However, this is one of the problems still remaining to be solved.

The general picture in the south is clear.

In the north one town, Hazor (Josh. 11), is singled out for special mention. Here a coalition of Canaanite kings was defeated. It is of great interest to us that only recently the excavation of Hazor was undertaken and the excavator has discovered that there was continuous Canaanite occupation of the town till the middle of the thirteenth century.[21] This, of course, fits in well with the picture we have given elsewhere.

There is no mention of conquest in the center of the land. Possibly the people here, like the Gibeonites, surrendered to Israel without fighting.

One final point of archaeological interest is that even after Israel had secured a good footing in the land there were many pockets of resistance that still remained: "There remaineth yet very much land to be possessed" (Josh. 13:1).

The extent of this unpossessed land is given to us in Judges 1. Some of the towns mentioned in this list have been excavated. Two in particular, Megiddo and Bethshan, tell the story that they were in Egyptian and Canaanite hands till some time after 1200 B. C. Only after the lapse of some years did the typical Israelite culture, as shown by pottery, appear in these towns. The Bible has quite rightly represented the conquest of the land by Israel as being incomplete at the time of Joshua.

With the story of the conquest we have already entered the days of the Judges. The land was divided among the various tribal groups both to the east and to the west of the Jordan. It was to be about 1020 B. C. before there was any semblance of stability and centralized control in the land. We turn then to the days of the Judges.

---

21. Y. Yadin, *BA,* XIX (1956), pp. 2-11; XX (1957), pp. 34-37; XXI (1958), pp. 30-47; XXII (1959), pp. 2-20.

Five:

SETTLING INTO THE LAND

ARCHAEOLOGISTS ARE AGREED THAT THE PERIOD FROM 1200 B. C. to about 1000 B. C. was one of the most disturbed of all periods in the history of Palestine. Excavations show clearly that many cities were burned and laid waste. Some towns were destroyed and rebuilt two or three times during these years. The town of Bethel, for example, suffered severely no less than four times in the two centuries. There is probably no single reason for these destructions, but the fact of considerable political instability in Palestine is clearly borne out by the archaeological evidence. This is, of course, quite in keeping with the picture we have in the book of Judges, where there are references to conflict between the various tribes of Israel and yet other references to conflict between Israel and her hostile neighbors.

ISRAEL'S HOSTILE NEIGHBORS

Modern archaeology has done a great deal to make clear to us the character of Israel's neighbors. On every side there were

77

foes. To the northeast were the Aramaeans. To the northwest were the Canaanites, later to become known as the Phoenicians. In the coastal areas to the southwest the Philistines were a grave menace, while on the southeast were the Moabites and the Edomites, as well as various nomadic groups.

On the purely human level it is a marvel that Israel ever survived the attacks of these peoples. On many occasions she very nearly collapsed before the assaults of her enemies. Yet Israel emerged at the last as a unified nation. It was in the purposes of God that she should survive.

From time to time these neighboring peoples made raids into the territory of the little nation of Israel which was fighting for a foothold in the mountain areas of the new land. On these occasions national leaders arose to defend the people. These leaders were the "Judges." Their resistance to Israel's enemies seems to have been confined to limited areas. Thus, in the southwest it was Samson who warded off the Philistines. Shamgar likewise opposed this enemy. In the north the resistance was led by the woman Deborah, who urged the men of Israel to undertake a great battle in which a Canaanite coalition was overcome. Again, Othniel threw back the oncoming Aramaeans, who had been led by Chushan Rishathaim (Judg. 3). Gideon dealt with the nomadic peoples — the Amalekites, the Midianites, and the Sons of the East (or the Sons of Qedem, as we must call them in the light of modern knowledge). When the Moabites invaded the areas near Jericho, it was Ehud who threw them back. Jephthah the Gileadite defeated the Ammonites. Other minor Judges were active in other areas.

It will be of value to undertake a brief review of the fascinating way in which these peoples around Israel have been brought to life in recent years. We know a great deal about each of them today, and it has become very clear that the Bible has preserved a remarkably reliable picture of their customs and achievements.

The Philistines

The Philistines were part of the great movement of peoples which flowed out of the general Aegean area in the years around 1200 B.C. They are referred to by the Egyptian writers as the "Sea Peoples." It was these Sea Peoples who destroyed the famous city of Troy.

PALESTINE
in the days of
THE JUDGES

ARAMAEANS

Damascus

OTHNEIL

Asher
CANAANITES
Naphtali
Zebulun
Issachar
DEBORAH
GIDEON
Manasseh
JEPHTHAH
AMMONITES

Megiddo
Taanach
Jezreel

Manasseh

Ephraim

Dan
Benjamin
Gad
Jerusalem
EHUD
kelon
Timnah
Reuben
PHILISTINES
za
SAMSON
SHAMGAR
Judah

AMALEKITES

MOABITES

EDOMITES

In Palestine these newcomers settled in the southwest and eventually gave their name to the land. They brought a distinctive culture with them. Their former areas of occupation are clearly recognizable today by the so-called "Philistine pottery." In the Bible, the towns where they are said to have lived are all in the southwest corner of the land. It is of great interest, therefore, to discover that it is precisely in this region that their very distinctive pottery is also found. Indeed, the occurrence of this pottery is quite rare elsewhere.[1]

The Philistines were skilled in the working of metals. Excavations have produced small smelting furnaces at a number of sites. Gerar in the region of Gaza is a case in point. More recently furnaces have been found at Tell Qasile near Tell Aviv. Both copper and iron were worked in these places. It seems to be clear that iron implements were used on the Philistine plains before they were used on the highlands where the Israelites lived.[2] We are reminded of the Biblical reference to the monopoly exercised by the Philistines over the working of metals for agricultural purposes:

> *Now there was no smith found throughout all the land of Israel: for the Philistines said, Lest the Hebrews make them swords or spears: But all the Israelites went down to the Philistines, to sharpen every man his share, and his coulter, and his ax, and his mattock* (I Sam. 13:19, 20).

One object commonly found in excavated Philistine towns is the beer mug. This item was well known in the east at this time. Vessels large and small, equipped with side spouts and strainers, were commonly used for the barley beer which was the popular drink of the day. Professor Albright has observed that from the widespread occurrence of these vessels it is evident that the Philistines were "mighty carousers."[3] This picture is entirely in accord with the picture we have in Judges where we see Samson meeting his death at a Philistine feast where there was a good deal of drinking (Judg. 16:23-25).

According to the Bible, Samson met his death in a house where he was able, by his strength, to cause the two middle pillars

---

1. W. F. Albright, *The Archaeology of Palestine* (London, 1954), pp. 114, 116.
2. *AJA*, Vol. XLIII, No. 3, pp. 458ff.
3. *Op. cit.*, p. 115.

to collapse and thus to bring about the destruction of the whole building. Excavations have shown that some of the large Philistine houses were built around a large central hall which was bisected by a row of pillars, used to support the upper story and the roof.[4]

The Philistines made considerable inroads into Palestine during the years 1200-1000 B. C. Finally they were able to overrun the whole land. At one stage they carried off the Ark of God from the little town of Shiloh. Excavation has shown that they did far more damage than merely to carry off the Ark. They burned the town to the ground at the same time. Shiloh was not occupied again for many a century. In the days of Jeremiah the ruins were still to be seen, and this prophet used them as a lesson to the people of Judah who were pinning their hopes of deliverance simply on the fact that the Temple of God stood in Jerusalem (Jer. 7:12-14).

Further evidence of the versatility of the Philistines is to be seen in their sea trade. It is clear from Egyptian records that some of the Philistine towns were engaging in a lively mercantile industry, exploiting the sea lanes between Egypt and Phoenicia. A fascinating story of the adventures of a certain Wen-Amon,[5] who was sent by the Pharaoh to buy timber from Phoenicia, gives us a remarkable insight into the great activity in shipping along this coast at the time of the Judges. The Canaanites, too, were mixed up in this business. We also have an important hint in the Bible that Israelites were engaged in some way in this traffic, although it seems certain that they were working with the Canaanites rather than with the Philistines:

> *Gilead stayed beyond the Jordan; and Dan, why did he abide with the ships? Asher sat still at the coast of the sea, settling down by his landings* (Judg. 5:17, R.S.V.).

This trading activity was well organized with groups of ships under one control, suggestive of a mercantile organization.

Our general picture of the Philistines is thus one of great technical advance and quite obvious advantage over the Israelites. It is little wonder that they all but overcame the people of Israel. Only the efforts of the great King David were at last successful in subduing this very powerful foe.

4. *BA* (May, 1951), p. 44.
5. J. B. Pritchard, *ANET* (Princeton, 1955), pp. 25-29.

The Jordan River, although the most famous and well-known river in the world, is not an imposing one, particularly not in the region of its origin, in northern Israel. (Courtesy, Trans World Airlines)

THE CANAANITES

In the minds of many Bible readers the Canaanites constituted the main population of Palestine at the time of the judges. They were indeed a very important element but by no means the only element in the population. The Bible refers to other groups, such as Amorites, Jebusites, and Hivites (Judg. 3:5). The Canaanites, however, were a highly cultured people and stood far in advance of Israel at the time.

When the incoming Israelites first met the Canaanites they destroyed many of their towns in a most ruthless fashion. An excellent lesson in comparative architecture is to be gained by setting the fine Canaanite town of Bethel, which the Israelites destroyed, alongside the succeeding towns which the Israelites subsequently built on the site. There were three such towns in the course of two centuries. W. F. Albright remarks that the change in culture is extraordinary. The new towns were quite rude in their construction in comparison with their Canaanite predecessors. Indeed, each phase of the new town deteriorated in construction. The third phase was by far the worst.[6]

This is not by any means an isolated case. There is an over-all superiority of the Canaanite towns on the physical level. Such cities as Megiddo, Bethshan, and Salmonah in the north gave evidence of considerable wealth. Megiddo, for example, had a large and richly ornamented palace at the time. Although there was a degree of looting when it was finally destroyed, many fragments of what were once beautiful objects of gold, ivory, and alabaster remained strewn about the floors of the palace to gladden the hearts of the excavators.

There was, of course, a number of Canaanite towns that were not captured by the Israelites, as a study of Judges 1 will reveal. We have solid evidence to show that towns like Megiddo had no sign of the typical Israelite culture till well on into the eleventh century.

The Canaanites, too, were engaged in trade by sea and, as we have seen, shared with the Philistines the export and import trade with Egypt. In the sphere of religion the Canaanites constituted a more serious menace to Israel. We know a great deal today about the religion of these people. The important documents which were found at Ras Shamra have given us a remarkable picture of the gods and goddesses, the temples and religious rituals, the hymns,

6. *BASOR*, No. 56, pp. 11, 12.

Photograph and drawing of an ivory plaque, showing the prince of Megiddo receiving prisoners and tribute. (Courtesy, The Oriental Institute, The University of Chicago)

prayers, and myths of the Canaanites. Many of their hymns were not unlike the later Psalms of Israel. The sacrifices offered in Canaanite temples resembled those which the Israelites offered to Jehovah both in the names of the sacrifices and the beasts offered, as well as in the ritual observed. But the religion was polytheistic, and highly sensuous, with a strong emphasis on fertility rites. In the temples of the Canaanites there were male and female prostitutes ("sacred" men and women) and all sorts of sexual excesses were practiced. It was believed that in some way these rites caused the crops and the herds to prosper. Baal was the god who cared for the rain and the growth of the crops and the flocks. The goddess Asherah, the goddess of passion and the consort of Baal, was the inspiration of every form of passion whether in love or in war. Even during the days of the Judges the worship of these gods was already finding favor in the eyes of many of the Israelites. The writer of the book of Judges makes the point that it was because Israel served the Baalim and forsook the Lord that they were delivered into the hands of oppressors (Judg. 2:11, 13, etc.).

Archaeological excavations at Gath in the Lachish region. The picture shows foundations that date back to the Early Bronze Period. (Courtesy, Israel Office of Information)

Display of pieces of pottery discovered at Gath, dating from the Bronze Age.
(Courtesy, Israel Office of Information)

One of the outstanding contributions of the Canaanites in the realm of culture was that they were the real originators of the alphabet as a usable medium for writing. It was probably about 1700 B. C. when the first efforts were made to develop an alphabet. Flinders Petrie, the English archaeologist, found some of the earliest attempts at alphabetic writing in the general area of the Sinai peninsula. Certainly by the time of the Judges this new form of writing was widely in use. The Canaanites, however, were versatile enough to be able to use several types of writing for their literature. At Ras Shamra excavators found several scripts in use, including the cumbersome old Akkadian cuneiform (wedge-shaped) script which had been used in lower Mesopotamia in the land of Akkad for the past two thousand years. An attempt to use a special type of cuneiform alphabet was one of the unusual experiments being tried here. A good deal of material was written in this type of script, even though it did not persist in later centuries.

The Canaanites, then, were a most dangerous group of enemies for Israel. Their clear superiority in art, in architecture, in trade, and in many other departments of life must have been most impressive to many of the Israelites. It is little wonder that some began to imagine that their superiority may have had a connection with their religion. This made it easier for some of the Israelites to accept the religion of Canaan.

From the point of view of military conquest Israel, as we have seen, did not succeed in taking all the Canaanite towns. The one major victory reported in the Bible came on the occasion when Deborah was able to urge the tribes of Israel to attack a Canaanite coalition in the north near the waters of Megiddo. Some scholars have seen in the information given in the Bible material for dating this event. The battle took place at "Taanach by the waters of Megiddo" (Judg. 5:19). It has been argued that the mention of Taanach in preference to Megiddo points to a period when Megiddo lay in ruins, but when Taanach was in existence. A date of about 1125 B. c. would fit the facts of archaeology and the facts of Biblical history alike. After this battle the organized resistance of the Canaanites ceased, although many independent towns still remained to be captured by the Israelites.

One final feature of Canaanite life at the time of the Judges should be mentioned. Excavations have uncovered the important

The foundations of the Canaanite temple of the god Mekal (fourteenth century B.C.), the oldest of no less than five temples discovered at Beisan in Palestine, showing the characteristics both of a temple and of a "high place." (Courtesy, The University Museum of the University of Pennsylvania)

Perspective drawing of the sanctuary of Thothmes III (1501-1447 B.C.) at Beth-shan, dedicated to the local god Mekal (see illustration on page 86). (Courtesy, The University Museum of the University of Pennsylvania)

temple of Baal Berith, which stood at Shechem and which featured in the story of Abimelech, the son of Gideon (Judg. 9:4). The ruins of this temple produced evidence to show that it was used during the days of the Judges, although its original foundation goes back to an earlier date. It was a massive structure about twenty-five meters by twenty-one meters in size and was surrounded by a wall about five meters thick (nearly seventeen feet).[7] We can picture the sort of worship that went on there in view of the information to be found on the Ras Shamra texts.

THE ARAMAEANS AND THE NOMADIC GROUPS

To complete the picture of Israel's neighbors we must add to the Philistines and the Canaanites the very important Aramaeans, and also some of the groups such as the Amalekites, the Midianites, and the Qedemites (Sons of the East).

The Aramaeans are rarely mentioned in the book of Judges. Yet they were to become a very significant group in later days. They are known in the English Bible as Syrians. From the days of King David onwards they were a continual menace to the state of Israel.

Their origin is becoming clearer to us in recent times.[8] Already in about 1900 B.C. they were known in lower Mesopotamia. In the centuries that followed they were moving towards the west

7. W. F. Albright, *op. cit.*, p. 104; R. J. Bull, "A Re-examination of the Schechem Temple," *BA* (Dec., 1960), pp. 110-119.
8. A. Dupont Sommer, *Les Araméens* (Paris, 1949); "Sur les debuts de l'histoire araméenne," *VT, Supp. I* (1953), pp. 40-49.

and finding new homes for themselves in the general area which we know today as Syria. The tablet records refer to them in the centuries before the period of the Judges. By 1300 B. C. they were well settled just to the northeast of the land of Canaan. It was one of their kings who invaded Palestine early in the days of the Judges. He is known in the Bible as Chushan Rishathaim (Judg. 3:8, 10).[9]

Interesting material has also come to light in recent years about the domestic use of the camel in the East from about 1200 B. C. onwards. The camel, by no means unknown in previous centuries but used only spasmodically, now came to be widely used as a beast of burden.[10] There are increasing references to camels in the literature of the East after 1200 B. C. The picture of the desert nomads, Midianites, Amalekites, and the Children of the East, using camels to conduct raids into Israelite lands in order to carry off crops and flocks, seems to be entirely in accord with the picture we have from archaeology (Judg. 6:5, 7:12, etc.).

Incidentally, we may have some idea of the type of "pitcher" used by Gideon since the discovery in a tomb near Amman in Transjordan of a peculiar vessel with a handle, standing about ten inches high with an opening in the side about five inches by four inches. A small platform inside was used to support the typical open lamp of the day.[11]

ISRAELITE EVIDENCE FROM THE DAYS OF THE JUDGES

Israel's neighbors, as we have seen, left a good deal of archaeological evidence behind them. The Israelites themselves left some tangible evidence as well. Many new settlements arose in the hill country between 1200 and 1000 B. C. For the first time this part of Palestine became dotted with towns, a circumstance indicating an increase in the population.[12] A number of these towns have been excavated and their ruins show that the Israelite culture was quite different from that in Canaanite towns. In general the houses were much poorer. Indeed, the whole picture is one of comparative

---

9. A. Malamat, "Chushan Rishathaim and the Decline of the Near East Around 1200 B.C.," *JNES* (Oct., 1954).

10. W. F. Albright, *The Biblical Period* (1950), p. 21; J. P. Free, *JNES* (1949), pp. 187-193.

11. *Quarterly Department of Antiquities Palestine*, Vol. XI, Nos. 3, 4, Plate 17.

12. G. E. Wright and F. V. Filson, *The Westminster Historical Atlas* (London, 1953), p. 45.

poverty. The pottery is rougher, the city fortifications are poorly built and scarcely likely to have been of much use in war, and there is a lack of the wealth so often evident in the Canaanite towns. W. F. Albright has noted:

> The archaeologist can scarcely be faced with a greater contrast than that between the well-built and well-drained patrician houses of the last Canaanite Bethel and the rustic constructions and lack of drainage of the earliest Israelite period of buildings.[13]

One fairly new feature of life on the highlands was the widespread use of cisterns. Pottery deposits in cisterns in excavated towns indicate that the art of storing water in rock cisterns came into general use about the thirteenth century B. C.[14] Thereafter many towns were able to exist in the hill country where previously life had been very difficult by reason of the lack of water. These cisterns were for the most part constructed with a narrow neck opening out to a large bulbous reservoir in the limestone below. Water was

13. W. F. Albright, *op. cit.,* pp. 17, 18.
14. *Ibid.,* p. 22.

A large cistern cut into the high rock near Masada, west of the Dead Sea. This particular cistern dates from the days of Herod (see page 279) but serves as a general example of such water storage places. (Courtesy, Israel Office of Information)

drained into these cisterns from the roofs or from the ground around the house. The cistern was generally made watertight by a facing of lime plaster (cf. Jer. 2:13).

We have already made brief reference to the fact that some of the Israelites seem to have engaged in seafaring activities in the north. There is no actual archaeological evidence of this fact but as we have seen, the Bible record is not at all out of keeping with the non-Biblical evidence of sea trade between Egypt and Palestine during these centuries.

There is some further interesting information available from the excavation at ancient Gibeah whose ruins are to be seen today about six miles north of Jerusalem. This town had at least four periods of occupation during its history. These periods can be fitted in very clearly with the literary data in the Bible and elsewhere. It has been demonstrated that the original Gibeah was built on virgin soil sometime during the thirteenth century B. C.[15] It continued on into the next century but was destroyed in the twelfth century B. C. by a fire which left a good deal of ash about in the ruins. The second city was built in the eleventh century in the days of Saul.

The book of Judges tells the story of an attack on Gibeah by the men of Israel as a reprisal for the brutal handling of the concubine of a certain Levite by the Benjamite inhabitants of Gibeah. The town was assaulted and burned to the ground according to the Bible record (Judg. 19, 20).

THE PLIGHT OF ISRAEL AND THE NEED FOR UNITY

Sufficient has now been said to make it clear that the picture in the book of Judges is greatly enlarged by our latest archaeological evidence. It becomes quite clear that the general historical, geographical, cultural, and religious backgrounds of the book are consistent with the general Palestinian setting for the period 1200-1000 B. C.

It might be well to recall, even if only in outline, that Israel's plight at the time was serious indeed. She was, in the first place, torn by disunity. The geographical problems were great. In these days of fast transport we do not realize how difficult it was for the various tribal groups to maintain any sort of cohesion. Imagine the difficulty of maintaining contact between the tribe of Reuben in Transjordan, the tribe of Dan in the southwest, and the tribe of

15. *AASOR,* Vol. IV, (1924).

Asher in the north when it involved traveling long distances on foot or by slow-moving animals over unmade roads along the hilly terrain of Palestine. Local disturbances could get quite out of hand before other tribal groups would know of the trouble. Misunderstandings would easily arise, and did arise, as we see in such incidents as the schismatic altar of Reuben and Gad (Josh. 22), or the jealousy of Ephraim when she was not included in the force that Gideon took to drive out the Midianites and their allies (Judg. 8). Further evidence of intertribal misunderstandings and actual clashes is to be seen in the story of the massacre of the men of Benjamin by men from the surrounding tribes after the concubine of the Levite who stayed overnight at Gibeah had been cruelly killed (Judg. 19).

There was another serious factor causing disunity during these years. This was the tendency for many to follow the religion of the Canaanites. This declension of the Israelites may have been due in part to the subtle attraction of the wealth of the Canaanites. They had fine homes, splendid art, a fine literature, good trade connections around the East, and an apparent superiority in every way over the people of Israel. The unthinking Israelite may have been inclined to associate this wealth with some imagined favor of the gods of Canaan, and as a result he may have forsaken the simpler non-sensuous faith of Israel. Once there was religious apostasy in some areas, there was the possibility of serious disunity. This undoubtedly took place.

The forces for disintegration were thus very strong indeed. There was, as W. F. Albright points out, a strong centrifugal tendency, which was only increased by the assaults of Israel's hostile foes on every hand.[16] For not only did these enemies attack the tribes in isolated areas, but they compelled some of them to leave their homes in order to find new safe areas in which to live. The tribe of Dan is a case in point (Judg. 18:1ff.).

Throughout the land, both east and west of Jordan, there were aggressive moves from surrounding peoples. It was indeed a day when "every man did *that which was* right in his own eyes" (Judg. 17:6). This descriptive phrase, applied to the Israelites themselves, characterized the whole political condition of the land at this time.

As against these disruptive forces, however, there were some unifying forces. The people of Israel possessed, after all, a common language, common customs, a common religion and loyalty to Jehovah,

16. W. F. Albright, *op. cit.*, p. 19.

91

and a common Mosaic tradition of law. Moreover, despite apostasy, there was a central sanctuary at Shiloh which must have exercised some sort of cohesive force. What Israel needed was a great leader who would command the respect of all the tribes, and who would unite Israel's resources of manpower in order to throw off her aggressors. It was left to the last judge, Samuel, to gather together the national hopes for a king and to focus these on Saul, who emerged as Israel's first monarch.

ONE NATION – ONE KING

BEFORE ISRAEL FINALLY REACHED THE STAGE WHERE SHE WAS ABLE to choose a king who would be acceptable to all the tribes at once, there were a number of experiments in kingship. Perhaps the best known of these was the attempt of the tribes to make Gideon king after his success in beating off the marauding nomadic groups. On his return home the men of Israel said, "Rule thou over us, both thou, and thy son, and thy son's son also." Gideon was unwilling to undertake such a responsibility and said, "I will not rule over you, neither shall my son rule over you: the Lord shall rule over you" (Judg. 8:22, 23).

A second abortive attempt at kingship was that of Gideon's son Abimelech, who conspired with the Canaanites of Shechem (Judg. 9:6ff.). He had all his brothers put to death, except the one who escaped, and after a short-lived rule he was killed when a woman dropped a millstone on his head while he was attacking the besieged city of Thebez.

ARCHAEOLOGY AND THE DAYS OF KING SAUL

It was in the days of the Judge Samuel that general agreement among the tribes was obtained. The need for a king had become quite clear in the minds of the people and they began to cry out for a king "like all the nations" (I Sam. 8: 5). At first Samuel seemed to be unwilling to agree to their request, realizing, no doubt, that the people had a wrong motive. They wanted a king at all costs. What they needed was a ruler who would recognize that God was their Sovereign and that any other ruler should be but the vice-regent of God. Israel was essentially a theocracy whose kings needed to be men after God's own heart. After a time, Samuel was able to choose Saul the son of Kish, a man Israel needed. Saul was indeed God's choice. In due course Saul was anointed and was able to demonstrate both his physical prowess and his spiritual qualities. In his defeat of the Ammonite king at Jabesh Gilead (I Sam. 11), he showed that he could lead men in battle. In his sharing the experience of the prophets (I Sam. 10) he showed that he had a heart to yield to the influences of God's Spirit. He was accordingly acclaimed as king and widely accepted by the people.

Saul's life was one long struggle against the hostile neighbors that surrounded Israel. As we read the story of his life in the first book of Samuel we trace the steps of a life which began with promise and ended in tragedy. There were several serious acts of rebellion against God. Many of his actions earned the contempt and keen opposition of the best men in Israel. Finally he met his death by falling on his sword after the battle of Mount Gilboa in which the Philistines defeated the army of Israel (I Sam. 31).

Archaeological research has given us some useful light on certain aspects of the story recounted in the book of Samuel. His chief opponents, the Philistines, are now more clearly delineated for us after the many excavations in the Philistine plains. There is no need to repeat the detail given in the previous chapter. We can, however, add a note to the Philistine story as it touches on the last part of the story of Saul. When Saul died after that tragic battle at Mount Gilboa, the Philistines desecrated his body, which they found lying where it fell. His head was cut off and placed in "the temple of Dagon," and his armor was taken to "the house of Ashtaroth" in Bethshan, and his body was fastened to the wall of the same city.[1]

---

1. I Sam. 31:9, 10; I Chron. 10:9, 10.

The mighty mound of Bethshan (present-day Beisan) which once supported the city of Bethshan. It was occupied intermittently for five thousand years. Most likely the battle of Mount Gilboa, in which Saul and his three sons perished, took place near here, whereupon their bodies were fastened to the walls of Bethshan. (Religious News Service Photo)

We can be fairly certain that one of the two temples excavated at Bethshan during the years 1921 to 1933 by C. S. Fisher, Alan Rowe, and G. M. Fitzgerald was this actual temple. Here were typical temples of the day where the cult of the gods of Canaan was carried out. Numerous items of religious significance were found in these temples. Which of the two temples was the one referred to in the story is, of course, impossible to say. It is now quite clear, however, that there was a temple in Bethshan at the time.

The most important single item of archaeological interest is the fortress of Gibeah, which was excavated by W. F. Albright.[2] It was the second occupation at Gibeah and replaced the little town that had been destroyed by fire in the days of the Judges (Judg. 19, 20). After the destruction of the first town the site remained unoccupied for about a century. It was succeeded by this little fortress, which probably served as Saul's headquarters during the

2. W. F. Albright, *Archaeology of Palestine* (London, 1954), pp. 120-122.

A pastoral scene near the mound of Megiddo, taken from the east. (Courtesy, The Oriental Institute, The University of Chicago)

Philistine wars. It was larger than the subsequent fortress which eventually rose on its ruins.[3] It was not a luxurious place, although it was marked by a "certain measure of rustic luxury."[4] It was a two-storied building and contained a variety of pottery vessels, including a number of large cooking pots, and an iron plough point which suggested that some sort of agriculture was carried on in the area. The fortress was a rectangular building with double walls and a tower at each corner as far as we can judge from the ruins today.

David, Israel's Greatest King

Bible history relates how David had to flee from Saul and find a home among the Philistines (I Sam. 27). It seems that David became a sort of vassal of these enemies of Israel. When Saul was killed in battle, David was allowed to become king in Hebron (II Sam. 2:1-4), while Saul's son fled across the Jordan and became king in Mahanaim (II Sam. 2:8). From the Philistine point of view it was probably a desirable thing to have two kings ruling over

3. See above, p. 90, n. 15.
4. *AASOR*, Vol. IV, pp. 51f.

Israel. "Divide and conquer" is an old principle. The arrangement was, however, short-lived. After seven years the two parts of the kingdom were reunited and David became king over all Israel (II Sam. 5). Although he was forced back by the Philistines to his fortress (II Sam. 5:17), he was able eventually to fight his way out and deliver his whole nation as well.

David's life was filled with a number of magnificent achievements. On every side he was able to push back Israel's enemies. Philistines, Moabites, Edomites, Arameans, Ammonites, all suffered at his hands (I Sam. 5, 8, 10, etc.). At his death, David left a kingdom at peace from her foes. In addition to these military achievements there were remarkable advances in the spheres of government, commerce and trade, religion, and international affairs. The whole organization of government was undertaken in a workmanlike fashion. Officers were appointed over the several departments of state (I Chron. 27:25-34). Trade connections were made with the Phoenicians and perhaps with others. In matters of religion the Temple services were organized and the music of the Temple was arranged. It was one of David's greatest hopes to build the Temple but he was denied this privilege (I Sam. 7). It was left to his son Solomon to complete the task according to the pattern of his father David. One of David's greatest achievements, however, was the setting up of Jerusalem as the national capital. But it had to be captured from the Jebusites (I Sam. 5). There was shrewd design in choosing this site, for it lay outside the borders of Judah, and therefore a member of the tribe of Judah could not be accused of partisanship in the choice of a site for his capital. The place was, moreover, strategically placed in the central hill country, and rather inaccessible to an invading foe. It was in all probability a place which had honored associations with Abraham.

Excavations at sites in the general southeastern areas of Palestine have revealed several towns with a well-known type of fortification, the so-called casemate walls, which are really two comparatively thin walls braced across by transverse walls and giving the appearance of great solidity. These date to about the start of the tenth century B. C. and can be attributed either to Saul or to David.[5] The Biblical picture would seem to suggest David rather than Saul, since Saul was far too busy with his enemies to be able to devote his energies to building. The sites are strategically placed in regard to the

5. W. F. Albright, *op. cit.,* p. 122.

97

Philistines. There is nothing at all surprising in the fact that David should feel it necessary to undertake some sort of fortification against the Philistines in this area. Such a system would provide some check on their inroads.

One of the clearest pictures we have of David in the Biblical record is that of a musician and an organizer of the Temple music (I Chron. 25). It is now clear that Palestine was well known around the East for many centuries as a land where music was widely enjoyed. As early as 1900 B.C. Egyptian artists painted Palestinian nomads who visited their land with asses and goods for trade.[6] Among the people pictured were some who carried stringed instruments like harps. Egyptian monuments of the New Empire from about 1550 onwards refer to a variety of examples of music from the land of Canaan.[7] The Ras Shamra texts from Ugarit, the famous Canaanite town on the mainland opposite Cyprus, have produced an abundance of religious poetry and a number of references to a class of temple personnel known as *sarim*.[8] These appear to have been more or less similar to the Hebrew "singers" of the days of David and after. Later records of the Assyrians also refer to considerable musical activity in this land.

Further evidence is probably to be obtained from a study of the names of some of the men employed by David in this service. At least some of these have Canaanite names[9] and others are said to have been "aboriginals"[10] of the land. It is legitimate to think that David compelled some of the local inhabitants to serve him in the capacity of musicians in much the same way as he forced other conquered people to do other work.

The tantalizing reference to the capture of Jerusalem in II Samuel 5:6-8 speaks of David's men reaching the gutter (water shaft). David said on that day, "Whosoever getteth up to the gutter, and smiteth the Jebusites . . . *shall be chief and captain*" (II Sam. 5:8). The translation of the Hebrew word here is open to various interpretations. If the reference is to some kind of water tunnel we may find an explanation in the wonderful water systems of the Canaanites. At a variety of places in Palestine underground tunnels,

6. On the Beni Hasan wall paintings, see p. 20. See also W. F. Albright, *op. cit.*, p. 209.
7. W. F. Albright, *Archaeology and the Religion of Israel*, p. 125.
8. C. H. Gordon, *Ugaritic Manual*, III (Rome, 1955), p. 327.
9. W. F. Albright, *op. cit.*, p. 127.
10. Hebrew *ezrah*: aboriginal (I Kings 4:31; I Chron. 2:6).

which enabled the people to take water into the city, have been brought to light. The best of these was that at Megiddo. We may imagine that the Jebusites of Jerusalem exploited a similar kind of arrangement. What was necessary for David's men was to find the entrance to this water tunnel, enter it, slay its defenders, and then wait there till other people from the town came for their water. By eliminating them one by one the final surrender of the town through thirst was assured.

There is, however, one other possibility. W. F. Albright translates the word gutter as "hook" by comparison with a similar word used by the Assyrians.[11] He imagines the use of some kind of climbing apparatus where hooks were used to grasp the wall. He translates the sentence: "Whoever getteth up with the hook and smiteth the Jebusites." In that case the capture of Jerusalem was by quite a different method. Whatever the method, the stronghold of the Jebusites was at last taken. The method by which it was captured is probably still one of those secrets which must be left to the archaeologist to explain as his knowledge of ancient methods of warfare is enlarged.

11. W. F. Albright, "The Old Testament and Archaeology," *Old Testament Commentary*, H. C. Alleman and E. E. Flack (Philadelphia, 1954), p. 149.

A view of Mount Zion, Jerusalem, religious and national center of the kingdom of David and Solomon and symbol of the presence of the Lord. (Courtesy, Israel Office of Information)

One final reference to archaeological evidence from David's time comes from Gibeon, now known as El-Jib. It has been under excavation since 1956 by J. B. Pritchard. In the course of the excavation, one of those things happened that every archaeologist hopes for. Inscribed materials in the form of Hebrew writing on the handles of large jars gave the exact name of the place as *gb'n*, that is, Gibeon.[12] These jar handles were found among the debris in a very large pool excavated into the native rock inside the north wall of the city. The pool was 11.3 meters in diameter and 10.8 meters deep and was in use from shortly after 1200 B. C. it would seem. It was therefore there in David's time. The excavator has suggested that this is the pool referred to in II Samuel 2:12-17 where the servants of David and the servants of Ishbosheth, Saul's son, met and did battle.

The Achievements of Solomon

Archaeological discoveries relating to Solomon's time are quite remarkable. Professor Albright has observed in his useful volume on the archaeology of Palestine that "the age of Solomon was certainly one of the most flourishing periods in the history of Palestine. Archaeology, after a long silence, has finally corroborated Biblical tradition in no uncertain way."[13]

Solomon entered on the marvelous inheritance left to him by his father David. It lay in his hands to make a great nation out of the now united tribes. At first he succeeded in a measure. By the end of his life he had ruined his work and allowed the growth of such serious discontent that shortly after his death the whole structure which had been built up so carefully by David came tumbling down.

At the time when Solomon ruled over Israel, Phoenicia was one of the greatest powers in the East. Its people, who represented the northern section of the Canaanites, had by now given up military ambitions and were concentrating on trade. The Phoenicians were excellent technicians and were evidently in great demand all around the East to judge by the widespread occurrence of clearly Phoenician influences in art and architecture in all the surrounding countries. The Bible makes it clear that Solomon availed himself of the skills that these Phoenician tradesmen were ready to offer to anyone who

---

12. J. B. Pritchard, *BA* (Dec., 1956), pp. 66-75; *Illustrated London News* (Oct., 1956), pp. 695-697, (March, 1958), pp. 505-507; *Vetus Testamentum,* Supp. VII (1960), pp. 1-12.
13. W. F. Albright, *The Archaeology of Palestine,* p. 123.

was able and willing to pay. Hence, in building, in metal working, in shipbuilding, in the manning of ships, and indeed in many other ways the influence of these people became important during the days of Solomon.

A study of the description of the Temple and of the art work used in it in chapters 6 and 7 of I Kings will reveal many remarkable resemblances between the work of the Phoenicians and the artistry in the Temple. Chapter 6 makes a special reference to the woodwork which lined the Temple. It was largely cedar which had been imported from the king of Tyre (I Kings 5:10). Solomon used a great deal of this cedar to build the house of the Lord (I Kings 6:9, 10, etc.). Woodworkers carved cherubim, palm trees, open flowers, and the like (I Kings 6:29, etc.) into the cedar boards. A similar picture is given in the case of the metal work as described for us in chapter 7. The details here are a good deal more complete. The copper used in the various items was fashioned into the same kinds of patterns. Reference is made to cherubim, lions, oxen, palm trees, pomegranates, network, flowers of lilies, and so on (I Kings 7:18, 26, 29, 36, etc.). Now a study of the motifs used in the Phoenician ivory inlay work, which has been discovered in many ancient sites excavated in recent decades, will make it quite clear even to the non-technical reader that the motifs used in both the woodwork and the metalwork of Solomon's Temple were strongly influenced by Phoenician patterns. This is to be expected since there is specific reference in the Bible to the employment of Phoenician tradesmen in each case.

There are important references to Solomon's building activities in the Bible:

> And Solomon's builders and Hiram's builders and the Gebalites did fashion them, and prepared the timber and the stones to build the house (I Kings 5:18).

Again in reference to the metalwork, we learn that Solomon sent and fetched Hiram, a tradesman from Tyre, a man filled with wisdom and understanding and cunning to work all works in brass (I Kings 7:13, 14).

It is little wonder, therefore, that the Bible narratives betray the strong Phoenician traits referred to. Phoenician workmen were bound to leave behind products of their workmanship that bore their own characteristic imprint. The Bible here has preserved a remarkable and reliable description of Phoenician art motifs.

101

In the matter of the architecture of Solomon's buildings we have some interesting material from modern excavations. Perhaps the most striking fact that has emerged is that the whole pattern of the Temple of Solomon is very close to that of other temples in the East at this time. The idea of two main parts in the Temple, a holy place and a most holy place, although it follows the arrangement of the ancient Tabernacle in the wilderness, can be paralleled in a number of places.[14] Even the two big, free-standing pillars referred to in Solomon's Temple as Jachin and Boaz have their parallels in the temples of the East. It seems clear that Solomon relied in part on the Phoenician architects in the actual design of the Temple. Even if Solomon's Temple followed in a general way the ancient Tabernacle model, the working out of these details in an actual Temple seems to have followed patterns that were fairly usual all around the East at the time.

Another feature of the architecture of Solomon's buildings on which we have archaeological light is described in the following terms:

> *And the great court round about had three courses of hewn stones, and a course of cedar beams; like as the inner court of the house of Jehovah, and the porch of the house* (I Kings 7:12 R.V.).

This passage gives us a feature that was used in other places besides the Temple. In the great excavation at Megiddo, carried out during the years 1925 to 1939, precisely this arrangement was found in the town that was there in Solomon's day. It was commented on at the time by R. S. Lamon and G. M. Shipton, the excavators. In describing a certain building they wrote:

> One feature of the building . . . is that the piers of its podium consist of three rows of hewed stones. Wherever the third course was preserved, the upper surface was burned black, and therefore some combustible material, presumably wood, must have overlain the stones. On the floor of the courtyard, near the northwest corner of the building, there was found a large piece of wood charcoal in a deposit of ash which lay along the west wall of the building and which, when analysed, proved to be that of cedar. In addition to indications of timber above

14. G. E. Wright and F. V. Filson, *The Westminster Historical Atlas* (London, 1945), p. 48.

stonework there were still to be seen lying on top of the podium walls sufficient remains of mud brick to show that this material too entered into the composition of the super-structure. This evidence accords well with the type of construction in Solomon's temple in Jerusalem as described in I Kings 7:12.[15]

The occurrence of the so-called proto-Ionic capitals in the buildings of Solomon's time, and for that matter in later buildings as well, is a further indication of the strong influence of the Phoenicians at the time.[16]

It is further to be noted that the use of wood in the interior of the Temple of Solomon can be compared with the contemporary usage of wood in several structures in the area of Syria.

During his lifetime Solomon strengthened Israel's army. In particular he built up a considerable force of chariots. These were concentrated at strategic points where chariot cities were built and where horsemen were trained (I Kings 4:26, 10:26-29, etc.). The nature of these chariot cities is now much clearer to us since the excavations at Megiddo, one of Solomon's chariot cities. In 1928 P.L.O. Guy found a remarkable set of ruins at this site.[17] Here were a great number of units in a complex group of buildings each of which consisted of a central passage about three meters wide, flanked by two rows of stone pillars which seem to have served both as tie-posts and as supports for the roof. Behind each row of posts was an area of some three meters wide for the horses. Each unit accommodated about thirty horses. Similar groups of stable units are known at Taanach, Hazor, Tell el Hesi (Eglon?) and Gezer. While it is true that more recently some doubt has been expressed as to whether these ruins at Megiddo did in fact belong to Solomon, and not rather to Ahab, the appearance of Solomons's stables may be understood from the ruins at Megiddo.[18]

Solomon had to import horses from other lands. According to I Kings 10:28, 29, Solomon obtained his horses from Egypt. This passage in the Authorized Version of the Bible has an odd ring about it: "And Solomon had horses brought out of Egypt and linen yarn"

15. R. S. Lamon and G. M. Skipton, *Megiddo I* (Chicago, 1939), p. 59.
16. W. F. Albright, *op. cit.*, pp. 126f.
17. *Ibid.*, pp. 123f. Cf. Y. Yadin, "Hazor Ruins," *IEJ*, 8 (1958), pp. 80-86.
18. Y. Yadin, "New Light on Solomon's Megiddo," *BA* (May, 1960), pp. 62-68.

Remnants of the floors and hitching posts of the stables of Solomon, as excavated at Megiddo.
(Courtesy, The Oriental Institute, The University of Chicago)

(I Kings 10:26). The word for "linen yarn" might well mean "from QWH," where QWH refers to a country. At the time of the translation of the Authorized Version of the English Bible such a land was unknown but today we translate this passage rather differently in the light of our discovery of the ancient land of Que (QWH), which lay in the area of Asia Minor at the time of Solomon. The Hebrew of the passage can now be translated as follows: "And Solomon had horses brought out of Egypt and out of Que."

It is clear from the Bible that Solomon must have had considerable sources of copper. Many tons of copper would have been required for all the brass (Hebrew "copper") items used in the Temple. The Bible has a specific reference to the casting of metals in the plains of Jordan (I Kings 7:46). There can be no doubt about the existence of mines and metal-working furnaces in the area of the Jordan in

104

these times. Nelson Glueck has made this clear in a variety of ways. In his delightful book *The River Jordan* he remarks:

> I found fragments of slag on some of the tells north of Admah and especially upon the site of ancient Succoth. In Solomon's time this entire district in the Jordan Valley hummed with industrial activity devoted to the turning out of finished metal articles for the adornment of the new Temple.[19]

Further evidence of the great activity in the smelting and working of metals at this time is to be found in the discovery of deposits of copper ore in the areas south of the Dead Sea. These were quite clearly worked in the days of Solomon. Nelson Glueck found a great deal of evidence to show that the mines in this area were worked from about the days of David onwards for several centuries. But the activity was particularly intense in the days of Solomon. Quite apart from the many small furnaces found in the area below the Dead Sea, Glueck was able to excavate the ancient site of Ezion

19. Nelson Glueck, *The River Jordan* (Philadephia, 1946), p. 146.

A beautiful view of the Dead Sea and the mountains of Moab as seen from the Wilderness of Judah; it is a scene similar to that of the surroundings of the Qumran community. (The Matson Photo Service)

Geber.[20] Here he found that a flourishing town existed in the days of Solomon. The most important discovery was that this town was a center of copper refining. An amazing building was uncovered in which the ancient crucibles were still to be seen in place. The smelting was carried out by making use of the strong winds blowing from the north. Draughts were led into the furnaces, and the refining process was carried on in a highly technical manner. There must have been a good deal of copper produced in this factory. Very likely Solomon used a lot of it for trading purposes.

It is interesting to learn from the Bible that Solomon had a port on the Red Sea at precisely this point. That a port existed here is borne out by the excavations at Ezion Geber. The town produced various pieces of evidence which pointed to the existence of a port there. In the first place, there were many items which may very easily be reconciled with sea activity, such as copper and iron nails, pieces of rope of various kinds, and pieces of tar. Further, there were items found here which came from other lands. Some were of Egyptian origin and yet others came from southern Arabia. All of this points to a center of trade in which the sea played a great part.

A linguistic item points in an interesting way to the activities at this port. The Bible tells us that Solomon had a "navy of Tarshish" here (I Kings 10:22). The very word "Tarshish" may betray the purpose for which the port was used. Professor Albright has suggested that this word has linguistic links with a Semitic root which is used of the flow of liquids or, perhaps by a metaphorical use, of the flow of molten metals.[21] In that case a Tarshish fleet may well be a refinery fleet. The activity of the Phoenicians here can be compared with their activity in the island of Sardinia where activity in the production of copper at this time is now established.[22]

Incidentally, this work seems to add point to the story in the Bible that the Queen of Sheba paid a visit to Solomon (I Kings 10). There is clear evidence that there were trade connections between Palestine and southern Arabia at the time. The ancient kingdom of Seba (Hebrew "Sheba") was situated in the southwest corner of Arabia. Quite recently this area has been visited by a party of archaeologists. A great deal of evidence was obtained, but unfor-

20. N. Glueck, *The Other Side of Jordan*, pp. 50-113.
21. W. F. Albright, "New Light on the Early History of the Phoenician Colonization," *BASOR*, No. 83, pp. 21ff.
22. *Ibid.*, pp. 14ff.

tunately the local Arabs made continuance of the work impossible.[23]
Sufficient has been discovered, however, to show that this area was
a flourishing place in the days of Solomon. If we are to have further
evidence of the Queen of Sheba it will probably come from this area.

One valuable piece of written evidence from this age is the
now famous Gezer calendar written in the old Phoenician script on
a piece of limestone. The writing gives us valuable insight into the
agricultural activities of the land at the time. A recent translation
by W. F. Albright reads as follows:

> His two months are [olive] harvest,
> His two months are planting [grain],
> His two months are late planting;
> His month is hoeing up of flax,
> His month is harvest of barley,
> His month is harvest and feasting;
> His two months are vine-tending;
> His month is summer fruit.[24]

The Close of Solomon's Life

Solomon's reign which began with such promise was to end
tragically. We have seen how very remarkably the Biblical account
of his reign has been corroborated by modern archaeological discovery. The Bible gives us a sad picture of the collapse of the
kingdom at Solomon's death. Yet it is not to be wondered at that
the revolution came. In a variety of ways Solomon sowed the seeds
of revolt by his own foolish methods of government. It was not
altogether wise to divide the land into new zones in the way he
did (I Kings 4). Some of the new boundaries cut across the old
tribal boundaries and this led to certain tribal disagreements. Moreover,
the king resorted to heavy taxation and to a sort of forced labor
in order to carry out his work of erecting great buildings, like his
own palace and the Temple. Israelite men were sent in courses to
Lebanon to cut the cedar trees — a month in Lebanon and two months
at home. There was something of extravagance in the royal building
program. In addition to this, the king offended the religious scruples
of many of the people by allowing his foreign wives to erect their
shrines in the very shadow of the Temple of God (I Kings 11).

23. Wendell Phillips, *Qataban and Sheba* (London, 1955).
24. J. B. Pritchard, *ANET* (Princeton, 1955), p. 320.

Many foreign favorites were apparently encouraged in the court, the most notable among them being the Phoenicians.

All of these grievances were the basis for considerable dissatisfaction among the people. On Solomon's death the people quite naturally hoped for some relief from his son Rehoboam. Had this son been wise he might have made concessions so as to overcome the many legitimate grievances of the people. But he unwisely followed the advice of his friends and as a result the whole kingdom collapsed. Thereafter there were to be two kingdoms in the land (I Kings 12).

Seven:

THE KINGS OF ISRAEL

Aﾠ FTER THE DEATH OF SOLOMON THE NORTHERN KINGDOM OF ISRAEL
founded by Jeroboam set out on its disturbed course which was
to come to a sad end after only two hundred years of independent
existence. In that time there were to be no less than nineteen kings.
These belonged to nine different families in all. There was great
insecurity in government. If we use the term "dynasty" for a
ruling house, then we can say that only the Fourth and the Fifth
Dynasties achieved any stability at all.

Three features about these days are important to remember.
In the first place, Israel had periods of conflict and periods of
friendship with her neighbor and brother Judah. Secondly, the great
nation Assyria lay in the background of the history of these days
like an ogre and was to cause a great deal of trouble to Israel and
Judah alike. Thirdly, these were the days of the great preaching
prophets – Elijah, Elisha, Hosea, Amos, Micah, and Isaiah.

Before we discuss the kings of Israel it will be necessary to
give some account of the Assyrians so that we may appreciate their
significance for the history of Israel. We owe a great deal to

Assyrian records in interpreting the story of Israel since information was recorded in the Assyrian palaces about at least six of Israel's kings. Furthermore, several of the Assyrian kings are known to us in the Bible. It was not for nothing that Israel referred to the Assyrians as a rod (Isa. 10:5), a razor (Isa. 7:20), and a flood (Isa. 8:7, 8). We turn, then, to give a brief review of the history and culture of the great Assyrian nation.

THE ASSYRIANS: THEIR HISTORY, CULTURE, AND SIGNIFICANCE FOR BIBLE HISTORY[1]

The heart of the Assyrian nation lay in the very fertile region surrounding the middle Tigris River in the general area of modern Mosul. In the days of the Israelite patriarchs the Assyrians were already a recognizable group. They were trading with the old Hatti people in Asia Minor. One of their remarkable king lists[2] tells of their earliest kings who "lived in tents." The second group comprised kings "whose fathers were known." The third group, of only six, had three foreigners. From king number 33 on to the last king, number 107, we have a good deal of detail for each. One of the great kings of early times was Shamshi-Adad, a contemporary of Hammurabi. He reigned from about 1748 to 1716 B. C. This was about the time of the Hyksos kings in Egypt. The great Dynasty Eighteen, which was so powerful in Palestine and in western Asia generally, was prevented from expanding too far to the east by the Assyrians. In the days when the religious reformer Akhenaton neglected his empire in Asia, the Assyrians were able to push to the west and occupy the land between the Tigris and the Euphrates rivers. This was in the time of the strong Assur-Uballit (1354-1318 B. C.).

During the days when Israel was moving into the promised land, and all through the unsettled period of the Judges, the Assyrians were consolidating their position at home. At the time of the Exodus there was a very strong king, Adad-Nirari (1304-1273 B. C.), who subdued the king of Babylon. With the collapse of the powerful nations like Egypt and the Hittites at the time of the invasion of the Sea Peoples about 1200 B. C., Assyria was ready to exploit the

1. W. L. Hallo, "From Qarqar to Carchemish, Assyria and Israel in the Light of New Discoveries," *BA* (May, 1960), pp. 34-61.
2. *JNES* (July, 1942; October, 1942; January, 1943).

new situation. Just at the start of the eleventh century the first Tiglath Pileser (1118-1078 B. C.) was pushing into the areas occupied by the Aramaeans (Syrians). From that time onwards it became quite a regular feature of Assyrian practice to invade lands to the west for plunder and economic gain.

The great figure in Assyrian expansion was King Ashur-nasir-pal (883-859 B. C.). He moved the capital from Ashur to Calah (Nimrud), and set about to organize the Assyrian army into a tremendous machine. Nimrud was the base where the army was recruited and trained. Bowmen, spearmen, and slingers made up the infantry. The more mobile units were the cavalry, armed in much the same way. Then there were the charioteers, one of the most dreaded units of the Assyrian army, whose thunder from afar struck terror into many a nation. These were vividly described by the prophet Nahum (Nah. 2:3, 4; 3:2, 3). Other units were trained in

One of the first and greatest kings of the Assyrians was Ashur-nasir-pal II (883-859 B.C.), who built himself a military capital at Nimrud, twenty miles south of present-day Mosul, on the east bank of the Tigris, and fortified it with a citadel and towered city wall, remnants of which are seen in this photograph. (Courtesy, Consulate General of the Republic of Iraq)

siege warfare, which the Assyrians worked out to a fine art. Siege apparatus included battering rams, large wooden or cane shields to protect the attackers before the walls, scaling ladders, and great slings. There were special techniques for building earth ramparts on which the battering rams could be run up. Still other units of the army were trained to cross rivers, to climb mountains, to undertake anything

This huge (ten and a half feet high) human-headed winged bull guarded the gateway to Ashur-nasir-pal's palace in Nimrud. Note that it has five legs so that observers from the side would always see at least four. (Courtesy, The British Museum)

that was necessary for the transport of the Assyrian army. All this Ashur-nasir-pal established on firm foundations, building on the past no doubt, but providing that final drive that made the whole war machine the wonder and the terror of the East. He campaigned in a great half-circle around his land. Although he did not reach the little kingdoms in Palestine, he did mention many states in the vicinity,

This is part of the monument Ashur-nasir-pal set up in the courtyard of his palace. In the 154 lines of the text surrounding his image he tells that he built this city Calah with the labor of his prisoners of war, and that on the completion of the work he made a royal banquet of celebration for all the inhabitants of the new city, 64,000 in number, and for another 5,000 distinguished guests from the farther parts of his empire. Around his head are the symbols of the great gods of Assyria. (Courtesy, Consulate General of the Republic of Iraq)

like Tyre and Sidon, from whom he took tribute, and although he did not refer to the contemporary King Omri of Israel, it is of some significance that the Assyrians referred to Israel by the term "Bit-Humria," that is, "House of Omri."

The successor of Ashur-nasir-pal was Shalmaneser III (859-824 B. C.). He is not known in the Bible but his records tell us that King Ahab was involved in a war with him. He left us a picture of King Jehu on a large black obelisk to be seen today in the British Museum. It is the only picture of a Bible king that we have.[3] In his day the great prophet Elijah was preaching in Israel.

3. J. B. Pritchard, *ANET* (Princeton, 1955), pp. 280f.

Tiglath Pileser III, accompanied by his driver and captain, standing in his war chariot, no doubt a representation of his going on one of his campaigns in Syria or Palestine. In Babylonian texts he is known by his native name Pul, the same name by which he is known in the Bible (II Kings 15:19, I Chron. 5:26). (Courtesy, The British Museum)

After the death of Shalmaneser III the Assyrians lost very much of their vigor for the best part of a century. During these years they had troubles nearer home and were unable to raid lands to the west. This provided a respite for little Syrian and Hebrew states and they were able to indulge in some local wars. We can say that from 823 to 745 B. C., except for a few years around 800 B. C., the Assyrians were of no great danger in western Asia. In 745 B. C., however, one of the Assyrian generals usurped the throne and took the name of one of the great kings of the past, calling himself Tiglath Pileser III. He reigned from 745 to 727 B. C. At home he was able to restore control, subdue some of the enemies who had kept Assyria from expansion all those years, and then turn once again to the west. He came into vital touch with Israel and is referred to in the Bible (II Kings 15:19, 29; 16:7, 10). At a time of dispute between Israel and Judah, the king of Judah foolishly called on the king of Assyria for help. This led to the overthrow of the king of Syria,[4] who at the time was an ally of Israel. Then Tiglath Pileser invaded Israel and took many captives (II Kings 15:29, 30). At the same time Judah herself had to pay tribute and, in effect, lost her liberty. The king of Israel at the time was Pekah. When he died in 732 B. C., Israel had only ten more years of independence remaining. They were sad years in which Pekah was murdered and his successor was taken captive to Assyria by Shalmaneser V (727-

4. The "Syria" of the Bible is strictly "Aram." Generally it refers to Damascus.

Ashur-bani-pal (668-626 B.C.) was one of the last kings prior to Assyria's fall before the combined attacks of the Medes and Chaldeans around 610 B.C. Here he is seen bringing a libation after a lion hunt. (Courtesy, The British Museum)

722 B. C.). It was in the year 722 B. C. that Israel fell, and her capital Samaria was captured by the next Assyrian king, Sargon by name (II Kings 17).

Judah continued alone as great Assyrian kings continued to rule in the East — Sargon II (721-705), Sennacherib (704-681), Esarhaddon (680-669), Ashur-bani-pal (668-626). Finally Assyria herself fell before the combined attacks of the Medes and the Chaldaeans during the years 612 to 609 B. C. The kingdom of Judah outlasted the great Assyria by over twenty years.

Artists were encouraged in Assyria. We still delight in some of the wonderful ivory work that was produced by the artisans of those days. But excellent work was also done in metals, precious stones, and other artistic media. Perhaps the most spectacular art work from Assyria was that done by the stone masons. Huge winged lions and bulls with human heads, weighing several tons, adorned the entrances to palaces and temples. Splendid flat slabs of alabaster were used to line the walls of the palaces. These were carved with detailed pictures taken from the whole range of Assyrian life. Here we can see the nation at war, at work, and in the daily round of life. From such bas-reliefs we gain a great deal of information about the equipment of the army and the methods of battle and siege warfare. We see the hundreds of slaves engaged in hauling great carved bulls into the palaces, and we observe the tools of the workmen. We see the king engaged in hunting lions (Nah. 2:11, 12). We learn something of the gods of Assyria and the procedures in the

115

Detail of the scene depicted on page 114. Tiglath Pileser III made several references to Old Testament characters in his royal annals, such as Azariah (Azriau), Menahem (Menihimme), and Jehoahaz (Iauhazi). He further claimed to have replaced Pekah (Paqaha) by Hoshea (Ausi') during his campaign in Palestine. (Courtesy, The British Museum)

temples. All this and much more is still to be seen today by the visitor to the great museums of the world where these excavated bas-reliefs are on display. In addition to the pictures there were literally miles of written records which preserved valuable historical information.

Some of the Assyrian kings were men of literature who went to great pains to collect the stories of the ancient world into their palaces. Thanks to this, the world is able to read the ancient flood story and the Babylonian story of creation, carefully recorded on baked clay tablets. There is a great number of local historical records on which we can draw today for our history of this great nation.

Assyrian architecture was a great achievement in itself. The first stage in the erection of a palace was the construction of a huge raised terrace covering several acres. This was made of large unbaked bricks and for added stability was built with sloping sides and sometimes faced with stone slabs. On this terrace the king constructed his palace of massive baked mud bricks. Some of the palaces contained over one hundred rooms. The inside walls were lined at the bottom with slabs of alabaster carved in the way we have indicated. The upper parts of the walls were decorated with bright paint and glazes. Huge carved-stone figures stood at the entrances. An impression of splendor and power must have been created in the mind of the visitor from a foreign land. Incidentally, the pictures on the walls would have a good propaganda effect on the foreigner. Perhaps these things might happen in his land some day!

The religion of the Assyrians was polytheistic. There was a great deal of religion of a formal kind, with prayers for every occasion. Some of the Assyrian gods are known in the Bible — Tammuz, Ishtar, Nebo, and Nisroch. It was quite a common practice for the Assyrian kings to set up in a captured town an Assyrian altar and other religious symbols as a sign of conquest. It was probably such an altar that Ahaz of Judah saw in Damascus. He had a copy of it made in Judah (II Kings 16:10-11).

In contrast with all this culture, there was unspeakable cruelty in the nation. As a regular practice after a battle, hundreds of the conquered people were taken off to a strange land. Many were selected for torture. Heads were removed, hands cut off, ears taken off, tongues pulled out, eyes gouged out, skins taken off in one piece and often tacked to the walls of the town as a warning. Indeed, it seems that there was no piece of brutality known to man that the Assyrians did not use. Not only did they do these things, but they portrayed them on the bas-reliefs and described them in some detail in their official records. The cruel Ashur-nasir-pal described his dealings with the city of a certain Khulai in these words:

> Six hundred of their warriors I put to the sword; three thousand captives I burned with fire; I left not a single one among them alive to serve as a hostage. Khulai their governor I captured alive. Their corpses I piled into heaps; their young men and maidens I burned in the fire; Khulai, their governor,

flat slabs of alabaster that lined the walls of the palaces were carved with detailed *s taken from the whole range of Assyrian life. In spite of a certain conventional-* *n these representations, they at the same time display a stark realism as is evident* *the various postures of the dead and dying lions and lionesses in one of Ashur-* *pal's hunts.* (Courtesy, The British Museum)

I flayed and his skin I spread upon the wall of the city of Damdamusa; the city I destroyed, I ravaged, I burned with fire.[5]

Assyria remains in the memory of men today as possibly the supreme example of a nation with the highest culture, with a highly formal religion and skill in all the arts of mankind, but which lacked in its inner soul that love of righteousness and that fear of God of which the prophets of Israel spoke so fervently. Of what use is culture if a man or a nation lacks righteousness?

THE FIRST THREE DYNASTIES OF ISRAEL

The first house began with Jeroboam I (922-901 B. C.).[6] His son Nadab ruled after him for only two years and was then slain by a certain Baasha (I Kings 15:25ff.). This was the first of many conspiracies that removed kings from the throne in Israel.

We have some interesting achaeological light from the days of Jeroboam. Reference is made in the Bible to the invasion of Palestine by Pharaoh Shishak of Egypt, five years after the death of Solomon (I Kings 14:25-28, II Chron. 12:2-12). The story in Kings refers only to the attack on Jerusalem. More detail is given in Chronicles where the walled cities of Judah are mentioned (v. 4). In actual fact the invasion touched Israel rather severely.[7] We know from the records of Shishak in Egypt that his campaign seriously affected Israel also. A list of the towns he attacked is given on the walls of his partly ruined temple in Karnak, close to modern Luxor in Egypt. This list includes many towns in Israel. In particular the town of Megiddo is mentioned. When Megiddo was excavated some years ago, one of the striking finds was part of a broken stele (inscribed stone slab) bearing some of the names of Shishak, and showing that he had probably set up here in Israel a commemorative inscription.

We have nothing else at present to enlarge our Biblical picture of the house of Jeroboam, excepting that we may have some light

---

5. E. A. Budge and L. W. King, *The Annals of the Kings of Assyria* (London, 1902), pp. 291f.

6. We follow the dates of W. F. Albright in *Biblical Period* (Pittsburg, 1950), p. 66. The alternative chronology in R. Theile, *The Mysterious Numbers of the Hebrew Kings* (1958), pp. 74ff., differs in some respects.

7. B. Mazar, "The Campaign of Pharaoh Shishak to Palestine," *VT*, Supp., Vol. IV (1957), pp. 57-66.

on the golden calves set up by him in Bethel and Dan (I Kings 12:29). It has often been suggested that these were objects of worship. We think today that this may not be the correct picture, although no doubt many of the unthinking Israelites would worship these images, and to that extent Jeroboam "made Israel to sin." It has become clear, however, that people like the Hittites and the Canaanites symbolized the presence of their gods by animals. There are in existence a number of pictures and statues where gods are standing on the backs of animals.[8] Perhaps Jeroboam agreed that the God of Israel could not be represented in any form, but he wanted to symbolize God's presence in some way. So he chose the method of the pagans. This was a most dangerous procedure for it led many to attach significance to an image and, in fact, broke the second commandment.

The Second Dynasty of Israel was introduced by Baasha when he slew Nadab, the son of Jeroboam. He and his son Elah ruled from 900 to 876 B. C. Of the twenty-five years, Elah ruled only two before he was murdered by the usurper Zimri.

8. W. F. Albright, *From Stone Age to Christianity* (Baltimore, 1940), p. 228; O. R. Gurney, *The Hittites* (Pelican, 1961), Fig 8, pp. 142, 143.

"Jeroboam the son of Nebat, who made Israel to sin" is an ominously recurring phrase in that part of the Old Testament that deals with the history of the kings. He had made two golden calves and placed them in Dan and Bethel. Earlier, the Israelites had turned to the worship of a golden calf at Sinai. These golden "calves" may have looked like the god Apis, the bull calf of Memphis. (Courtesy, The British Museum)

Baasha was soon involved in a war with Judah (I Kings 15:16-22). Two features about this story in the Bible can be illuminated from archaeology. Asa of Judah found that Baasha was building a fortress on his frontier. In fear, he sent to the neighboring king of Damascus for help. This king, Ben-hadad son of Tabrimon (v. 18), is now known from an inscription found in Syria.[9] It is an Aramaic text telling of a vow made by "Bir-hadad, son of Tab-ramman, king of Aram."

The second item concerns the fortress of Geba (v. 22). When the Syrian armies arrived at the invitation of Asa, Baasha left off his building of the fortress and retired to fight. Asa immediately crossed the border, pulled down the fortress of Baasha, carried the materials to his own side of the frontier, and erected two fortresses there! One of these was Geba or Gibeah. It was the third fortress on this site. There had been a building here in the days of the Judges. When the surrounding tribes attacked the tribe of Benjamin on the occasion of the physical humiliation of the Levite's concubine, the town of Gibeah was burned (Judg. 19, 20). King Saul built the second fortress here, as we have seen.[10] It was Asa who built the third. Excavation has revealed a remarkable correlation between the Biblical information and the extant remains at this site.[11] It is still possible to view some of the remains of the fortress of Asa at Gibeah.

The end of Israel's Second Dynasty came when Elah was slain. His murderer, Zimri, did not rule more than a week (I Kings 16:11-20). We must, however, count him as a third ruling house in Israel. Archaeological discovery adds nothing to the Bible narrative. The army captain who slew Zimri was Omri, the father of Ahab, and a great man in his own right. It looked as if there was to be some stability at last in Israel, for this house was to rule for over thirty years.

THE DYNASTY OF OMRI

This Dynasty comprised four kings in all: Omri (876-869 B. C.), Ahab (869-850 B. C.), Ahaziah (850-849 B. C.), and Joram (849-842 B. C.). It is a family that is described in the Bible in derogatory terms. Very little is given about Omri, and only the worst features

---

9. W. F. Albright, "A Votive Stela Erected by Ben Hadad I of Damascus," *BASOR* (Oct., 1942), pp. 23ff.
10. See above, pp. 95f.
11. *AASOR*, Vol. IV, xxxivf.

of Ahab are mentioned. Ahaziah and Joram were probably of little account in any case. Modern discovery has a different picture to give, and adds considerably to the Bible picture. It is a principle of Biblical interpretation that the Bible deals with people from the religious angle. Very often it says little about other aspects of their life such as their political and economic significance. Kings like Omri and Ahab merit only denunciation in the religious sphere, but archaeology shows that the case is quite different in the political and economic spheres.

The story of Omri is given in but six verses in the Bible apart from the account of his murder of Zimri (I Kings 16:23-28). Two things are mentioned about him. He bought a field from Shemer and founded the capital of Israel there. He was a wicked man and "did worse than all that were before him." There is only a hint of "the might that he shewed."

Thanks to archaeological work we can now enlarge this picture a great deal. The town of Samaria has been excavated. The foundations of the city were laid by Omri, although the bulk of the first city was probably built by his son Ahab. But it is in the realm of international politics that Omri is best known. Both the Assyrians and the Moabites knew him and his name was recorded in their annals.

We have no details in Assyrian records about Omri himself but we think that he was not merely known, but also respected, forever after, for Palestine became known in Assyrian records as Bit-Humria, that is, House of Omri. The Assyrian king at the time was the great and cruel Ashur-nasir-pal (883-859 B.C.). Just why Omri was esteemed thus becomes clear from the wonderful record left in Moab by her famous King Mesha (II Kings 3:4). Moab had been conquered by David and held by Solomon. After Solomon's death it was lost again. The Bible tells us that King Mesha of Moab paid tribute to Israel (II Kings 3:4). It was never known who had subdued Moab again till an English missionary in 1868 visited ancient Dibon in Moab and found a large black basalt stone with thirty-four lines of writing on it. Every effort was made to get this stone to Jerusalem but the local Arabs proved difficult and finally destroyed it in 1873. Fortunately a copy of the stone was made before it was destroyed and this told the story of how King Mesha of the Bible had at last been able to throw off the yoke of Israel. The special interest to us here is that the stone tells us that it was Omri, king of Israel, who had subdued Moab and humbled it for many years, and that this state of affairs had carried on under his son. But then

121

After the death of Ahab, Mesha the king of Moab successfully revolted against Israel, which is recorded on the so-called Moabite Stone. This record contains a list of the villages which Mesha "with the help of Chemosh," the god of the Moabites, was able to take from Israel. (Courtesy, The Oriental Institute, The University of Chicago)

Chemosh the god of Moab had again occupied the land. We infer that Mesha had been able to free Moab from Israel. This revolt began in the days of Ahab. Probably Mesha at first refused to pay tribute at a time when Ahab was busy with his Syrian wars. Mesha declared that this was the time when Moab gained her freedom. The Bible states that it was after the death of Ahab that Moab rebelled. The two accounts are not contradictory. They look at the events from two different angles. From the viewpoint of Moab the revolt dated from the refusal to pay tribute to Ahab. But from Israel's point of view Moab did not gain her freedom until after the failure of the punitive expedition recorded in II Kings 3.

This valuable non-Biblical record from Moab reads as follows:

I [am] Mesha, son of Chemosh-(. . .), king of Moab, the Dibonite — my father [had] reigned over Moab thirty years, and I reigned after my father, — [who] made this high place for Chemosh in Qarhoh (. . .) because he saved me from all the kings and caused me to triumph over all my adversaries. As for Omri, king of Israel, he humbled Moab many years [lit., "days"], for Chemosh was angry at his land. And his son followed him and he also said, "I will humble Moab." In my time he spoke [thus], but I have triumphed over him and over his house, while Israel hath perished for ever! [Now] Omri had

122

occupied the land of Medeba, and [Israel] had dwelt there in his time and half the time of his son [Ahab], forty years; but Chemosh dwelt there in my time.

And I built Baal-meon, making a reservoir in it, and I built Qaryaten. Now the men of Gad had always dwelt in the land of Ataroth, and the king of Israel had built Ataroth for them. but I fought against the town and took it and slew all the people of the town as satiation [intoxication] for Chemosh and Moab. And I brought back from there Arel [or Oriel], its chieftain, dragging him before Chemosh in Kerioth, and I settled there men of Sharon and men of Maharith. And Chemosh said to me, "Go, take Nebo from Israel!" So I went by night and fought against it from the break of dawn until noon, taking it and slaying all, seven thousand men, boys, women, girls and maid-servants, for I had devoted them to destruction for [the god] Ashtar-Chemosh. And I took from there the (. . .) of Yahweh, dragging them before Chemosh. And the king of Israel had built Jahaz, and he dwelt there while he was fighting against me, but Chemosh drove him out before me. And I took from Moab two hundred men, all first class [warriors], and set them against Jahaz and took it in order to attach it to [the district of] Dibon.

It was I [who] built Qarhoh, the wall of *the forests* and the wall of the citadel; I also built its gates and I built its towers and I built the king's house, and I made both of its reservoirs for water inside the town. And there was no cistern inside the town at Qarhoh, so I said to all the people, "Let each of you make a cistern for himself in his house!" And I cut *beams* for Qarhoh with Israelite captives. I built Aroer, and I made the highway in the Arnon [valley]; I built Beth-bamoth, for it had been destroyed; I built Bezer — for it lay in ruins — with fifty men of Dibon, for all Dibon is [my] loyal dependency.

And I reigned [*in peace*] *over* the hundred towns which I had added to the land. And I built (. . .) Medeba and Beth-diblathen and Beth-baal-meon, and I set there the (. . .) of the land. And as for Hauronen, there dwelt in it (. . .) [And] Chemosh said to me, "Go down, fight against Hauronen." And I went down [and I fought against the town and I took it], and Chemosh dwelt there in my time . . . .[12]

12. J. B. Pritchard, *ANET*, p. 320.

So Omri was a man of importance after all. We are able to discover the full picture today with the help of the archaeologist.

The story of Ahab is told in some detail in the Bible, the best part of six chapters being devoted to it. The emphasis, however, is on those aspects of Ahab's life that are important from the religious point of view. His clash with Elijah, his theft of the vineyard of Naboth, his evil wife Jezebel, his encouragement of the false prophets, his conflict with the prophet Micaiah, and his final defeat in battle are the main points of interest for the Bible writer. There are hints of other achievements in the account of two successful wars against Syria, and in the reference to "the ivory house which he made and all the cities that he built" (I Kings 22:39). These matters are recorded in "the book of the chronicles of the kings of Israel," but since this work is now lost we have no record of them. If we are to learn more about Ahab, then, we are dependent on the discoveries of the archaeologist. In this we are not disappointed. A variety of additional pieces of information is available for us from this source.

The story of the conflict of Ahab with Elijah gains much from modern discovery. It was at a time of severe drought. This drought is attested in the writings of Josephus[13] who quoted from the Greek writer Meander, who had drawn on some Phoenician sources. Of greater interest, however, is the fact that the god Baal, who features so much in this story, is now depicted for us in very great detail as a result of the tablet discoveries from Ras Shamra, the former Ugarit, a great Canaanite town and the site of several temples. Baal was peculiarly the god of fertility. He controlled the seasons and was responsible for the storm and the rain. If a drought was upon the land, it was due to Baal's working. The devotee would appeal to him for a relief of these conditions. With scorn, Elijah, on Mount Carmel, exposed the emptiness of this belief (I Kings 18). If Baal failed, the God of Israel would not. At the word of Elijah, and in answer to his prayer, the rain came.

There is another feature of this story. In the Hebrew text there are in fact two gods referred to in I Kings 18:19. These are Baal and Asherah (translated in the Authorized Version as "the groves"). The documents excavated at Ugarit show us that Asherah was a female goddess, the consort of Baal, a sensuous, lustful creature. She, like Baal, had her prophets in Israel, four hundred of them (I Kings 18:19). The Authorized Version of the Bible needs to be

13. Josephus, *Antiquities*, Book 8, cp. 13.

revised here to read: "the prophets of Baal four hundred and fifty, and the prophets of Asherah four hundred."

The story of Naboth receives some explanation, too, in the light of Canaanite mythology. One of the myths of Canaan told of a goddess who found a young hunter one day with a beautiful bow, the gift of another god. She tried all she could to persuade him to give her the bow. He would not part with such a precious possession. Then she gained permission from El, the chief of the gods, to take measures to obtain the bow. She selected a man of brutal character, turned him into an eagle, placed him in a flight of eagles, and had him swoop down one day to peck the young hunter to death. She then took the bow with impunity. Might was right in Canaanite mythology, and if gods and goddesses behaved in this selfish fashion, could it be expected that their worshippers would be any better? Naturally, Jezebel, a Canaanite woman, believed that her husband had the right to possess a man's vineyard regardless of his claim that it was a family possession, and so she said to him: "Dost thou now govern Israel? arise and eat bread and let thine heart be merry. I will give thee the vineyard of Naboth" (I Kings 21:7).

Ahab is known on the Assyrian monuments as one of a coalition of twelve kings who opposed the great Shalmaneser III at the battle of Karkar in 853 B. C. The Assyrian claimed to have won the battle. It is significant, however, that he did not make war for a few years afterwards. It is probable that both sides were badly mauled. In the Assyrian account of the battle we are given a list of the forces of the coalition. The following extract from the annals of Shalmaneser gives interesting details of the participants in the coalition.

> . . . I approached Karkara. I destroyed, tore down, and burned Karkara, his royal residence. He brought along to help him 1200 chariots, 1200 cavalrymen, 20,000 foot soldiers of Adad-'idri (Hadadezer) of Damascus; 700 chariots, 700 cavalrymen, 10,000 foot soldiers of Irhuleni from Hamath; 2000 chariots, 10,000 foot soldiers of Ahab the Israelite; 500 soldiers from Que, 1000 soldiers from Musri. . . .[14]

Other places are listed, including Arabia and Ammon. It is clear that Ahab provided the greatest contingent of chariots and the second largest number of soldiers. If the stables discovered at Megiddo belonged to Ahab and not to Solomon, we understand where some

14. J. B. Pritchard, *op. cit.*, p. 278, column 2, and p. 279, column 1.

125

of his horses and chariots were kept.[15] This significant battle is not even referred to in the Bible. The forces of Israel since the days of Solomon must have been considerable. It was probably as a result of this battle that Ahab's army was so weakened as to give encouragement to Moab to rebel and to refuse to pay tribute. No doubt Ahab intended to subdue Moab again, but he died before he was able to accomplish this.

15. See above, p. 103

Professor Nelson Glueck discusses with interested members of his crew unearthed pottery dating from the time of Abraham. (Courtesy, Israel Office of Information)

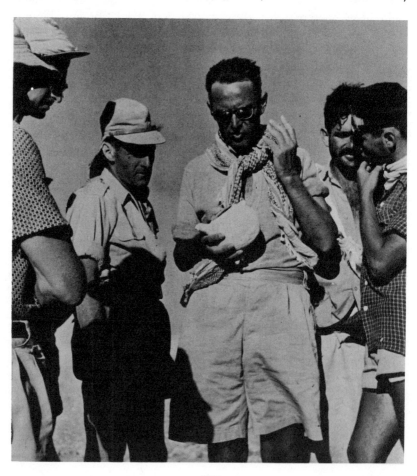

Excavations have given us a good deal of insight into the building programs of Ahab. The first palaces at Samaria were very fine indeed. Some of the finest masonry of all time was laid down by the builders of Ahab. Another feature of the palace ruins here was the clear Phoenician influence, revealed particularly in the type of carved capital at the top of the columns used to support the roof. In the same palace area a considerable amount of carved ivory was found. It was the fashion of the day to decorate the interior walls with ivory friezes and to ornament the palace furniture in the same way. Palaces of this type have been found in Assyria and in Phoenicia. The magnificent ivories found at Nimrud in ancient Assyria include numerous pieces from the time of Ahab, that is, in the ninth century B. C. Ahab's ivory house (I Kings 22:39) in particular now finds a good parallel and an explanation in a room in one of the palaces of Nimrud where the mud-brick wall was once overlaid with a great ivory screen.[16]

Incidentally, Ahab's archenemy Ben-hadad was eventually slain by a certain Hazael (II Kings 8:15). This fact is attested in the records of Shalmaneser III who referred to Hazael as the "son of a nobody," the usual description of a usurper. The annals of Shalmaneser read thus:

> I defeated Hadadezer of Damascus together with twelve princes, his allies . . . . Hadadezer himself perished. Hazael, the son of nobody [a commoner], seized the throne . . . .[17]

We have nothing of real importance to add to our picture for the two successors of Ahab. Joram tried to subdue Moab again with the help of Judah and Edom, but failed. It was probably in these years that Hazael became king of Damascus and began his raids on Israel. It was at the time of one of the Syrian raids, perhaps before the reign of Hazael, that the Syrians were besieging Samaria and fled at the sound of what they thought were the armies of the Hittites and the Egyptians. More recently we have discovered that there was a land to the north of Palestine known as Musur. This land features often on the tablets. It is thought that what the Syrians

---

16. M. E. L. Mallowan, *Iraq*, Vol. 13, pp. 1-20; Vol. 14, p. 8; and succeeding volumes. Note Vol. 20, p. 104. Illustrations of the ivories occur in *Illustrated London News*, No. 221, p. 256, No. 223, pp. 199ff., No. 228, pp. 130ff., No. 231, pp. 869-873, 934-937, 968ff. J. W. and G. M. Crowfoot, *Early Ivories from Samaria* (1938).

17. J. B. Pritchard, *op. cit.*, p. 280, column 2.

feared was a coalition of Hittites and Musurites rather than a coalition of Hittites and Egyptians. In the days of the first translations of the Bible into English, the word MSR was mistaken for Egypt, since the two words have the same consonants. There are other places in the Bible where we are able to make changes like this in the light of more recent knowledge. Indeed, the Bible has an intimate knowledge of ancient geography and we are only now coming to understand its value as a source of ancient geography.

Here we must leave the dynasty of Omri. It is clear that modern archaeology has done much to increase our knowledge of the times, and to give us a fuller picture of the kings of Israel in this period.

THE DYNASTY OF JEHU

Various groups in Israel grew tired of the weak successors of Ahab, and a change was imminent. There was a revolution, supported by the prophet Elisha and the prophetic party as well as by other faithful adherents to the faith of Israel. Finally an opportunity came and an army captain named Jehu decided to act after the armies of Israel had been mauled in a battle in which the king was wounded. Jehu slew the king as he lay at Jezreel recovering from his wounds. The same day he caused the death of the king of Judah who happened to be visiting the king of Israel. The wicked Jezebel was sought out and cast to the dogs (II Kings 9 and 10). Jehu thus commenced a new dynasty which was to have five kings who ruled from 842 to 745 B. C., nearly a century in all.

Jehu is best known to us as the one king in either Israel or Judah whose picture we have today. The great Shalmaneser III was still reigning at the time of Jehu's accession. He evidently had some dealings with Jehu in the year 842 B. C., for the large black obelisk found by the early excavator Sir Henry Layard at Nimrud in 1840 has a picture of Jehu bowing before Shalmaneser and offering: "Silver, gold, a gold beaker, golden goblets, pitchers of gold, lead, staves for the hand of the king, javelins."[18] This incident happened when Shalmaneser, who had been busy for some years and had allowed the king Hazael of Damascus to get a little out of hand, decided to pay a visit to the west. Hazael was subdued, as were others. The rulers of Tyre, Sidon, and Israel thought it better to pay tribute. This fact passes unnoticed in the Bible. We have nothing else to

18. *Ibid.,* p. 281.

Two of the four sides of the Black Obelisk of Shalmaneser III. They show Israelites carrying gifts, described as "the tribute of Jehu, son of Omri," and consisting of silver, gold, golden vessels, tin, the royal staff, and fruits. (Courtesy, The British Museum)

-up view of the second panel of the side depicted to the left, showing "Jehu, son of ;" bowing before Shalmaneser III. It is the only contemporary "portrait" we have of king of Israel, and dates from 841 B.C. (Courtesy, The British Museum)

report about Jehu from archaeological discovery, but in a general way the Assyrian story brought to light by the excavators helps to explain much in the next century.

Events in the eastern parts of the Assyrian domains kept their kings busy from about 837 B. C. till 802 B. C. The Syrians were able to molest Israel a great deal when they had no fear of the Assyrians. Thus, despite early promise, Jehu suffered at the hands of Hazael and lost Israel's lands in Transjordan (II Kings 10:32, 33). His son Joahaz was practically a subject of Hazael and his successor Ben-Hadad (II Kings 13:1-7). Then in the year 802 B. C. Damascus herself was prostrate before the Assyrians. Joash, the third king of the Jehu dynasty (801-786 B. C.), seized the opportunity to regain the lost lands of Israel (II Kings 13:25). The days were auspicious from another point of view. Events in the general area of Damascus of which we have been ignorant till recent years provided Israel with further welcome relief. An important monument found near Aleppo tells of struggles between Zakir, the Aramaean king of Hamath, and a strong coalition headed up by Ben-Hadad of Damascus.[19]

This monument, in the form of a stele, tells of a siege of Hazrek, the Biblical Hadrach (II Chron. 9:1). It commences with these words:

> The stela which Zakir king of Hamath and Lu'ash set up in honor of 'Ilu-wer . . . . I am Zakir, king of Hamath and Lu'ash. I am a humble man, but Baal-Shamain (Lord of Heaven) called me and has held to me, and Baal-Shamain has caused me to reign over Hazrek. And Benhadad, son of Hazael, king of Aram, united against me twelve [?] kings — Benhadad and his army, Bar Gush and his army, the king of Que and his army, the king of 'Umq and his army, the king of Gurgum and his army, the king of Sam'al and his army, and the king of Meliz and his army . . . and all these kings besieged Hazrek and raised up a rampart higher than the rampart of Hazrek, and digged a ditch deeper than its ditch. Then I raised my hands to Baal-Shamain and Baal-Shamain heard me and Baal-Shamain spoke to me by seers and . . . Baal-Shamain said to me, "Fear not! It is I who caused you to reign and it is I who will be with you. It is I who will deliver you from all these kings which have set up siege against you . . . ."

19. *Ibid.*, p. 501. Cf. A. Dupont-Sommer, *Les Araméens*, pp. 45ff.; M. F. Unger, *Israel and the Arameans of Damascus* (1957), pp. 85-89. Cf. also M. Black, *Documents from Old Testament Times*, ed. D. Winton Thomas, p. 246.

Zakir was delivered. But the preoccupation of so many of these Aramaean kings in the general period 800-775 B.C. meant that Israel and Judah were not troubled by them. Indeed it was because of these troubles in Syria that Joash of Israel (about 801-786 B. C.) was able to re-establish Israel's prestige. On his death, his competent son Jeroboam II set out on a period of remarkable prosperity for Israel.

During these years also the great Assyrian nation was more or less immobilized. Adad-nirari III (811-783) was occupied with the powerful Urartu people from the Caspian region for the first quarter of the eighth century, and his son Shalmaneser IV (783-773) was still fighting defensive actions against this people. Even Assyrian governors close to home were virtually independent. Among these, Shamshi-ilu of Bit-adini ruled in royal style. He is probably the one Amos had in mind as "him that holdeth the sceptre" in Bit-adini ("house of Eden"), in Amos 1:5. Ashur Dan III (773-775), and Assur-nirari V (755-745), the two rulers who followed, could do no better. Owing to the discovery of written records in the excavations of Assyrian cities, we now have this picture.[20]

Thus while the Assyrians, the Aramaeans, and the Urartu people fought one another to a standstill, Israel and Judah with the long-lived rulers Jeroboam II and Uzziah were able to regain something of the economic strength and the territorial extent they had known in the days of Solomon.

The Bible record in Kings dismisses Jeroboam II in very few verses (II Kings 14:23-29). His reign was a sad one from the religious point of view, for apostasy and insincerity abounded, and the king allowed the worship of false gods to continue unchecked. Yet these were days of great economic prosperity. Evidence of this is given in the words of the great eighth-century prophets. The more sober records in Kings do not give this impression. Something of the splendor of the days and of their prosperity can be gained from excavations.

The buildings in Samaria and in Megiddo dating from this time give evidence of careful planning. The excavators refer to the remarkable layout of the town of Megiddo in these days. It is, however, the town of Tirzah that gives what is perhaps the best picture of the times. Here the great gate into the city led at once into a massive structure which was evidently the palace of the local governor. Nearby were two large buildings with fine stone founda-

20. W. W. Hallo, *op. cit.*, pp. 41-46, summarizes the material.

tions. Behind these three buildings lay the rest of the town, which was of a very ragged style and spoke of poverty. No better picture of the considerable class distinction in Israel could be hoped for. The excavator, Père de Vaux, made special reference to this fact.[21]

One sign of the prosperity of the times was a great grain-storage pit at Megiddo. Here was a pit some twenty-three feet deep, some thirty-seven feet across at the top, and some twenty-three feet across at the bottom. Its capacity was about twelve thousand eight hundred bushels. It had two sets of winding stairs inside. Chaff was found between the chinks in the uncoursed stones that made up the sides.

Another suggestion of prosperity comes from Samaria. Just inside the gate, about seventy receipts written on pieces of broken pottery (ostraca) were found by the excavators. These records, known as the Samaria Ostraca, date in all probability to the reign of Jeroboam and tell of oil, barley, wine, and so on, being received in the city.[22]

One important feature of these receipts is the considerable variety of names on them. Many of these were composed with the element Jah or Iah, showing some link with the name of Israel's God. Such names as Elijah, Jedaiah, and so on, are typical. Alongside these were many names with the element Baal, like Elibaal, Abibaal, Jeribbaal. In fact, for every eleven Jah names there were seven Baal names. This points to a certain popularity for the names involving Baal and suggests a widespread devotion to this pagan god. While it is true that many people do not pay much attention to the meaning of a name, yet it is evident that these names were common in Israel and were used without much compunction by the people. All of this fits in with the picture of apostasy given in the prophets.

We have the feeling that there is much yet to be discovered about these days in Israel. What we have is of great importance in explaining and in corroborating the Biblical narratives referring to this age.

At the close of Jeroboam's life a new terror appeared in the East. The Assyrians had a new king, Tiglath-Pileser III, who ruled from 745 to 727 B.C. It was the end of liberty for the small kingdoms to the west. Before a quarter of a century was over the kingdom of Israel had fallen. When Jeroboam II of Israel died he was replaced

21. R. de Vaux reports in *Revue Biblique* almost annually from 1946. See especially Oct., 1951, pp. 558ff., and plate x; also Oct., 1952.

22. D. Winton Thomas, *Documents from Old Testament Times* (1958), pp. 204-208.

by his son Zechariah. But this king ruled for only six months and was killed in a revolt. It was the end of the Jehu dynasty.

THE LAST KINGS OF ISRAEL

After the death of Zechariah in 745 B. C. Israel was to have only about a quarter of a century of independence remaining. In that time there were five kings of whom three were murdered, one was taken captive, and only one died naturally. Our information for these days, apart from the Bible, comes from the Assyrian records. Three of the last kings were referred to in these records.

The usurper who slew Zechariah was Shallum. He reigned only a month and was himself liquidated by Menahem. It was in the days of Menahem that the Assyrian inroads became serious. Tiglath Pileser made a move towards Israel but Menahem was able to buy him off. The figure of fifty shekels referred to in II Kings 15:20 is now known to be the average price for a slave. Menahem was asked to assess his men at the price of slaves and to buy his freedom thus. It was probably in the year 743 that Tiglath Pileser referred to Menahem as paying tribute to him. It almost seems that Menahem was captured and then released. The account of Tiglath Pileser refers to his attack on Gaza, and then he adds:

> As for Menahem I overwhelmed him like a snowstorm and he fled like a bird alone, and bowed to my feet. I returned him to his place and imposed tribute upon him. . . .[23]

There follows a list of the tribute collected.

Menahem died in his bed and was succeeded by his son Pekahiah (II Kings 15:22). We know no more about this man and in any case, after two years he was slain by an army captain named Pekah.

Pekah is a notorious character in Bible history, for he made an alliance with Rezin, king of Damascus, and sought to invade Judah. Rezin had paid tribute to Tiglath Pileser as early as 743 and his name is mentioned in the list which quotes Menahem in these words:

> I received tribute from Kustashpi of Commagene, Rezon of Damascus, Menahem of Samaria, Hiram of Tyre, Sibitti-bi'li of Byblos, Urikki of Que, Pisiris of Carshemish, I'nil of Hamath . . . [etc.].[24]

23. J. B. Pritchard, *op. cit.*, pp. 283f.
24. *Ibid.*, p. 283, col. 2.

But Rezin, emboldened by Tiglath Pileser's preoccupation elsewhere, headed up a new anti-Assyrian coalition in which Pekah of Israel joined. They sought to bring Judah in and planned to set up a certain Ben Tabeel (Isa. 7:6) in place of King Ahaz. The place name *Tab-el* has now been discovered on a tablet from Nimrud so that the Ben Tab'al of Isaiah 7:6 may well have been the son of Ahaz and a princess from Tab-el.[25]

When Pekah and Rezin moved on Jerusalem (II Kings 16:5, II Chron. 28:5-8), King Ahaz of Judah in a panic called on Tiglath Pileser for help. The Assyrians marched west, imposing tribute on Judah, Ammon, Edom, and Moab, and taking large numbers of people from the Galilee and Gilead areas of Israel into captivity (II Kings 15:29). At that time the fortress of Hazor was destroyed and the proud kingdom of Israel was reduced to a tiny vassal state only part of its original size.[26] It is strange that both Hosea and Isaiah refer to Ephraim, which would have been fairly correct geographically. These events took place in the years 734-732.[27]

In 732 Tiglath Pileser turned to Damascus. The Bible tells us of the attack of the Assyrians on this ancient foe of theirs (II Kings 16:9). The city which had held out so long finally fell. In the same year a pro-Assyrian revolt in Samaria cost Pekah his life and brought Hoshea to the throne as a loyal Assyrian vassal, at least for a short time. If Tiglath Pileser did not actually put Hoshea on the throne, he seems to have approved. His record reads:

> They overthrew their king Pekah (Paqaha) and I placed Hosea (Ausi') over them as king.

The strain of the Assyrian annual tribute was too much for Hoshea and he began to intrigue with Egypt. Retribution was swift. The new king of Assyria, Shalmaneser V (726-722), took action in 725 B. C., and the Assyrian armies came to Israel. Shechem was captured and Samaria was besieged. Hoshea the king was captured outside the city and deported before the fall of Samaria (II Kings 17:4). The siege went on for nearly three years but in August or September of 722 the city fell. Shalmaneser died in December, 722, that is, after the fall of Samaria. Sargon his son and successor claimed

---

25. H. W. F. Saggs, *Iraq*, 17 (1955), pp. 131-133; W. F. Albright, *BASOR*, No. 140 (1955), pp. 34ff.

26. Y. Yadin, *BA*, No. 20 (1957), pp. 34-37.

27. The record of Tiglath Pileser is damaged but the general sense is clear. See J. B. Pritchard, *op. cit.*, p. 283, col. 2.

the final capture of the city on his monuments, and no doubt he was present, and possibly even in command of the armies, so that he had a share in the fall. The Babylonian Chronicle notes the destruction of Samaria (Sa-ma-ra-'i-in), as the outstanding event of the reign of Shalmaneser. It is of interest to note in Ezra 4:10 that Samaria, normally spelled in Hebrew as *Shomron*, is spelled *Shamrayin*, as in the Babylonian Chronicle.

Shalmaneser V took exiles off to Assyrian lands like Guzana (Gozan) and Haran (I Chron. 5:26). In due course these exiles evidently reached the capital cities of Nimrud (Kalah) and Nineveh, where Israelite names have been found on written records. Ostraca from Nimrud and Nineveh carry twenty-two Israelite names, like Menahem and Hoshea.[28]

The story of the capture and destruction of Samaria as told by Sargon in his annals reads as follows:

> I besieged and conquered Samaria, led away as booty 27,290 inhabitants of it . . . . The town I rebuilt better than it was before and settled therein people from countries which I myself had conquered. I placed an officer of mine as governor over them and imposed upon them tribute as is customary for Assyrian citizens.[29]

There are parallels between this narration and the story in the Bible in II Kings 17.

So ended the kingdom of Israel. The importance of archaeology for the enlargement of our knowledge of these Bible kings and for the corroboration of many of the statements in the Bible is evident. Perhaps the most important feature of this additional material is that it enables us to place the kings of Israel in a true perspective. In that light they appear politically to be of far more significance than we would think them to be were we dependent on Bible history alone. As to their worth in the eyes of God, the Bible writers had a true perspective. It remains a fact that mere physical achievement has no justifying worth before God.

28. J. B. Segal, "An Aramaic Ostracon from Nimrud," *Iraq,* 19 (1957), pp. 139-145; W. F. Albright, *BASOR,* No. 149 (1958), pp. 33-36.
29. J. B. Pritchard, *op. cit.,* pp. 284f.

Eight:

THE KINGS OF JUDAH

W HEREAS ISRAEL CEASED AS AN INDEPENDENT NATION IN 722 B. C., Judah continued until 586 B. C. Factors similar to those which influenced Israel are found in the case of Judah: the continual menace of Assyria, the possibility of conflict with her own sister state, and the ministry of the prophets. To these we may add conflict with Edom, which acted as a natural rival to Judah in much the same way as Syria did for Israel. Modern archaeology has added to our knowledge of Judah in ways similar to those we have seen for Israel. Judah had but one line of kings during all this period. There was a short interregnum when the woman Athaliah ruled, but the royal prince was in hiding and came to the throne after six years. It will be convenient to treat the story of Judah in three sections, the period contemporary with Israel's first four dynasties, the period contemporary with the rest of Israel's history, and the period when Judah stood alone.

ᵤstration on page 136: Panorama of Bethlehem, where both David and "the Son of ᵃvid" were born. (Courtesy, Trans World Airlines)

The First Eighty Years: 922 B.C. to 842 B.C.

Rehoboam (922-915 B.C.) was involved in the campaign of Shishak of Egypt. The Bible refers only to the invasion of Judah and, indeed, Judah appears from I Kings 14:25 to have been the principal target of Shishak, although, as we have seen, the campaign was far more extensive. Shishak mentioned several towns of Judah on his temple at Karnak. At this time the important town of Ezion Geber on the Red Sea, the port of Solomon, was destroyed by fire. This was a loss to Judah, but later, in the days of Jehoshaphat, when the Egyptian menace was past, the people of Judah were able to rebuild the port.

From the time of Asa (913-873 B.C.), we have evidence of the building of the fortress of Gibeah. This has been referred to in our account of the kings of Israel. Thanks to the discoveries of Ras Shamra we are able to understand the reforms of Asa more clearly: "He took away the sodomites out of the land . . . and Maachah his mother . . . he removed from *being* queen, because she made an idol in a grove" (I Kings 15:12, 13). We now know that these sodomites were sacred male prostitutes. The Canaanites had these in their temples along with sacred women. These men and women performed rites in the temples designed to encourage fertility in flock and field. The very name *qedeshim* is the same in Hebrew and Canaanite and means "holy men," although the practices of these men were far from holy. The other reference to Asherah the goddess we have discussed already. Here, too, the Authorized Version of the Bible needs to be revised.

Jehoshaphat (873-840 B.C.) came to the throne about the same time as King Omri of Israel. There began a period of friendship between Judah and Israel which lasted for thirty years. There was close co-operation between Ahab and Jehoshaphat during their reigns. They were present together at the battle in which Ahab was slain.

The main archaeological interest in these years lies with Israel up to the present. The one feature we have for Judah concerns the rebuilding of the port of Ezion Geber. The Bible indicates that Jehoshaphat "made ships of Tharshish to go to Ophir" (I Kings 22:48). Though the ships were wrecked, the Biblical statement suggests that the port was rebuilt. This seems to be supported by Nelson Glueck's excavation there. The second city of Ezion Geber is datable from pottery to the early part of the ninth century.

From the Revolution of Jehu to the Fall of Samaria

The revolt of Jehu in Israel brought about the death of Judah's king also (II Kings 9:27). This enabled the queen mother, Athaliah, the sister of Ahab of Israel (II Kings 8:26), to seize the throne for herself and to destroy the seed royal. Fortunately, the king's sister rescued his baby son Joash and brought him up. During the six years that Athaliah ruled, Canaanite worship was encouraged. In particular Baal was worshipped and Mattan, a priest of Baal, was installed. The name of Mattan is Canaanitish, typical of many others ending in "an" to be found on the baked clay tablets unearthed in recent years.[1] Perhaps Mattan was actually a Canaanite who was brought to Israel by Athaliah to lead the sensuous Canaanite worship which has been revealed to us by such documents as those found in the Ras Shamra (Ugarit) library.

There is little of archaeological interest during those years. Assyrian evidence for Judah is lacking, although the king of Syria, Hazael, who invaded the area around Gath and thought of turning to Jerusalem, is known to the Assyrians. He was the "son of a nobody," that is, a usurper.

With the ascent of Uzziah to the throne, Judah embarked on a period of great prosperity. It was the eighth century. External foes were occupied elsewhere and both Judah and Israel were free to exploit the days of freedom. The narrative in Kings, as we have seen, dismisses Jeroboam very quickly. Its treatment of Uzziah is almost as brief (II Kings 15:1-7). However, the account in II Chronicles 26:1-23 is quite detailed. The days were prosperous, as we learn from this chapter. In particular there was expansion in the southern parts of Judah towards the Negeb. Recent discovery and excavation in this area have shown how true the picture in Chronicles is. A good deal of surface survey has been carried out in the Negeb in recent years and it is now clear that during the eighth century, settlement extended over almost the whole area. This was an important transit area between the coast and the Arabian lands behind.[2] Uzziah had good contacts with the Arabs at the time.

One other point of interest is that the Bible speaks of the restoration of Eloth or Ezion Geber in the days of Uzziah. This

---

1. W. F. Albright, *Archaeology and the Religion of Israel* (Baltimore, 1953), p. 127.
2. N. Glueck, *Rivers in the Desert,* gives details.

The Government of the State of Israel has conducted extensive archaeological research in historical sites. Essential to the determination of the significance of any find and its identification is on-the-spot photography. This scene shows such activity in Central Negev. (Courtesy, Israel Office of Information)

was the third city on the site. For the first time in its history the place assumed the semblance of a real village and not merely a large fortified industrial plant. Pottery dates the town to the days of Uzziah. In its debris was a royal seal bearing the name Jotham, which was probably the seal of the crown prince.

There is still some dispute about the name "Azriyau of Ya'udi" referred to in records of the Assyrian king Tiglath Pileser III. This name has been interpreted as Azariah of Judah. Azariah was an alternative name of Uzziah (II Kings 15:1-17). Writers like W. F. Albright are inclined to identify the two.[3] Other scholars associate this name with a ruler of the little state of Sam'al to the north of Israel on the Syrian coast. This state was also known as Ya'udi.

At any rate, there is some additional evidence from excavation to supplement the narratives of the Bible for the days of Uzziah.

3. W. F. Albright, *The Biblical Period* (Pittsburg, 1950), p. 40.

Another view of archaeological activity at Wadi Kurnub in the Negev. The fact that armed protection is necessary indicates the political unrest in this area of the Near East. (Courtesy, Israel Office of Information)

After Uzziah's death in 742 B. C. the Assyrian menace became severe. The great Tiglath Pileser was soon to begin his attacks on Israel, and Judah was caught up in the struggle very quickly.

It was in the days of Ahaz (735-715 B. C.) that Judah became seriously involved with Assyria. The threat of Pekah of Israel and of Rezin of Damascus caused Ahaz to call on the Assyrians for help despite the advice of Isaiah to the contrary (Isa. 7:1-9). Ahaz was summoned to Damascus to pay homage and to witness the symbols of Assyrian lordship set up there. We have suggested that a pagan altar was among these, and that Ahaz had a copy of this made in Jerusalem (II Kings 16:7-11). Ahaz, under his alternative name Jehoahaz, is mentioned in a list of tributaries of Tiglath Pileser, a list which, incidentally, includes rulers of such countries as Edom, Moab, Gaza, Askelon, and Ammon.[4] All of these were in the vicinity

4. J. B. Pritchard, *ANET* (Princeton, 1955), p. 282.

141

of Judah and suggest the seriousness of the Assyrian inroads at this time.

Tiglath Pileser's list reads as follows:

> ... in all the countries ... I received tribute of Kushtashpi of Commagene, Urik of Que, Sibitti-be'el of Byblos, Enil of Hamath, Panammu of Sam'al . . . Sanipu of Bit-Ammon, Salamanu of Moab, . . . Mitinti of Ashkelon, Jehoahaz [Ia-u-ha-zi] of Judah [Ia-u-da-a-a], Kaush-malaku of Edom . . . Hanno of Gaza . . . .

There is strong evidence in the Bible that Ahaz was inclined to receive religious influences from the east. The reference to the passing of his son through the fire (II Kings 16:3) links up with the discovery that the god Muluk or Malik was widely worshipped in the lands to the east of Palestine.[5] One of the rites associated with this god was that of offering children in sacrifice. The deity Adrammelech, referred to in II Kings 17:31 as being the god of those people whom the Assyrians settled in Samaria after the exile of the Israelite population, is now attested in Syria as Adad-milki. There are references to the sacrificial cremation of sons to the god Adad in documents from northern Mesopotamia extending from the tenth down to the seventh centuries.[6] If we would understand the significance of the religious practices of Ahaz we will need to call on the discoveries of the archaeologist.

It was during the days of Ahaz that Israel finally fell, leaving Judah alone in the land as a more or less independent Hebrew state, although there was a degree of subservience to Assyria.

FROM HEZEKIAH TO THE DOWNFALL OF JUDAH

From the days of Hezekiah (715-687 B.C.) we have some valuable material. The Assyrian records are a great help here. Quite early in the reign of Hezekiah, King Sargon of Assyria came to the areas to the southwest of Judah where the king of Ashdod was causing trouble of some kind. Ashdod had even tried to obtain the aid of Judah, but without success. In 712 B.C. Sargon sent troops to attack Ashdod. The event is referred to in the Bible in Isaiah 20. This reference is of special interest because it was the sole

---

5. W. F. Albright, *Archaeology and the Religion of Israel,* p. 163.
6. *Ibid.,* p. 221.

reference to Sargon preserved in the records of the ancient world until the excavations in old Assyria showed what a great king he was. In his records he made reference to the revolt of Ashdod of 712 B. C. Sargon's annals speak thus:

> Azuri king of Ashdod had schemed not to deliver tribute [any more] and sent messengers [full] of hostilities against Assyria to the kings in his neighbourhood. On account of the misdeed which he [thus] committed, I abolished his rule over the inhabitants of his country and made Ahimiti, his younger brother, king over them. But these Hittites always planned treachery, hated his reign, and elevated Iamani [or Iadna] over them, who, without claim to the throne, knew, just as themselves, no respect for authority. [In a sudden rage] I marched quickly — in my state chariot and with my cavalry which never, even in friendly territory, leaves my side — against Ashdod, his royal residence, and I besieged and conquered the cities Ashdod, Gath, and Asdudimmu. . . . I reorganized these cities and placed an officer of mine as governor over them and declared them Assyrian citizens and they bore my yoke.[7]

An interesting letter from Nimrud, mentioning tribute from Egypt, Gaza, Judah, Moab, Ammon, Edom, and Eqron, may well date from this campaign.[8]

In 701 B. C. the next Assyrian king, Sennacherib, invaded Palestine and crushed a rebellion. In the southwest, Egyptian forces were defeated and the town of Lachish was besieged. This siege is vividly depicted in the bas-reliefs found in the palace of this king at Nineveh. He followed up his success at Lachish by attacking the walled cities of Judah, forty-six in all, according to the Assyrian record. The Bible tells of the promise of Hezekiah to Sennacherib to pay heavy tribute. The Assyrian king was not content and proceeded to besiege the capital, Jerusalem. The prophet Isaiah urged Hezekiah to hold out. This he did and the Assyrians retired. The Bible account in II Kings 18:1 to 19:7 has many parallels with the account of Sennacherib. Here are a few extracts from the annals of Sennacherib:

> As to Hezekiah the Jew, he did not submit to my yoke. I laid siege to forty-six of his strong cities, walled forts and to

7. J. B. Pritchard, *op. cit.*, p. 286, col. 1.
8. H. W. F. Saggs, *Iraq*, Vol. 17 (1955), pp. 134ff.

In II Kings 18:13-16 we read: "In the fourteenth year of king Hezekiah did Sennacherib king of Assyria come up against all the fenced cities of Judah, and took them. . . . And Hezekiah gave him all the silver that was found in the house of the Lord, and . . . cut off the gold from the doors of the temple of the Lord . . . and gave it to the king of Assyria." This hexagonal clay prism, found at Nineveh, and dating from 686 B.C., confirms that Sennacherib received such tribute from "Hezekiah the Judaean." (Courtesy, The British Museum)

countless small villages in the vicinity and conquered them by means of well-stamped earth-ramps and battering rams brought thus near to the walls . . . . Himself I made a prisoner in Jerusalem, his royal residence, like a bird in a cage. I surrounded him with earthwork in order to molest those who were leaving his city's gate . . . . I reduced his country but I still increased the tribute and the presents due to me as his overlord which I imposed upon him beyond his former tribute to be delivered annually . . . . Hezekiah did send me later to Nineveh . . . thirty talents of gold, eight hundred talents of silver . . . .[9]

9. J. B. Pritchard, *op. cit.,* p. 288.

The correlations between the two records are quite remarkable and have often been noticed. Among the more important we could draw attention to the mention of Hezekiah the Jew in both records, the attack on his walled cities (the exact number being given by Sennacherib), the siege of Jerusalem, in which Hezekiah was living, the tribute imposed, especially the thirty talents of gold, which is mentioned in both records, and Sennacherib's return to Nineveh (II Kings 19:36). Each record gives additional facts as well, so that the complete picture is obtained from a combination of the two.

There is some possibility that there was another visit by Sennacherib to Palestine. Some writers feel that the Bible record requires this, and the external facts allow it. The second visit is said to be recorded in II Kings 19:8-37. This remains a subject for debate, however. The Assyrian records are silent in the matter. But since they are silent for Sennacherib after 689 B.C., we await future discovery to clear up the point.

The death of Sennacherib at the hand of assassins, referred to in the Bible (II King 19:37), is known in Assyrian records.

> I tore out the tongues of those whose slanderous mouths had uttered blasphemies against my god Ashur and had plotted against me, his god-fearing prince; I defeated them. The others I smashed alive with the very same statues of protective deities with which they had smashed my own grandfather Sennacherib — now as a belated sacrifice for his soul. I fed their corpses, cut into small pieces, to dogs, pigs, zibu-birds, vultures, the birds of the sky and to the fish of the ocean.[10]

One final detail from the days of Hezekiah is concerned with the way in which "he made a pool and a conduit and brought water into the city" (II Kings 20:20). German students in 1880 found a long tunnel connecting the pool of Siloam and the Virgin's Fountain. On exploring it they found an inscription on the wall inside, in a script that was in use in the days of Hezekiah.[11] The writing is only the scratching of one of the workmen as he described how the last few blows were struck before the waters flowed. There is, however, no reason for doubting that the workman's remarks are true and that this tunnel is indeed the conduit of King Hezekiah. The so-called Siloam inscription, now housed in the Museum at Istanbul

10. *Ibid.,* pp. 288f.
11. *Ibid.,* p. 321.

in Turkey, still provides some excitement for the reader as he senses the thrill of those who finally broke through the wall of rock:

> (. . .) [when the tunnel] was driven through. And this was the way in which it was cut through: — While (. . .) [were] still (. . .) axe [s], each man toward his fellow, and while there were still three cubits to be cut through, (there was heard) the voice of a man calling to his fellow, for there was *an overlap* in the rock on the right (and on the left). And when the tunnel was driven through, the quarrymen hewed [the rock], each man toward his fellow, axe against axe; and the water flowed from the spring toward the reservoir for 1,200 cubits, and the height of the rock above the head[s] of the quarrymen was one hundred cubits.

Hezekiah's successor, Manasseh, who had one of the longest reigns in Judah, ruled from 687 to 642 B.C. He is referred to briefly in the annals of Esarhaddon (681-668 B.C.) where he is listed with others who paid tribute to help in the building of a royal palace.

> I called the kings of the country of Hatti and of the region on the other side of the river: Ba'lu king of Tyre, Manasseh [Me-na-si-i] king of Judah [Ia-u-di], Qaushgabri king of Edom, Musuri king of Moab, Sil-Bel king of Gaza, Metinti king of Ashkelon, Ikausu king of Ekron, Milkiashapa king of Byblos, Matanbaal king of Beth-Ammon, Ahimilki king of Ashdod — twelve kings of the seacoast.[12]

The religious practices of Manasseh can be better understood from a knowledge of Eastern religion in those centuries. Archaeology has much to say about these. We have no other information about Manasseh apart from the account in the Bible and the one reference in the annals of Esarhaddon. Evidently Judah was still under some sort of allegiance to the Assyrians.

A significant collection of documents from this same Assyrian king, Esarhaddon, has been found in recent years in the form of some three hundred fragments of baked-clay cuneiform writing which, when assembled, proved to comprise eight large tablets, practically identical in content, which constituted the written document of a treaty Esarhaddon had made with his vassals to the east of Assyria

---

12. *Ibid.,* p. 291.

A limestone lintel of a tomb of a certain Shebna, dating from the seventh century B.C., and inscribed with archaic Hebrew. It is not impossible that this is the Shebna whom Isaiah rebuked for the very fact of having prepared an elaborate sepulcher (Isa. 22:15ff.). (Courtesy, The British Museum)

in which they swore to support the accession of Ashurbanipal's sons after his death.[13] No doubt such treaties were drawn up for all of Esarhaddon's vassals. Certainly after his death there was a period of seventeen years of peace which was only broken when the sons Assurbanipal in Nineveh and Shamash-shum-ukin in Babylon fought each other in a bloody war, and though Assurbanipal won, it was at the price of Assyria's strength. She was in decline from 648 to her fall in 609 B.C.

These documents, apart from their historical interest in showing something of the procedures of government, give a very clear picture of the formal structure of a covenant between a suzerain and his vassal, and provide important parallels between the Biblical covenants and the secular covenants of the day. It would seem that these non-Biblical covenants may have provided a useful illustration of the way in which Yahweh, Israel's King, was related to Israel, who was His vassal.

But to return to the internal strife between the two sons of Esarhaddon, it is to be noted that there were repercussions all over the Assyrian world and many peoples took the opportunity to revolt. Already in 641 Elam was in revolt. In 640 in Judah, Amon, a pro-Assyrian king, was murdered (II Kings 21:20ff., II Chron. 33:21ff.). Assurbanipal marched west to deal with Judah and other rebels in the area. He may have had to punish Samaria again, for Ezra 4:9ff. speaks of foreigners being settled in that town by Asnapper.[14] In Judah the "people of the land" punished the rebels and made Josiah

13. D. J. Wiseman, *The Vassal Treaties of Esarhaddon* (London, 1958).

14. A. Malamat, "The Historical Background of the Assassination of Amon, King of Juda," *IEJ*, No. 3 (1953), pp. 26-29.

king, thus avoiding Assyrian retribution (II King 21:24, II Chron. 33:25).

But Josiah began to pursue an anti-Assyrian line both in politics and religion, one that had already been followed by Hezekiah when he sent an invitation to the Israelites in the Assyrian province of Samaria to join in the Passover (II Chron. 30:1-31:1). The death of Assurbanipal in 627 assured Josiah of success and he extended his reforms to all Israel. The last kings of Assyria were powerless to resist. Indeed it was in Josiah's reign that the end came for Assyria. The great coalition of Media and Babylon on the east and the hostile groups like Judah on the west encircled Assyria. In 612 Nineveh, Nimrud, Assur and Dur-Sharrukin had fallen. Only Egypt remained loyal to Assyria in her dying throes and Pharaoh Necho set out to assist her at Harran whence her last king Assur-uballit II had fled after the fall of Nineveh. Josiah's little army opposed him as he passed through Palestine, but Josiah lost his life (II Kings 23:29, 30). By 609 the collapse of Assyria was complete. The words of the prophets of Judah concerning Assyria's doom were fulfilled (Isa. 10:12-15, Zeph. 2:13-15, Nahum).

Thanks to modern knowledge from Assyrian excavations, we can now translate the small Hebrew preposition '*al* in II Kings 23:29 more accurately. The word has several meanings, "above," "upon," "beside," "against." The translators of the A.V., assuming that Egypt was going to fight against Assyria on this occasion, translated accordingly. We now translate, the king of Egypt went up "*alongside* the king of Assyria," rather than "*against* the king of Assyria."

Necho had deposed the son of Josiah, who naturally became king after his father's death, and chose another son, Eliakim, whom he renamed Jehoiakim. This man was probably pro-Egyptian in his sympathies (II Kings 23:34). By 605 B. C. the Egyptian armies were defeated at Carchemish in Syria and the Babylonian general was marching into Palestine. Jehoiakim was allowed to rule, but as a tributary of Nebuchadnezzar who by now was king in Babylon. This state of affairs continued till the death of Jehoiakim in 598 B. C. Within three short months his son Jehoiakin had to face an invasion from Nebuchadnezzar. It is not clear whether this eighteen-year-old king was being punished for the intrigues of his father or whether he was involved in some personal intrigue. In any case, the Babylonian armies marched on into Judah, besieged Jerusalem, and took the king into captivity. At the same time by a shrewd move all the men of ability, the leaders and technicians, were taken away. In this way Nebuchadnezzar hoped to weaken the rebels (II Kings 24:12-16).

Two valuable inscriptions bear on these times. Quite recently, important texts have been published by D. J. Wiseman.[15] One of these gives the first non-Biblical reference we have to this first attack of Nebuchadnezzar on Jerusalem. The record reads:

> In the seventh year, the month of Kislev, the king of Akkad mustered his troops, marched to the Hatti-land and encamped against the city of Judah and on the second day of the month of Adar he seized the city and captured the king. He appointed there a king of his own choice, received its heavy tribute and sent them to Babylon.[16]

The second record comes from the archives unearthed by the German excavator Koldewey in Babylon. Here were hundreds of receipts for oil issued to various captives in the city. The name Yaukin (Jehoiakin), king of Judah, appears on three of these.[17] One of them refers to his five sons as well.

> 1½ sila [oil] for 3 carpenters from Arvad, ½ sila each; 11½ sila for 8 carpenters from Byblos, 1 sila each . . . . 3½ sila for 7 carpenters, Greeks, ½ sila each; ½ sila to Nabu-etir the carpenter; 10 [sila] to Ia-ku-u-ki-nu [Iaukin] the son of the king of Ia-ku-du [Judah], 2½ sila for the 5 sons of the king of Ia-ku-du [Judah].

These receipts date about the year 592 B. C. and testify to the presence of Jehoiakin and his family in Babylon some years after his captivity.[18]

The king appointed by Nebuchadnezzar to replace Jehoiakin was the latter's uncle Zedekiah. For several years he gave his allegiance to the Babylonian king. Then he, too, began to intrigue with Egypt. As a result Nebuchadnezzar came to Palestine, bent on destruction. We have a very full account in the Bible of the last days of Judah (II Kings 25). Some very valuable materials bearing on the last eighteen months of Judah's history have been brought to light from excavations.

Both excavations and surface surveys conducted in southern Judah have confirmed the fact that there was considerable destruction carried

15. D. J. Wiseman, *Chronicles of Chaldean Kings* (London, 1956).
16. *Ibid.,* p. 73.
17. J. B. Pritchard, *op. cit.,* p. 308.
18. W. F. Albright, *The Biblical Period,* p. 47.

out here at the start of the sixth century B. C. Numerous excavated mounds revealed that they were occupied till just after 600 B. C. but that there was a drastic break in their occupation after that, so that they were not occupied again till post-exilic times. Some of them were never again occupied.[19]

In Lachish we have the best picture of the destruction. Indeed, there were two destructions close together. The final destruction was violent, and so fierce was the fire which destroyed the city that the limestone of the buildings turned to lime. The most important item in the town of Lachish was the collection of inscribed potsherds or ostraca, known as the Lachish ostraca. These turned out to be military letters quickly written out in the days of feverish haste as the Babylonian armies were closing in. As we read these short notes we gain the impression that southern Judah was in a state of stress. There were urgent orders passing to and fro, special arrangements being made for fire signals, the sending of a military mission to Egypt (Jer. 26:20-23), the inspection of guards, and general increase of military activity. The whole correspondence suggests an atmosphere of nervous tension in the early stages of the war before Jerusalem fell. Here is the letter that speaks of messengers going to Egypt:

> Thy servant Hoshaiah hath sent to inform my lord Yaosh: May Yahweh cause my lord to hear tiding of peace! And now thou hast sent a letter, but my lord did not enlighten thy servant concerning the letter which thou didst send to thy servant yesterday evening, though the heart of thy servant hath been sick since thou didst write to thy servant. And as for what my lord said, "Dost thou not understand? call a scribe!" as Yahweh liveth no one hath ever undertaken to call a scribe for me; and as for any scribe who might have come to me, truly I did not call him nor would I give anything at all for him!
>
> And it hath been reported to thy servant, saying, "The commander of the host, Coniah son of Elnathan, hath come down in order to go into Egypt; and unto Hodaviah son of Ahijah and his men hath he sent to obtain (. . .) from him."
>
> And as for the letter of Tobiah, servant of the king, which came to Shallum son of Jaddua through the prophet, saying, "Beware!", thy servant hath sent it to my lord.[20]

19. W. F. Albright, *Archaeology of Palestine* (London, 1954), pp. 140f.
20. J. B. Pritchard, *op. cit.*, p. 322.

Another letter tells that the soldiers in an unnamed post were looking for the fire signals of Lachish, because those of Azekah were already not visible. It would seem that the state of affairs was already more advanced than that described in Jeremiah 34:7, where all the cities of Judah had fallen except Lachish and Azekah. The letter reads as follows:

> May Yahweh cause my lord to hear this very day tidings of good! And now according to everything that my lord hath written, so hath thy servant done; I have written on the door according to all that my lord hath written to me. And with respect to what my lord hath written about the matter of Beth-haraphid, there is no one there.
>
> And as for Semachiah, Shemaiah hath taken him and hath brought him up to the city. And as for thy servant, I am not sending *anyone* thither [today (?), but I will send] tomorrow morning.
>
> And let [my lord] know that we are watching for the signals of Lachish, according to all the indications which my lord hath given, for we cannot see Azekah.[21]

Unfortunately, there is nothing yet available about the events in Jerusalem apart from what we have in the Bible. This town has been more or less continuously occupied through the centuries, and has in any case been destroyed many times. Further, it is a sacred city for three great faiths. It would be impossible today to do a great deal of excavation in the vital areas of the town.[22]

Thus Judah came to an end and the land passed under the control of the Babylonians. Not all the Jews by any means were taken to captivity, although only the poorer people remained in the land to care for it (II Kings 25:12). Some of the Jews, including Jeremiah the prophet, went to Egypt (Jer. 43). It was perhaps fifteen hundred years since Abraham had left Ur of the Chaldees to come to Palestine. It was surely a strange thing that after all those years some of his descendants should be returning there, not as free men, but as captives. Yet they learned many lessons from this captivity, and after their return were to undergo further experiences that were to take them on to the "fulness of times" when the Messiah would come.

21. *Ibid.*
22. See note, p. 9

PART TWO:

ARCHAEOLOGY AND
THE PRE-CHRISTIAN CENTURIES

Nine:

DAYS OF EXILE

W HEN THE PEOPLE OF JERUSALEM WENT INTO EXILE IN THE days of Nebuchadnezzar, a period of history closed for Israel. The tribal units that had entered Palestine in the time of Joshua had been united under King Saul about 1050 B. C. Following the death of Solomon and the division of the land into two kingdoms, each had gone its own way and had fallen in turn before a great conqueror — Israel in 722 B. C. before the Assyrians, and Judah in 586 B. C. before Nebuchadnezzar and the Babylonians (or Chaldeans).

After each disaster thousands of captives were taken to lands far away from the homeland. We know little of the fate of the exiles from Israel, but we do have some knowledge of the exiles from Judah.

THE HOME OF THE EXILES IN BABYLONIA

Bible history makes it clear that the people of Judah were invaded more than once by the armies of Nebuchadnezzar, and each time captives were taken. In 597 B. C. King Jehoiachin and many

155

of his notables, among whom was the prophet Ezekiel (Ezek. 1:2), were taken away to Babylonia. When Jerusalem fell to Nebuchadnezzar in 586 B. C., another group of people from Judah joined the party that had been exiled some eleven years before. It is of great interest to us to read the letter that the prophet Jeremiah wrote to these first exiles. Jeremiah stayed behind in Jerusalem and was still there when the city finally fell to the Chaldeans. But he wrote to the first group of exiles words of encouragement, urging them to build houses, plant gardens, take wives, raise children, and pray for the peace of the city to which they had gone (Jer. 29:1-7). All of this argues for a degree of freedom for the exiles in that foreign land.

The first group was already settled in the region of the River Khebar. Thanks to archaeological discovery, the general area where these people lived can now be identified with some certainty. Much of our information comes from the ancient site of Nippur in southern Mesopotamia, which will be referred to again in this book. This town has been excavated in part, and excavations are still proceeding there. Among the cuneiform tablets discovered in the ruins were two, dating respectively to 443 B. C. and 424 B. C., which refer to a waterway named *naru kabari* or *nehar kebar* which in English is "River Khebar."[1] This waterway was evidently an artificial canal which started from the Euphrates River just north of Babylon, and which can be traced further south until it joins the Euphrates again south of Ur of the Chaldees. Nippur itself is some sixty miles southeast of Babylon and the canal flowed through Nippur. There was therefore a connection by water between the general area where the exiles lived and the capital of the great Nebuchadnezzar.

It is interesting to note that the place name Tel Abib (Ezek. 3:15) is a Hebrew adaptation of a Babylonian name Til Abubi.[2] The Babylonian words mean "the mound of the flood." The actual site is not known but it was no doubt one of the many old mounds or tells formed from the debris of ruined cities. These had been long unoccupied and some of them were thought to go back to the days before the great Bible flood. Apparently some of these mounds were resettled. Other similar sites, for example Tel Melah and Tel Harsha (Ezra 2:59, Neh. 7:61), are referred to in the Bible as having been occupied by the exiled Jews. G. A. Cooke says that the name Tell Abubi was a common name in Babylonia at all periods. It was known

---

1. G. A. Cooke, *The Book of Ezekiel, ICC* (Edinburgh, 1936), p. 4.
2. *Ibid.*, p. 42.

in Hammurabi's code and on one of the inscriptions of the Assyrian king Tiglath Pileser.[3]

Actually in the vicinity of Nippur there are several old mounds and, as we shall see later, there is clear evidence that there were Jews living in this area between 500 and 400 B.C.[4] We may conjecture that these later Jews were descendants of the earlier exiles deported from Judah just after 600 B.C.

We can picture the Jewish exiles then, settled in a foreign country among the heathen, and engaged in some sort of forced labor under Nebuchadnezzar. Here they were to dwell for many years until finally many of them returned home just after 540 B.C. as a result of the decree of the conqueror Cyrus. Their lot may not always have been hard, for preachers like Ezekiel were evidently free to preach to the people who seem to have had some sort of limited local government with "elders." Their true condition remains largely a matter of conjecture. F. F. Bruce has made the fascinating suggestion that the exiles were drafted into a forced-labor gang working on the Babylonian irrigation system.[5]

BABYLON THE GREAT

The great capital was about sixty miles away from the exiles. Very likely few of them ever saw the great city. Yet it is of some importance for us as Bible students to know something about this city which is described in such glowing terms in several passages in the Bible. Thus the book of Isaiah refers to it as "Babylon, the glory of kingdoms, the beauty of the Chaldees' excellency" (Isaiah 13:19).

Babylon was an ancient city with a long history of occupation. Nebuchadnezzar determined to restore and to extend it so as to make it one of the most wonderful of all the cities in the East. In this he succeeded. Today, thanks to the work of Robert Koldewey and his team of German archaeologists, we have a good idea of the splendor of the city of those days.[6] During the years between 1899 and World War I the ruins of the inner city of Babylon were thoroughly excavated. A vast system of fortifications, streets, canals, palaces, and temples was brought to light. Well might Nebuchadnezzar have described this city in the words of Daniel 4:30, "Is

---

3. *Ibid.*
4. See below, pp. 215-218.
5. F. F. Bruce, *Bible Study Notes* (Jan.-Feb., 1951), p. 34.
6. R. Koldewey, *The Excavations at Babylon* (1914).

That Babylon deserved to be called "the Great" is evident even from the ruins that have come to light. Here are the well-preserved remnants of the imposing Ishtar Gate which convey clearly the great dimensions of the buildings that made the Babylonians boast of their accomplishments. (Courtesy, Consulate General of the Republic of Iraq)

not this great Babylon, that I have built for the house of the kingdom [royal dwelling place] by the might of my power, and for the honour of my majesty?"

The inner city where the king had his palaces is seen today as a remarkable complex of ruins. Entrance was gained through the great Ishtar gate, a double gate leading through double fortification walls. It was adorned with magnificent enameled bricks into which patterns were worked, patterns of flowers, geometrical figures, life-size animals, bulls, lions, and dragons. The Ishtar gate must have been startling in its beauty. Once inside this magnificent gate, the visitor would pass along the stone-paved procession way in the heart of the city proper. This way was walled up with enameled bricks decorated with life-size lions. To the right of the procession way

158

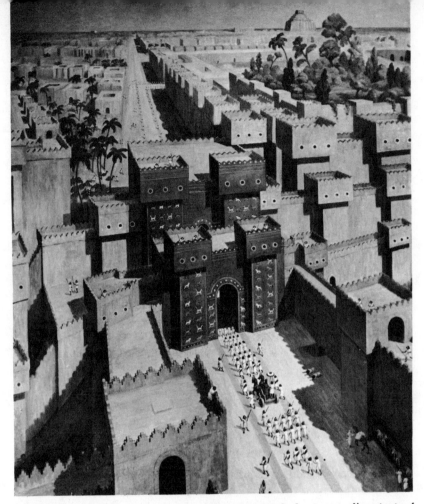

An artist's conception of what the Isthar Gate and the surrounding part of Babylon may have looked like. This is a reproduction of a painting by Maurice Bardin of the reconstruction according to Unger. Note the so-called "hanging gardens" to the right and the ziggurat behind them in the distance. (Courtesy, The Oriental Institute, The University of Chicago)

lay the palace area, likewise adorned with beautiful enameled bricks. One fine room decorated with bricks of gold and blue must have been the throne room. Some writers have made the suggestion that this was the place where the finger wrote on the wall, although the Bible does not actually assert this. In the same general area is a strange structure, thought by some to be the remains of the famous "hanging gardens." Whether or not this particular set of ruins can be identified with this well-known world wonder, it remains true that one of the features of the mighty Babylon was a remarkable set of gardens supported on terraces and thrust up into the air. They were built, according to tradition, for the wife of the king, a woman from the

159

cool mountain regions to the north, to give her both beauty and coolness.

Further down the procession way on the right lay the temple area where the priests' quarters as well as the temple of Marduk, known as Esagila ("house whose top is lofty"), were to be found. The most spectacular of all the buildings in the sacred area was the great ziggurat or temple tower which rose up into the sky in eight stages, according to the Greek historian Herodotus.[7] There were other notable buildings in the heart of this splendid city. Outside the main city area were various fortification walls at intervals of miles apart, all designed to make Babylon impregnable. Truly this was an outstanding city and one to be proud of.

And Nebuchadnezzar was proud indeed as the inscriptions show. Among the ruins of the city Koldewey found a good deal of inscribed materials, partly on bricks and stones and partly on baked clay tablets. Many of the written records indicate the pride and confidence of Nebuchadnezzar, as a selection of these inscriptions will show:

> A great wall which like a mountain cannot be moved I made of mortar and brick. . . . Its foundation upon the bosom of the abyss I placed down deeply . . . its top I raised mountain high. I triplicated the city wall in order to strengthen it, I caused a great protecting wall to run at the foot of the wall of burnt brick . . . .[8]

> When Marduk the great lord named me the legitimate son and to direct the affairs of the land . . . Babylon his mighty city . . . , its great walls I completed. Upon the thresholds of their great gates strong bulls of bronze, and terrible serpents ready to strike, I placed. That which no king had done my father did in that he enclosed the city with two moat-walls of mortar and brick. As for me, a third great moat wall, one against the second, I built with mortar and brick, and with the moat-wall of my father joined and closely united it. Its foundation upon the bosom of the abyss I laid down deeply, its top I raised mountain high . . . .[9]

> The produce of the lands, the products of the mountains, the bountiful wealth of the sea, within her I gathered . . . great quantities of grain beyond measure I stored up in her. At that time

7. Herodotus, *The Histories* (London, 1954), p. 86.
8. W. H. Lane, *Babylonian Problems* (London, 1923), p. 179.
9. *Ibid.*, p. 178.

the palace, my royal abode . . . I rebuilt in Babylon . . . great cedars I brought from Lebanon, the beautiful forest to roof it . . . .[10]

Concerning one of the temples, Nebuchadnezzar spoke in the following terms:

Huge cedars from Lebanon, their forest with my clean hands I cut down. With radiant gold I overlaid them, with jewels I adorned them . . . the side chapels of the shrine of Nebo, the cedar beams of their roofs I adorned with lustrous silver. Giant bulls I made of bronze work and clothed them with white marble. I adorned them with jewels and placed them upon the threshold of the gate of the shrine . . . .[11]

In contrast to all these grandiose words we listen to the words of the prophets of Israel with something of awe:

And Babylon, the glory of kingdoms, the beauty of the Chaldees' excellency, shall be as when God overthrew Sodom and Gomorrah. It shall never be inhabited, neither shall it be dwelt in from generation to generation (Isa. 13:19, 20).

Babylon shall become heaps, a dwellingplace for dragons, an astonishment, and an hissing, without an inhabitant.

Though Babylon should mount up to heaven, and though she should fortify the height of her strength, yet from me shall spoilers come unto her, saith the Lord.

Thus saith the Lord of hosts; The broad walls of Babylon shall be utterly broken, and her high gates shall be burned with fire (Jer. 51:37, 53, 58).

Babylon was not beaten down by an enemy. It was taken by the Persians in 539 B.C. and became a sort of second capital. In the days of Alexander the Great it was still occupied, although Alexander undertook the clearing up of certain deserted areas. In Roman times there was a town here. The town, however, was slowly abandoned and today the state of ruin of the once magnificent city is a telling commentary on the proud words of the man who made it in his day the wonder of all the East.

10. *Ibid.,* p. 181.
11. *Ibid.,* p. 187.

ARCHAEOLOGY AND THE PROPHET EZEKIEL

It was during the days of exile that the prophet Ezekiel sought to show the exiles that they were suffering the just consequences of their sins. It has been the traditional view of the Christian Church that the book of Ezekiel should be taken at its face value so that we regard the prophet as having done his preaching during the period 597 to 573 B. C. in the land of Babylonia. More recently there have been those who have sought to show that this prophet lived in Palestine for at least part of his ministry. Others have tried to show that the prophecy came from a date much later than the exile. In these discussions archaeology has done a good deal to support the traditional view.

A reproduction of another painting by Maurice Bardin of Babylon the Great. Here the ziggurat area is depicted with the river in the foreground. When this illustration and the one on page 159 are contrasted with the dismal sight of the area now, the veracity of God's predictive word concerning Babylon is driven home forcefully. (Courtesy, The Oriental Institute, The University of Chicago)

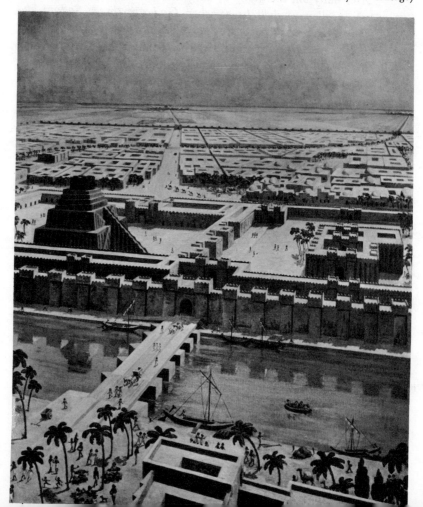

Already we have made reference to some of the place names which are not inconsistent with a Babylonian residence for Ezekiel. Indeed, they require it, if the geographical data are to have meaning. But there are other pointers. In Ezekiel 4:1 the prophet is commanded to take a brick and draw on it a map of Jerusalem. The Hebrew word here refers to a sun-dried brick, and while it was quite usual to draw sketches on such mud bricks in Babylonia, we are not aware that this sort of thing was ever done in Judah.[12] Again, the fact that Ezekiel was commanded to "dig through" the walls of the house as he acted a parable of the removal of people from the doomed city of Jerusalem points to Babylonia (Ezek. 12). Excavations show that the usual medium used for house construction in these lands was mud or adobe. In Palestine, on the other hand, the walls were made of stone, and the act of digging through a wall would invite the collapse of the wall (Ezek. 12:5-7).[13] It has been maintained that walls of mud were non-existent in Palestine in the sixth century B. C. but were in fact the only walls in use in Mesopotamia.[14] Other passages in Ezekiel's prophecy refer to the same type of house. Thus Ezekiel 13:10-15 refers to a house where the rainstorms will wash away the plaster. The same picture of adobe walls in the houses is found in Ezekiel 22:28.

Evidence that Ezekiel wrote at the time of the Exile comes from a most unusual source, namely the description of the east gate in the ideal temple described in Ezekiel 40:5-16.[15] There is enough data here for the careful reader to be able to reconstruct the ground plan of the gateway. It turns out to be a gate with provision for three doors, one behind the other, in a space of twenty-five cubits. Archaeologists point out that this type of gate was of a very old pattern. It was quite common in the days of King Solomon, for example, and is known in excavations at Megiddo, Ezion Geber, and Hazor, in the towns that go back to the days of Solomon. Another interesting fact is that this type of gate disappeared in the ancient Near Eastern scene in the ninth century B. C. and was replaced by a new style of gate altogether. A certain number of the older type of gate must have remained in use for years after their construction, but sooner or later they would all disappear, so that by Ezekiel's day it would be almost impossible to find one. How then would Ezekiel

---

12. Edward Chiera, *They Wrote on Clay* (Chicago, 1938), pp. 160-164.
13. Mud houses are to be seen, however, in Palestine in some places today.
14. C. C. Howie, *The Date and Composition of Ezekiel* (1950), p. 18.
15. *Ibid.,* pp. 43ff.

in a vision see a gate, the like of which was known in Solomon's day, but which had long since gone out of use in the East? The answer is that he must have seen the Solomonic gate in the Temple in Jerusalem prior to its destruction by Nebuchadnezzar in 587 B.C.[16] The destruction of the Temple would have removed what was probably the last gate of this kind to be seen in the East. In any case, here is a reasonable explanation of why Ezekiel would see such a gate in his vision, and incidentally a reason for thinking that he lived at the time of the Exile.

There is another possible link with Babylonia which, although not accepted by all commentators, seems to the present writer to have some value. It is that the strange imagery in Ezekiel 1 owes something to the Babylonian environment. In his vision Ezekiel saw strange creatures with human heads and wings, and in the imagery we hear of the face of a man, a lion, an ox, and an eagle (Ezek. 1:5-11). The partly human, partly animal forms are reminiscent of the guardian figures of the Babylonian temples, which may have been known to Ezekiel. It is quite within the range of the facts of Biblical history and also of our own experience today that God takes up the events and experiences of life as a starting point for speaking His mind to us. It was the storm that gathered on that day that was the prelude to God's revelation to Ezekiel. The storm was merely an attendant on God's throne. So, too, God called on the visual impressions so familiar to Ezekiel to grant to him a vision of the divine splendor.

SOME LATER MILITARY EXPLOITS OF NEBUCHADNEZZAR

Bible readers are familiar with those military events that concern the fall of Jerusalem. We referred in an earlier chapter[17] to the recent publication of an important document which refers to the campaign of Nebuchadnezzar in 598 B.C., which led to the captivity of Jehoiachin (II Kings 24:10-16). Reference has also been made to the valuable receipts from Babylon which refer to the presence of Jehoiachin here in 592. Unfortunately, written evidence of the campaigns of Nebuchadnezzar is sparse at present. That he had other

16. The size of the gate described in Ezekiel 40 is not significant because it is in any case visionary. It is the pattern that concerns us. There is little point to argue, as some have done, that the size of Ezekiel's doorway would have been too big for the temple known in Solomon's time and still standing in Ezekiel's earlier years.
17. See above, p. 149.

campaigns is certain, and some of these are referred to in the Bible. Thus he had dealings with both Tyre and Egypt. Ezekiel 29:18 speaks of his siege of Tyre, but we still await archaeological evidence of this event. Concerning Egypt, however, we have one inscription which, though far from complete, does tell of a campaign in that land.[18] The prophet Ezekiel spoke in several places of the judgment God intended for Egypt at the hands of the Babylonian king (Ezek. 29:19, 30:10, 32:11). A fragmentary historical text dating from the thirty-seventh year of Nebuchadnezzar, which is the year 567 B. C., speaks of fighting between Pharaoh Amasis and the king of Babylon. Unfortunately the tablet is so badly damaged that we can draw little reliable information from it. It may have been confined to the area of the Delta only, and again we await further archaeological light.[19] By this date Nebuchadnezzar was already old and his days of fighting were over.

A further tantalizing inscription from these days refers to an expedition to the general area of Syria and Lebanon.[20] This, too,

18. J. B. Pritchard, *ANET* (Princeton, 1955), p. 308.
19. There are useful discussions in H. L. Ellison, *Ezekiel* (Grand Rapids, 1958), p. 102, and H. R. Hall, *The Ancient History of the Near East,* (London, 1950), p. 549.
20. J. B. Pritchard, *op. cit.,* p. 307.

The fifth paragraph of this Babylonian chronicle of the sixth century B.C. tells of the capture of Jerusalem on March 16, 597 B.C., by Nebuchadnezzar, and of the appointment of Zedekiah as king and the removal of Israelite prisoners, among whom Jehoiachin, to Babylonia. (Courtesy, The British Museum)

is incomplete and lacks definite evidence as to the date and the occasion. What interests us is that the prophet Ezekiel infers that for many years after the fall of Jerusalem the Babylonians were active militarily. It is Babylon that is to be the agent of divine judgment on Tyre and Egypt. The inscriptions, though meager in number and content, do at least point to a continuation of the campaigns of the great king for a number of years. We live in hope that yet further excavation will bring to light additional significant evidence about these times which are so vital in Bible history.

THE CLOSING YEARS OF CHALDEAN POWER

When Nebuchadnezzar died in 562 B. C., after a reign of forty-two years, he was followed in quick succession by three weak kings, first by his son Amel Marduk (562-560 B. C.), whom Jeremiah calls Evil Merodach (Jer. 52:31, II Kings 25:27), then by Nergal-shar-usur (Neriglissar), one of the nobles and a son-in-law of Nebuchadnezzar, who replaced the inefficient Amel Marduk in a revolution and reigned from 560 to 556, and finally by the weak son of this last king, Labashi Marduk, who was expelled after a second revolution a few months after he came to the throne. One of the conspirators, Nabonidus (Nabunaid), then ruled as the last king of Babylon (556-539 B.C.).

The names of these three kings are known in written records. Thus Neriglissar's name appears on contract tablets as early as 596 B. C. Apart from Evil Merodach, who according to the Bible released King Jehoiachin (II Kings 25:27), we have no special interest in these rulers. The last king of Babylon is, however, of very real interest to us, for it was in his time that the collapse of Babylon became imminent.

Nabonidus ascended the throne amid bloodshed. Already the people of the land had shown considerable discontent with the Chaldean rulers and in two revolutions had managed to replace them. The new ruler was a man of culture with such a keen interest in antiquity that he has been described as the world's first archaeologist. He restored the temple of the moon in Haran where his mother was probably a priestess. Perhaps he was in fact a Syrian and from the outset stood little chance of gaining popular approval. But he took steps at once to make an impression on the people. An important basalt stele, now preserved in Istanbul, tells of his rise to power. He declared:

I am the real executor of the wills of Nebuchadnezzar and Neriglissar, my royal predecessors. Their armies are entrusted to me and I shall not treat carelessly their orders . . . .[21]

Referring to the previous king he declared that

Labashi Marduk, a minor who had not yet learned how to be-have, sat on the royal throne against the intention of the gods.[22]

The inscription goes on to tell how one night in a dream Nebuchad-nezzar and his attendant appeared to Nabonidus on Marduk's com-mand, to interpret strange signs in the heavens as a portent of a long reign. Other gods, too, sent favorable signs. It is evident from the inscription that the new king wished to indicate to the people that he had the personal approval of both Marduk the god, and the former Nebuchadnezzar.

Important new inscriptions from Haran were found in 1956 during an examination of the mosque which now stands on the old site.[23] Three basalt stelae about two meters high by about a meter wide had been found and reused in the mosque, but they were ancient and carried cuneiform inscriptions relating to the days of Nabonidus. Two of these tell of the reign of this ruler and of his restoration of the temple of the moon goddess Sin at Haran. Naboni-dus said that it was Sin "who called him to kingship." It would seem, however, that he earned the hostility of the people for his support of Sin, and it may have been partly for this reason that he retired to Teima for several years. The third stele is an account of the life of Nabonidus' mother who was a votaress of the moon goddess.

In an attempt to win the esteem of the priests, Nabonidus under-took various works of restoration in the temples of Babylonia. He richly endowed many of these, restored the temple of Marduk in Babylon, and journeyed through the land bestowing gifts on the gods of each sacred shrine: Sin at Ur, Shamash at Larsa, Ishtar at Uruk. Before long, however, he offended the priests greatly and paved the way for his own downfall. The year after his accession he was called to the west to quell a revolt. Moving on to Hamath and turning south towards Edom, he discovered the oasis at Teima where he settled down, to remain till perhaps his sixteenth year as king.

---

21. *Ibid.,* p. 309.
22. *Ibid.*
23. These documents have been published by C. J. Gadd in *Anatolian Studies,* Vol. VIII.

This was a fatal mistake, for it was necessary for the king to be present each New Year in Babylon for the special annual procession of the gods. In his absence the procession could not be held. It was an occasion when pilgrims flocked to the great city and when the coffers of the temples profited greatly. As the king stayed away year after year, the anger of the priests grew.

Back home in the capital the king appointed his son Belshazzar to be the actual ruler. One cuneiform inscription reads as follows:

> He entrusted a camp to his eldest, first-born son; the troops of the land he sent with him. He freed his hand; he entrusted the kingship to him. Then he himself undertook a distant campaign, the power of the land of Akkad advanced with him; toward Teima in the midst of the westland he set his face . . . . He slew the prince of Teima . . . then he himself established his dwelling in Teima . . . .[24]

The important Nabonidus Chronicle, issued later, in all probability at the inspiration of Cyrus, makes the point that in the seventh, ninth, tenth, eleventh years "the king was in the city of Teima. The son of the king, the princes, and his troops were in Akkad . . . . "[25] More important is the repeated statement that "the king did not come to Babylon for the ceremony of the month of Nisan."

It is interesting to comment here that since it was Belshazzar who exercised the co-regency in Babylon, and probably did so to the end, the book of Daniel is correct in representing him as the last king of Babylon (Dan. 5:30). A man like Daniel who was honored would thus be "third" in the kingdom.[26] Incidentally, the reference in Daniel 5:18 to Nebuchadnezzar as "father" of the king may simply follow Semitic usage which allows language like this in the case of family relationships, or it may follow on the claims of Nabonidus that he was the legitimate heir of Nebuchadnezzar.

The days of Babylon were drawing to a close. Further to the east a petty king, Cyrus the Persian, had in a remarkable way become ruler of both Media and Persia and had embarked on a program of expansion. In 546 B. C. he had conquered Lydia. In the

---

24. Quoted in J. Finegan, *Light from the Ancient Past* (Princeton, 1947), pp. 189f.
25. J. B. Pritchard, *op. cit.*, p. 305.
26. The Aramaic word means literally "third" but it came to mean, more generally, a prominent officer of state.

following years he was able to bring most of the East under his control, leaving only Babylonia as a last pocket of resistance. These ominous events led to some action on the part of Nabonidus. The Nabonidus Chronicle tells us that the king was still at Teima in the eleventh year, that is, 546 B. C. He may have stayed there longer, for the chronicle has a gap at this point and does not resume till the seventeenth year, which was the last year of his reign. There must have been something of a panic, for the record tells us that "Bel went in procession," that is, the New Year festival was held. Moreover, the gods from neighboring cities were entering Babylon. We think that in a vain hope to gain some protection from them Nabonidus gathered gods into Babylon. Some cities resisted this summary carrying off their gods to Babylon, if we are to judge from the chronicle: "The gods from Borsippa, Kutha . . . and Sippar did not enter."[27]

In October of 539 Babylon fell to the Persians. There were battles in the outskirts of Babylon some days before. On the fourteenth day Sippar was seized and "on the sixteenth day Gobryas ['Ugbaru] the governor of Gutium and the army of Cyrus entered Babylon without battle. Afterwards Nabonidus was arrested in Babylon when he returned there."[28]

The end of the two co-rulers Nabonidus and Belshazzar was death at the hands of the Persians. A new age had dawned for the people of the East and in particular for the Jews in exile. It was to usher in days of return and restoration.

ARCHAEOLOGY AND THE PROPHET DANIEL

We do not intend here to enter the lists and fight a battle with the literary critics about the date of this important book in the Old Testament. That decision rests on a number of considerations. There are, however, a number of comments that may be made from the archaeological angle, for undoubtedly the author of this book was reliably informed on a number of issues. In particular the fifth chapter has a number of items which suggest a well-informed writer.

The references in various places in this book of Daniel to soothsayers, magicians, astrologers, and the like (Dan. 1:20, 2:10, 4:7, 5:11, etc.), are all authentic items in the background of the times. Excavations have produced a good deal of material about the religion

---

27. J. B. Pritchard, *op. cit.,* p. 306.
28. *Ibid.*

of Babylon, and it is clear that magic and divination played a large part.

Another feature of the book of Daniel which has an authentic ring is the great importance attached to dreams. We have already noticed how Nabonidus made a strong point of the dream in which he saw Nebuchadnezzar. Dreams figure in the authentic records of Mesopotamia from the earliest times, forming an integral part of the kings' actual accounts of their own reigns.[29] It is quite wrong to write off all dreams as apocryphal accretions. Even if ancient rulers invented the dreams, they were accepted by the people as one of the ways in which the gods spoke to men. Hence the many references to dreams in the context of Babylonia are quite in keeping with the facts of the case.

Up to the present the enigmatic figure of "Darius the Mede" of Daniel (5:31, 6:1-28, 9:1, 11:1) is quite unknown to the archaeologist. Concerning this man W. F. Albright wrote, "The elusive problem of Darius the Mede remains exactly as puzzling as ever; it certainly cannot be solved merely by hypercriticism."[30] Perhaps we have to do here with a title.

One of the texts of Nabonidus found at Haran and dated to 546 B. C. refers to the "King of the Medes."[31] This statement opens up the whole question afresh. D. J. Wiseman asks whether this phrase may not have been another name for Cyrus.[32] Certainly the people of Haran spoke of the king of the Medes in 546 B. C. But by this time there was no such king, his place having been taken by Cyrus the Persian who went on to conquer Babylon. Wiseman suggests that we should translate Daniel 6:29 as "in the reign of Darius, even in the reign of Cyrus the Persian."

We have already referred to the place of Belshazzar in the closing days of the Chaldean rule in Babylon. The writer was correctly informed in this matter. The relationships between Nabonidus and his son and the achievements of each have been made the subject of a valuable piece of research by R. P. Dougherty in his

29. Cyrus Gordon, *Introduction to Old Testament Times* (Ventor, 1953), pp. 66f.

30. W. F. Albright, *Journal of Biblical Literature* (Dec., 1949), p. 375. Cf. H. H. Rowley, *Darius the Mede* (1960); J. C. Whitcomb, *Darius the Mede* (1959).

31. See p. 167.

32. D. J. Wiseman in *Documents from Old Testament Times* (London, 1958), ed. D. Winton Thomas, p. 83.

book, *Nabonidus and Belshazzar*, which contains a wealth of valuable material about these times.[33]

The story of the three young men who were thrown into a fire because they refused to worship the image of the king (Dan. 3) reminds us of the large brick kilns outside the city where Nebuchadnezzar's workmen baked bricks for his buildings. Some of these have been uncovered in excavations. A strange comparison with this very incident comes from the days of Rim Sin, a former king in these lands (1750 B.C.). This king once decreed concerning four men of Larsa: "Because they threw a young slave into an oven, throw ye a slave into a furnace." Although the precise significance of the decree is not clear, E. G. Kraeling remarks about this incident, "Clearly, that sort of thing was nothing new in Babylonia."[34]

While these items do not settle the date of composition of the book of Daniel, they show that the author was in possession of a good deal of authentic background material. Archaeological research can do much to establish the value of the background material appearing in an ancient document such as this.

THE EXILES LOOK HOMEWARD

Ezekiel the prophet had spoken of days of restoration and had told the people of his vision of the valley of dry bones (Ezek. 37). Earlier still the prophet Jeremiah had spoken of restoration after seventy years (Jer. 25:12) under the kings of Babylon. Magnificent passages in the latter part of the book of Isaiah gave strong hope of restoration. Here, too, Cyrus was referred to as the Lord's shepherd, the Lord's anointed (Isa. 44:28, 45:1). As the years went by, and more especially as the progress of Cyrus the Persian was witnessed, there must have been a spirit of keen anticipation among those exiles who still held to the faith of their fathers. The Lord was about to turn again the captivity of Zion (Ps. 126). No longer need the exiles sit down and weep by the waters of Babylon (Ps. 137). To the exciting story of Cyrus and his decrees which granted freedom to all exiles, we now turn.

33. R. P. Dougherty, *Nabonidus and Belshazzar* (Yale, 1929).
34. E. G. Kraeling, *Bible Atlas* (Chicago, 1956), p. 323.

Ten:

THE RETURN OF THE JEWS FROM EXILE

THE FALL OF BABYLON IN 539 B.C. USHERED IN TWENTY-FIVE years of significant history for the Jews. After the restoration of their Temple in 516 B.C. or early in 515 B.C. we enter upon a period of comparative silence. But these early days were vital in setting the pattern for a good deal of the subsequent history of the Jews. In actual fact considerable numbers of the exiles did not return from Babylonia and those who did were faced with tremendous hardships in their own land. There were droughts, there were enemies on every hand, the land to which the Jews were returning had been devastated and required much attention before it would yield the fruits of the field, and finally heavy taxation was exacted by the Persian overlords. By perhaps March, 515 B.C., the Temple was completed in Jerusalem. This gave to the returning exiles a tangible focal point in their national life. There is quite an amount of archaeological material referring to these days, far more indeed than there is for the subsequent centuries.

173

Illustration of page 172: *Assyrian court attendants from the palace of Sargon II, at Khorsabad. This bas-relief dates from c. 710 B.C.* (Courtesy, Consulate General of the Republic of Iraq)

The Decrees of Cyrus

The book of Ezra opens with an account of the decree of Cyrus which allowed the exiles to return to their land:

> *Thus saith Cyrus king of Persia, The Lord God of heaven hath given me all the kingdoms of the earth; and he hath charged me to build him an house at Jerusalem, which is in Judah. Who is there among you of all his people? his God be with him, and let him go up to Jerusalem, which is in Judah, and build the house of the Lord God of Israel, (he is the God,) which is in Jerusalem* (Ezra 1:2, 3).

There is an alternative form of this decree in Ezra 6:3-5.

Historians of a former day approached these simple Biblical statements with suspicion.[1] Some writers argued that we had no evidence that Cyrus made a decree of this kind, much less that he paid any sort of honor to the God of Israel. He was a Persian who worshipped Persian gods and could hardly be expected to pay honor to the God of the Jews. We no longer raise questions of this kind

1. W. O. E. Oesterley and T. H. Robinson, *A History of Israel*, (Oxford, 1932), II, 75, 81.

In Babylon a baked clay cylinder of about nine inches long was found that dates from 536 B.C. This document is now known as the Cylinder of Cyrus, who was king of Babylonia from 538-529 B.C. On it is recorded his capture of Babylon without a battle, his return of prisoners to their own countries, and his restoration of treasures to the native temples. (Courtesy, The British Museum)

since we have given due weight to important documents from the days of Cyrus which show us that he was a master of propaganda and knew how to exploit every occasion to the best advantage for himself. A study of the so-called Nabonidus Chronicle, of the famous Cyrus Cylinder, and of the verse account of Nabonidus helps a great deal in understanding the true state of affairs at the time.

The Nabonidus Chronicle referred to in our previous chapter[2] was almost certainly prepared under the direction of Cyrus. We have seen how it tells us of the last years of Nabonidus and of how he neglected his duties to the gods in Babylon. It is clear that Nabonidus in a last panic gathered many gods into Babylon as a sort of protection in his time of desperation. It was all to no avail. The chronicle tells us that the noble Cyrus was welcomed into the city with real joy.

> In the month of Arahshamnu, the third day, Cyrus entered Babylon, green twigs were spread in front of him . . . the state of peace was imposed upon the city . . . . From the month of Kislimu to the month of Addaru, the gods of Akkad which Nabonidus had made come down to Babylon . . . returned to their sacred cities . . . .[3]

It is evident from this document that Cyrus had a policy of returning the gods to their own homes. This fact is borne out by a study of the important Cyrus Cylinder which was especially prepared for the occasion. The document, which is really a baked clay cylinder, begins with a strong piece of propaganda in which the new king shows how he has the approval of the gods. After some broken lines in the record it goes on to say:

> . . . the correct images of the gods he removed from their thrones, imitations he ordered to place upon them . . . . he interrupted in a fiendish way the regular offerings . . . . the worship of Marduk, the king of the gods, he changed into an abomination, daily he used to do evil against his city . . . . Upon their complaints the lord of the gods became terribly angry . . . . he scanned and looked through all countries, searching for a righteous ruler willing to lead him [Marduk] in the annual procession. Then he pronounced the name of Cyrus, king of Anshan, declared him to become the ruler of all the world . . . . Marduk the

2. See above, p. 168. See also J. B. Pritchard, *ANET* (Princeton, 1955) , p. 305.
3. *Ibid.,* p. 306, col. 2.

great lord, protector of his people, beheld with pleasure his [Cyrus'] good deeds and his upright mind and ordered him to march against Babylon.[4]

This must have been of tremendous value in establishing the prestige of the new king in the eyes of the Babylonians. Here then was the legitimate king of the region, who had the approval of the gods. Cyrus wisely entered Babylon without destroying the city and gave careful instructions to his troops to respect the people and their property. The story is told in considerable detail on the cylinder. More was needed, however, in order to secure the goodwill of the people, and especially of those who were slaves in that land. It would be wisdom indeed to free all captives and restore them to their homes. This Cyrus did. The decree reads:

> As to the inhabitants of Babylon who against the will of the gods (. . .) I abolished the corvee [yoke] which was against their social standing. I brought relief to their dilapidated houses, putting an end to their main complaints.[5]

It is not hard to see in these words the intention of the king that enslaved peoples should be freed, although it must be admitted that these words might have applied only to the local Babylonians. Later on in the document, however, we have a possible reference to the return of exiles of various kinds to their lands:

> I also gathered all their former inhabitants and returned to them their habitations.[6]

Concerning the treatment of the gods we have some clear statements. The gods were to be returned to their homes and restored to their temples which were to be repaired:

> I returned to the sacred cities on the other side of the Tigris, the sanctuaries of which have been ruins for a long time, the images which used to live therein and established for them permanent sanctuaries. I also gathered all their former inhabitants and returned to them their former habitations. Furthermore I resettled on the command of Marduk, the great lord, all the gods of Sumer and Akkad whom Nabonidus has brought into

4. *Ibid.*, p. 315, col. 2.
5. *Ibid.*, p. 316, col. 1.
6. *Ibid.*, p. 316, col. 2.

Babylon . . . . May all the gods whom I have resettled in their sacred cities daily ask Bel and Nebo for a long life for me . . . .[7]

It was clearly the policy of the Persian ruler to allow freedom of worship. It is to be noticed that although Cyrus was not a worshipper of the gods of Babylon, he knew how to make a show of honoring them in order to win his way with the Babylonian people. We need not conclude that because he spoke in terms such as we read in this document he necessarily worshipped the gods of Babylon.

In the light of material like this we may conclude that Cyrus prepared similar documents for other people. In the case of the Jews there were no images to be restored to the Temple, but there was a Temple to be rebuilt and sacred vessels to be returned. It is sheer hyperskepticism to deny that Cyrus granted to the Jews privileges similar to those that were allowed to other people. We argue that the brief decrees in the book of Ezra are extracts from longer decrees issued for the Jews by the great king. We need not pay particular attention to the fact that Cyrus seems to pay honor to the God of the Jews. He probably paid no more respect or worship to this God than he did to others.

That Cyrus did in fact restore temples is borne out by some of the inscriptions found in excavations. Thus, at Uruk the German excavations of E. Heinrich, H. Lentzen, and others showed that the sanctuary of Ishtar was rebuilt by Cyrus, who left inscribed bricks on which this claim was made.[8] At Ur also, although inscribed bricks show that some restoration was done by the former ruler Nabonidus, it is of special interest to us to find that Cyrus himself authorized and completed a great deal of restorative work in the sanctuaries of Ur.[9] Both inscribed bricks and an important baked clay cylinder found near to the great ziggurat refer to this fact.

Further information along this line is obtained from a baked clay tablet in the British Museum, unfortunately badly damaged, which presents in verse form the information contained in the Nabonidus Chronicle.[10] We now know it as the "Verse Account of Nabonidus." It was evidently prepared by the priests of Babylon, and gives in

7. *Ibid.,* p. 316.
8. R. P. R. de Vaux, "Les Décrets de Cyrus et de Darius sur la reconstruction du Temple," *RB* (Jan., 1937), p. 33.
9. *Ibid.,* p. 34.
10. J. B. Prichard, *op. cit.,* pp. 312-315.

The impression (left) of the cylinder seal (right) shows Darius I on a lion hunt. The cuneiform inscription gives his name and title, "The Great King," in three languages — Old Persian, Elamite, and Babylonian. The agate cylinder dates from c. 500 B.C. (Courtesy, The British Museum)

panegyric form an account of the victories of Cyrus. Despite the gaps we can still read that Cyrus, after the capture of Babylon, was occupied with sacred works. He multiplied the offerings to the gods and prostrated himself before them. He restored the gods and the goddesses to their sanctuaries and sent back the people with them.

There can be no doubt that Cyrus showed a great deal of tolerance towards the various religious sections in the community. It is against the background of these facts that we must read the decrees of Cyrus found in the Bible. Quite clearly there is every reason to regard the Biblical accounts as authentic. W. F. Albright has written, "The substantial historicity of the edict of Cyrus in 538 has been confirmed by modern archaeological discoveries."[11]

One further point is relevant to our discussion. The two accounts of the decree of Cyrus in the Bible are in two different languages. The passage in Ezra 1:2-4 is in Hebrew, and the passage in Ezra 6:3-5 is in Aramaic. This fact may well be significant because on the one hand Persians used Aramaic in their official and international documents, and on the other hand it seems clear that they often used the local languages for the promulgation of information in given areas. In Ezra 6:2 there is a specific term used, *dikronah*, which we now know to have been an Aramaic term for an official memorandum "which recorded an oral decision of the king or other official and which

11. W. F. Albright, *The Biblical Period* (Oxford, 1952), p. 49.

This golden model of a Persian chariot resembles strongly that of the seal impression on page 178 where even the knobs on the wheels are shown. Note the prominence the human figures and the lion are given in comparison with the horses. (Courtesy, The British Museum)

initiated administrative action. It was never intended for publication but solely for the eye of the proper official, following which it was filed away in government archives."[12] This will explain why the document was later found in the official archives at Achmetha or Ecbatana (Ezra 6:2).

The Hebrew document of Ezra 1 would refer to information for local national consumption. It was a proclamation in Hebrew, to be made possibly by the royal heralds, and it was addressed to those who claimed to be worshippers of Yahweh, God of heaven. Precisely the same sort of thing happened elsewhere in Persian times as we know today from documents brought to light by the archaeologists in which the wishes of the Persian king were made known to the people in written form in their own tongue. For example, there are records from Egypt, not precisely from the days of Cyrus, but from the days of his successor Darius, who instructed the Egyptians in matters affecting their religion. He sent a message to the satraps (governors) of Egypt to assemble the wise men, priests, and scribes

12. G. E. Wright, *Biblical Archaeology* (London, 1957), p. 200.

to undertake the publication of the ancient laws of Egypt, as they affected in particular the Pharaoh, the temples, and the people. Again, there are inscriptions in the local Egyptian script referring to the work of Darius in restoring temples and the like.[13] There are also several references to the beneficent acts of the Persian kings in the general area of Asia Minor. The name of these rulers was long remembered in these areas, and one notable inscription found near Magnesia in Asia Minor, written in Greek, refers to a letter from Darius to his local satrap, expressing grief that damage had been done to his reputation because the satrap had charged impost on sacred vessels of the god Apollo. These cases point to the possible use of local scripts and writings in certain cases where the Persian king wished to express his will.

In the light of all this evidence there seems no reason to doubt that the decrees of Cyrus recorded in the Bible give the substance of the originals. In any case, much of the background we have been able to discover from archaeological research lends support to the Biblical picture. Thus it was that Jews who lived in Babylonia found themselves in the year 539 B.C. in the happy position of being able, if they so desired, to return to the land of their fathers.

The Land of Judah at the Time of the Return

It has been pointed out more than once in recent years that at the time of Nebuchadnezzar's final assault on Judah in the years 587-586 B.C. there was considerable destruction in all the cities of Judah. W. F. Albright has written in this connection:

> A fair number of towns and fortresses of Judah have now been excavated in whole or in part; many other sites have been carefully examined to determine the approximate date of their last destruction. The results are uniform and conclusive: many towns were destroyed at the beginning of the sixth century B.C. and never again occupied; others were destroyed at that time and partly reoccupied at some later date; still others were destroyed and reoccupied after a long period of abandonment, marked by a sharp change of stratum and by intervening indications of use for non-urban purposes. There is not a single

13. R. P. R. de Vaux, *op. cit.*, p. 40.

BIBLE LANDS *in the days of the* PERSIANS
(THE EARLIER KINGDOMS ARE ALSO SHOWN)

MEDITERRANEAN SEA

BLACK SEA

AEGEAN SEA

KINGDOM OF LYDIA

Sardis

Memphis

Thebes

RED SEA

Tyre

AREA OF THE FIFTH PERSIAN SATRAPY

Jerusalem

Ammon

Damascus

Haran

Teima

Dedan

KINGDOM OF THE MEDES

Babylon

Nippur

Uruk

Ur

Ecbatana (Acmetha)

Susa

CASPIAN SEA

PERSIAN GULF

KINGDOM OF THE PERSIANS

Persepolis

This is a picture of the eleventh tablet of the Assyrian version of the Epic of Gilgamesh, the Babylonian account of the flood. The tablet was found at Nineveh and dates from c. 650 B.C. (Courtesy, The British Museum)

case known where a town of Judah proper was continuously occupied through the exilic period.[14]

The destruction does not seem to have extended to the former territory of Israel. North of Jerusalem we have evidence, based on excavations, that towns were occupied there throughout the sixth century. In particular the town of Bethel, which really lay outside Judah proper, in the area of Benjamin, was occupied till about 500 B. C., when it was destroyed. The reason for its destruction is still unknown. Further north, towns like Samaria, Megiddo, and Tell en Nasbeh, whose Biblical name is not now known, were all occupied in the sixth century. All of this points to the fact that Nebuchadnezzar confined his destruction to the area of Judah, although, as the quotation from Albright shows, he ravaged that land thoroughly.

It seems evident, therefore, that when the Jews returned from their exile they returned to a land that had little in the way of towns, houses, or farms awaiting them. It has been suggested that only one other period in the history of the land showed such a tragic picture, and that was before the days of Abraham, at the close of the Early Bronze Age.

The actual area occupied by the returning Jews was a small one. Its limits can be partly worked out from the material supplied in the lists given in Ezra 2 or in Nehemiah 7. It extended from

14. W. F. Albright, *Archaeology of Palestine* (London, 1956), pp. 141f.

Bethzur, which is just north of Hebron, to a point not far north of Jerusalem, perhaps twenty-five miles from north to south along the central ridge. Nehemiah 7:66f. gives a population of just under 50,000.

Were it not for the generous attitude of Cyrus and his successors, we may well wonder how the returning Jews survived. Hostile neighbors were likely to cause trouble, and the burden of a land which had lain waste now for over half a century was a big one. It was to this task that the returning exiles now set their hands.

A BRIEF REVIEW OF THE KINGS OF PERSIA UP TO 500 B. C.

In order to obtain a correct perspective for our study, we should now give some attention to the story of the Persian rulers and their methods of government during these years, since these facts are important for our understanding of the Biblical narrative.

The first of these rulers was Cyrus. Already in 549 B. C. he had united the peoples of Media and Persia under his rule and by 546 he had subdued Croesus, the king of Lydia. In 539 B. C. he entered Babylon, which he was to rule till 530 B. C. We think of him today as the founder of the great Persian Empire. In order to govern his great domain he established twenty provinces called satrapies, each ruled by a satrap (protector of the kingdom). These officers were kept under his eye by means of his personal secretaries, financial officers, and generals, who owed allegiance directly to him although they served in the capitals of the satraps. The vast expenses of such an empire were raised from taxation which was often unkind. This taxation was to be a source of trouble to the people in Judah who, as subjects of the Persian rulers, had to pay their share. There are Biblical references to this burden of taxation as, for example, in Nehemiah 5:4.

In the year 530 B. C. the great Cyrus was killed in battle, fighting some tribal peoples to the northeast of his land. His son Cambyses rescued his body and buried him in a tomb that was already prepared and which can be seen today, although it has since been plundered.

Cambyses had helped his father to govern Babylon and was an experienced ruler. During his short reign he was able to conquer Egypt, and by 525 Memphis, the capital of Egypt, was in his hands. We remember this king in Jewish history because of his kindness to the Jewish settlement away down the Nile at Elephantine. Here there was a military post manned by Jews to protect the southern

183

borders of the land. We have no idea of the origin of the Jews here, but they had a temple erected for worship. When Cambyses destroyed the local temples of the Egyptians, he spared the temple of the Jews, a fact which is mentioned in important documents from a later day to which we shall refer later.[15] When the task was completed in Egypt, Cambyses set out on the return journey. As he reached Mount Carmel in Palestine, he heard that a usurper had risen up in Persia and claimed his throne. Whether due to shock or, as some claim, by his own hand,[16] he died there.

In the service of Cambyses was a younger relative, Darius by name. He left Palestine at once and organized opposition to the usurper. Before the year 522 had passed, the usurper Bardiya, whose real name was Gaumata, was slain.[17] Meantime, revolts broke out all over the empire and Darius began a struggle for recognition. After two years he was able to subdue all his opponents and rule supreme. He commemorated his success by having a mountainside smoothed off and a huge inscription carved on its face, with a picture of himself placing his foot on the head of one of his conquered foes. This inscription is still to be seen at Behistun. Darius had a long reign, lasting till 486 B. C., during which he did much to reform the laws of Persia and to extend his domains. It was he who built the first canal to join the Mediterranean Sea to the Red Sea.[18] He also undertook the invasion of Greece but was defeated at the battle of Marathon in 490 B. C. His work as a builder is seen in palaces from his time which have been excavated in Babylon, Susa, and Persepolis, although his successors extended his building program considerably. Finally, we remember him as an outstanding financier who standardized the weights and measures of Persia, developed the coinage, which in his day was of comparatively recent invention, and began to interfere in the commercial life of the people.[19] Some economists say that owing to the government interference price levels rose with a jump at the start of the reign of Darius and contributed in the end to the economic disintegration of the great empire.[20] Numerous documents

15. See below, p. 224. See also J. B. Pritchard, *op. cit.*, pp. 491f.
16. Herodotus, iii, 62f.
17. The original Bardiya was a brother of Cambyses but was executed for rebellion. Gaumata, a Magian, claimed to be this Bardiya whose death was never announced.
18. A. T. Olmstead, *History of the Persian Empire* (Chicago, 1948), p. 145.
19. F. A. Banks, *Coins of Bible Days* (New York, 1955), p. 16. A. T. Olmstead, *op. cit.*, pp. 186f.
20. A. T. Olmstead, *op. cit.*, pp. 193f.

of the period found in excavations show the extent to which the king was taking an undue share of the profits of the traders.[21] This led to price rises and to the distress of the poor people. We have traces of this trouble in the Bible, for example in Nehemiah 5:1-4.

THE RETURN OF THE EXILES

The Bible has two lists which give the composition of the group that finally left Babylonia to return to Judah, one in Ezra 2 and one in Nehemiah 7. These lists differ slightly from one another, and various attempts are made to explain this. Many writers are inclined to think that the lists refer to the state of affairs at the time when the story in Ezra and Nehemiah was finally committed to writing.[22] More recent study has sought to show that the difference between the two lists can be explained best in terms of slight scribal variations in lists which were compiled from an actual original which made use of a numerical notation such as we have found in several Aramaic documents from Persian times. This system of notation, which was widely used both among the Persians and also among the later Nabataean and Palmyrene scribes, consisted of a series of strokes and other special marks which could lead to minor scribal variants. It is suggested that the Jews themselves had a similar system and, indeed, there is a hint of this on some of the ostraca from Samaria dating back to the eighth century B. C. A recent writer on this subject has said:

> As for the lists in Nehemiah 7 and Ezra 2, while at first glance these textual numerical differences may seem detrimental, actually they greatly enhance the value of the lists, as they bring out much of their real nature and age — remains of ancient census lists made by the builders and supporters of the restoration and reform sometimes called "the Second Temple," documents vested with reality and antiquity by the very blemishes and signs of use they exhibit.[23]

It seems clear that the returning company of Jews wished to remain exclusive and required that a man should have his name on

21. *Ibid.*
22. W. F. Albright, *The Biblical Period* (Oxford, 1952), p. 62, Note 122.
23. H. L. Allrik, "The Lists of Zerubbabel (Nehemiah 7 and Ezra 2) and the Hebrew Numeral Notation," *BASOR* (Dec., 1954), p. 27.

the official list before he could gain recognition in the community. For this reason many of the local people were excluded (Ezra 4:1, 2).

It is evident from documents unearthed at Nippur that many Jews did not return at this time.[24] Those that did were led by Sheshbazzar (Ezra 1:8, 11). This man had a Babylonian name, perhaps Sin-ab-usur or Shamash-ab-usur, but there is some dispute as to who he was. There is a name like this among the sons of Jehoiachin (Jeconiah) in the list in I Chronicles 3:17, 18, Shenazar, and it has been thought that the strangeness of the name caused scribal confusion. It was not at all impossible that in 538 B.C. there should be a son of Jehoiachin alive. He had five sons in 592 B.C. according to tablets found in Babylon, and they could not have been very old at the time of the return.[25] There may well have been a son still alive aged sixty or so.

On the other hand, some writers have held that we may have here a Babylonian official in Persian employ to whom was entrusted the task of leading the Jews home.[26] Another Persian official, Mithredath, handed to him the sacred vessels of the Temple (Ezra 1:8), and presently the party set out for their homeland. In the subsequent story, the Bible tells us only of the work of Zerubbabel (Zer-babil, "offspring of Babylon") and Jeshua the priest. What happened to Sheshbazzar we do not know. Perhaps he was frustrated by the groups that later troubled Nehemiah, or perhaps his task was only of limited duration and having completed it he returned to Persia. In any case, Zerubbabel and Jeshua alone feature in the Bible story.

This Zerubbabel had a Babylonian name but he was the son of Jehoiachin's eldest son Shealtiel. It was these two men, Zerubbabel and Jeshua, who led the national life. Although the first aim was to build the Temple, they were sidetracked and did little about it till the days of Darius.[27] They seem to have done some preliminary work and to have made arrangements to obtain cedar logs from Tyre. Just here we can add an archaeological note. Ezra 3:7 refers to cedar trees being brought by sea to Joppa. It is of real interest to us today to learn that there was a town at the mouth of the little Yarkon River in those days, originally founded about 1200 B.C.,

---

24. G. E. Wright, *Biblical Archaeology* (London, 1957), pp. 205f.
25. J. B. Pritchard, *ANET* (Princeton, 1955) p. 308, col. 2.
26. E. G. Kraeling, *Bible Atlas* (Chicago, 1956), p. 329.
27. The writer is well aware of the many unsolved problems about the foundation of the Temple.

but still in use in Persian times. Today it is known as Tell Qasile. It was excavated in part in 1948-1950.[28]

When the time was ripe to take up again the building of the Temple, it was Zerubbabel who was to the fore. In the exciting days that followed the death of Cambyses, the prophets Haggai and Zechariah called on this man, who is described as "governor of Judah" (Hag. 1:14), or as "the Tirshatha" (Ezra 2:63), a Persian word meaning "his excellency" and known from Persian documents of those days. Haggai gave his first message in August 520 and called on Zerubbabel to commence work on the Temple. The foundation was laid and the work put in hand. At once there were local objections from Tattenai, governor of the province "Beyond the River."

This governor is known in a document from Babylon dating from a few years later, actually 502 B. C.[29] The name is also known from a text referring to "Tattenai prefect of Susa."[30] This latter is not the man in the Bible, but the text shows that the name was a common one in those times. E. G. Kraeling has suggested that the name Tattenai may have been confused with Ushtanni, who is known in Babylonian texts as governor of "Babylon and Beyond the River" and whose first recorded date is March 21, 520 B. C.[31]

The objections of Tattenai led to the search for the original memorandum of Cyrus to which we have already referred.[32] This was found in the archives at Ecbatana (the Biblical Achmetha, Ezra 6:2). Permission being granted to continue, the work went on and was finally completed in March, 515 B. C. (Ezra 6:15). Some have seen in the willingness of Darius to accede to the request of the Jews a desire on his part to win over yet another part of his domains. The work of the prophets Haggai and Zechariah fell at the time when Darius was just recovering from the revolts of recent days. Perhaps indeed Zerubbabel was a loyal supporter of the new king at first. There is more than a hint, however, that he allowed himself to become the center of hopes for the restoration of the throne of David (Haggai 2:20f. and Zech. 4:6f., 6:12f., etc.).[33] The opinion of W. F. Albright is of interest:

28. B. Maisler, "The Excavation of Tell Qasile," *BA* (May 1951), pp. 43ff.
29. E. G. Kraeling, op. cit., p. 331.
30. *Ibid.*
31. *Ibid.*
32. See above pp. 178f.
33. The prophecies were made in all sincerity and under divine inspiration, but some change in conditions must have led to the postponement of God's purposes. See Jeremiah 18:6-10 for an important principle.

Haggai's second oracle . . . exults in the approaching downfall of Persia and the coming of a new Jewish state; in his fourth oracle (Hag. 2:20-23) dated in December, while the Babylonian rebellion still appeared to be successful, he explicitly declared that the imperial throne would be overturned and implied that Zerubbabel was the Lord's anointed . . . . Whether Zerubbabel died a natural death or was removed, we cannot say; there is not the slightest reason to suppose that he committed any overt act of disloyalty to the crown . . . . evidently the Persian authorities contented themselves with depriving the Davidic family of its political prerogatives, which were turned over to Joshua and his successors. We may safely credit Joshua with political astuteness in the difficult situation in which he found himself.[34]

Unfortunately we have no archaeological evidence about the Temple. If there are remains today, they lie beneath the present ground level. The whole Temple area has suffered greatly through the centuries, and while no doubt there would be much to bring to light if the archaeologists could only excavate on the site where the great Mohammendan mosque now stands, we must await the future before we can discover what lies buried there.[35]

It is significant that the state of Judah seems to have been ruled internally by the high priests from this time onwards. We know quite a number of the high priests between these days and New Testament times. Perhaps for political purposes the Persians appointed governors, but they seem to have allowed the normal internal affairs of state, like taxation, to be supervised by the high priests. That the Persians did allow some sort of priestly rule in their empire is shown by the fact that the priests of Hierapolis in northern Syria were able to levy their own taxes and strike their own coins.[36]

THE PROVINCE OF JUDAH IN 500 B. C.

It is evident, then, that the little province of Judah was closely linked with the great Persian administration from the time of Cyrus onwards. In political status it was only a small part of a much larger

34. W. F. Albright, *The Biblical Period* (Oxford, 1952), p. 50.
35. The announcement that excavations will be undertaken by the British School of Archaeology in Jerusalem under Dr. Kathleen Kenyon inside the old walled city in the old Jewish quarter should provide valuable evidence about old Jerusalem.
36. *Ibid.,* p. 55.

satrapy. We have seen that the Persians organized their vast domains into large units called satrapies which were ruled by satraps. Persian inscriptions like the great biography of Darius on the rock at Behistun list these satrapies. A. T. Olmstead in his *History of Persia* refers to other lists at various periods in Persian history which make it possible to trace changes in the disposition of these satrapies. Many of these satraps replaced former kings and became little monarchs themselves, and for this reason the Persian authorities needed to keep them in check. These larger units were then divided into smaller provinces, each with its own administrator. One of these satrapies defined by Herodotus as the fifth, "Beyond the River [Transpotamia]," seems to have been subdivided into several provinces, among them being Judah, Samaria, Ammon, Ashdod, and Arabia.[37] The province of Judah was surrounded by these others, whose governors quite naturally viewed any sign of expansion with suspicion. The complete satrapy thus included Syria, Palestine, and other areas to the west of the Euphrates, all united into the one large area of "Babylon and Ebir-nari [Across the River]."[38] We know some of the satraps who ruled this vast area, men like Gobryas and Ushtani (or Hystanes). A. T. Olmstead describes the position of Zerubbabel in this complex system as "only a governor of the third rank." His immediate superior was Tattenai, governor of "Across the River," who in turn was under the authority of Hystanes, satrap of "Babylon and Across the River."[39] In later years, following a revolt in Babylon in 482 B.C., the satrapy of "Across the River" was detached from Babylon. This was the state of affairs when Nehemiah was governor, and we shall take up the point again later.

At the end of the sixth century B.C. we must picture a little province under the control of the returned exiles, protected by royal decree, but surrounded by hostile neighbors, and opposed even by those Jews who had never gone into exile but who had stayed in the general area to which the exiles returned.

37. Herodotus, iii, 89ff.
38. A. T. Olmstead, *op. cit.*, pp. 56f.
39. *Ibid.*, pp. 138f.

Eleven:

THE PERSIAN PERIOD IN PALESTINE
FROM 500 B.C. TO 330 B.C.

AFTER THE BUILDING OF THE TEMPLE THE JEWS ENTERED ON A period of history which is for us today obscure, to say the least of it. The darkness is penetrated at one or two points only, notably in the days of the governor Nehemiah who rebuilt the wall of Jerusalem. A certain amount of material is available from excavations in towns that were occupied in Palestine during Persian times and from these we gain some insight into the types of buildings in use, the pottery, the coinage, and in particular the growing influence of Greek culture in the land. But we have no clear idea of the way in which the Persians ruled the land, for we know of only two governors of these times, Nehemiah and Bagoses, although we have some reason to think that the priests did a good deal of the routine work of government, notably in the area of tax collection. Modern archaeological work gives some insight into the neighboring peoples who feature in the Biblical narrative. Outside of Palestine we know something about the Jews in Mesopotamia and Egypt, and we shall devote a special chapter to these groups, but it would be well first of

191

ustration on page 190: This beautiful piece of Persian craftsmanship is a golden nking horn. It recalls the words of Nehemiah 2:11 — "For I was the king's cup-rer." (Courtesy, The British Museum) all to review the history of the Persians during the period 500 B. C. to 330 B. C. This will provide a good background against which to view the story of the Jews as far as we can reconstruct it today.

PERSIAN KINGS FROM 500 B. C. TO 330 B. C.

At the close of the sixth century B. C. the great Darius was still ruling and was to continue till 486 B. C. We have referred to his attack on Greece and to his defeat at Marathon in 490 B. C. His achievements were great indeed and his successor Xerxes I (486-465 B. C.), who had been trained in the art of government by being allowed to rule as viceroy in Babylon, carried on his work. In the light of this experience he was able at a later date to carry through some vital administrative changes in government. His father had commenced to build several great palaces, perhaps the most notable of all being that at Persepolis, but it was left to Xerxes to bring the whole magnificent plan to completion, and to change it in certain respects. He alone seems to have been responsible for the magnificent reliefs which surpass all the earlier work of his father's craftsmen. He had many military successes in all parts of his own empire despite the fact that he did suffer defeat at the hands of the Greeks in the battles of Thermopylae and Salamis in 480 B. C. and again at Plataea the next year. Perhaps in actual fact these successes of the Greeks were not so great as subsequent Greek writers made them out to be, but they did arouse Greek patriotism and had a tremendous effect on the morale of the Greeks. We know Xerxes best in Biblical history from the story of Esther, which took place in the old Elamite town of Susa, conquered by Cyrus, but at the time of the Biblical story the site of a beautiful palace built by Darius, and later enlarged and completed by Xerxes. That this monarch lived there for at least some of his reign is evidenced by documents found in Susa, although there were other palaces, the best loved of them being that at Persepolis.[1]

The next king was Artaxerxes I (465-424 B. C.) during whose reign the famous Nehemiah was governor of Judah and Ezra the scribe was active.[2] Important documents from Egypt and Mesopotamia, dating partly from the reign of Artaxerxes and partly from

1. A. T. Olmstead, *The History of the Persian Empire* (Chicago, 1948), pp. 230f. and pp. 266f.
2. The writer is not unaware of the problem of Ezra but holds that Ezra and Nehemiah were contemporary. See below pp. 196ff.

Darius the Great (522-486 B.C.) moved his capital from Pasargadae to Persepolis, where he erected a magnificent group of buildings on a huge artificial platform. The illustration shows the exquisite stairway leading to the reception hall, called the Apadana. (Courtesy, The Oriental Institute, The University of Chicago)

the reign of his successor Darius II (423-404 B. C.)[3], give us evidence about the Jews for these years. There was a brief period of two years between these two kings, during which Xerxes II (424-423 B. C.) occupied the throne, but this king is relatively unimportant.

The last four kings were Artaxerxes II (404-358 B. C.), Artaxerxes III (358-338 B. C.), Ares (338-336 B. C.), and Darius III (336-331 B. C.). Persia collapsed finally in 331 B. C. before the Greek invader Alexander the Great.

ARCHAEOLOGY AND THE BOOK OF ESTHER

The little book of Esther is placed in the days of Xerxes, whose Biblical name is Ahasuerus. It is a puzzling book in some ways because

---

3. Some Egyptian documents come from the reigns of Darius I and Xerxes I as well. See below p. 221.

it is difficult to identify most of the people concerned from external evidence. The chief characters of the book, Vashti, Haman, and Mordecai are unknown in non-Biblical history. Excavations, however, as well as general historical evidence make it clear that there is much in the book that shows the writer to have been correctly informed on many of the background details of the story.

Xerxes (Ahasuerus) was a historical person. The picture given in the book of Esther of a king who was a despot and thoroughly sensuous in character corresponds with the account given by the Greek historian Herodotus.[4] He greatly enlarged his harem at Persepolis, as excavation shows,[5] and became involved in a shameful affair with his brother's wife and later with the daughter as well.

The description of the ornate palace with its bright curtains is quite in the manner of the gaudy palaces of the Persians. Excavations at Susa (Biblical Shushan) have yielded abundant evidence of the rich ornamentation of the walls of the palace and of the richly colored glazed bricks used there.[6] This palace, commenced by Darius, was

4. Herodotus, *The Histories* (London, 1955), pp. 594ff., or *Herodotus*, ix, 107ff.
5. A. T. Olmstead, *op. cit.*, chap. 20.
6. *Ibid.*, pp. 166-171. Also R. Ghirshman, *Iran* (London, 1954), pp. 165-167.

This aerial view gives an impression of the extent of the area Darius' palaces covered. Persepolis remained the Achaemenian spring capital until Alexander overthrew the Persian empire. (Courtesy, The University Museum of the University of Pennsylvania)

Detail of the Tripylon Relief, showing Darius on his throne and his son Xerxes standing behind him. This son is no doubt the Ahasuerus mentioned in the book of Esther, while his successor, Artaxerxes, is the king who sent Nehemiah to Jerusalem. (Courtesy, The Oriental Institute, The University of Chicago)

described in glowing terms. It was built of special timbers and adorned with gold, lapis lazuli, turquoise, silver, and ebony, and was erected by men who came from all over the empire.[7]

The story of Esther could well fit into the time of Xerxes, for he reigned for twenty years, and the events of this book do not go beyond the twelfth or possibly the thirteenth year (Esther 3:7, 12). The banquet in the third year may coincide with the great council that Xerxes held before the invasion of Greece, and the four years that intervened before Esther became queen may well fit into the time that the king was absent in Greece (Esther 1:3, 2:16).[8] The standard commentaries on the book of Esther point out that many of the customs referred to in the story are quite in keeping with Persian practice.[9] Thus the arrangements for the banquet (1:6-8), obeisance before the king and his favorites (3:2), belief in lucky and unlucky days (3:7), exclusion of mourning garb from the palace (4:2), hanging as the death penalty (5:14), dressing a royal benefactor in the king's robes (6:8), dispatching couriers with royal messages (3:13, 8:10) are all customs that are now well known from the written records that have come to light.[10] There are, moreover, a good number of Persian words in the book, largely from the language of government and trade. All of these facts show that, at the very least, the author

7. R. Ghirshman, *op. cit.,* pp. 165f.
8. *Herodotus,* vii, 8.
9. For example, L. B. Paton, *The Book of Esther, ICC* (Edinburgh, 1951), pp. 64ff.
10. *Ibid.,* p. 65.

195

of the book of Esther was well informed on numerous matters of Persian practice and Persian life, and while there are difficulties of interpretation and identification still remaining, we may hope to find yet more archaeological evidence to clear up the historical situation. It is risky to adopt the view that has been adopted by many modern writers that the whole story is pure fiction, especially when we have to argue so much from silence, a very uncertain basis for argument in any case.

EZRA THE SCRIBE

The date at which Ezra did his work is not clearly specified in the Bible, which merely says that it was in the seventh year of Artaxerxes the king (Ezra 7:7, 8). The question immediately arises as to whether this was the first or the second king of this name. If it was the first, the date would be 458 B.C., but if it was the second, it would be 397 B.C. The Bible certainly gives us the impression that Ezra preceded Nehemiah. There is little in the way of archaeological evidence to help us solve the question of dating. This is in striking contrast with the case of Nehemiah where we have convincing evidence for a date of 444 B.C. One possible reconstruction which allows of Ezra preceding Nehemiah, and which appeals to the present writer, is as follows:

Artaxerxes I in his seventh year, following the practice of other Persian kings, decided to investigate the religious condition of the Jews in Judah. Such inquiries were not unusual and there is in existence today an important document from Egypt which tells of a similar inquiry into the religious observances of the Jews in Egypt towards the end of the fifth century B. C.

> To my brethren Yedoniah and his colleagues, the Jewish garrison, your brother Hananiah. The welfare of my brothers may God seek at all times.
>
> Now, this year, the fifth of King Darius, word was sent from the king to Arsames saying, "Authorize a festival of unleavened bread for the Jewish garrison."
>
> So do you count fourteen days of the month of Nisan and observe the passover, and from the fifteenth to the twenty-first of Nisan observe the festival of unleavened bread. Be ritually clean and take heed. Do not work on the fifteenth or the twenty-first day, nor drink beer, nor eat anything in which

there is leaven from the fourteenth at sundown until the twenty-first of Nisan. For seven days it shall not be seen among you. Do not bring it into your dwellings, but seal it up between these dates.

By order of King Darius.

To my brethren Yedoniah and the Jewish garrison,

Your brother Hananiah.[11]

In the present instance, Ezra, a Jew living in Persia, was selected by Artaxerxes I because of his reputation in matters of Jewish law, and he was given a strict commission to go to Judah and inquire concerning the way the people obeyed the law of their God. He was to take free-will offerings from the Jews in his own land and have access to government funds if he needed extra money.

11. J. B. Pritchard, *ANET* (Princeton, 1955), p. 491.

Gateway flanked by human-headed winged bulls are characteristic of the palaces of the great rulers. Darius had his at Persepolis. Although the gateway depicted here is from an earlier period (c. 700 B.C.) and several hundred miles removed from Persepolis, namely at Khorsabad, it gives a clear impression of the dimensions of such gateways. Usually behind the bulls appeared winged human figures bearing the symbols of fertility and prosperity in the right hand. (Courtesy, Consulate General of the Republic of Iraq)

After inquiry, he was to teach the ignorant, and then enforce the law with penalties (Ezra 7:11-26). He duly arrived in Judah and delivered his commission to the local rulers.

About the same time some illegal building was being carried on in Jerusalem and a complaint went to the king that a wall was being built around the city (Ezra 4:11-16). A prayer recorded from the lips of Ezra makes reference to God giving the people a wall in Judah and in Jerusalem (Ezra 9:9). The next thing we know is that Artaxerxes had forbidden the building of a wall and the work of Ezra was cut short. Ezra did indeed attempt some reforms, but little attention is paid to these in the record and we may conjecture that not much was achieved. Perhaps Ezra was disgraced and his commission taken away because he became involved in the matter. It is here suggested that he went into retirement to reappear when Nehemiah came as governor. If this is not the true picture, then we have to place Ezra after Nehemiah, or at least allow that Nehemiah preceded him to Judah and that he followed a little later. This is the view taken by W. F. Albright, who holds that Ezra came in the thirty-seventh year of Artaxerxes.[12] The fact is, however, that we lack external evidence of an archaeological kind to solve the problem.

NEHEMIAH THE GOVERNOR AND RESTORER OF THE WALLS OF JERUSALEM

At first reading of the Biblical records we are in a similar quandary about the date of Nehemiah, for the start of his story is in the twentieth year of Artaxerxes. Now is this the first or the second king of this name? The discovery of Aramaic documents at Elephantine[13] in Egypt has placed it beyond all doubt that it is the first of these kings that is referred to in the Bible. The details of this argument will be given in the next chapter, so for the present we shall accept the fact.

It was late in 445 B. C. that Nehemiah learned from his brother Hanani and other Jews who had come from Jerusalem that the situation there was bad. The lack of a wall made attacks from hostile neighbors inevitable. At the time there was a ban on the building of the wall (Ezra 4:17-24). By careful pleading Nehemiah was able to have this order reversed and was himself appointed governor of Judah (Neh. 5:14). Provided with letters to the governors of

---

13. For detailed discussion, see below, pp. 218-227.

"Beyond the River," a Persian province (Neh. 2:7, 9), and with a military escort, Nehemiah set out for Judah. Three days after his arrival he went by night on a tour around the city walls. The account of this journey in 2:12-15, together with the accounts of the walls in chapter 3 and 12:31-40, makes a striking picture when compared with the reports of excavations conducted at various points around the walls in recent times. While it is not possible to sort out the picture completely, the disposition of the places mentioned on the eastern side of the city is fairly well agreed upon today. One recent writer said:

> The topographical texts of Nehemiah are likewise of exceptional value, even more so than any passages in Josephus, not only because they present us with a thrice-repeated wall description by an eyewitness more detailed than that of Josephus (Neh. 2:11-15, 3; 12:31-39), but especially because they deal with the city of the Old Testament itself, before as well as after the Exile. When Nehemiah arrived in Jerusalem, Herod's extensive levelling and enlargement operations in the sacred quarter were still far off.[14]

It is true that there is some discussion going on about the exact site of the Valley Gate and the whole matter hinges on whether the pre-exilic city included the southwestern hill.[15] This can only be decided after more excavation. The writers of two large works on Jerusalem in recent years, L. H. Vincent and J. Simons, both include the southwestern hill in the pre-exilic city. A good discussion of the minimal view of the walls has recently been given by M. Avi-Yonah in the *Israel Exploration Journal*.[16] In certain areas it has been possible to understand some of the features brought to light in the excavations by reference to the Biblical narrative. Captain Weill, excavating in the southeast corner of the city, revealed a remarkable staircase which was evidently set in a sort of postern gate in the wall. The Bible reference to Nehemiah's procession at this point reads:

> *And at the fountain gate, which was over against them, they went up by the stairs of the city of David* (Neh. 12:37).

14. J. Simons, *Jerusalem in the Old Testament* (Leiden, 1952), pp. 437f.
15. E. G. Kraeling, *Bible Atlas* (Chicago, 1956), p. 336.
16. M. Avi-Yonah, "The Walls of Nehemiah — A Minimalist View," *IEJ* (1954), IV, 239f.

This seems to suit the staircase revealed in the excavation, since the stairs ran between two walls which joined the main outer wall at right angles and then led up into the heart of the city of David. In this same area Charles Warren in 1867 found evidence for a tower, perhaps the tower of Nehemiah 3:25-27.

An opening in the wall here has been taken to be the Fountain Gate. J. Simons has written:

> The real importance and practical value of Nehemiah's wall descriptions consist first of all in the fact that to them we owe the knowledge of a very considerable number of features, especially on and near the city's fortified perimeter, which are not mentioned even in passing by any other Biblical writer, and these features are so numerous that without them our picture of biblical Jerusalem would lose half or more than half of its contents. The Dung Gate, the "Mishneh" Gate, the Water Gate, the Inspection Gate, the Fountain Gate, and the Sheep Gate would all be entirely unknown to us but for the texts of Nehemiah . . . . The same would be true as regards the Tower of the Furnaces, the "wall of the square," the "wall of the pool of Shiloah," the "stairs of the city of David" and several features connected with the water supply, e.g., the Dragon Well and the King's Pool.[17]

Now the fact that several of these features have been discovered in excavations leads us to believe that if ever extensive digging can again be carried out all around the area where the walls once ran, we shall find the descriptions of Nehemiah most valuable in interpreting the discoveries.[18]

The Biblical narrative tells of the completion of the work of rebuilding, a task in which men from various areas played a part. Perhaps the towns referred to in chapter 3, which makes reference to the men of Tekoa, Beth-zur, Keilah, Zanoah, Jerusalem, Gibeon, Mizpah, Jericho, and Beth-haccerem, give us the best idea we have of the extent of Judah at the time. By placing these on a map it is possible to see at a glance the area from which Nehemiah drew his helpers.

17. J. Simons, *op. cit.*, p. 44.
18. The recent work (1961) of Dr. Kathleen Kenyon in this area has provided significant new evidence on the whole problem.

ARCHAEOLOGICAL LIGHT ON JUDAH'S NEIGHBORS

As Nehemiah began his task he was greatly troubled by the opposition of various neighbors. The most troublesome of these were Sanballat the Horonite, Tobiah the Ammonite, and Geshem the Arab (Neh. 2:10, 19; 4:1, 3, 7; 6:2; etc.) who plotted against Nehemiah, but he was able to frustrate them (Neh. 2:19f., 4:6).

Archaeological discovery in this century has produced evidence about these neighbors and in the case of Sanballat and Geshem has brought to light some actual written evidence. The name of Sanballat is now known on one of the Elephantine papyri dating to the year 407 B. C., which can be shown quite clearly to be later than Nehemiah.[19] We shall see that Sanballat had a long life and remained governor in Samaria some years after Nehemiah ceased to be governor in Judah. The name Sanballat is probably a Babylonian name, Sin-ubal-lit. The man was governor of Samaria under Persian overlordship, but almost certainly he was not a Babylonian. The names of his sons Delaiah and Shelemiah are Hebrew, not Babylonian. Both names include the element IAH, which stood for Yahweh, the name of the God of the people of Israel. It is, however, possible, and even likely, that Sanballat followed a syncretistic kind of religion not unlike the religion of the Jews in Egypt. The Elephantine documents, to be discussed in detail in the next chapter, show us that there were other groups who followed a syncretistic religion not unlike that of the Jews.

The name Geshem is now known from two sources, one being a contemporary inscription found at Hegra in Arabia, and the other found in a temple on the borders of Egypt, belonging probably to Arabs who worshiped there at a time when their influence extended to this point.

At the time of Nehemiah the kings of Dedan were the rulers of a vast area to the east of the Jordan and extending away to the south, and although naturally under Persian domination they had some sort of control over a wide area. They left behind them a variety of inscriptions, one of which reads as follows:

> Niran, son of Hadiru, inscribed his name in the days of Gashm, son of Shahar, and Abd, governor of Dedan.[20]

19. See below, p. 227.
20. A. T. Olmstead, *op. cit.,* p. 295.

The phrase "Abd [servant], governor of Dedan" is reminiscent of the one in the Bible, "Tobiah, the servant, the Ammonite" (Neh. 2:10, 19). Tobiah is described as "the servant," and the governor of Dedan is "servant." Another feature about the inscription is the use of the word PHT for *governor*. This same word occurs in the books of Ezra and Nehemiah as an element in a proper name, Pahat-Moab.[21] W. F. Albright has suggested that the name, which means "governor of Moab," may well have come from such a governor who gave his name to the family. The word *pahah* would not have been correct until the time of the Babylonians or Persians, since Moab had its own tributary kings till at least 645 B. C.[22] These facts, quite apart from the name Geshem, point to a Persian date for the inscriptions of Hegra.

Until very recently this reference stood alone, but now we have some most valuable confirmatory evidence from the Arab temple referred to above. On the outskirts of the area, controlled by the kings of Dedan, there was a temple where offerings were made to the North Arabian goddess Han-'Allat, and in which worshippers had deposited long ago a number of silver vessels, three of which bore inscriptions in Aramaic. The proper names on these are, with one exception, all north Arabic. One of them is of special interest to us because it carries the words "Qainu son of Geshem [Gusham] king of Kedar." These inscriptions are securely dated to the end of the fifth century B. C. by converging lines of evidence. Professor I. Rabinowitz who published the material traces the objects to the Arab shrine at Tell el-Maskhutah (ancient Succoth) in the Wadi Tumilat on the eastern part of the Nile delta.[23]

It is becoming increasingly evident that the Arab kingdom ruled over by Geshem was quite considerable and included northern Arabia, old Edom, the Sinai area, and part of the Nile delta, with possibly even a part of southern Judah, where small altars very like those found in southern Arabia have been discovered.[24] This large Arab kingdom was brought under some sort of Persian control and added to the satrap of "Across the River," but its local ruler was evidently allowed to continue as the Persian governor, probably on condition

21. Ezra 2:6, 8:4, 10:30; Neh. 3:11, 7:11, 10:14. Compare W. F. Albright, *The Biblical Period*, p. 64, note 131.

22. W. F. Albright, *loc. cit.*

23. F. M. Cross, "Geshem the Arab, Enemy of Nehemiah," *BA* (May, 1955), p. 47.

24. W. F. Albright, *Archaeology of Palestine* (London, 1956), pp. 143f.

that he paid annual tribute. The discovery in such a context of an inscription such as that we have quoted points with some certainty to the son of the Biblical Geshem.

The third of Nehemiah's troublesome neighbors was Tobiah the Ammonite. While we have no direct evidence of this man at present, we do know quite a deal about his family. His very name suggests that he worshipped Yahweh because of the element IAH at the end. His family was of political importance in Transjordan from the fifth century to the second century at least. At the important site of 'Araq el Emir in central Transjordan there are some fine rock-cut tombs, one of which bears the name *Tobiah* deeply cut in the rock, in Aramaic letters of the third century B. C. used during the rule of the Ptolemies in Egypt.[25] In the same region we find the remains of what some writers call a palace and others a mausoleum, built evidently by the last of the Tobiad rulers.[26] Earlier on in the third century B. C. we know of an Ammonite governor of this family, because of a letter which he wrote to an Egyptian official named Zeno employed in the government of Ptolemy II, Philadelphus (285-246 B. C.). The letter stated that Tubias (Tobiah) was sending to Ptolemy a number of animals, including horses, dogs, and camels.[27]

While therefore there is no direct evidence at present for the Tobiah of Nehemiah's day, it is clear that there was a Tobiah family in Transjordan in the centuries that followed, and we have good reason to link these later Tobiahs with the man of Nehemiah's time.

SOME ITEMS OF GENERAL CULTURE

Excavations in Palestine have produced a variety of items of general culture which make their contribution to our understanding of these centuries.

We refer first of all to the pottery of the period. There is a distinctive type of pottery for this so-called Persian or Iron III period, as there is for all archaeological periods. But what is of special interest to us is that at this period a good deal of very distinctive Greek pottery appeared in Palestine, bearing witness to the growing influence of the Greeks in the Eastern Mediterranean

25. *Ibid.*, p. 149.
26. G. E. Wright, *Biblical Archaeology* (London, 1957), p. 204. Cf. W. F. Albright, *op. cit.*, pp. 149f.
27. G. E. Wright, *op. cit.*, p. 204. See also L. H. Vincent, "La Palestine dans les papyrus ptolémaique de Gerza," *RB* (April, 1920), pp. 161ff.

A beautiful example of Greek red-figure ware. Sherds of both black-figure and red-figure ware were found in various places in Palestine, indicating that the Greek traders, who were the precursors of the Greek conquerors, visited these parts from the fifth century onwards.

lands. It was during the sixth century B. C. that the Athenian and other Greek potters set out to master the art of representing the human figure and its drapery in great detail on their pottery pieces. At first they perfected the art of working black figures on a red background, using a technique that itself was old but was now brought to perfection. About 530 B. C. a new technique appeared in which the potters represented figures in red on a lustrous black background. The Athenians held their art as a secret and attained a brilliance in their vases not equaled elsewhere.

The black-figure ware which has been found in many lands in the East, including Egypt, Syria, and Palestine, argues for Greek trading at some time before 500 B. C. There is also a good deal of red-figure ware now known from excavations, showing that the Greeks were active as traders from the fifth century onwards. Actually, once the trading began, it continued on through the centuries, the Greek traders being only the precursors of the Greek conquerors. The excavator of the site of Tell en Nasbeh to the north of Jerusalem has written concerning the presence of Greek pottery in this town as follows:

> In a small hill town, even if it was, or had been, the capital of the minute Persian province of Judah, the presence of such ware

204

is significant, telling of close commercial relations between Attica and Palestine in the period of Athens' greatest glory.[28]

In all, some thirty sherds of Greek pottery consisting largely of Attic black-figure ware, although there was some red-figure ware, were found in this excavation. Greek traders evidently visited this town before 500 B. C.

The most recent work at Shechem has produced evidence of Greek influences in the center of Palestine before 500 B.C. Pieces of Greek black-figure ware, probably of the sixth century B.C., were discovered in one area.[29]

As we turn to coinage we have further significant material. Coinage as we know it today was probably first used by the kings of Lydia when Croesus, their most famous king, stopped minting lumps of so-called white gold about 550 B. C. and changed over to pure gold coinage. The kings of Persia took the lead from him, and Lydian coins served as patterns for the coinage of Persia. On the golden daric and the silver shekel of the Medes and the Persians appeared the picture of the great king. The Greek colonies of the Ionian isles and of Italy copied the idea, and not long after, Greek traders in the eastern Mediterranean started to make coins. The men of old Greece soon followed suit, although they used silver for their coins because they lacked gold. Significant emblems were used on the coins by many of the Greek states. Aegina had a turtle, and Athens, the home of beautiful vases, had a vase. Later, when the Athenian dictator Peisistratus came on the scene, he used the head of the patron goddess of Athens, Athene, on the front of the coins, and a small owl and a twig of olives on the back. The Athenians thought that Athene appeared at times in the guise of an owl, and so they associated this bird with the goddess. The Greek coins were minted in multiples of the drachma.

Both of these latter facts about Greek coinage, namely, that they were minted in multiples of the drachma and that they carried the picture of an owl, are important for our study of the coinage of Palestine in these times. Coins began to appear in Palestine in the fifth century B. C. and excavations reveal that by the third century they had become abundant. W. F. Albright has noted:

28. C. C. McCown, *Tell en Nasbeh* (Baltimore, 1947), I, 62.
29. E. F. Campbell, *BASOR*, No. 161 (Feb., 1961), pp. 52f.

> Silver coins, struck in imitation of Attic drachmas, but with the Hebrew or Aramaic inscription *Yehud*, "Judah," are being found in increasing numbers.[30]

In the same discussion this writer observes,

> We have hinted above at the importance of the Attic currency, which became the standard medium of exchange in Palestine more than a century and a quarter before the Macedonian conquest. Attic coins were locally imitated in the second half of the fifth century, and in the following century we find all sorts of barbaric modifications of the figures on the drachma, the owl of Athena being kept until it became unrecognisable.[31]

In the light of these facts it becomes of real interest to discover that several passages in the books of Ezra and Nehemiah, refering to events in the latter half of the fifth century B.C., show that the gifts to the Temple were assessed in terms of coins of some kind (Ezra 2:69, 8:27; Neh. 7:70-72). On any system of dating Ezra and Nehemiah, these passages fit into the fifth century B.C., by which time the drachma standard had already penetrated into other lands besides Greece. It is true that there has been some discussion about the exact nature of this coinage, and the Hebrew word *darkemon* has been variously interpreted as *drachma* or *daric*.[32] In either case, these two standards of coinage were in use at the time, and either would suit the Biblical passages.

It is evident from these considerations that the Persians must have granted considerable local autonomy to the Jews, with the right to strike their own coinage. This was not a unique occurrence, for we know today that the priests of Atargatis at Heliopolis in northern Syria received permission to strike their own coinage and to levy their own temple taxes.[33]

Light on the Persian system of taxation comes from a most unusual source. In order to carry out its tremendous program of government the Persians worked out an elaborate fiscal scheme, and taxation was levied in all parts of the empire. We gain a brief glimpse into this program in Nehemiah 5, where we learn that people in Palestine had to mortgage their property in order to meet the

---

30. W. F. Albright, *Archaeology of Palestine* (London, 1956), p. 143.
31. *Ibid.*
32. Cf. G. E. Wright, *op. cit.*, p. 203, and W. F. Albright, *loc. cit.*
33. W. F. Albright, *loc. cit.*

requirements of the government. When we come to investigate the methods of collecting taxes we find light from the seal impressions left on the handles of large jars dating from the fifth and fourth centuries B. C. There are several kinds of seals now known. One type consists of three consonants, YHD, in ancient Hebrew script, together with a small circle in which there is often a cross. This last sign is known from Egypt where it is associated with the letters *lmlk*, meaning "belonging to the king." It was evidently associated in Egypt with some official collection for the king. The letters YHD on the seals found in Palestine signify "Judah," and it is a reasonable conclusion that if at Elephantine in Egypt the symbol of a circle and a cross was associated with the king's portion, it was so in Judah also.

Another group of seals has a circle inside of which is a five-pointed star, between the points of which are the letters YRShLM, which would spell out "Jerusalem" in Hebrew. The writing is again in the old type of Hebrew script. A third group of seals written in a more clearly Aramaic script had only the letters YHD on an oval seal without any decoration. Finally, there is a group of seals mostly from Tell en Nasbeh which carry the three letters MTsH, referring possibly to the town of Mizpah.[34] This was evidently an important town in Persian times, for the text in Nehemiah 3:7 may be translated "Mizpah, belonging to the throne of the governor of this Side of the River." The town apparently had some official connection with the satrap of the whole area.

The jar stamps have been found in various places. J. D. Duncan found twenty of them at Ophel (Jerusalem), others were found at Gezer, some twenty-eight others at Tell en Nasbeh. The existence of such a variety of these stamps on the handles of large jars bearing the names of Judah, Jerusalem, and possibly Mizpah, suggests very strongly that there was in use some sort of local method of collecting taxes in kind. Potters were evidently required to make certain jars of standard capacity for the collection of the king's portion.

When we turn to architecture and to building remains of the Persian period in Palestine, we are not very well off. The most spectacular of these is a building at Lachish, on the summit of the mound, which dates from the late fifth, or early fourth century, and which according to several opinions has a number of features

---

34. As an abbreviation. See G. E. Wright, *op. cit.,* p. 203; also H. L. Ginsberg, *BASOR,* No. 109, pp. 20f.; N. Avigad, "New light on the MSH seal impressions," *IEJ,* Vol. 8, pp. 113ff.

that are reminiscent of Parthian buildings in Mesopotamia.[35] Certain new features in architecture are to be found here, suggesting that the ideas were imported from further east. It has been conjectured that we have here one of the residences of the Arab kingdom of which the most famous Biblical representative was Geshem.[36] Certainly Lachish was rebuilt in the fifth century, at a time when the Jews were hardly in a position to build so far to the south. Near to the structure was a small temple that was not destroyed till the second century, probably when the Jews conquered the area. This adds support to the idea that the building may have been an Arab palace. It is further to be noticed that in the same general area of southern Palestine, at the ancient site now known as Tell Jemmeh on the edge of the Negeb, and also at Gezer in the plains of Sharon, small cube-like limestone altars resembling those found in southern Arabia were excavated. It is possible that these came in through trade, but quite likely also that there was Arab control in these areas at this time.[37]

Beautiful works of art have been found in some sites. Sir Flinders Petrie discovered a tomb at Tell el Far'ah in the Negeb which contained a beautiful silver bowl and a dipper, the latter having for a handle the figure of an undraped maiden.[38] Art of this kind is known in other parts of the Persian Empire. Other finds of bronze figures of gods and animals bear witness to the well-developed art of the period in some places. The art may not, however, have been the work of the Jews themselves, since they normally refrained from representing the form of men and animals in any way at all.

LIGHT ON JUDAH UNDER DARIUS II

Nehemiah left Judah to return to the king in 433 B. C., although he was to go back later and continue his work as governor. We do not know how long he continued in this post, but possibly with the death of Artaxerxes in 423 B. C. he may have been replaced. He was able to carry out reforms and persuade the people to enter into a covenant with God (Neh. 10), in which, among other things, the people agreed to pay an annual contribution to the upkeep of the

---

35. W. F. Albright, *Archaeology of Palestine* (London, 1956), p. 145.
36. G. E. Wright, *op. cit.*, pp. 203f.
37. W. F. Albright, *op. cit.*, pp. 143f.
38. *Ibid.*, p. 145.

Temple (Neh. 10:32). A similar payment seems to have been undertaken at Elephantine in Egypt where there was a list of those who contributed to the Temple upkeep.[39] The idea was, of course, very old in Israel, going back to Moses' time.

From the days of Darius II (423-404 B. C.) we have some interesting material on the state of affairs in Judah, with the names of some of the significant people who lived at the time.[40] The information comes from the Aramaic papyri of Elephantine and carries our story down to the close of the fifth century B. C. Before the next century had closed the Persians were overthrown and the Greeks were in the ascendancy. We are now in a position to turn to the fortunes of the Jews in lands outside Palestine, and to study the remarkable documentary evidence that has been brought out of the earth by the modern excavator in both Mesopotamia and Egypt.

39. A. Cowley, *Aramaic Papyri of the Fifth Century B.C.* (1923), pp. 65-73.
40. See below pp. 224-227.

Twelve:

THE JEWS OUTSIDE PALESTINE IN THE FIFTH CENTURY B.C.

T HERE WERE MANY JEWS LIVING OUTSIDE PALESTINE IN THE FIFTH century B. C., partly as a result of enforced exile and partly because of voluntary migration. We know of several occasions in Bible history when the people of Israel were taken into captivity. Even before the collapse of the northern kingdom in 722 B. C. there were captives taken from the Galilee area by Tiglath Pileser (II Kings 15:29). When Samaria fell, a further group of exiles was taken (II Kings 17). In the case of Judah, King Manasseh was captured and later released but we may conjecture that some Jews accompanied him into exile (II Chron. 33:11). Then came the various visits of Nebuchadnezzar (II Kings 24:1, 2; 24:10-16; 25:1-21; Jer. 52:31), which led to the exile of other groups of Jews. It would be impossible today to estimate the total number of people of general Israelite stock that eventually reached Mesopotamia.

But other lands such as Egypt had their complement of exiles from Palestine.[1] One wonders whether Pharaoh Shishak just before

1. E. G. Kraeling, *The Brooklyn Museum Aramaic Papyri* (Yale, 1953), pp. 41-48, discusses the origin of the Jewish colony at Elephantine.

Illustration on page 210: Present-day native craft on the River Nile, Delta area. (Courtesy, Trans World Airlines)

900 B. C. took any captives to Egypt (I Kings 14:25). Certainly Pharaoh Necho, just before 600 B. C., took King Jehoahaz to Egypt (II Kings 23:34), and we may believe that he took also some of his subjects. It is not unlikely that after Nebuchadnezzar's first visit to Jerusalem in 598 B. C. Pharaoh Hophra gave encouragement to Jews to rebel against the Chaldeans. An inscription of one Nesuhor, a prince under Hophra, tells of Syrians, Greeks, and Asiatics at Elephantine, and it is possible that there were Jews among these also. A further group of Jews, among whom was the prophet Jeremiah (Jer. 41-44), reached Egypt after the fall of Jerusalem in 586 B. C., although, unlike the exiles to Babylon, these came voluntarily and settled in the delta area (Jer. 43:7). An interesting message is recorded in Jeremiah 44 in which the prophet addressed remarks to all the Jews in Egypt, both to those at Tahpanhes, Noph, and Migdol, all of which are in the northern part of the land, and to those in the country of Patros, the region of southern or Upper Egypt. From this it would appear that at the time of Jeremiah there were Jews in both northern and southern Egypt.

Without doubt the people of Palestine were to be found in other areas too, in the post-exilic period, and we shall not be surprised if future research reveals this to be so. Against the background of exile and dispersion of the people of Palestine, we can understand why it is that modern archaeologists have discovered important evidence of Jewish colonies in both Babylonia and Egypt during the present century.

THE DEVELOPMENT OF ARAMAIC AS AN INTERNATIONAL LANGUAGE

It will be wise before we discuss the Jewish colonies of Egypt and Babylonia to give some brief review of the way in which the Aramaic language came into prominence until it eventually became the medium of international correspondence in Persian times.[2] A group of people that may be regarded as one of the less important groups in the East, and which never rose as a people to the status of an empire, nevertheless gave to the great conquerors of their day a language and a script which provided them with the means of communication with their vast empire.

The Aramaeans are known from early times, possibly as early

2. A. Dupont-Sommer, *Les Araméens* (Paris, 1949), gives a good outline, chap. 6.

as 2000 B. C., when there is evidence of them in southern Mesopotamia.[3]
The Assyrian inscriptions refer to them in 1320 B. C., and after the
tenth century B. C. there is an abundance of written material in
Aramaic. Certainly in the ninth, eighth, and seventh centuries B. C.,
and from then onwards, there is a good range of material from
diverse regions in the general area represented today by Syria. This
indicates that it was possible to write standard Aramaic from the
first half of the ninth century B. C. We may say that before the
little Aramaean states were finally destroyed by the Assyrians, their
language had attained such maturity that not only did it survive,
but it was actually able to impose itself on the conquerors. From the
ninth and eighth centuries onwards the Assyrian scribes needed to
know Aramaic because of their dealings with the Aramaeans. The
Bible in II Kings 18:26 makes reference to the fact that the Jewish
leaders in Jerusalem invited the Assyrians to speak to them in Aramaic:
"Speak, I pray thee, to thy servants in the Syrian language [Aramaic];
for we understand it."

That Aramaic was known in Assyria is shown by a long letter
written on a piece of pottery (an ostracon) in the days of Ashurbanipal, about 650 B. C. There are in addition standard weights in the
shape of a lion from the ancient site of Nimrud marked with the
names of Shalmaneser V, Sargon, and Sennacherib, and bearing some
marks in Aramaic. At Nineveh the excavations brought to light
numerous contracts dating from the seventh century B. C., written
in the laborious cuneiform script, but carrying also a short summary
in Aramaic to facilitate classification.

Two reasons for this widespread use of Aramaic may be suggested.
It was a language that had a simple alphabet in contrast to the syllabic
cuneiform (wedge-shaped) script of the Assyrians and others. It was
also the language of the virile Aramaeans, thousands of whom had been
taken captive through the centuries. Men of business began to use
the script and the language, and once this step had been taken,
progress was rapid.

Throughout the seventh century B. C., long Aramaic inscriptions
were made in Syria proper. When the Chaldeans took over after
the Assyrians they, too, knew Aramaic, as we know from numerous
cuneiform tablets from the days of Nebuchadnezzar and Nabonidus,
which carry notes in the Aramaic script, although the bulk of the

---

3. A. Dupont-Sommer, "Sur les débuts de l'histoire araméenne," *Congress
Volume* (Copenhagen, 1953), pp. 40f.

Aramaic was a widely used language and eventually became the lingua franca *of the Near East. Around the middle of the first century A.D. there existed a little kingdom comprising the province of Hatra, which was known by the name of Arabia. The statue to the right represents the richly dressed Princess Washfari, daughter of King Sanatruq, who lived in the fortress city Hatra. To the left is a basrelief of the eagle, bird of the firmament, the patron of the armies of Hatra, which is evident from the military standard. Both statues have Aramaic inscriptions.* (Courtesy, Consulate General of the Republic of Iraq)

tablets is written in cuneiform. There was clearly a complex linguistic situation in which Aramaic took its place alongside Akkadian.

A most interesting document from Egypt dating to the early years of the sixth century B. C., perhaps about 586, is written in Aramaic and is addressed to the Pharaoh by a Phoenician king named Adon who asked for help against the king of Babylon.[4] Evidently the Phoenician prince believed that the Egyptian scribes could read Aramaic.

4. H. L. Ginsberg, "An Aramaic Contemporary of the Lachish Letters," *BASOR*, No. 111, pp. 24f.

When Cyrus took over Babylon in 539 B. C. and the whole Chaldean empire fell, Aramaic became the official language of Persian diplomacy. Under Darius I the empire spread from India to Egypt, and in order to keep in touch with this vast area, Aramaic was used as the one language that would facilitate international contacts. It will suffice to state here that Aramaic documents from Persian times are known in abundance and have been found in almost all the provinces of the great empire from Egypt to India.[5]

A note of caution may be added just here. We have good evidence that the Persians used local languages at times along with Aramaic.[6] In Asia Minor there are inscriptions in Greek, including two stelae on the Bosporus, one in Greek and one in cuneiform, which Herodotus says were erected by Darius. In Egypt a set of laws was drawn up in demotic, the script of the common people, and correspondence between a satrap and the priests of Khnum was in demotic also. So it seems that there was flexibility in practice.

According to Esther 1:22, 3:12, and 8:9, Xerxes issued edicts to each of the peoples in its own tongue. Although this was evidently done at times, nevertheless the tremendous importance of Aramaic cannot be overlooked. We shall see in this chapter that the Jewish colony at Elephantine in southern Egypt used Aramaic a great deal during the fifth century B. C.

THE JEWISH COLONY AT NIPPUR IN BABYLONIA

In 1889 an American excavation conducted by the University of Pennsylvania began excavations in the ancient site of Nippur to the south of old Babylon.[7] In the northwest area of the ruins the excavators discovered a remarkable collection of baked-clay tablets in a room about eighteen feet by nine feet. There were some 730 tablets in this room comparable in quality of writing and appearance with those found in the library of the great Assyrian ruler Ashur-bani-pal. These tablets were dated to the reigns of Artaxerxes I (465-424 B. C.) and Darius II (423-404 B. C.), but there was one tablet also from the reign of Artaxerxes II. The cache turned out to be the archives of a family of Babylonian businessmen, the Murashu family.

5. These are listed in A. Dupont-Sommer, *Les Araméens*, pp. 79-102.
6. A. T. Olmstead, *History of the Persian Empire* (Chicago, 1948), pp. 116, 297. Also R. P. R. de Vaux, "Les décrets de Cyrus et de Darius," *RB* (Jan. 1937), pp. 38-41.
7. See above, p. 156.

At the time of the discovery, tablets from this period were rare, and the find created a good deal of excitement because it gave a remarkable insight into the business methods of those years. For the most part the tablets are plain commercial documents, contracts, receipts, lists of witnesses, letters, and the like. Much of the business was concerned with matters of agriculture, lands, crops, workmen, canals, public works, cattle, tools, vines, and trees. Payment was made by weighing out silver or occasionally gold.

The Murashu family ran a sort of banking business for exchange of moneys and for payments at a time when a new system of taxation had come into force in Persian lands.[8] Introduced by Xerxes, its full rigor was experienced under Artaxerxes I. In many areas in Mesopotamia agricultural lands were held by what was called "bow" tenure, that is, the owners were obliged to furnish a bowman for the armed forces. This was an ancient custom, and as the years went by it became possible to commute the service to a money payment. With the rise of a new class of Persian officials, much of the land passed into the hands of the Persians by a clever trick. The former holders of "bow" lands, no longer required to send a bowman to the army, but required now to pay a money equivalent, often had to borrow money at forty percent per annum from such profiteers as the Murashu family. Their pledged lands were then worked by those rogues for their own advantage, until the title was completely lost to the original owners. When additional fields fell into the hands of the state, because owners were unable to pay the taxes, there were corrupt officials who leased these lands to the same dishonest money lenders. We have already referred to the passage in the book of Nehemiah where some of the people complained that they were unable to help in the building of the walls because of the claims upon them for money and the necessity for them to devote all their time to working their fields.

> *We, our sons, and our daughters, are many; therefore we take up corn for them, that we may eat, and live. Some also there were that said, We have mortgaged our lands, vineyards, and houses, that we might buy corn, because of the dearth. There were also that said, We have borrowed money for the king's tribute, and that upon our lands and vineyards* (Neh. 5:2-4).

8. A. T. Olmstead, *op. cit.,* pp. 299, 356, *passim.*

In the troubled days following the death of Artaxerxes I the Murashu family needed to gain the goodwill of the new king whoever that might be. When finally Darius II emerged supreme, Enlil-nadinshum, the head of the firm, made a trip to greet his new master and to see that the privileged position of the Murashu family was maintained. He evidently succeeded. Documents show that in the years that followed the Murashu sons acquired "bow" lands on an unprecedented scale. It would seem, however, that at last the authorities caught up with the rogues and after 417 B.C. the firm suddenly disappeared. It has been suggested that the royal commissioners finally ran the villains to earth, recovered the crown lands, and punished the wrongdoers.

We have given this detail in order to underline some of the problems that confronted the people under the Persian administration, and to stress the way in which the small farmers were exploited by unscrupulous officials and bankers.

But there is another point about the archives of the Murashu bankers. These bankers recorded a great variety of names in their receipts and contracts. It is clear that they did business with many different peoples, Persians, Medes, Chaldeans, Aramaeans, and what is of special interest to us, Jews, who seem to have been free citizens by then. There is a considerable number of Jewish names in the documents, pointing to the fact that many of the exiles did not return to Palestine but remained in the land, following the advice of Jeremiah (Jer. 29:1-7) to build houses and to seek the welfare of the city to which they had been exiled. Many of the names have the element YAH in them, like Yahulamu, Dadiya, Hananiah, Gedaliah and Pedaiah. Other well-known Jewish names occur, like Gadalyama, Ahiyama, Haggai, Benjamin, Natunu, Shabbata, and Mordecai. Over

This limestone tablet, discovered at Uruk, and dating back to c. 3300 B.C., is considered the earliest known example of Sumerian pictorial writing. (Courtesy, Consulate General of the Republic of Iraq)

sixty Jewish names are known from the days of Artaxerxes, and over forty from the time of Darius II. It is of some interest to discover that the name Mordecai was especially common in the days of Artaxerxes I. It was, of course, in the time of his predecessor Xerxes that the Bible places the story of Esther and the Jew Mordecai.

LIFE IN "YEB [ELEPHANTINE] THE FORTRESS"

There was a contrast between this settlement at Nippur in Babylonia and that at Elephantine in Egypt. The Nippur residents were part of a community that was engaged largely in agriculture and commerce, whereas the Elephantine colony had no agricultural pursuits to speak of, their means of livelihood being trade, shipping, stone quarrying, guarding the border, and attending to the taxes on goods that passed through this frontier post. In other words, the Elephantine colony was a military and administrative post.

The Aramaic texts of Elephantine speak of "Yeb the Fortress," and of "Syene the Fortress." Yeb was situated on a narrow island in the Nile, opposite modern Assuan, and Syene was on the site of Assuan itself. Syene was regarded as the southern limit of Egypt, and the phrase "from Migdol to Syene" is one that is known in the Bible (Ezek. 29:10, 30:6). In 1893 Charles Wilbour, an American traveler, acquired some valuable Aramaic papyri while visiting Assuan. A few years later, in 1904, Lady Cecil and Sir Robert Mond, two English visitors, bought some more, while yet others fell into the hands of German scholars. By 1914 a goodly number of these had been published and the world was given a remarkable glimpse into the life of a Jewish colony on this island in the Nile in the period 500 to 400 B.C. The documents were written in Aramaic on papyri which, thanks to the dry climate of Egypt, had been preserved all these years. They consisted of deeds, contracts, and letters, both private and official. The translation of these documents enabled the scholars to form an idea of how the affairs of daily life were conducted and by what laws the people of this colony were governed.[9]

All transactions were safeguarded by agreements and contracts were drawn up in proper manner, attested by witnesses, and then

---

9. Discussions and translations are available in J. B. Pritchard, *ANET* (Princeton, 1950), pp. 222f., 491ff., E. G. Kraeling, *op. cit.,* and A. Cowley, *Aramaic Papyri of the Fifth Century B.C.* (Oxford, 1923).

rolled up and sealed. Finally a note was added to the outside of the document to identify it. The procedure is not very different from that followed by Jeremiah in the purchase of his field (Jer. 32:8-14), and is basically the Babylonian method which was adopted by the Persians. Most of the documents at Elephantine carry two dates, one in Egyptian style and one in Babylonian style, so that we have no doubt about the date at which they were written.

Marriage contracts, as we might expect, are numerous and show that marriages were generally arranged between the bridegroom and someone acting for the bride. It was usual for the groom to give a bridal gift. In case of a divorce (which seems to have been rare, to judge from the few documents referring to it), the husband lost his marriage gift. It was possible for the wife also to sue for divorce. One woman whose name was Mibtahiah was involved in more than one marriage.

Slavery was known in Yeb and slaves were bought and sold, or perhaps inherited. One poor female slave, with three sons, had her children divided on the death of her master. There is, on the other hand, a case where a slave was freed and seems to have become the heir of his master.

Many of the documents deal with loaning and borrowing, and it is evident that both men and women were able to engage in business. The interest rate on loans was high, as much as sixty percent in some instances, with the threat that if the sum were not repaid the interest would be added to the capital and the same rate of interest charged. Modern wives will find interest in the case of a husband who used his wife's money and had to write out a promissory note to repay within a month. To the lady's credit it should be added that she charged no interest. Other business contracts deal with all manner of things. One case is recorded where two men signed a receipt for a load of barley they received from a boatman and promised to deliver it to a certain company of soldiers.

Real estate transactions were common. The Jews could buy and sell houses and make legal transfer of gifts of houses and lands. Daughters seem to have been specially favored as the recipients of houses, but more particularly on the occasion of marriage.

Litigation was common in Elephantine for all kinds of reasons. It is clear that Jews could go to law in civil matters, and the case would be heard before the Persian-Egyptian courts, although in internal matters affecting the Jewish community the matter was dealt with

Folded and sealed contracts found at Elephantine. Note the writing in Aramaic on the outside, which was done for quick and easy identification. The characters on the top docu-ment stand for: spr bi zi ktb, "letter concerning a house, written by. . . ." (Courtesy, The Brooklyn Museum)

by the priests. Typical civil cases were disputes about land, boundaries, possession of stock, and stealing.

Regular correspondence was sent and received by the people in the colony. Letters generally began with salutations to the temple of the deity, followed by the name of the addressee, the name of the writer, and the wish that God might permit them to see the face of the addressee in peace. After all these formalities came the formal requests, some of which are very modern. One man asks a friend to visit him; another complains that since his friend came to live in Syene he had not seen him; yet another sends greetings from several friends. So the simple matters of the common life are dis-cussed. Generally the letters were written on papyrus, but some were written on broken pieces of pottery (ostraca).

Among the most interesting of the papyri are several that consist of little more than lists of people. One contains the names of those who contributed gifts to the temple at Yeb. There are 123 names on the list, many of them being women, and it may be regarded as a sort of "Who's Who" in the colony of Yeb. The correspondence relating to government affairs, and especially the important letter addressed to the governor of Judah, requires a special discussion.

Glimpses into the Persian government that was in existence in Egypt at the time are also to be gained from these papyri.[10] Thus the satrap at the time of Xerxes was Achaemenes. His successor, who features a good deal in the documents and who functioned under both Artaxerxes I and Darius II, was Arsham (Greek, Arsames). In matters of government there were various departments, each of which had a presiding individual assisted by a group of colleagues. At the head of the chancery from which the orders of Arsham were issued was a chancelor, who is called in Aramaic, *be'el te'em*, which is precisely the name found in the Bible in Ezra 4:9 for Rehum, who is there associated with a number of other officials, "the scribe and the rest of the companions." It was this group that took action as a body against the builders of the wall of Jerusalem early in the reign of Artaxerxes I. It is of interest also to learn that at Elephantine there was another Rehum, who occupied much the same sort of post. In the provinces, the head man was a *pekid* or "officer," a title known both in Persian contexts and in the Bible (Esther 2:3, Neh. 11:9, etc.) and which had a variety of connotations.[11] It is clear that the Persians in Egypt used peoples of various nationalities in this and similar posts. In the letter addressed to the governor of Judah, the term is *peha*, which is also a Biblical word. Other Persian titles that appear either here at Elephantine or elsewhere occur in the Bible. One common Persian title for "treasurers," *gizbarayya*, does not happen to occur in the Elephantine texts, but it is found in the Bible in Ezra 7:21. The list in Ezra 4:9, which commences with Rehum and goes on to speak of the *Dinaites*, is really referring to the "judges." The Aramaic texts before us throw a great deal of light on the function of these "judges" in a typical Persian colony. All of these insights into Persian methods of administration add at the same time to our understanding of the Biblical records, for time and again we discover that the Bible has used a title that has a specific Persian connotation.

THE RELIGION OF THE JEWISH COLONY

The Jews in Egypt still worshipped Yahweh, the God of Israel. They built a temple for worship on the island of Yeb, and contributed to its upkeep. They observed the feast of unleavened bread, for we

10. E. G. Kraeling, *op. cit.*, pp. 27-40.
11. Hebrew, *pakid*, used in Gen. 41:34, Jer. 20:1, II Chron. 24:11, Judg. 9:28, etc.

learn from a document dated in 419 B. C. that Darius the king had sent to Arsham the satrap a letter ordering the Egyptian Jews to celebrate the feast from the fifteenth to the twenty-first of Nisan. While there is no reference to the Passover as such, it is likely that the Jews observed this also. There are one or two texts that show that the Sabbath was observed also. For example, one sentence on an ostracon reads: "Tie up the ass tomorrow on the sabbath lest he stray."

It is not certain that the Jews of Elephantine had copies of the Jewish Scriptures with them. There are some sentences in the papyri that suggest that they had parts of Deuteronomy, and perhaps of Genesis, but this is not beyond doubt.[12] The only literary piece that we know for certain that they possessed was the story of Ahikar, an ancient worthy who had various exciting adventures and acquired a good deal of sound wisdom which he passed on to his son. The story comprised a piece of wisdom literature rather like some of the literature of the Bible and the sacred books of other peoples.[13]

We cannot, of course, argue from silence and conclude that the Jews here had no Biblical literature simply because no pieces of the Bible have been found. It may be one of the accidents of preservation that it is chiefly documents of a business character that have been found.

It is to be further noted that in the temple of Yahu (Yahweh) sacrifices were offered. Reference will be made below to the letter addressed to the governor of Judah in which it is pointed out that when this temple at Yeb was destroyed, it was no longer possible to offer meal offerings, incense, or burnt offerings. Two priests are mentioned as well as a servant of Yahu, which indicates that there was evidently a well-organized ritual in use at the temple of Elephantine.

One disconcerting feature of the Jewish religion at Yeb is the fact that evidently some kind of syncretism was tolerated. The long list of contributors to the temple of Yahu indicates that of the total sum collected, certain moneys were earmarked for Eshem-bethel and 'Anat-bethel. The distribution was, Yahu, 246 shekels, Eshem-bethel, 140 shekels, and 'Anat-bethel 240 shekels.[14] The element "bethel" in the latter two names frequently occurs as the name of a

12. E. G. Kraeling, *op. cit.*, pp. 97-99.
13. J. B. Pritchard, *op. cit.*, pp. 427-430.
14. W. F. Albright, *Archaeology and the Religion of Israel* (Baltimore, 1956), p. 169.

god from the seventh to the fourth century B. C. in Canaanite-Aramaean contexts. A third name that has a divine connotation, Herem, is found on other documents from Elephantine. The conclusion of W. F. Albright, whose discussion we have followed here, is as follows:

> There can, accordingly, be no reasonable doubt that we are confronted with Aramaic syncretism, arising about the seventh century B. C. in Jewish circles which were under strong pagan influence.[15]

In another place the same writer discusses the possibility that these names may represent substitutes for the name of God:

> The three divine names Eshem-bethel, Herem-bethel, Anat-bethel (Anat-Yahu), meaning respectively, "Name of the house of God" (God), "Sacredness of the house of God," and "Sign (?) of the house of God" would reflect pure hypostatizations of deity . . . .[16]

Possibly the same happened here as in later Judaism, where a fence was built around the holiness of God by substituting words denoting aspects or qualities of God, such as Divine Wisdom, or the Divine Word, or the Divine Presence, for the name of God. There remains, however, something of uncertainty about the exact nature of the religion in Elephantine. We naturally think of the picture of the religion of the Jews in the years just before and just after the exile in Judah itself. Indeed, at various times syncretism was very serious in both Judah and Israel and was strongly assailed by more than one prophet. If that happened in the homeland, there is no reason why it should not have happened in a foreign land like Egypt.

15. *Ibid.,* p. 171.
16. W. F. Albright, *From Stone Age to Christianity* (New York, 1957), p. 373.

Another Elephantine papyrus before unrolling. (Courtesy, The Brooklyn Museum)

Such divergences from the official orthodox view of the priests in Jerusalem would not be tolerated by them for a moment, and it was unthinkable that there should be a second temple beside the one in Jerusalem. This comes out clearly in the letter which we now take up for discussion.

LETTER TO THE GOVERNOR OF JUDAH FROM THE PEOPLE OF YEB

One of the most striking of the letters found among the Aramaic documents at Yeb was one dated in 407 B. C. It was a petition to the governor of Judah to assist in the rebuilding of the temple in Yeb. The circumstances seem to be these. At some earlier time, even before the days of Cambyses, the Jews had built a temple in Elephantine.

> Our forefathers built this temple in the fortress of Elephantine, back in the days of the kingdom of Egypt, and when Cambyses came to Egypt he found it built. They knocked down all the temples of the gods of Egypt but no one did any damage to this temple.[17]

When Darius II came to the throne after violent measures, his brother rose against him and there were uprisings in many of the provinces, such as Asia Minor, Media, and Egypt, in the years 410 to 408 B. C. It is possible to deduce from the documents available that, whereas the Jews were formerly in the service of the Egyptians and served them loyally, they were now in the service of the Persians and served them loyally too. In the troubles of these years, when the satrap Arsham was recalled for consultation with Darius II at the start of his reign, the local Egyptians took the opportunity to attack the Jews. There was conspiracy with the local officials, Widrang (Vidarang), the local Persian chief, and his son co-operating with the Egyptians, probably for personal gain.

> In the month of Tammuz, in the fourteenth year of King Darius, when Arsames departed and went to the King, the priests of the god Khnub, who is in the fortress of Elephantine, conspired with Vidarang, who was commander in chief here, to wipe out the temple of the god Yaho from the fortress of Elephantine. So that wretch Vidarang sent to his son Nefeyan who was in

---

17. J. B. Pritchard, *op. cit.,* p. 492, col. 1.

command of the garrison of the fortress of Syene this order: "The temple of the god Yaho in the fortress of Yeb is to be destroyed."[18]

The temple was duly razed, its pillars of stone, its five gateways, and its roof of cedar-work were destroyed and fire set to the ruins. The basins of gold and silver and other articles in the temple were taken off. Subsequently, after a long period of fasting and praying to Yaho, the God of heaven had allowed them to have some cause of rejoicing over their enemy, for the Persians had duly punished him and demoted him.

The next part of the story concerns the letter which was written by the Jews of Elephantine to the priests in Jerusalem. This letter, though no longer in existence, is referred to in the letter to the governor. There was no answer to this, so the people wrote to the governor himself, and this is the letter we now have. Its main purpose is to ask the governor Bagoas (Bigvai) to give some help in the rebuilding of the temple in Elephantine since the Egyptians "do not allow us to build."

> Your servants Yedoniah, and his colleagues, and the Jews, the citizens of Elephantine, all thus say: If it please our lord, take thought of this temple to rebuild it, since they do not let us rebuild it. Look to your well-wishers and friends here in Egypt. Let a letter be sent from you to them concerning the temple of the God Yaho to build it in the fortress of Elephantine as it was built before.[19]

If Bagoas would do this they offered to pray for him, and to offer meal offerings and incense and sacrifice to Yaho. They assured him that merit would be stored up before Yaho by this act, greater than the merit of those who sacrificed the value of one thousand talents.

Two other important facts are given in the letter. First, these Jews of Elephantine stated that they had written to the high priest in Jerusalem, Johanan and his colleagues the priests, and to Ostanes (Ustan), the brother of Asani, and the nobles of the Jews. To this letter there had been no reply. Secondly, they stated that they had

18. *Ibid.,* col. 1.
19. *Ibid.,* col. 2.

written to Delaiah and Shelemiah, the sons of Sanballat the governor of Samaria.

These two facts are most significant, for they give us a glimpse into Judah and Palestine at the close of the fifth century B. C. We learn that Bagoas was governor, Johanan was high priest, and Sanballat was still alive, although his two sons were of some importance, owing no doubt to the age of their father. It was useless for the people of Elephantine to ask further help from the religious leaders at Jerusalem for that door was evidently closed. It has been argued by some scholars that the Jerusalem priests regarded the Jews in Egypt as semi-heretical, and therefore did not encourage them in their apostasy.[20] If that was so, the only hope of help for the Jews at Yeb was to work through the Persian political leaders, Bagoses and Sanballat.

The outcome of this letter is full of interest. Request was made that Bagoas should write to the Jews in Egypt and inform them of his plans to help. What happened was that the emissary brought back some verbal information.

> Memorandum of what Bagohi and Delaiah said to me. Memorandum. Let it be an instruction to you to say in Egypt before Arsham concerning the altar house of the god of heaven which in Yeb the fortress was built formerly before Cambyses, which Widrang, the evildoer did cast down in the year 14 of Darius the king, that it should be rebuilt in its place, as it was formerly, and that meal offerings and frankincense should be brought upon that altar corresponding to what formerly was done.[21]

It is not clear just how the Jewish colony in Egypt stood under the protection of the governor of Judah, but he agreed that they should go to Arsames and report these facts. It is interesting to note that the new temple was to be a place where the only offerings were to be the non-blood offerings. This has led some writers to suggest that the governor of Judah may have consulted the priests in Jerusalem, as well as the nobles, before giving his opinion. In the end it seems that the temple in Elephantine was finally rebuilt. One document dated to 402 B. C., in referring to a certain house that changed owner-

20. Logically, of course, other answers may be given. The writer assumes that the worship in Jerusalem, despite certain defects, was essentially true to the divine intention in that age.
21. E. G. Kraeling, *op. cit.,* p. 106.

ship, located it on the west of the temple of Yaho, which suggests that the temple and the cult were still in existence then.

This is the last we hear of the Jewish colony. Persian control in Egypt ceased just at the turn of the century.[22] The Jewish colony "which burst mysteriously into the historical picture with the coming of Cambyses, disappears from it equally mysteriously a few years after the eclipse of Persian rule."[23]

THE DATE OF NEHEMIAH

The material in the papyri from Elephantine enables us to date Nehemiah very firmly in the reign of Artaxerxes I. The high priest referred to in the papyri is Johanan, who, according to Nehemiah 12:22, was the second high priest after Eliashib, the priest referred to in the days of Nehemiah. Again in Nehemiah 12:10, 11 we have a list which places Johanan (or Jonathan) after Eliashib. Another significant reference is to be found in Josephus, who speaks of an officer of the Persians, Bagoses, and a high priest named John (Johanan).[24] According to this reference, Bagoses, living in the days of Johanan, must have ruled after Nehemiah. Bagoses is the governor referred to in the Aramaic letter we have just considered from the year 407 B. C. Evidently the Sanballat referred to is the same man whom we meet in the days of Nehemiah, but now grown older. We are led to the conclusion that Nehemiah lived before 407 B. C. Since he went to Jerusalem in the twentieth year of King Artaxerxes, we look for a king of this name who ruled prior to 407 B. C. This is, of course, Artaxerxes I, who reigned from 465 to 425 B. C., which means that Nehemiah's arrival in Jerusalem is to be dated in 444 B. C. In a most exciting way, the discovery of some Aramaic papyri in Egypt, hundreds of miles away from Palestine, enables us to give an exact date to an important Bible character.

After the close of the fifth century B. C. we enter upon a period of great obscurity for the Jews. Yet there were important things happening all around them which had a vital bearing on their future history. Thanks to archaeological research we can pierce the darkness just a little.

22. *Ibid.,* pp. 111-119.
23. *Ibid.,* p. 115.
24. Josephus, *Antiquities,* Book XI, vii, 1.

Thirteen:

THE COMING OF THE GREEKS

THE FOURTH CENTURY B.C. WAS TO WITNESS THE COLLAPSE OF Persian power in the East and the rise of the Greeks. At the close of the fifth century the Persian ruler was Artaxerxes II (404-361 B. C.), whose reign was not without merit, although he lost control in Egypt following the revolt of his brother Cyrus. The famous Greek expedition in which the Greek writer Xenophon took part contributed to the Persian loss of Egypt. Thirty years after the death of Artaxerxes II the great Persian Empire collapsed. But before the final collapse Artaxerxes III (Ochus), a brutal man, had a measure of success and was able to restore some of the lost fortunes of the Persians. He recovered Egypt in 342 B. C. and was able to quell revolts in the general area of Phoenicia. There are hints in some ancient records that the Jews were involved in these revolts and that some of them were exiled to the area of the Caspian Sea.[1] The last Persian king, Darius III, was faced with the impossible task of opposing the might of Alexander the Great. By 331 B. C. the Persians were no more and

1. For example, the Chronicle of Eusebius.

229

the East fell into the hands of the Greeks. In this chapter we shall follow the fortunes of the Jews in Palestine for the period 331 B.C. to 63 B.C., during which Greek rulers controlled the land, and at the end of which Palestine fell into the hands of the Romans.

BRIEF HISTORICAL OUTLINE, 331 B.C. TO 63 B.C.

Alexander the Great, son of Philip of Macedon, was born in the year 356 B. C. At the age of twenty he came to the throne of Macedon on the assassination of his father. The various states around Macedonia seemed to think that the treaties with Philip ended on his death, but they were to learn that the young Alexander was as strong as his father. Very soon he subdued all these and decided on an invasion of Persia. By 331 B. C. he was master of the East. Yet his

Coin portrait of Alexander the Great from a silver drachm. (Courtesy, The Oriental Institute, The University of Chicago)

life was to ebb away in June 323 B. C. before he was thirty-three years old. Almost at once his empire was divided between his generals. The senior general Perdiccas tried to hold the empire together and the various generals were assigned to satrapies. We are especially interested in Ptolemy, who went to Egypt, and Seleucus, who went to Babylon. But the scheme did not work and before long war broke out. There was fighting for several years, but by 315 B.C. four leaders had emerged. Ptolemy Lagi ruled in Egypt, the most compact of the four kingdoms, where he was assisted by General Seleucus who had been forced out of Babylon by the second leader, Antigonus, who ruled in Syria and central Asia. Then Cassander held Macedonia, and Lysimachus held Thrace. When Antigonus tried to exert greater claims in the Palestine area, he came into conflict with Ptolemy and Seleucus, and in 312 B. C. these two defeated him at Gaza and obtained control of Palestine and parts of Syria. Seleucus seized this moment to dash across the desert to Babylon and to reinstate himself in his old satrapy. This was the commencement of the Seleucid dynasty. Eleven years later Antigonus was again defeated and Seleucus extended his boundaries to the north and established his capital at Antioch. The final outcome of all this strife, as far as Palestine was concerned, was that from now on the Ptolemies and the Seleucids were to strive for the possession of the Holy Land. For the first hundred years till 198 B. C., Palestine was ruled by the Ptolemies, but after this it passed into the hands of the Seleucids and remained, nominally at least, a Seleucid possession till the Romans took over the land in 63 B. C.

We can distinguish three periods in the Seleucid rule: (1) from 198 B. C. till 175 B. C., a period of undisputed Seleucid rule; (2) from 175 B. C. till 135 B. C., the period of the Maccabaean struggle; and (3) from 135 B. C. till 63 B. C., the period of nominal Seleucid rule during which there was a great deal of real independence for the Jews. With the coming of the Romans in 63 B. C. Jewish independence was finally lost.

We have some valuable archaeological evidence for the years 400 B. C. to about 50 B. C., and even if it is not great in quantity, it does help to fill out the written records.[2] The latter part of the period is better supplied with such evidence than the earlier.

EDOMITES, IDUMAEANS, AND NABATAEANS

During the three centuries under consideration, the history of the Jews, though incomplete in many places, touches again and again on the Edomites, now known as Idumaeans, and a newer group called Nabataeans. Archaeological work in Transjordan has given some additional information about the Edomites during these years. It will be remembered that at the time of the fall of Judah in 586 B. C. these people exploited the situation in southern Judah

2. W. F. Albright, *Archaeology of Palestine* (London, 1956), p. 147.

That Greek influence reached far and wide is evident from the finding of this charming statue of Hermes, the Greek god of travelers, at Nineveh. (Courtesy, Consulate General of the Republic of Iraq)

231

and invaded the area. They were to be overwhelmed in their own homeland by other Arab groups before the end of the fifth century. Excavations at the old port of Ezion Geber, which was originally founded by Solomon, have produced seal impressions from City IV which contain names that are clearly Edomite.[3] But by the fifth century ostraca carry names that are Arab in character.[4] We may conclude that with the rise of the Arabs belonging to the group that produced the Geshem of Nehemiah's day, the Edomites quite lost their power. Many moved to Judah, while others were absorbed. In

3. Nelson Glueck, "The Topography and History of Ezion Geber and Elath," *BASOR*, No. 72, pp. 11f.
4. Nelson Glueck, "Ostraca from Elath," *BASOR*, No. 80, pp. 3-10.

The Nabataean rock-cut temple of El-Khazne in Petra. Note its dimensions by comparing them with those of the human figure in the doorway. (The Matson Photo Service)

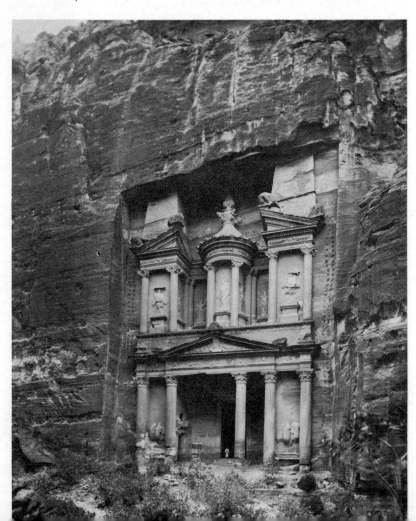

southern Judah they lived on and became known as the Idumaeans. We have valuable evidence about them here from some tombs found at Marisa which date to the middle of the third century B. C. These will be described in some detail later.[5] A variety of inscriptions, containing many names, indicates that Edomites lived alongside other types of people, like the Phoenician settlers. The names are recorded in Greek for the most part, but there are some in Aramaic, among which there are those with the divine element *Qos*, the name of the chief god of old Edom. Interestingly enough, Josephus refers to the husband of Salome, the sister of Herod, as "Kostobaros, an Idumaean by birth . . . whose ancestors had been priests of Koze, whom the Idumaeans had formerly worshipped as a god."[6]

In due course the Arab group that replaced the Edomites was itself replaced by the Nabataeans, who appear first in recorded history in 312 B. C., when Antigonus the Greek decided to attack them.[7] His general actually took the high rock behind Petra, the refuge of the ancient Edomites, but success was short-lived because the troops were wiped out as they were returning home. The researches of Nelson Glueck have shown that the land of Edom had no serious sedentary occupation during the whole Persian period.[8] Then came the Nabataeans, who gave up their own Arabic tongue for Aramaic, as thousands of inscriptions show today, and slowly settled down to build towns and to live an urban life. Petra became their great center, and here they undertook the remarkable task of carving out homes and temples in the red sandstone of the valley. There is a good deal of inaccurate talk in some circles where, in order to show how the prophecies that foretold the downfall and desolation of Edom at last came true, pictures of rock-cut dwellings and temples in Petra are shown as Edomite buildings. These structures are undoubtedly Nabataean. The only Edomite site in the area is on the hill behind Petra, where there is evidence of occupation in Edomite times.[9] Of special interest in the Nabataean areas are the "high places" where these Nabataeans offered sacrifices to their gods. These may give some idea of the kind of thing referred to so often in the days of the great prophets of Israel. Quite a deal of excavation has gone on in Naba-

5. See below, pp. 236f.
6. Josephus, *Antiquities*, XV, vii, 9.
7. Jean Starcky, "The Nabataeans — A Historical Sketch," *BA* (Dec., 1955).
8. Nelson Glueck, Reports in *AASOR*, Vol. 15. Also, *The Other Side of Jordan* (New Haven, 1940).
9. W. H. Morton, "Umm el-Biyara," *BA* (May, 1956), pp. 26f.

taean sites, so that today we know something of the coinage, the splendid pottery, the architecture, and the fortresses erected in strategic places to guard their frontiers. One of their kings, Aretas, is known in the New Testament in II Corinthians 11:32 as the king who controlled Damascus at the time Paul escaped over the wall in a basket.

At the period under discussion in this chapter, the Nabataeans were just coming into their own. They were to have dealings with the Greeks, the Maccabees, the Idumaeans, and the Romans before they were finally overcome by the Romans just after A.D. 100.

ARCHAEOLOGICAL EVIDENCE FROM THE DAYS OF THE PTOLEMIES

There were five Ptolemies who controlled Palestine from Egypt in the third century B.C.: Ptolemy I, Soter (323-285 B.C.), Ptolemy II, Philadelphus (285-246 B.C.), Ptolemy III, Euergetes I, (246-221 B.C.), Ptolemy IV, Philopater (221-203 B.C.), and Ptolemy V, Epiphanes (203-180 B.C.). There was a good deal of conflict with the Seleucids during the century when the Ptolemies ruled, and Palestine again became a battlefield over which two empires fought. Under the first of these rulers many Jews were taken to Egypt and

The famous Rosetta Stone which, because of its inscriptions in Egyptian hieroglyphics (top), Demotic (middle), and Greek, gave Thomas Young (1773-1829) and J. F. Champollion (1790-1832) the necessary clues to decipher the old Egyptian language. This black basalt stone is nearly four feet high and is named after Rosetta, where soldiers in Napoleon's army discovered it in 1799. It lists, among other things, the royal titles of Ptolemy V, as well as the name of Cleopatra. (Courtesy, The British Museum)

forced to live in Alexandria, where Greek soon became their language. Ptolemy II released many of them in view of troubles with the second and third Seleucid rulers, Antiochus I (280-262 B. C.), and Antiochus II (261-247 B. C.). Finally a treaty was made and a marriage arranged between Antiochus II and the daughter of Ptolemy II. This soon failed when the daughter of the Egyptian was murdered, and soon after, his son Ptolemy III waged war on the Seleucid ruler. Further wars followed till finally the Seleucid king Antiochus III, the Great (223-187 B.C.), was able to overwhelm all Egyptian resistance and enter Judaea as ruler in 198 B. C. The story is told in a peculiarly disguised fashion in Daniel 11.

Points of archaeological interest during these years may now be mentioned. We have referred already to the important papyri discovered in Egypt from the archives of Zeno, an official in the government of Ptolemy II.[10] Tobiah, an Ammonite who sent gifts of animals to the Pharaoh, features among these documents, and as we have seen, the find gives valuable insight into the condition of Transjordan at the time. Another Egyptian papyrus dated to 259 B. C. refers to the purchase of a "Babylonian slave girl" of seven years in Birta of Ammantis, which is identical with the fortress of Tobias. The witnesses to this document are described as "clerechs of the cavalry of Tubias," that is, they were soldier settlers with plots of land. Evidently, then, Tobias had military forces at his disposal and guarded this part of Ptolemy's domains. Perhaps the position of this Tobias under Ptolemy of Egypt was similar to that occupied by his forefather, Tobiah the Ammonite, under Artaxerxes I, the Persian.[11]

Further evidence from Egypt concerns the presence of a considerable Jewish colony there at the time. Epigraphic evidence from the third century B. C., including two Jewish-Aramaic papyri and at least eight ostraca from Edfu in Upper Egypt and from the site known as Zawiyet el-Meitin, all point to the presence of Jews in the land. That there were Jews in the region of Alexandria is clear from the Zeno papyri which contain Jewish names. To these may be added Aramaic tomb inscriptions from Alexandria and Aramaic writing on coins from Demanhur nearby. The personal names revealed are partly Biblical names, partly Aramaic, and partly Greek.[12]

---

10. See above, p. 203. See also, C. C. McCown, "The Araq el-Emir and the Tobiads," *BA* (Sept., 1957), pp. 63f.
11. C. C. McCown, *op. cit.*, p. 70.
12. W. F. Albright, *From Stone Age to Christianity* (New York, 1957), p. 349.

It was during the years of Ptolemy II that, according to the story told in the spurious letter of Aristeas, the king called together Jewish scholars to translate the Torah into Greek for inclusion in the great library that he founded at Alexandria. The names of the men supposed to have been chosen are certainly in line with the names revealed in the epigraphic evidence we have already referred to. While we have none of the original manuscripts of this Septuagint translation into Greek, it is fairly clear that in the period 300 to 250 B. C. the Torah was translated.

One other important find from Egypt from these days is a small piece of papyrus containing the ten commandments in Hebrew, the so-called Nash papyrus.[13] Evidently some of the Jews in Egypt in the third century B. C. could still read Hebrew.

Some of the sites excavated in Palestine have produced coins of this period, and naturally there is an abundance of pottery to show that many sites were occupied. The one group of important monuments of the period is the painted tombs of Marisa in south-western Judah, the Old Testament Mareshah, and the modern Tell Sandahannah. The tombs, discovered in 1902 by J. P. Peters and H. Thiersch, lay near to the tell which represented the most important town in the area. They were originally excavated from the soft limestone rock and painted inside in a most elaborate fashion. Free spaces on the walls were occupied by inscriptions and graffiti (drawings and writing scratched on the walls) in Greek and Aramaic. The personal names were Greek, Phoenician, and Edomite (Idumaean). We are especially interested in the site because Ptolemy II established a Sidonian colony here under an official named Apollophanes, whose epitaph is preserved in one of the tombs. When the tombs were first opened the colors of the frescoes on the walls were quite bright, but they have now faded. One tomb had a long procession of animals, some of which were real while others were imaginary. W. F. Albright has suggested that they may have been based on some book of illustrations of wild life sketched from the zoological gardens of Alexandria.[14] The predominance of Greek names on the walls may simply mean that the Phoenicians and the Idumaeans who lived there were Hellenized by that time. One of the tombs had a remarkable painting of tall cressets for carrying torches or lamps. These were painted on opposite piers in the vestibule of one of the tombs and may have represented

13. *Ibid.,* pp. 345, 350.
14. W. F. Albright, *Archaeology of Palestine* (London, 1956), p. 149.

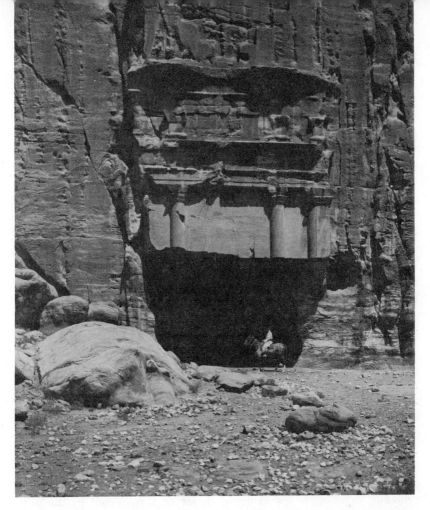

A view of another monument in Petra — a corniced tomb with Nabataean inscription, a rare exception among the numerous rock-cut tombs in the Petra area. (The Matson Photo Service)

incense stands, the like of which are known from pictures and from carvings on coins from the general area of Phoenicia. Albright sees in them a possible source of information about the two tall pillars that stood outside the temple of Solomon.[15] The worship of the region was evidently syncretistic, with elements of Edomite, Phoenician, and Greek religion. The town of Marisa was a well-planned town of Greek pattern, with streets at right angles forming blocks

15. W. F. Albright, *Archaeology and the Religion of Israel* (Baltimore, 1956), pp. 144-146; also, "Two Cressets from Marisa and the Pillars of Jachin and Boaz," *BASOR* (Feb., 1942), pp. 18f.

of houses.[16] There was a market place next to the gate, rectangular in shape, open at one end and with shops on three sides. The material from the tombs in the area combines to give the impression that this area was thoroughly Hellenized by the middle of the third century B. C. It was this Hellenization that was to lead to much of the Maccabaean trouble in the second century, when the orthodox Jews resisted the changes.

The town of Bethel at this time shows three phases of occupation between the fourth century and A. D. 70. The first phase covers the Ptolemaic and the Seleucid period down to the reign of Antiochus IV, and it presumably came to an end with the campaigns of General Bacchides about 160 B. C. The coins give the story, for there were ten Ptolemaic coins from the years 285 B. C. to 182 B. C. and four coins of Antiochus IV.

The town of Tell en Nasbeh, north of Jerusalem, produced coins of Ptolemy II as well as coins of both earlier and later periods.

The important town of Shechem in central Palestine which played a prominent part in the earlier history of Israel was apparently unoccupied between the eighth and the fourth centuries B. C. But towards the end of the fourth century it was reoccupied. Coins of all five Ptolemies have now been found and bear witness to the occupation of the town in the century 300-200 B. C. One small jug unearthed in the Hellenistic area contained thirty-five beautifully preserved Ptolemaic coins, all of them silver tetradrachms. The excavation report reads as follows: "One of Ptolemy I, sixteen, and probably three more, of Ptolemy II; six of them dated to the year of issue; one of Ptolemy III (246-221 B. C.), two of Ptolemy IV (221-204 B. C.); four, and probably eight more, of Ptolemy V (205-181 B. C.). Two of the Ptolemy V coins were dated: one in 198 B. C., and the other in 193 B. C."[17]

ARCHAEOLOGICAL EVIDENCE FROM THE PERIOD 198 B.C. TO 134 B.C.

When the Seleucid ruler Antiochus III entered Palestine in 198 B. C. there commenced an era of great trouble for the Jews which was aggravated by the fact that some of the Jews were sympathetic to the desire of the Greek rulers to introduce Greek culture all over

16. W. F. Albright, *Archaeology of Palestine* (London, 1956), p. 153.
17. E. F. Campbell, "The Third Campaign at Balatah (Shechem)," *BASOR*, No. 161 (Feb., 1961), p. 44.

the East. When Antiochus was defeated by the Romans in Asia Minor and was required to pay heavy indemnity to them, the Seleucid ruler sought ways and means to raise the money.

This need for money brought conflict with the Jews. There was in Jewish circles a serious tactical struggle going on between groups within the priestly circle, and different parties were contending for the power of the supreme priestly office. One group was inclined to court the favor of the Seleucids by offering money to assist them in their problem. This group was willing, too, to promote Hellenization. Under Seleucus IV (187-175 B.C.), the high priest Onias, representative of the so-called Oniads, and regarded as a worthy occupant of the high-priestly office by the conservative Jews, was made the subject of slanderous reports to the king by the other party (II Macc. 3:4ff., 4:1ff.). Seleucus did not respond, however. But when he was murdered by the ambitious Antiochus IV (175-163 B.C.), troubles began in earnest. Antiochus had been taken as a hostage to Rome as a boy and had learned the ways of Rome. He had also learned to fear Rome. Anxious to obtain more funds, he responded to the appeal of one Jason to remove Onias. Jason promised the new king rich gifts of money and a vigorous promotion of Hellenization in Jerusalem (II Macc. 4:7ff.). So Onias was removed and Jason appointed in his stead. Three years later a certain Menelaus offered still larger sums and Jason was removed and Menelaus appointed in his stead. The appointment of the high priest had been taken over by a pagan ruler, much to the offense of the pious Jews. When in 169 B.C. Antiochus invaded Egypt, and it was reported that he had been killed, the exiled Jason seized Jerusalem and the office of high priest and banished Menelaus. When Antiochus, very much alive, returned, he forcibly replaced Menelaus and at the same time took valuable treasure from the Temple in Jerusalem. He himself entered the Temple, an act of desecration in the eyes of the pious Jews. A year later, during a renewed campaign in Egypt (168 B.C.), he was ordered to leave Egypt by the Roman representative Popilius Laenus and to abandon all designs on Egypt. Perhaps in spite, he gave orders for his officer Apollonius to make a surprise attack on Jerusalem. Many Jews lost their lives and much damage was done. This was followed up by repressive measures. Antiochus forbade the Jews to read their Scriptures and to practice their religion. Worst of all, he desecrated their Temple and offered pagan sacrifices there. Then he set up a fortress near the Temple, often referred to in the books of Maccabees as "Akra," a veritable symbol of foreign domination. Its position is not known with certainty today, although archaeological and topographical considerations suggest the southeast hill on the ridge south of the sanctuary.[18]

The Jews could bear the insults no longer and rebelled under the family of the Hasmoneans, whom we know as the Maccabees, a name given to one of their leaders and possibly derived from a Hebrew word meaning "hammerer." From 168 B. C. till 142 B. C. the Jewish patriots waged incessant war against their enemies, being led at first by the aged Mattathias, and then in turn by his three sons, Judas (166-160 B. C.), Jonathan (160-142 B. C.), and Simon (142-134 B. C.).

Judas was able to defeat a number of Seleucid armies, and by the end of 165 B. C. the Jews were allowed to return to the Temple and were granted religious freedom. But they wanted political liberty too, and the war went on. To strengthen the hand of the Jews, Judas built forts, one of the most interesting of which was the fort at Bethzur to the south of Bethlehem. By 161 B. C. this was taken by the Seleucid general Bacchides, who destroyed it and rebuilt it on the site to a Greek plan.

When Judas was slain in battle, Jonathan took his place. Before his death he was able to consolidate the position of the Jews greatly. He was actually appointed high priest by a usurper of the Seleucid throne to whom he gave support. This usurper, Balas by name, made many concessions, and when he died and a new king took control in Antioch, Jonathan besieged Jerusalem, which was in the hands of the Seleucids. The price of lifting the siege was a lightening of taxation and the granting of certain areas near Samaria to Jonathan. When further troubles in Antioch brought a change in Seleucid policy, Jonathan supported another rebel, named Tryphon, and proceeded at once to Bethzur, the Seleucid fortress, and took it. But Tryphon was afraid of Jonathan and had him trapped and imprisoned. The leadership passed to his brother Simon. Before long Simon had captured Gezer, another Seleucid stronghold, and had taken the fortress in Jerusalem itself. The Jews were so pleased at these successes that they accepted Simon formally as high priest, even though he was not of the correct family. Simon also gained recognition by the Roman Senate of the day, but he met his death by treachery at the hands of his son-in-law. It was under Simon that the Jews emerged again into real independence. The family to which he belonged, the

18. J. Simons, *Jerusalem in the Old Testament* (1952), pp. 144ff.

Hasmoneans, was now both the ruling family and the high-priestly family. Civil and religious authority were vested in them. This had its problems, but from 142 B. C. till 63 B. C. the Jews preserved their independence, even though the Seleucids at times endeavored to exert control over them. The Jews had an ambition to recover lands lost to their enemies, and the Seleucids made one or two abortive attempts to regain control of the Jews. But before we take up that story, we shall collect the archaeological material for the period 198 B. C. to 134 B. C.

Our information comes from the excavation of several important sites, among which Bethzur, Samaria, Marisa, and Gezer feature as especially valuable. We must remember that the Greek conquerors, in pursuance of their Hellenizing policy, built towns all over their domains. In Palestine several towns were repeopled and numbers of Greek colonists settled there. Thus Samaria was repeopled by colonists from Macedonia, and coastal towns like Gaza, Ascalon, Caesarea, Dor, and Ptolemais became Greek cities. East of Jordan there were numerous Hellenized towns and in the mountain areas such places as Bethshan (Scythopolis) and Gezer became Greek cities in addition to Samaria. The Ptolemies had previously been active in Transjordan where Amman had been renamed Philadelphia by one of these rulers.

Reference has already been made to the ruins at 'Araq el Emir in Transjordan, where the rock-cut tomb of one of the Tobiads carries an inscription in Aramaic. The building in the vicinity, called by some a mausoleum and by others a palace, was built in a vigorous Hellenistic style with carved lions and Corinthian capitals. More recently it has been argued that we have here the remains of a fortress. It was built of huge blocks of limestone and was set upon a slight elevation, surrounded by a small lake, and almost completely surrounded by walls.[19] This whole building is probably to be referred to the time of Hyrcanus, the last of the Tobiads, for Josephus described the layout in great detail and credited it to Hyrcanus who, he says, lived across the Jordan and built this remarkable place for himself.[20] If that is so, the building would date from about 175 B. C., just before the days of the Maccabees.[21]

The town of Bethzur is full of interest because it provides an interesting correlation between the documentary evidence and the

---

19. C. C. McCown, *op. cit.*, pp. 66, 68.
20. Josephus, *Antiquities*, XII, iv, 11.
21. W. F. Albright, *Archaeology of Palestine* (London, 1956), pp. 149f.

GREAT

SEA

GALILEE

Straton's
Tower
(Caesarea)

SAMARIA

Scythopolis

Samaria
Shechem

Modein   Bethel
Gezer   Michmash   Philadelphia
Emmaus   Beth-   Mizpah   Jericho
Horon
Jerusalem

Marissa
Beth-zur
Gaza   Hebron

IDUMAEA

PALESTINE in the days of the MACCABEES

excavated evidence. It was the scene of several battles during the Maccabaean wars. The earliest town here was probably built during the Persian period as a protection for the Jews against the Idumaeans. In the days of the Ptolemies it was a prosperous place, to judge from the range of coins found in the excavation. Fifty-two coins from the days of the first six Ptolemies were brought to light, the earliest dating to 252 B. C. and the latest to 210 B. C. There were other coins found in the site, but they tell a different story.[22] There were in all nearly three hundred coins found in the excavation, but the greater part of them come from the days of the Seleucids and the Maccabees. In detail, the story is as follows. There were 126 coins of Antiochus Epiphanes (175-163 B. C.), none from his successor, five from Balas (150-145 B. C.), thirteen from Demetrius II (145-139 B. C.), ten from Antiochus VII (139-129 B. C.), only two Seleucid coins from the years 125-121 B. C., but sixteen Jewish ones from the days of John Hyrcanus the Jewish ruler (134-104 B. C.). This story in coins tells us that Bethzur was occupied in the days of Antiochus IV, with a decline in occupation between 160 and 145 B. C. There was a revival, then, from 145 B. C. till late in the reign of John Hyrcanus. After about 100 B. C. the coin story ceases.

On the summit of the mound of Bethzur the excavators discovered the foundations of a large fortress which gave evidence of three periods of occupation. The first, built in the days of the Ptolemies, was almost completely destroyed and rebuilt into a much larger fortress. It can be attributed to Judas Maccabeus, who built it between 165 and 163 B. C. Soon after, it was captured, destroyed, and rebuilt on a Hellenistic plan by the Seleucid general Bacchides about 161 B. C.[23] The archaeological picture thus follows closely the literary picture.

The coin story shows a gap in occupation again till 145 B. C., which takes us to the days of Jonathan and Simon, when the fortress again fell into the hands of the Jews.

One interesting sidelight on the excavations in Bethzur is that there was a considerable collection of jar handles from large wine jars that normally came from Rhodes, and which have become known as Rhodian jar handles. Each of these bears the name of the potter or magistrate for the year. The presence of so many of these here testifies to a Greek garrison in the town, and as G. E. Wright says,

---

22. O. R. Sellars and W. F. Albright, "The First Campaign of Excavation at Beth-Zur," *BASOR*, No. 43, p. 10.
23. W. F. Albright, *op. cit.*, pp. 151f.

"They certainly preferred this imported wine to the native product of the local vintage."[24]

Our next site, the town of Gezer, was finally taken by Simon. It was in a strategic position, guarding the approaches to Judaea from the west and commanding the great coast road. From the literature we learn that the town was taken after a desperate struggle and the heathen population deported and replaced by Jewish colonists. Then Simon "made it stronger than it was before and built therein a dwelling place for himself (I Macc. 13:43-48). An important inscription found in the debris reads, "Pampras says: May fire overtake Simon's palace."[25]

This Pampras, with a Greek name, was probably one of those dispossessed by Simon, and left a curse scratched on a wall.

Ruins at Gezer were interpreted by R. A. S. Macalister as a Maccabaean castle, but more recently Y. Yadin has shown them to be the remains of a Solomonic gate.[26] However, the Maccabaean town has been exposed and among other interesting features in the town was a building which seems to have been a town bathhouse. It was built of stone lined with cement, with benches around the walls, a drain beneath the floor, and a heating room at one end. It is possible, however, that the building was some sort of industrial plant.

We have already made reference to the town of Marisa, the site of the Moresheth-gath of the Old Testament (Josh. 15:44, Micah 1:15, Jer. 26:18, etc.).[27] Excavations produced Ptolemaic coins, showing occupation at that time. During the days of the Seleucids the town was in the hands of these hated foreigners (II Macc. 12:32ff.), until it finally fell into the hands of the Jews during the reign of John Hyrcanus, about 110 B. C.

Samaria was an important town during the Greek period and there are several indications of Greek occupation here. Some two thousand Rhodian jar handles, for example, are a strong testimony to the presence of Greek soldiers.[28] In the actual building remains we may refer to the fine Hellenistic wall built astride the earlier Israelite wall, and especially the magnificent round towers which are dated nowadays to the time of Alexander the Great who settled Greek colonists there. His representative Perdiccas is said to have rebuilt

---

24. G. E. Wright, *Biblical Archaeology* (London, 1957), p. 209, col. 1.
25. R. A. S. Macalister, *Gezer*, I, 212f.
26. Y. Yadin, "Solomon's City Wall and Gate at Gezer," *IEJ*, Vol. 8, pp. 80ff.
27. See above, pp. 236ff.
28. G. E. Wright, *op. cit.*, p. 209.

Samaria.[29] He repaired the old Israelite walls and strengthened them by these round towers. There is a line of walls built around the summit of the mound about four meters thick, which is dated about 150 B. C. and points to the time of the Maccabaean troubles. The town of Samaria fell finally to the sons of John Hyrcanus, when a ditch was built around the city, as well as a double line of walls, to starve the people out. All relief from Syria was cut off and Samaria returned at last to Jewish hands in 107 B. C.

The town of Shechem suffered a violent destruction during the course of these years and it has been conjectured that this may have been due to John Hyrcanus in 107 B. C. A coin of Antiochus VIII dated about 121-120 B. C. and another from 112-111 B. C. point to an occupation of Shechem extending into the period of Jewish freedom which preceded the Roman occupation.[30]

Evidence from the Period 135 B. C. to 63 B. C.

When Simon was foully slain at the instigation of his son-in-law, his son John Hyrcanus, who was governor at Gezer, came at once to Jerusalem and took over control of the government. In 130 B. C. he was attacked by the Seleucid ruler Antiochus VII, who was making a bold bid to regain control over Judaea. He actually succeeded momentarily and took John Hyrcanus off to Mesopotamia to war against the Parthian hordes who were becoming a menace at this time. Very soon Antiochus died and John was free. He returned to Jerusalem and reigned for thirty years, during which time he extended the boundaries of Judaea greatly. He was able to take Shechem, subdue the Samaritans and the Idumaeans and, as we have seen, retake Samaria by the hands of his two sons. He was keen to proselytize neighboring peoples and forced many to be circumcised. He was high priest as well as ruler and offended many by his carelessness in the priestly office and by his political ambition. He offended such new groups as the Pharisees, for example. In order to provide some protection against the Seleucids he strengthened the links with Rome. His reign saw the start of tension between two groups that we later know as the Pharisees and the Sadducees.

John's successor was his son, who took the title "king" but he reigned only one year as Aristobulus I. It was a busy year and he

29. W. F. Albright *op. cit.*, p. 150.
30. G. E. Wright and L. E. Toombs, "The Third Campaign at Balatah (Shechem) ," *BASOR,* No. 161 (Feb., 1961) , pp. 45f.

kept his brothers out of the way by casting them into prison. On his death in 103 B. C., his brother Alexander Jannaeus (103-76 B C.) succeeded him and married his widow, much to the disgust of the pious groups. He turned out to be an ambitious and successful ruler, but he was cruel and unpopular. Although he extended the boundaries of Judaea still further to the east of Galilee and into Philistia and central Transjordan, he had serious clashes with the religious groups, especially with the Pharisees. It was in this general period that the sect of Qumran, to be discussed in the next chapter, founded their monastery in the wilderness near the Dead Sea. Before Alexander died he advised his wife to divide the priestly and the kingly functions. This she did, ruling the country herself as Alexandra (76-67 B. C.), and having her son Hyrcanus appointed high priest. Her younger son Aristobulus was bold and enterprising and quite unlike his weak and irresolute brother Hyrcanus. But Aristobulus was restrained for the time being. When Alexandra died in 67 B. C. she left the Hasmonean dominions to the dissensions of her two sons. At first, Hyrcanus was both king and high priest. But Aristobulus refused to submit. He collected an army and defeated the army of Hyrcanus at Jericho. Much of the army of Hyrcanus then joined him. He then proceeded to Jerusalem where he shut up Hyrcanus and forced him to surrender. Hyrcanus gave up both the throne and the high-priesthood and retired to private life in Jerusalem. There might have been peace had not Antipater, the governor of Idumaea, espoused the cause of Hyrcanus and intrigued with the Nabataean king. Hyrcanus was persuaded to leave Jerusalem and go to Petra, to Aretas the king of the Nabataeans. Aretas then led his army against Aristobulus in Judaea and defeated him in battle. He was finally besieged in Jerusalem. In such circumstances Pompey the Roman general, at the time in Syria, who had been approached by both parties, took the initiative, postponed his projected attack on the Nabataeans, and proceeded to Jerusalem. The outcome was that Aristobulus was taken to Rome, Hyrcanus was allowed to remain as high priest and was given the title of ethnarch, while the wily Antipater continued as an agent of the Romans, in the capacity of an adviser, until he was murdered in 43 B. C.

These years, from the accession of John Hyrcanus to the conquest by the Romans, have left some archaeological material. The town of Bethel was occupied during this period and has yielded coins of John Hyrcanus, Alexander Jannaeus, and later rulers, but a lack of coins from the time of Herod suggests a period of non-occupation.

Tell en Nasbeh tells a similar story, although it was occupied in Herod's time. One of the greatest hoards of coins yet found in Palestine comes from Joppa where, in 1949, some 851 coins of Alexander Jannaeus were unearthed, all of them of one type, bearing the inscription "Alexander, King." There was evidently a mint at Joppa which supplied coins for Alexander.[31]

The final collapse of Samaria came during these years, and other towns, like Marisa and Bethshan, fell to the Hasmonean kings. We have reviewed the archaeological material for these towns above. One general feature for the three towns, Bethzur, Gezer, and Marisa, is that the series of Jewish coins comes to an end about 100 B. C. The reason is not clear, but it may mean that soon after the aggressive policy of Alexander Jannaeus (103-76 B. C.) these towns were abandoned because it was no longer necessary to maintain garrisons at these points.[32]

It is of considerable interest to us to follow the story of the coins of the Hasmonean rulers through these years. A letter from a Seleucid ruler, referred to in I Maccabees 15:6, tells how Simon was given leave to coin money. There is some debate about whether coins that have been found are really to be attributed to Simon or not. One recent writer suggests that it was only after the death of Antiochus VII in 129 B.C., when the Seleucid power in Palestine was finally broken, that Maccabaean coinage began to be minted.[33] It is clear that John Hyrcanus (134-104 B. C.) did make coins, using as symbols on their face flowers, fruit, stars, anchors, and such items as would not offend a people that held to the divine authority of the second commandment. On the reverse side he commonly used the cornucopia, the pomegranate, and a wreath, with the inscription in archaic Hebrew letters reading, "John the High Priest and the Community of the Jews." One of the common coins was the tiny bronze *lepton*, which was made in Judaea more than any other coin. It is the widow's mite of which the value was one-four-hundredth part of a shekel.

Alexander Jannaeus had the title "King" put on his coins, and used Greek letters on some of them as well as the old Hebrew letters. His symbols were the palm, the lily, the pomegranate, the cornucopia, and the wheel. By the time of Hyrcanus II (63 B. C. ff.) the coins

---

31. A. Kindler, "The Jaffa Hoard of Alexander Jannaeus," *IEJ*, Vol. 4 (1954), pp. 170ff.
32. W. F. Albright, *Archaeology of Palestine* (London, 1956), pp. 153f.
33. L. Kadman, "The Hebrew Coin Script," *IEJ*, Vol. 4, p. 150.

bear only the title "High Priest," but by then the Romans were in control. The last of the Hasmoneans was Antigonus, who seized the throne in 40 B. C., at the time when the Roman Empire was in a turmoil. In the years immediately preceding the appointment of Herod as king, Antigonus actually had coins minted with the title "King Antigonus" on one side and the words "Mattathias, the High Priest and the Community of the Jews" on the other. These coins were significant because they give us the Jewish name of Antigonus. They were, however, poor coins, being seriously adulterated, with twenty-seven percent copper, thus reflecting the deterioration due to Roman extortions and continual warfare. The symbols on these coins were the usual ones, but in addition we now find for the first time the seven-branched candlestick that was to become so common in later synagogue art.

We might be permitted to make one concluding remark to this chapter. It is that although the archaeological evidence, apart from the magnificent finds at Qumran and in other areas nearby, is by no means spectacular, our knowledge of these times is provided by a good deal of written evidence for most of this period, particularly for the latter part, thanks to writers like Josephus. To a large extent Greek remains lie near the surface of the mounds and tells of Palestine, and have either eroded away or have been removed for the buildings of the Romans, Arabs, and later builders. Nevertheless, such material as is available is of considerable value in supplementing the written records.

Fourteen:

THE RELIGIOUS COMMUNITY OF QUMRAN

I T WAS DURING THE GREEK PERIOD WE HAVE BEEN DISCUSSING THAT a remarkable community of Jews settled in the barren hills to the west of the northern end of the Dead Sea. The sect flourished here from the last part of the second century B. C. until about A. D. 70, living, so it seems, partly in a monastery whose remains have now been excavated, and partly in the caves nearby. Valuable manuscripts were left behind by these people, to be discovered in recent years and thus to provide the world with what is in some ways the most spectacular archaeological discovery of our times.

When Muhammed ed Dhib, a young Bedouin shepherd, threw a stone into a small circular hole in a cliff in these hills bordering the Dead Sea, and heard something crack and break, he could have had no idea of the train of excitement he was to set in motion in the lands far away to the west. He had discovered a treasure trove of ancient manuscripts the like of which had never been found before and which was but the prelude to yet other discoveries of a similar kind. Since that first exciting discovery in perhaps March, 1947, each year has brought to light yet more amazing discoveries. Now that we have the story unfolded, at least in part, we can reconstruct the setting with some clarity. We shall do this in order to make the significance of the find clearer.

HELLENIZATION AND THE PIOUS JEWS OF THE SECOND CENTURY B. C.

In our last chapter we outlined the growth of the Greek influence in Palestine to the point where it led to a Jewish revolt. It was an influence that began back in the fifth century B. C. when Greek traders visited the land and Greek influences in agriculture, coinage, pottery, art, thought, ways of living, indeed in nearly every aspect of life, were imbibed by the people of Palestine. Then came the days of the Ptolemies and the Seleucids, who had the specific intention in most cases of Hellenizing the East. The Jews themselves were divided in their reaction to these influences, for, although on the purely cultural level Greek ways might be acceptable, there were dangers for the spiritual life of the Jews. Acceptance of Greek influence in some areas was likely to lead to repercussions in other areas, and perhaps finally to a destruction of the Jewish way of life which, after all, was based on the very law of God. Pious men who became known as the Hasidim banded together to resist these sinister influences. When Antiochus IV (Epiphanes) came to the Seleucid throne in 175 B. C. he, too, had the policy of Hellenizing the East and so providing a unifying force for his empire. Because of this he soon interfered with the legitimate priesthood of the Jews, replacing the descendant of Zadok by Menelaus, who was sworn to assist the progress of Hellenization. Antiochus finally decided to prohibit the distinctive features of the Jewish faith, and this led, as we have seen, to the Maccabaean revolt. Many Jews were slain, others resisted by fighting back. It was 142 B. C. before the pagans were finally driven out by the efforts of the Maccabaean leaders. At first these leaders were supported by the Hasidim, who were anxious above all else to secure religious liberty, but once this had been obtained they were not at all interested in the political aspirations of the Hasmonean family and they withdrew their support. A particular evil from their point of view was that the Hasmonean family had taken the position of high priest as a gift from the pagan Seleucid rulers and had then endeavored to combine with it political ambitions. When finally Aristobulus I took the title "king," and Alexander Jannaeus seemed to go into the depths of wickedness, many of the Hasidim seem to have organized themselves into a group to resist such evils. From such a setting the Pharisees were to emerge. One of the groups found a leader whom they called the Teacher of Righteousness,[1] withdrew into the wilderness of Judaea, and organized themselves into a religious community in the region of what we know today as Wadi Qumran.

There are perhaps some elements of conjecture in the story as we have outlined it here, but it is essentially correct. Archaeologically some important points have been established. The record of coins found at Qumran starts with the coins of John Hyrcanus (134-104 B.C.), and it continues until the time of Antigonus (40-37 B.C.). There was a break at this point, with a lack of evidence from the days of Herod the Great, but the story resumes in the reign of his son Archelaus (4 B.C.-A.D. 6), and carries on till about A.D. 70, when there is another break. Finally, there are some coins from the period A.D. 132-135.

It appears that the site was abandoned about 37 B.C. for a reason that is not yet known. An earthquake wrecked a good deal of the building in 31 B.C., but after Herod's death the people returned and stayed then till A.D. 70 at which time the Romans finally devastated the place. It was at this period, when the Roman legions were moving towards Qumran, that we think the inhabitants hid their precious documents in the caves nearby, hoping to return later. But they never did. Who occupied the site in the days of the second Jewish revolt is not certain, although the coins from A.D. 132-135 suggest an occupation of some kind. Although this strange community had come to an end, the nature of the people and of their beliefs and hopes were carefully portrayed for us in their documents.

WRITTEN TREASURES FROM THE CAVES OF QUMRAN

The first cave that was entered produced a number of amazing documents, some of which were acquired by the Syrian monks in Jerusalem, and others by the Hebrew University of the State of Israel. The main documents were a complete roll of the book of Isaiah, a second roll of Isaiah complete from chapter 41 onwards but with fragments of earlier chapters, a commentary on the first two chapters of Habakkuk, the Rule of the Community, an expanded Aramaic paraphrase of Genesis, chapters 5 to 15, a book now known as the *Wars of the Children of Light Against the Children of Darkness*, and a book of Thanksgiving Psalms.

1. Or "Right Teacher." See T. H. Gaster, *The Dead Sea Scriptures* (New York, 1957), p. 5.

The caves in the cliffs near Wadi Qumran have proved to be veritable storehouses of archaeo-logical treasures. Cave 4, shown here, yielded many fragments of manuscripts that came from the library of the monastic community that lived in this area. (Courtesy Dr. Bernhard W. Anderson and Prentice-Hall, Inc.)

These finds were startling enough, and they may be followed up by the reader in some of the excellent accounts now available, but they were only a start.[2] The cave from which these original documents came was subsequently discovered in January, 1949, by trained archaeologists, and a systematic search was undertaken by experts in February to March, 1949. Unauthorized persons had been there before them and had disturbed the cave a good deal, but many fragments were found on the floor of the cave, including

2. F. F. Bruce, *Second Thoughts on the Dead Sea Scrolls* (Grand Rapids, 1956) ; Millar Burrows, *The Dead Sea Scrolls* (London, 1956) ; C. T. Fritsch, *The Qumran Community* (New York, 1956) ; Yigael Yadin, *The Message of the Scrolls* (London, 1957) ; J. M. Allegro, *The Dead Sea Scrolls* (London, 1957) .

scraps of Genesis, Leviticus, Deuteronomy, Judges, Samuel, Isaiah, Ezekiel and Psalms. There were also portions of commentaries on Micah, Zephaniah, and Psalms, all in very fragmentary form, and some pieces of other books, such as the Book of Noah, the Book of Jubilees, and the Testament of Levi.

Towards the end of 1951 a second cave was found by the Bedouin, containing yet more fragments, which they sold to the Museum in Jerusalem. At once an expedition of scholars set off to search the area. They were able to investigate forty caves. It was in March, 1952, that pottery of the type found in the first cave was found in several others, pointing to occupation by the same people at about the same time. Two of the caves, Cave 2 and Cave 3, contained fragments of the Old Testament, but Cave 3 yielded strange inscribed copper rolls, which were subsequently found to contain mysterious lists of treasures and the places where they were buried.

Cave 4 was the most startling of all in some respects, for here in September, 1952, the archaeologists cleared a cave that had been disturbed by the Bedouin. It contained many thousands of pieces representing over three hundred books, Biblical and non-Biblical, including every book in the Old Testament except the book of Esther. Commentaries on Psalms and Daniel and some of the Minor Prophets

The entrance to Cave 1. (Photo by the author)

The author standing beside the entrance to Cave 1, a close-up view of which appears on page 253. Note the circular hole through which the Bedouin shepherd threw a stone that broke a jar and thus led to the discovery of the ancient manuscripts which this and similar caves contained. (Photo by the author)

were represented, as well as hymns, apocryphal and apocalyptic writings, and fragments of other books known from Cave 1.[3]

Cave 5 was found in September, 1952, also, but the archaeologists themselves were the discoverers this time. It yielded a good harvest of non-Biblical works in fragments, as well as some phylacteries.

Cave 6, high up in the cliffs behind the settlement, had some pieces of manuscripts, but the most interesting item here was a fragment of a work known as *The Damascus Document of the Sons of Zadok,* which was discovered earlier in this century in an old synagogue in Cairo. It is evident that the Qumran people knew this writing and had a copy of it in their library.

Caves 7 to 10 were found by the archaeologists, but contained very little material. Then, early in 1956, Cave 11 was discovered by the Bedouin.[4] It contained material comparable in quality to that found in the first cave, including a small roll of Psalms, many pieces of the *Apocalypse of Jerusalem,* an Aramaic Targum of Job, and two

3. The contents of the various caves can be found in *RB* for the years 1953ff. See also, F. F. Bruce, *op. cit.,* p. 31, and J. M. Allegro, *op. cit.,* pp. 35-40.
4. Editorial in *Evangelical Quarterly* (Oct.-Dec., 1957), pp. 193f.

copies of the book of Daniel already known in fragment form from Caves 1, 4, and 6.

In addition to the work in the caves near Qumran, the excavation of the ancient ruin which represented the original monastery of the sect was undertaken. The work began in November, 1951, and soon it revealed a connection between Cave 1 and the ruins when a jar of the same type as was found in the first cave came to light, along with pottery and coins of the first century A.D. In the spring of 1953, 1954, 1955, and 1956 this work went on. The excavations revealed a building that had experienced three periods of occupation. Its dimensions and plan are now known.[5] Pottery and coins assist in dating the periods of occupation. The building had a water supply which came in by way of a conduit from springs in the hills behind. A considerable number of cisterns and more shallow receptacles for holding water links up with statements in the writings which show that these people laid a great emphasis on ritual washings. One room in the monastery was evidently the scriptorium where the scrolls were written, for here were found the remains of benches where men sat, and even two of the inkwells. The whole building was a complex one with many rooms. It was here that the members of this strange

5. The overall area was some 260 feet square.

This illustration gives a view of the ancient ruins of Qumran on the shores of the Dead Sea where the Essene-like community flourished at the beginning of the Christian era. (Courtesy, Dr. Bernhard W. Anderson and Prentice-Hall, Inc.)

community lived and worked to produce the manuscripts and rolls found in the caves.[6]

Quite apart from the finds directly connected with the Qumran community, there were important discoveries in other areas of the wilderness of Judaea. As early as January, 1952, there was a six-week campaign of excavation in the Wadi Murabba'at eleven miles to the south, which produced evidence of occupation in the Chalcolithic age (before 4000 B. C.), the Middle Bronze Age (2000-1550 B. C.), the Iron Age (1200-550 B. C.), and the Roman period. In all, four caves were investigated. The texts, coming mostly from the second cave, were of various types. One non-Biblical text in Hebrew was written over an earlier text, probably in the centuries B. C., while other texts came from the post-Christian centuries. Some fragments of Genesis, Exodus, Deuteronomy, and Isaiah were from the first and second centuries A. D. Included among the finds were also a complete phylactery, several ostraca, and a sensational find of two letters of the leader of the second Jewish revolt of A. D. 135, the well-known Bar Kochba, whose real name, as revealed by the letters, was Simon ben Kosebah. In the same caves were fragments of Latin and Arabic manuscripts. None of these finds is to be related in any way to the Qumran material.

Further discoveries at the end of 1959 brought to light yet other letters of Bar Kochba. Reports from Jordan led the Israeli Department of Antiquities to undertake careful investigations in caves to the north of Massada, with the result that a variety of objects was discovered including jugs, bowls, jars, cloth, food, but in particular a bundle of papyri and wooden slats all carrying writing. These proved to be letters written either by Bar Kochba or by his secretary to some of his officers, Jehonathan and Masabala, at a time when Bar Kochba was still commanding his forces. Evidently these two men took the precious documents with them to the cave where they were found.[7]

In yet another area, in the Wadi en Nar, which is the extension of the Brook Kedron, a ruined site was investigated in February to April, 1953. It yielded fragments of Greek New Testament texts, as well as Syro-Palestinian and Arabic texts. The place was formerly an early Christian monastery, now known as Khirbet Mird.

6. Details are to be found in J. T. Milik, *Dix ans de découvertes dans le désert de Juda* (Paris, 1957), pp. 41-44, and diagram 3. See also R. de Vaux, "Fouilles au Khirbet Qumran," *RB* (Jan., 1953), pp. 83-106.

7. Y. Yadin, "New Discoveries in the Judean Desert," *BA* (May, 1961), pp. 34-50.

As a result of all this searching and excavation, scholars have an embarrassing wealth of material which will occupy them in close study for many years to come. Not only do the finds throw light on the remarkable religious community of Qumran, but they also give valuable information about the thought of those times, the character of the Hebrew text, the background to the ferment of Biblical interpretation in which our Lord Jesus Christ preached and in which the Christian Church was formed, as well as insight into various aspects of the history of those times. We shall comment briefly on some of these items, indicating the lines which should be followed by the thoughtful reader.

THE CHARACTER OF THE QUMRAN COMMUNITY

The written material discovered in the caves, and especially the *Manual of Discipline*, or the *Rule of the Community* as some writers now call it, enable us to obtain a fairly clear impression of the basic ideas, the constitution, and the practice of the community.[8]

In the difficult days of the last part of the second century B. C. the pious group of Jews represented here was convinced that the end of this wicked age was at hand and that days of judgment spoken by the prophets of the Old Testament were about to commence. The very site of the monastery was at the point where the river described in Ezekiel 47 entered the Dead Sea. In such perilous times this society believed that God still had a remnant of faithful people who were in the line of the faithful remnants of past days, but that this one was the final one. The people of Qumran used names for themselves which remind us of the names of God's covenant people in the Old Testament, such as "the Elect," "the Saints of the Most High," "the Sons of Light," "the Holy People," "the Poor of the Flock," and "the Community of Israel and Aaron." As members of the covenant they believed that they were already in possession of the law of God, but they desired to live by its precepts. Their great aim was to study the Torah in order to discover its true interpretation along lines of procedure that had been given to them by the Teacher of Righteousness (or Right Teacher),[9] who had set out for them the

8. Simple outlines are to be found in F. F. Bruce, *op. cit.,* pp. 99-111, and T. H. Gaster, *op. cit.,* pp. 1-28.

9. F. F. Bruce, *The Teacher of Righteousness in the Qumran Texts* (London, 1957), has an excellent summary of present knowledge about this figure.

One of the most startling finds in the caves was a complete scroll of the book of Isaiah. (Courtesy, The American Schools of Oriental Research)

way of holiness and had shown them how to live and to serve God in such momentous days. They now awaited the dawning of the Messianic age in which there would be a new Jerusalem and a new Temple, where worthy sacrifices would be offered by a worthy priesthood. Until that day dawned, this community of God's elect was required to devote itself to the law of God, to submit to the discipline of the sect, and even to be prepared to suffer as an atonement for the sins of Israel that had gone astray. Indeed, they would make atonement for the whole earth and thus bring wickedness to an end.

The community was organized rather like a medieval monastery, with members composed of both the priests (sons of Zadok) and laity. At the head of the hierarchy stood the priests, who were supreme in all matters doctrinal and economic, and after them the Levites, the elders, and the rest of the people. The laity was divided into groups of thousands, hundreds, fifties, and tens, and the priests had authority over them in matters of law and property. Yet all members of the community were allowed to vote on matters of law and property in the general assembly which was conducted according to certain fixed rules. The priests in the assembly took their places first, then the elders, then the rest. No one was allowed to speak while his brother was speaking, and the supervisor who presided gave each man a clear opportunity to speak.

There was another important group, the council, a sort of supreme court, comprising twelve men, of whom three were priests, all skilled in the law, "to guard faithfulness in the land."

It seems that there were organized cells of this sect wherever ten men were found belonging to the order. Of these, one needed to be a priest who was able to interpret the law to them at any time of day or night, so as to preserve harmony.

It was not easy to become a member of this community. A man had to volunteer, and to agree to live by the regulations of the sect. He was first examined by the overseer as to his intelligence and character. After a time he appeared before the "many" and was examined. He was then required to serve a full year of probation during which he did not share either in the wealth of the community or in the purifactory rites. At the end of the year he was examined again, and if accepted, he deposited his property with the overseer, and was allowed the next year to share the purifactory rites of the group, but not its communal meal. When finally he was accepted, he surrendered all his property, which was merged in the common fund, and after confession and the reciting of blessings and curses by the priests, the applicant became a full member of the covenant community. He swore to follow the law of Moses, to live by it, and to shun all evil men and their ways.

Communal life was expressed in various ways. The two principal rites were baptism and the communal meal, and in these all members had a part. There were many occasions on which members of the sect had to carry out ritual washings, not only at their initial baptism but also on various other occasions which required outward lustrations. The community did not regard these washings as in themselves a substitute for purity of heart, for several portions in their writings insist on inward purity as the only way to win divine approval. The outward washing was only the symbol of inward cleansing.

The communal meal was another occasion where the whole group acted in unison, and where "all are to dine together, worship

259

together and take counsel together."[10] When they ate, the priest occupied the first place, and after that the members sat in their orders. Before meals, which evidently had a sacramental character, the priest gave thanks. In other ways, too, the society was communal. There was a good deal of work to be done on this basis, covering a great variety of occupations, so that the group could gain its daily bread. The excavations revealed the potters' corner and the room where the scribes worked, and it is believed that there is evidence of farming activity also in the area.

Time to these men was a sacred trust from God, and there were set times for prayer and meditation as well as for work. Throughout the night some of the men were engaged in the study of the Torah, the law of God, in three shifts. Wherever ten men were gathered, one of them devoted himself to the study of the law exclusively.

There were penalties imposed on those who broke the laws and offended in matters of community discipline. These were, for the most part, exclusion from the fellowship and reduction of the food ration. Details can readily be found in the *Manual of Discipline*.

It would appear that women as well as men might be admitted to the community, and that marriage and family life were not discouraged. The graves in the area gave evidence of the presence of women in the community, for a number of female skeletons was found and there are references in the documents to both women and children. The sect often took children in from outside and trained them along with other children for a period of ten years, after which the young adult could apply for membership in the society for which he was eligible at the age of twenty, admittance being in the usual way after examination and probation. Charles T. Fritsch has given an excellent summary of the character of the Qumran sect.

> The Qumran sect was a monastic community whose members practiced the common life according to strict regulations; it was a covenant community which lived according to the requirements of the New Covenant; it was a sacramental community in that every phase of life was lived in accordance with the divine ordinances; it was a priestly community in that its life was directed by priests, or sons of Zadok; it was a Bible-centered community, where the Scriptures were read and studied day and night, and

10. T. H. Gaster, *op. cit.*, p. 49; *Manual of Discipline*, col. vi, lines 2, 3.

where Biblical texts were continually copied by members of the group; and finally, it was an apocalyptic community, waiting expectantly for the quick overthrow of evil and the establishment of God's kingdom here on earth.[11]

We may suspect that the first settlers at Qumran believed the end to be very near, and no doubt they thought the time had come when the Romans came to the land in 63 B.C., for it seems certain that the Romans feature in their writings as one of the factors in the final victory. However, for a reason that is not clear, they vacated their settlement for some years and departed to "Damascus," returning after the death of Herod to await the time of the end. During these years John the Baptist was declaring that the time had come, and that Jesus Christ was the Messiah. This teaching did not influence the Qumran sect, and they were still in their monastery in A.D. 68 when the Roman armies began to quell the revolt of the Jews, who were led by the more violent elements of the nation, anxious to hasten on the downfall of the Romans. In the reprisals that followed, the whole of Judaea was subdued and along with it the Qumran settlement was destroyed. In a sense the end had come, but not in the way the community had hoped for.

THE QUMRAN APPROACH TO THE OLD TESTAMENT

The Qumran community believed that God had given them special insight into the meaning of the Old Testament scriptures, which were interpreted so as to enable the readers to see in the scriptures a description of their own times and circumstances. This became evident to modern scholars from the earliest days of the finds, for the commentary on Habakkuk, one of the rolls in the first cave, followed just these lines. The interpreter ignored the historical meaning of the text and read into it the present evil age, so that the text became a source of guidance for the present, an approach not unusual even in our own days. If the reader will take up one of the popular translations of the texts and read the commentary on Habakkuk or Nahum, he will see that the method is to quote the Bible text and then to add the words, "The interpretation of this concerns . . . ."[12] Sometimes the phrase used to introduce the interpretation may differ

---

11. C. T. Fritsch, *op. cit.*, p. 75.
12. T. H. Gaster, *op. cit.*, pp. 229-261. Millar Burrows, *op. cit.*, pp. 365-370.

slightly from this, but the meaning of the passage for "today" is stated after the Bible text in each case.

All of this material is valuable for us today because it throws light on the history of the times. Unfortunately at the present time we are still in the dark about the meaning of some of the references. For example, reference to the Kittim, which occurs in more than one place, seems to point to the Romans, but there are still some scholars who think differently, and we shall need more information before we can finally decide. When once the picture becomes clear, we shall have valuable material for dating the age at which these documents were written. Present indications are that the date of composition was between 135 B.C. and A.D. 70. That this approach to the interpretation of the Old Testament was used quite regularly seems to be implied by the fact that we now have this type of commentary for quite a number of Old Testament books, but notably the prophets.

THE QUMRAN COMMUNITY AND THE MESSIAH

The two centuries before the Christian era were centuries of speculation in many ways, as a study of the apocryphal, pseudepigraphic, and apocalyptic literature of those centuries will show. Such themes as the Messiah, the Day of the Lord, the final Judgment, the lot of the wicked were taken up by many writers, and the Qumran community, born in the midst of this sort of speculation, reflected the discussion of the day. There were, however, some novel ideas. The people believed that things would go on as they were till "the coming of a prophet and the anointed ones [Messiahs] of Aaron and Israel,"[13] and it was these duly anointed persons, one a high priest and one a king, for whom the community waited. Thus, they expected a prophet, a priest, and a king in that day. One document from Cave 4 showed that the teachers of Qumran made use of several passages from the Old Testament to justify their Messianic ideas. Here were collected Deuteronomy 18:18, 19, which refers to a prophet, Numbers 24:15-17, which refers to a king, and Deuteronomy 33:8-11, where Moses pronounced his blessing on the priestly tribe of Levi. The whole society was called "the community of Israel and Aaron,"

13. F. F. Bruce, *op. cit.,* p. 77, and *Rule of Community,* col. ix, line 11. Cf. T. H. Gaster, *op. cit.,* p. 58.

A reproduction of part of the scroll of the book of Isaiah. (Courtesy, Israel Office of Information)

and it evidently expected the two Messiahs to emerge from its own ranks. In another of the documents, the order of precedence of those who sit down at the banquet in the new age is given, and here the Messiah of Israel is subordinate to the priest. We are reminded of the inferior position of the prince in the latter chapters of Ezekiel.

263

It is noteworthy, in the light of these unusual Messianic ideas, that in Christianity the three figures of prophet, priest, and king are united in our Lord Jesus Christ whose Messiahship was achieved through the suffering of the cross.[14]

The Scrolls and the Text of the Old Testament

Prior to the discovery of these texts, our earliest Hebrew manuscripts were dated about A. D. 900. It has always been the desire of Biblical scholars to obtain earlier manuscripts in order to make a comparison with the present-day Hebrew text. In this way they could discover how well the text had been preserved. As a result of these wonderful Qumran discoveries we now have documents as old as 100 B. C., or perhaps even earlier.[15] How do they compare with the Masoretic text which we have in our Hebrew Bible, and which was fixed by the Rabbis according to the tradition (Masorah) which held in the early centuries of the Christian era?

A number of interesting facts has emerged. The most important is that in the main these ancient texts agree fairly closely with the text with which we are familiar. Where they diverge they not infrequently follow the Septuagint text more closely, and this diverges from the Hebrew text in a number of places. It is evident also that there were versions of the Hebrew Bible in existence in those days that differed from both the present Masoretic and the Septuagint texts.

From these discoveries certain facts are clear. It is plain that the Masoretic text, or at least the original form of it, is quite ancient. Although the standardization took place in early Christian times, the process was going on at least in the first century B. C. At the same time it is apparent that the translators of the Septuagint had a slightly different form of the text in Egypt, but it was a form that was not unknown in Palestine, for there is evidence of it in the caves of Qumran. Furthermore, the discoveries of these recent days show that there were still other forms (recensions) of the Hebrew Bible that were current in Palestine in those centuries. It became necessary for the Jews to decide on a standard text for their own

14. F. F. Bruce, *op. cit.,* pp. 76-84.
15. *Ibid.,* pp. 34, 44; Millar Burrows, *op. cit.,* pp. 73-122. A few persistent critics still seek to deny that the documents are pre-Christian and push them into post-Christian times.

use, and this the Rabbis did quite early in Christian times. It is probably because of these different texts that were in use in the days of the early Church that the quotations from the Old Testament occurring in the New Testament are difficult to trace exactly in many cases. Future work on the wealth of manuscript material will do much to show how our Hebrew Bible finally came into its present form.

THE QUMRAN SECT AND THE ZADOKITES

We have already made passing reference to the discovery many years ago, in an ancient synagogue in Egypt, of several fragments of a strange document which belonged to a sect of Jews known as the Karaites. The document was originally written by Jews who regarded themselves as a covenant group. Apparently they had migrated to "Damascus,"[16] where they were organized into a community by a leader called "the Star." The document found in Egypt has been called the Damascus document or the Zadokite fragment, because of its reference to Damascus and to the sons of Zadok. It gives details of a sect which, in many ways, resembled the sect we have come to know as the Qumran sect. The two lots of written material are related in style and terminology, and the two groups are similar in organization, in structure, and in many of their basic beliefs. Indeed, even before fragments of the Damascus document were found at Qumran some scholars were postulating a connection between the two groups. The question naturally arose whether the Qumran people knew of the writings of the Damascus group. The discovery of fragments of this Damascus document in Cave 6 makes it clear that the covenant community at Qumran was in possession of the rules and procedures of the Damascus or Zadokite sect. When a comparison is made between the two groups, it becomes clear that there are differences as well as resemblances. It was easier to enter the Damascus group than to enter the Qumran group for it was only necessary to take an oath and be enrolled by the supervisor. In the matter of personal goods, too, the Damascus sect had easier rules, for its members were required only to give two days' wages a month to community funds. Again, this group had closer connections with the Temple in Jerusalem, although it was stricter in its observance of

16. It is not agreed by all that this term is to be taken literally. See R. North, "The Damascus of Qumran Geography," *P.E.Q.* (1955), pp. 34ff.

many of the requirements of the law than the orthodox Jews of Jerusalem.

It seems that the two communities were closely related, if not identical. However, because of the differences, some scholars think that perhaps they represent two different stages, with the possibility that the Damascus group was the later. We cannot at this stage give a final answer as to the relationships between the two.[17]

THE QUMRAN SECT AND THE ESSENES

Several ancient writers, such as the Roman, Pliny, and the Jews, Josephus and Philo, give a good deal of detail about a sect that was in existence in their time, called the Essenes. Its members were scattered throughout Palestine and were celibates for the most part, although some did marry. They lived a very strict life, and in many ways conducted themselves like the community of Qumran. They had community meals, devoted themselves to prayer, engaged in ritual washings, were sworn to piety, and in general followed out a way of life that reminds us both of the Damascus (or Zadokite) sect and the Qumran sect. Pliny placed them in the Dead Sea area to the north of Masada and Engedi, which would bring them near to, if not actually one, the site of Qumran. Josephus, however, says that they were to be found all over Palestine. There are again many resemblances between the Essenes and the Qumran sect, and also some differences. Some scholars are ready to make an outright identification of the two groups; others feel that this is not warranted at present.[18] The fact seems to be emerging that there were a number of baptist and messianic groups in the Jordan Valley and in the Dead Sea area during the first centuries B. C. and A. D. John the Baptist founded one such group. It will probably turn out finally that all these groups were closely related, and traced their origins back to the same set of circumstances. We propose to regard them, apart from the group of John the Baptist, as basically Essenes.

THE QUMRAN SECT AND CHRISTIANITY

In the excitement of the early days of discovery, before the written materials could be properly assessed, there were those who noticed a number of superficial resemblances between the teaching

17. C. T. Fritsch. *op. cit.,* pp. 76-89.
18. F. F. Bruce, *op. cit.,* pp. 112-122; C. T. Fritsch, *op. cit.,* pp. 90-110.

and the practices of Qumran and those of Christianity. The conclusion was quickly formed that the origins of Christianity were to be sought in this sect. More mature consideration shows that this picture is quite false. There are vast differences between the two systems, and there is no ground at all to think that Christianity is related to the Qumran sect.

The reason for the superficial resemblances in teaching lies in the fact that Christianity touches time and again on the range of thinking of the Jewish people of those days, and offers its own solution. The coming of the Messiah, the significance of the Old Testament for understanding the purposes of God, discussions about the Day of the Lord, the problem of the wicked, and the final lot of the righteous, all of these, and many similar problems that occupied the thinking of the pious men of the times, fell for discussion among the early Christians. The writings of both the Qumran sect and of the early Christians abound in references from the Old Testament, so that similarity in language and theme by no means argues a dependence of one on the other. Both groups go back to the same basic source material in the Old Testament. There are, however, some important things to be said.

In the first place, there is at present no clear evidence of any direct contact between the Qumran community and either the Founder of Christianity or the early Christians. True, such scholars as J. M. Allegro and Professor Dupont-Sommer have argued that in the Teacher of Righteousness we have one who anticipated the teaching, passion, and messianic claims of Jesus Christ, and that the community of Qumran was a sort of shadow of the Christian Church. These ideas have been popularized by E. Wilson, but they have not met with widespread acceptance.[19] Rather, the majority of scholars have deplored the facile identification that this writer makes on the basis of insufficient evidence. The Teacher of Righteousness did not make Messianic claims for himself, nor did his followers regard him as Messiah, nor do we know how he died.

It would seem quite probable, however, that John the Baptist had contact with the Qumran sect. He lived in the deserts of Judaea when he was young and finally came preaching repentance, separation from this evil age, and the practice of a life of denial, while awaiting the coming of the Messiah whose forerunner he was (Luke 1:76-80,

19. E. Wilson, *The Scrolls from the Dead Sea* (London, 1957).

3:1-8). Much of this teaching is reminiscent of the teaching of Qumran. John also baptized and spoke of judgment, but he never identified himself with the Messiah. He preached to the masses rather than to a select group of people, and when Jesus came, John recognized Him as Messiah, although he still needed to learn the fuller implications of His coming and His ministry (Matt. 11:2-6).

There seem to be many points of contact between John and the Qumran people, but if he ever did belong to the sect, we would have to conclude that he broke with them in order to follow a new path set out for him by God.[20]

When we come to Jesus Himself, we find Him living a life that was very different from that of the covenanters of Qumran. There seem to be many parallels between His teaching and that of the Qumran sect, but this does not mean any more than that He accepted the same Scripture as they did, and lived in days when many were talking about the same great themes. It is a fact that the more we know about the literature and the discussions of these times the more we can place the teaching of Jesus in its setting, and in this regard much can be learned from the Dead Sea Scrolls. But in a thousand ways Jesus Christ was different from the people in the monastery of Qumran, both in His own life and in the peculiar emphasis of His teaching.[21] There is no trace in the teaching of this sect of those great doctrines that make Christianity really distinctive — the Incarnation, redemption through the death of One who was the Messiah, Himself Prophet, Priest, and King of Old Testament expectation, the Son of Man and the Suffering Servant alike.

There are, however, many resemblances in language and in thought between the writings of Qumran and those of the New Testament. This is only natural because the early Christians were showing how it was that Jesus Christ provided the answer to all the hopes, the strivings, and the questionings of those pious souls who, like the covenant community of Qumran, despaired of this present evil age. The last ten years of scholarly research on these documents have produced some thrilling discussions of the way in which Paul and others took up the challenge of the times, and showed how Christ, the true Messiah, had finally come in the fullness of time to make all things new.

20. C. T. Fritsch, *op. cit.*, pp. 112-116; F. F. Bruce, *op. cit.*, pp. 128-131.
21. C. T. Fritsch, *op. cit.*, pp. 116-124; F. F. Bruce, *op. cit.*, pp. 131-137. Cf. G. Greystone, *The Dead Sea Scrolls and the Originality of Christ* (London, 1955).

THE IDENTITY OF PEOPLES AND EVENTS IN THE SCROLLS

We have made reference in passing to several persons who appear in the literature of the Qumran sect but there are others besides these. Such people as the Teacher of Righteousness, the Wicked Priest, the Kittim, a certain Demetrius, king of Greece, and the house of Absalom, all demand an explanation. Then some of the events referred to in the scrolls, such as the reference to the attack of the Wicked Priest who pursued the Teacher of Righteousness to his place of exile on the Day of Atonement, will provide important clues to the true historical situation in which this literature arose. Many writers already feel that the Wicked Priest was Alexander Jannaeus (103-76 B. C.), who clashed with the Jews in his day and slew many. The Jewish rebels did invite Demetrius III, the Seleucid king at the time, to come to their aid, but just who the Teacher of Righteousness was is not at present clear, although suggestions are not lacking. Again, the Kittim would appear to be the Romans.

The fact remains, however, that at present we are uncertain about the identification of many of the people and events referred to in the scrolls. We are confident that within a very short time now the puzzle will begin to unravel. There is such a wealth of material still being examined, and still more coming to light, that it seems inevitable that we shall soon have a solution to our problems.

It does not seem that the well-known King Herod features at all in the Qumran documents. Yet we have reason to think that he had dealings with the community at Qumran. Archaeological evidence points to the fact that during Herod's time the monastery was deserted. The reason is not known, but it is conjectured that Herod may well have taken a strong dislike to these pious Jews so close to his Jericho palace. The Messianic teachings which they propounded could have been an offense to him and, further, the community seems to have had something of a military significance to judge from their document, *The War of the Sons of Light Against the Sons of Darkness.* If Herod set himself against them, he could do them harm, so it is quite possible that it was during these years that they went to "Damascus," to return after his death. However, here, too, we can do no more than speculate, since in any case "Damascus" may be used in a metaphorical sense, and the *War* scroll may not have referred to physical warfare any more than the Christian hymn "Onward, Christian Soldiers."

It is not without good cause that many have regarded these finds in the Qumran area as the most spectacular archaeological discovery of this age. The documents have widespread significance, touching on the text of both Old and New Testaments, and on the Messianic hopes of the age and the thinking of pious men in the years surrounding the birth of the Christian Church. We feel that here we meet face to face men whose whole being is vibrant with expectation of the coming of Messiah. Even if they were wrong, and even if their interpretations of Scripture were forced and unnatural, they have left for us a strong picture of a hope which only Jesus, the true Messiah, could fulfill. The Messiahship of the Lord Jesus stands out in thrilling contrast with the frustrated hopes of these people. And the story is not finished. We feel that much more light will yet break forth from the writings of this strange community.

Fifteen:

THE DAYS OF HEROD THE GREAT

With Herod's appointment as king by the Romans after the death of Antigonus, the last of the Hasmoneans, in 37 b. c., there was a new order in Judaea. Not being a true Jew, but an Idumaean by birth, Herod was despised by the Jews all his days. His reign was a tragic one and he died without a friend. But because of his tremendous building program, he left behind a great deal of material which is the delight of the archaeologist today. We shall first review the history of the times and then discuss the archaeological discoveries bearing on those days.

History of Palestine from 63 B. C. to 4 B. C.

In 63 b. c. Pompey entered Palestine and the Holy Land came under the direct control of Rome. This was in many ways an advantage, for it was to give the Jews peace, roads, aqueducts, and many fine buildings. Judaea itself was greatly reduced in size and it was included in the Roman province of Syria, with a local governor and Hyrcanus as high priest. Soon after, Scaurus, the Roman proconsul of Syria, had trouble with the Nabataeans, and Antipater, the father of Herod, was able to persuade the Nabataeans to pay tribute and in this way ingratiate himself with the Romans.

Just at this time civil strife, which was to have indirect repercussions on Palestine, was breaking out in Rome. When Gabinius became proconsul of Syria in 57 B. C. he had trouble in Judaea with a Hasmonean rebel, a son of the former Aristobulus. The revolt was quelled and the fortresses of Alexandrium, Hyrcania, and Machairus were demolished. In the campaign a young Roman named Antony distinguished himself. He met the young Herod and the two became firm friends. Gabinius divided the land into five areas in order to avoid troubles. When he planned an attack on Egypt, Antipater supplied his food and water as he passed through Palestine. In 54 B. C., following the success of Gabinius in Egypt, Antipater was able to bring about the collapse of another Jewish revolt by good advice to the rebels. As a reward for his efforts he became, in effect, the ruler of the land.

By this time the Roman world was ruled by a strange alliance of three men called a triumvirate, consisting of Pompey, Julius Caesar, and Licinius Crassus. In 53 B. C. Crassus met his death and Caesar and Pompey began to fight for supreme power. Caesar won, and by 48 B. C. Pompey was dead. In Palestine, intrigue among the descendants of the Hasmoneans led to serious conflict. The one man who finally profited by it all was Antipater. Whereas formerly he supported Pompey, now he supported Caesar, who at the time was needing help in Egypt. He was able to send three thousand Jewish troops and to persuade other Jews to assist. Hyrcanus the high priest accompanied him to Egypt. Caesar was well pleased and confirmed Hyrcanus as ethnarch of Judaea and high priest, while Antipater was made a Roman citizen and appointed to the position of procurator of Judaea. He proceeded to rebuild the walls of Jerusalem, and to appoint his son Phasael prefect of Jerusalem and his son Herod as governor of Galilee.

At once Herod proved his skill in battle and in the affairs of government. He put an end to banditry in the Galilee area and had the leader, one Hezekiah, and many of his followers, executed. In doing this he encroached on the jurisdiction of the Sanhedrin, and was summoned before this august body. He knew very well that he had the strong support of the Syrian governor and could afford to adopt an aggressive attitude in the presence of the Sanhedrin. Finally the Sanhedrin did not sentence him and Herod departed secretly from

Jerusalem. He reappeared with a body of troops, wanting to take vengeance on the Sanhedrin but his father Antipater restrained him and he returned to Galilee. But he had shown that he was a man to be reckoned with, as indeed it turned out. He proceeded at once to report the incident to the Roman proconsul of Syria, who forthwith appointed him governor of Coele-Syria. This greatly increased his power and enraged his enemies.

Then came the assassination of Caesar in March 44 B. C. The Roman senate confirmed the generous concessions Caesar had made to the Jews, but before long the proconsul of Syria, Cassius, an ambitious man, began to press the Jews for money and demanded that Antipater and his sons find it. They submitted, but earned the wrath of the Jews still more, so that when a Jewish conspirator, Malichus, arranged for the poisoning of Antipater, the nation was not grieved. Soon after, Cassius set off to Rome, hoping to gain the supreme place in the empire. Anarchy broke out in Judaea, and Antigonus, the son of Aristobulus and nephew of the high priest Hyrcanus, tried to seize the power but was frustrated for a time.

Eventually Cassius was overthrown, and Antony and Octavian emerged supreme. Antony returned to Asia, where Herod had in the meantime married Mariamne, the granddaughter of Hyrcanus, thus becoming a member of the royal family. When both parties in Judaea appealed to Antony, he favored Herod and Phasael. It was no advantage to Herod, for Antigonus called on the aid of the Parthian invaders from Persia, a great menace to Roman power in the East, and paid them money to invade Judah. This they did, and for the time being the Romans were unable to deal with them. They put Antigonus on the throne, who ruled from 40 to 37 B. C. This man, as we have seen, had his name placed on coins.[1]

The position of Herod was desperate and he appealed to Rome for help. There were others who were bargaining with Rome at that time, but in the end Rome ignored them all and appointed Herod as king. It took him three years to overthrow Antigonus and to enter into his possessions, but Antigonus was finally taken prisoner and executed. Thus ended the Hasmonean high-priesthood.

Herod's reign can be summarized in three stages.[2] From 37 to 25 B. C. he had a good deal of strife, with serious domestic trouble, most of which he overcame by executions. When in 31 B. C. Antony

1. See above, p. 248.
2. S. Perowne, *The Life and Times of Herod the Great* (London, 1956).

GREAT
SEA

Tyre

Ptolemais

GALILEE

Caesarea

SAMARIA

Sebaste (Samaria)

Shechem

Alexandrium

Philadelphia

JUDAEA

Jericho

Jerusalem

Bethlehem

Qumran

Hyrcanium

Herodium

Machaerus

Gaza

Hebron

Masada

PALESTINE
in the days of
HEROD

IDUMAEA

was defeated by Augustus, Herod managed to obtain the goodwill of the emperor.

From 25 to 14 B. C. there was peace for the most part, during which Herod's domains were greatly enlarged as a reward for loyal service to Rome. The last years of his life were again dogged by much strife during which he had several of his sons executed. Finally he contracted a disease and died in 4 B. C. at the age of seventy.

HEROD'S BUILDING ACHIEVEMENTS

Herod was one of the most passionate builders of antiquity. Today there is a great variety of ruined buildings to be found in Palestine which date back to Herod's reign. These remains are naturally of great interest to the archaeologist. They may be classified into four groups, the Temple in Jerusalem, other buildings in Jerusalem, buildings in the rest of his kingdom, and buildings in foreign countries.[3]

Herod made use of a particular type of masonry in his buildings which has become known to the archaeologists as Herodian masonry. It consists of huge blocks of stone, generally oblong, with a smoothed-

3. *Ibid.;* cf. pp. 18-21, 115-142.

The characteristics of Herodian masonry are the immense size of the stone blocks and the so-called marginal draft cut around their facing. This draft is not visible on the stones here that form part of a wall near Hebron. (Photo by the author)

out area cut down as a margin all around the outside of the block. This is referred to technically as a marginal draft. It is quite distinctive and can be easily recognized by the excavator. Much of his building showed a strong Hellenistic influence, and W. F. Albright has described it as the "fullest flowering of the Hellenistic architecture in Palestine."[4]

In the year 19 B. C. Herod decided to rebuild the Temple in Jerusalem. The exact bounds of the Temple as it was when Herod undertook his work are not known. He determined not only to reconstruct the Temple, but also to construct a huge courtyard in which pilgrims could gather. It was necessary to build a platform supported by columns and vaults over a portion of the hill to the southeast where the hill fell away. This area today is called Solomon's Stables, although it was built by Herod. Around the platform a tremendous retaining wall was built, sunk in places into bedrock. As early as 1867 to 1870 Sir Charles Warren excavated

4. W. F. Albright, *Archaeology of Palestine* (London, 1956), p. 154.

The so-called Jewish Wailing Wall in Jerusalem contains Herodian masonry. Here the marginal draft is visible around some of the stones. (Courtesy, The Oriental Institute, The University of Chicago)

around the existing wall down to bedrock. One of the best examples of the typical Herodian masonry is to be seen at the "Wailing Wall," where the huge blocks which make up the wall demonstrate the way in which Herod had his masons do their work. The largest of these blocks is sixteen and a half feet long and thirteen feet wide. In the early part of the last century Edward Robinson found the remains of two arches along the western side which mark the places where bridges connected the western hill to the platform. Unfortunately we have nothing of the Temple left today, although we suspect that if we could clear away the debris under the stone pavements in the old Temple area we might find some traces. We are dependent on the description of Josephus for such details as we have. The Temple was not completed till after Herod's death, as we learn from John 2:20. Possibly the only items we have today coming from the Temple are a complete and a partial inscription in Greek which forbids Gentiles to enter the inner precincts of the Temple. They were allowed to visit the outer court of the Temple, but they might not penetrate into any of the inner courts on pain of death.[5] The inscription discovered by Clermont-Ganneau in 1871 reads:

> No foreigner may enter within the barricade which surrounds the temple and enclosure. Anyone who is caught doing so will have himself to blame for his ensuing death.[6]

There are various structures around Jerusalem that give evidence of Herod's work, such as the wall around the city in which he built towers, some of which he included as part of his own palace. The words of W. F. Albright give a good summary of the position today.

> Almost the whole length of the Herodian First Wall of Jerusalem can be traced and remains of the Herodian masonry identified. The finest example of Herodian masonry with marginal draft, outside of the retaining wall of the Temple enclosure, appears in the so-called Tower of David at the Jaffa Gate.[7]

There are other traces of Herodian masonry in the heart of the old city and these are important in deciding the position of

---

5. F. F. Bruce, *Commentary on the Book of the Acts* (Grand Rapids, 1954), pp. 433f.

6. Details of the inscription are found in A. Deissmann, *Light from the Ancient East* (London, 1922) p. 80.

7. W. F. Albright, *op. cit.*, p. 154.

the so-called Second Wall of Herod, which protected the exposed northern side of the city. Two positions are advanced, one of which leaves the Church of the Holy Sepulcher outside the wall, and the other of which leaves it inside.[8] If the site of the Church of the Holy Sepulcher is the authentic site of Calvary, this wall should allow of its being outside the city proper of Herod's day. The matter is by no means settled.

Herod also built a fortress at the northern end of the Temple and named it the Tower of Antonia, after the Roman Antony. This was later to be used by Pilate as his Praetorium. It has been excavated in part in recent years, and a remarkable picture of the area has been brought to light. It contained the Gabbatha, the pavement which formed Pilate's Hall of Judgment, from which Christ was led to the cross (John 19:13).[9] This fortress first served as Herod's palace, but later he built a new palace to the west, referred to briefly already. On the north side were three towers: Hippicus, named after a friend; Phasael, after his brother; and Mariamne, after his wife. South of these lay the main palace. Of all these, little now remains, for they were destroyed by Titus at the fall of Jerusalem in A. D. 70. However, the so-called Tower of David probably preserves in its substructure part of the fortress of Phasael.[10] It is possible that part of Mariamne was discovered when an Anglican church was being built in 1901, and traces of Hippicus during the excavations of C. N. Johns between 1937 and 1948.

Of the buildings of Herod in other places in his kingdom we have today a great variety of remains available for study. One of the closest to Jerusalem was built about two miles away from the old Biblical Jericho, at the place where the Wadi Qilt opens out onto the plain. A good water supply from springs in the wadi made the place a delight. Some excavation has gone on in this area and it is possible that the work of the American Schools here in 1949 and 1950 uncovered part of a building of Herod's time, although it had been reused and extended by the later Arabs.[11] The exact nature of the original building is not easy to decide, although it may have been a palace or a large dwelling.

8. G. E. Wright and F. V. Filson, *Westminster Historical Atlas* (London, 1953), p. 99 and Plate XVII, c. See below, pp. 347f.
9. W. F. Albright, *op. cit.*, pp. 244-246. See below, pp. 345f.
10. *Ibid.*, p. 154.
11. *BASOR* (Dec., 1950, Oct., 1951).

But Jericho was not remote enough for Herod in his solitary moods, so he restored and re-equipped the fortress of Alexandrium, Hyrcania, Machaerus, and Masada. These were on high inaccessible peaks, Alexandrium high above the Jordan valley in central Palestine, Masada on the west of the Dead Sea, and Machaerus to the east, both high up and difficult to reach. More recently Masada has been excavated in part, with some striking results.[12] There was beauty here in the columns and general architecture. Great cisterns, storage space for food, and other remarkable features provided surprises for the excavators. There is abundant material for excavation in these fortresses as most of them have not been touched.

One of Herod's strangest structures was the Herodium, just south of Bethlehem, where he had an artificial top put on a hill and built there a castle which was reached by two hundred steps cut in the side of the hill. The ruins at the top are still to be seen, and traces of the stairway may still be detected on the side of the hill.

12. H. Avi Yonah and others, "The Archaeological Survey of Masada 1955-1956," *IEJ*, Vol. 7, No. 1, pp. 1-60.

Some of Herod's palaces were restored and re-equipped fortresses, one of which was located at Masada, west of the Dead Sea, built on an inaccessible rock. Part of the ruins can be seen atop this rock and extending to the left edge of it. The white ridge in the center of the photo is a Roman siege dam. (Courtesy, Israel Office of Information)

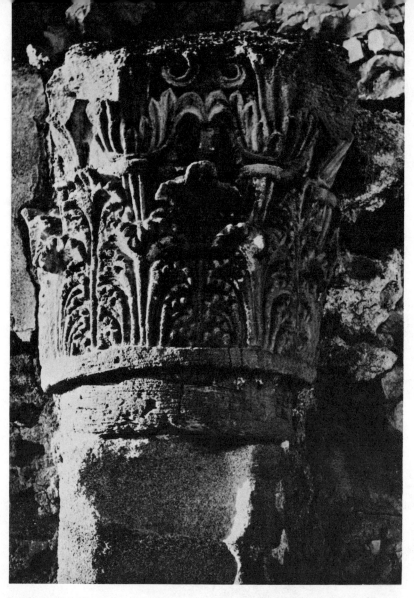

On the credit side of Herod's ill-reputed personality was his love for art, evidences of which are found in the ruins of his palaces. This photo shows a Corinthian capital found in the ruins at Masada. (Courtesy, Israel Office of Information)

Herod's work at Samaria must have been among his best. In 27 B. C. he undertook extensive work there. He first of all provided a new city wall, two and a half miles long, with towers at intervals. The chief gateway is still to be seen in ruins, with the two towers on either side. Herod called the new town Sebaste, the Greek name for Augustus, the emperor of the day, to whom this work was dedicated. Inside the wall Herod undertook the building of a magnificent temple in honor of Augustus. Built over earlier Israelite structures, it was about 225 feet square and stood on a platform (podium) that was approached by a fine flight of stairs. Today the ruins are the most imposing of all those to be seen in Samaria. The temple was high enough for one to view the Mediterranean Sea on a fine day. But there are other remains of interest in Samaria, such as the stadium, built at the edge of the valley that runs to the north of the town, and enclosed by walls. It was 638 feet long and 190 feet across. Traces of the forum are also to be seen in the heart of the town to the east of the temple.

Samaria retains many evidences of Herod's building activities in the ruins that are still visible today. The picture shows the main gateway with the two elegant towers. The marginal draft on the stones to the right of the human figure are discernible (The Matson Photo Service)

The town of Caesarea on the coast was another scene of Herodian activity. Here a fine port was constructed during a period of twelve years, from 25 to 13 B. C.[13] A wall, some two hundred feet wide and standing in 120 feet of water, formed the back side of the harbor. It was made of enormous blocks of limestone, some of them fifty feet by ten feet in size, and was furnished with towers here and there. On the shore a town was built with a semicircular wall that enclosed the main public buildings and served to protect them. When Laurence Oliphant visited the area in 1884 he reported that "the old Roman wall could still be traced for a mile and a half enclosing an area strewn with the remains of a theatre, hippodrome, temple, aqueducts and mole."[14] Today this material has largely disappeared, but already steps are being undertaken to excavate Caesarea, both on land and

13. Josephus, *Antiquities*, XV, 9, 6; *Jewish Wars*, I, 21, 5-8.
14. S. Perowne, *op. cit.,* p. 126.

Caesarea is rich in archaeological material dating from Roman times and later. Here the Roman hippodrome is being excavated and restored. (Courtesy, Israel Office of Information)

in the sea.[15] Caesarea, of course, was the place where the Roman governors lived from A. D. 6 to 66. Here, too, Paul was tried before Festus and spent two years in prison. Aerial photography has revealed some important features of this famous town.

Reference may be made finally to Hebron and its surroundings, where there are a number of evidences of Herodian building. In the town itself the present Moslem mosque preserves a very fine example of Herodian masonry. One outer wall is almost completely preserved and gives us an excellent idea of how the exterior of some of Herod's buildings would have appeared. At Ramat el Khalil, two miles to the north of Hebron, there are further examples of splendid Herodian masonry.

15. Brief report in *RB* (April, 1957), pp. 243-246, and various specialized discussions in recent issues of *IEJ*. C. T. Fritsch and I. Ben Dor, "The Link Marine Expedition to Israel, 1960," *BA* (May, 1961), pp. 50-59.

This photo affords a view of the huge moat that has recently been excavated at Caesarea. It was part of the wall that enclosed the port and extended far and deep into the water. (Courtesy, Israel Office of Information)

We shall not deal in detail with the building program of Herod in foreign lands. Among other gifts to foreign peoples we may note that he endowed Ptolemais (Acre) with a gymnasium, Damascus with a gymnasium and a theater, Sidon with a theater, Byblos with new city walls, Beirut with assembly rooms, temples, cloisters, and market place, Latakia with a new water supply, Antioch with a boulevard paved with marble and shaded with cloisters, and other towns with parks. His motive in all these works seems to have been his love for art, which was restricted in Judaea owing to the fact that representations of men and animals were forbidden by the commandments of Moses and, moreover, no inscription could be prepared dedicating an object to a man. Herod wanted to show his gratitude to his friends, too, and there may have been a desire also to commend the Jews in foreign lands. This could be done, he believed, if the ruler of the Jews showed these kindnesses to foreigners.

OTHER ARCHAEOLOGICAL EVIDENCE FROM HEROD'S TIME

The interested student can enlarge his knowledge of the times of Herod in other ways. It is possible, for example, by a visit to the Museum in Jerusalem, to become acquainted with the typical pottery of the times. We have referred to two inscriptions from the Temple, but there are other inscriptions of a secular nature available for study today. Then there is the coinage of the period with a good deal of interesting history preserved in an incidental way. Herod himself issued coins in bronze, with the inscription in Greek, his symbols being the pomegranate and leaves, the tripod and palms, the eagle, the cornucopia, and three ears of barley. He was wise enough to keep human figures off his coins since this would have been a serious offense in the eyes of the Jews.

In the valley to the east of the present wall of Jerusalem are a number of tombs bearing ancient names. An inscription on one of them, known as the tomb of St. James, mentions several members of the priestly order of Bene Hezir (I Chron. 24:15), three of whom seem to have been high priests in the reign of Herod.[16] The "Pyramid of Zacharias" and the "Tomb of Jehoshaphat" belong to the same period, which Professor Albright holds to be the time of Herod.

Outside Judaea there are the important remains of the Nabataeans, many of which were standing in the days of Herod, just at the

---

16. W. F. Albright, *op. cit.*, p. 157.

close of the Hasmonean era. We have seen how Herod's father was friendly with these people and indeed Herod spent some time with them in his youth. One of the greatest of the kings of the Nabataeans was Aretas IV, who ruled from about 9 B. C. till A. D. 40. It was he who did a great deal to modernize and adorn Petra, playing a similar role in his country to that of Herod in Judaea. Archaeologists distinguish a classical Nabataean period from the first century B. C. to the time of the Roman occupation in A. D. 106. This was well under way in Herod's day, but detailed discussion lies outside the scope of this book.

With the death of Herod in 4 B. C. we are already at the commencement of New Testament times. Jesus was born at the time of the great census which the emperor ordered (Luke 2:1-3) some time before the death of Herod. In Palestine a new arrangement in government followed quickly, and a somewhat different set of circumstances prevailed. To the discussion of that new environment we now turn.

Herod's palace at Masada had mosaic pavements. It is regrettable that the design of the mosaic shown here has been destroyed and hence we do not know what it represented. (Courtesy, Israel Office of Information)

HISTORY OF NEW TESTAMENT TIMES

W E SHALL FIRST PROVIDE A BRIEF HISTORICAL FRAMEWORK INTO which the events of the New Testament may be fitted and against which the items that have come to light in excavations may be studied. Only in that way can the excavated materials take on their correct meaning and significance. The story will be taken up to the time of the collapse of the second Jewish revolt in A.D. 135. For ease of presentation we shall break the period into two sections, the first up to the death of Emperor Claudius in 54 B.C.. and the second from the accession of Nero to the death of Hadrian.

THE HISTORY OF PALESTINE FROM 4 B.C. TO A.D. 54

When Herod died in 4 B.C., serious problems arose. In his will he had indicated that he wished his son Archelaus to be king in his place. But the people of Palestine had grown weary of the cruelties of Herod. Even before Archelaus visited Rome to have his appointment confirmed, a revolt had to be quelled with some degree of cruelty. Further, there were two other sons of Herod who might press

Illustration on page 288: *Ruins of a Roman temple in present-day Baalbek in Lebanon, the ancient city of Heliopolis, dating from the first century A.D.* (Courtesy, UNESCO/P.A. Pittet/1961)

Herod the Great was king of Judaea at the time of Christ's birth. This bronze coin of Herod dates from this period. The representation to the right may be an incense altar or a headdress between two palm branches. (Courtesy, The British Museum)

their claims to the succession.[1] In addition, the Jews of Palestine were asking that none of the sons of Herod should be king. The case needed wise handling and, after deliberation, Augustus decided to divide the domains of Herod into three, and to place one son over each part. Herod Archelaus was given the title Ethnarch and allowed to rule Samaria, Judaea, and the northern part of Idumaea; Herod Antipas was given Galilee and Peraea; and Herod Philip the area east and northeast of Jordan from the Yarmuk River to Mount Hermon. Thus it came about that in 4 B. C. Palestine had three Herods in place of one.[2] This arrangement continued in the case of Antipas and Philip for the rest of the reign of Augustus, that is, till A. D. 14, and for over twenty years after. In the case of Archelaus, however, a change was made after ten years because he offended the Jews greatly. He divorced his wife and married a woman who had been married twice before, undertook an extravagant building program, and in many other ways created dissatisfaction so that Augustus deemed it wise to remove him. We meet him in the gospel story on the occasion when Joseph and Mary and the child Jesus returned from Egypt. Discovering that Archelaus was ruling, they preferred to go on to Galilee rather than to remain in Judaea (Matt. 2:22).

In place of Archelaus the emperor appointed a Roman procurator who was directly responsible to the emperor himself, but dependent on the governor of Syria for military help and general supervision. Fourteen of these procurators are known for the period up to the fall of Jerusalem in A. D. 70, and three of them are of special interest to readers of the New Testament: Pontius Pilate (A. D. 26-36), Antonius Felix (A. D. 52-59 or 60), and Porcius Festus (A. D. 60-62).

In Roman politics the great Augustus died in A. D. 14 and was succeeded by his adopted son Tiberius, who was to rule till A. D. 37.

---

1. See genealogical table, p. 444.
2. See map, pp. 368, 369.

The "penny" brought to Christ by the chief priests and scribes in an attempt to trap Him was the silver denarius of Tiberius. The enlargement of this coin shows its obverse with "the image and superscription" of Tiberius, while the reverse shows Livia as Pax seated and holding a scepter and branch. (Courtesy, The British Museum)

This emperor was ruling during the period that Jesus was preaching in Palestine and at the time of His crucifixion. It was his "image and superscription" that appeared on the coin given to Jesus that day when the Herodians sought to trap Him (Matt. 22:20). Tiberius was never a popular man and ended life full of suspicion and cruelty. His successor was Gaius Caligula (A. D. 37-41), an amiable man, who won great public support at the start of his reign by granting many concessions to all sorts of people. Very soon, however, he began to show signs of mental disorder and insisted on being worshipped as a god. On one occasion, when Herod Agrippa was visiting Alexandria, some of the citizens tried to compel the Jews to worship the image of Caligula. The Jews appealed to the emperor, but his reply was to order his Syrian representative to set up his statue in the Temple in Jerusalem. The legate delayed to do so, and only the earnest pleas of Agrippa, followed by the death of Caligula soon after, prevented an ugly situation. At the last Caligula was quite mad and given up to all manner of excesses and extravagances. He was finally assassinated by a guard of the palace and was succeeded by Claudius (A. D. 41-54).

What was happening in Palestine in these years? Judaea was governed by the procurators, Coponius (A. D. 6-10), Ambivius (A. D. 10-13), Annius Rufus (A. D. 13-15), Valerius Gratus (A. D. 15-26), Pontius Pilate (A. D. 26-36), Marcellus (A. D. 36-38), Maryllus (A. D. 38-44). It was under Pontius Pilate that Jesus Christ was crucified. In the northeast, Philip ruled as tetrarch till A. D. 34. His subjects were a mixed lot, largely Greek and Syrian, with a rather small Jewish population. We have every reason to believe that Philip was a good ruler — wise, conscientious, and just. Like the other Herods, he was a builder and is remembered best in this regard for the two towns of Caesarea Philippi and Julias. The first of these (Matt. 16:13, Mark

8:27) was built on the site of the ancient Panias at the source of the Jordan River, and the other on the shores of Galilee close to the older town of Bethsaida. This latter town he called Julias, after the daughter of the Emperor Augustus.[3] It is the old town of Bethsaida that is known so well in the Gospels (Mark 6:45). Philip himself is mentioned only once in the New Testament in Luke 3:1. He died in A. D. 34 and his tetrarchy was placed under the governor of Syria until A. D. 37, when it was given by Emperor Caligula to Herod Agrippa I, the extravagant grandson of Herod the Great, about whom we shall comment briefly below.

The third son of Herod the Great, Herod Antipas, features a good deal in the New Testament. He was given the title of Tetrarch of Galilee and Peraea (Luke 3:1), two areas which were separated by the Jordan River (see map, pp. 368, 369). Peraea lay to the east of Jordan, and Galilee to the west of the lake of the same name. The special area of the Decapolis separated the two parts of his domain but was not under his control. It would seem that of the two parts, by far the less important and the less populated was Peraea, where Machaerus, the strong fortress of Herod the Great, was situated. It was here

3. See below, pp. 352f.

Archaeologists and visitors at the site of excavation at Ramat-Rahel near Bethlehem. (Courtesy, Israel Office of Information)

that John the Baptist was executed, according to Josephus.[4] But the main interest for us lies in the area of Galilee where Tiberias, the capital of Antipas, was situated and where the town of Nazareth was to be found. The first capital of Antipas was at Sepphoris, just to the north of Nazareth. This town was ruthlessly destroyed by the Romans in A. D. 6 following a rebellion, after which Antipas decided to move to a new site on the lake. But the new capital was never popular with the Jews because it was built on the site of a cemetery.

We know Herod Antipas, "that fox" (Luke 13:32), best in the New Testament for his murder of John the Baptist and for his association with Pilate in the crucifixion of Jesus (Luke 23:1-12). His marriage arrangements were not savory, for he married the daughter of the Nabataean king and then divorced her to marry Herodias, the wife of his brother. This woman and her daughter Salome joined him at Tiberias, and on one occasion, when John the Baptist rebuked him for his wrong, he cast John into prison. Subsequently, Antipas was induced by his wife and daughter to kill John. The story is given in some detail in the Gospels (Matt. 14:1-12, Mark 6:14-29, Luke 9:7-9). The scandalous infidelity of Herod Antipas towards his wife had serious consequences, for not only did it involve him in a war with the offended Nabataean king, but when Caligula became emperor he deposed Antipas and banished him to Gaul, giving his kingdom to the brother of Herodias, who now became Herod Agrippa I. Thus by the year A. D. 41, the grandson of Herod the Great became king over all the domains once ruled by his grandfather, as well as over some additional areas to the north of Mount Hermon.

Herod Agrippa I was the son of Aristobolus, one of the lesser sons of Herod the Great. Aristobolus had married his cousin Bernice, the daughter of Herod's sister Salome. So Agrippa I was closely linked into the Herodian family tree. He was educated in Rome, and in A. D. 23 returned to occupy a post under Antipas. He soon quarreled with him and fled to Antioch where he had a dispute with the governor and finally returned to Rome where he became tutor to the grandson of Emperor Tiberius and also a warm friend of Caligula. He soon found himself in prison for expressing too loudly the wish that Tiberius might die so that Caligula could become emperor. When the emperor died in A. D. 37, his friend Caligula, now the

---

4. Josephus, *Antiquities,* XVIII, v, 2.

occupant of the imperial throne, released him and appointed him king of the former tetrarchy of Philip, which for three years had been under the care of the governor of Syria. To this area was added the teritory of Abilene to the north of Mount Hermon. As we have seen, Agrippa was able to restrain Caligula from offending the Jews by setting up his image in the Temple in Jerusalem. When Herodias, Agrippa's sister, the wife of Herod Antipas, saw the honors bestowed by Caligula on her brother, she planned to gain some for her husband and urged him to ask the emperor to grant him the title of king. Accusations of plotting were laid by the representatives of Agrippa, and Antipas was banished and his domain added to those of Agrippa in A. D. 39. The final stage in Agrippa's progress towards the possession of the domains of his grandfather came when, following the assassination of Caligula, he supported the candidature of Claudius as the new emperor. When this came about and things settled down, Claudius confirmed all the other appointments which Agrippa filled, and then added to his domains Judaea and Samaria.

Agrippa took up his residence in Jerusalem and worshipped regularly at the Temple, suppressing all attempts to introduce pagan images or practices into the synagogues. As a strict Jew he soon came into conflict with the Christian Church, then in its infancy, and executed James and imprisoned Peter (Acts 12:2-4). When Peter escaped by divine intervention, Herod ordered the execution of the guards (vv. 11-19). He did not reign long over his large kingdom and met his death at Caesarea on the coast where he had gone to attend games in honor of the emperor. As he sat there in all the splendor of his royal garments, flatterers declared that he was a god. He died shortly afterwards (A. D. 44). The story in Acts 12:21-23, which is closely paralleled by that in Josephus, suggests that his death was an exceedingly painful one.[5]

His son Herod Agrippa II was only seventeen at the time and was regarded as too young to take over the responsible task of governing so great an area. Palestine returned to the control of the procurators. Six years later, in A. D. 50, following the death of his uncle, the king of Chalcis, a territory to the north of Abilene, the young Agrippa became the new king. This office carried with it the right to appoint the high priest of the Temple in Jerusalem. A few years later Agrippa II was transferred to the former territory

5. Josephus, *op. cit.*, XIX, viii, 2.

of Philip and ruled over lands to the east and northeast of Galilee, as well as the area of Abilene. His domains were enlarged still further by Emperor Nero in A. D. 54 by the addition of other areas in the region of Galilee and some areas in Peraea. Agrippa retained his position till his death, towards the close of the first century.

Emperor Claudius ruled till A. D. 54. His reign was significant for the Christian Church, for it was really under his rule that the great period of missionary expansion in the early Church began, with the missionary journeys of Paul as a central feature. Under Claudius, Jews were persecuted in Rome because of riots that broke out there "at the instigation of one Chrestus." Possibly Chrestus was the leader of the riots, but many commentators are convinced that the riot was caused by Jews who objected to the preaching of early Christian missionaries in Rome.[6] In any case, the Jews were expelled, and we learn from Acts 18:2 that among these were Priscilla and Aquila, who were to become pillars of the church in Ephesus.

From A.D. 54 to A.D. 138

Claudius was succeeded by Nero (A. D. 54-68), under whom Christian expansion continued. Later there was some persecution in Rome at least, when Nero laid the blame for the great fire at the door of the Christians. It was during his reign that Paul had his trials in Palestine under the procurators Felix and Festus, and finally met his death in Rome, probably in A. D. 67.

After Nero was slain at his own request, in order to avoid capture by the army, there were three short reigns in the years A. D. 68-69, namely, those of Galba, Otho, and Vitellus. Then Vespasian became emperor and ruled from A. D. 69 to 79. At the time of his appointment he was in Palestine quelling the Jewish insurrection that had broken out in A. D. 66. When the army heard of the death of Nero, they proclaimed Vespasian emperor, and he had to hasten back from Palestine to Rome to secure his emperorship. The task in Palestine was left to his son Titus who, after some delay, took Jerusalem in A. D. 70 but was cleaning up pockets of resistance in the country areas till A. D. 73. He eventually succeeded his father but had only a short reign of just over two years (A. D. 79-81). The remaining emperors that interest us are Domitian (A.D.

6. F. F. Bruce, *The Book of Acts* (Grand Rapids, 1954), p. 368.

Obverse (left) and reverse (right) of the silver tetradrachm of Bar Kochba, the leader of the second Jewish revolt. The obverse bears the name "Simeon," and the reverse has "Deliverance of Jerusalem" inscribed on it. (Courtesy, The British Museum)

81-96), Nerva (A. D. 96-98), Trajan (A. D. 98-117), and Hadrian (A. D. 117-138). It was under this last-named emperor that the second Jewish revolt broke out in A. D. 132, led by Ben Kosebah (Bar Kochba).

Palestine was ruled by the procurators from A. D. 44 onwards. Things moved along reasonably well at first, and Cuspius Fadus (A. D. 44 to perhaps 46) and Tiberius Alexander (perhaps A. D. 46-48) had no serious troubles. But from then on the Jews became increasingly troublesome, and under Cumanus (A. D. 48-52) riots broke out in Jerusalem and Samaria. Felix (A. D. 52-60), who had married Drusilla, the sister of Agrippa II, was suspicious of further troubles, and when Paul was sent to Caesarea by the officer of Jerusalem following a disturbance, Felix retained Paul in custody (Acts 21:27–24:27). He was succeeded in 60 (or perhaps 59) by Porcius Festus before whom Paul made his defense and appealed to Caesar (Acts 25:1-12). The narrative in Acts 25:13-26:32 refers to the occasion when Agrippa II, in company with his sister Bernice, visited Caesarea to welcome Festus to his new office. The new procurator, who found Paul something of a problem, called in Agrippa to advise him. Paul had appealed to Caesar, who at that time was Nero. It was not strange that in the early years of Nero Paul should appeal to him, for in the years A. D. 54-59 his administration was good, at any rate in the provinces, and there was little sign then of the persecution of the later years of his reign. It is clear from the narrative in Acts that Agrippa II, though a faithful Jew outwardly, had little knowledge of the deeper spiritual meaning of the faith he professed.

From the time of Festus the situation in Palestine grew worse. Trouble continued to brew during the procuratorship of Albinus (A. D. 62-64), but in the days of his successor Gessius Florus (A. D. 64-66) the whole thing flared up. At first Herod Agrippa II tried to advise the Jews against the rebellion, and Florus tried to use his power to quell the revolt. The Roman legate in Syria sent troops to assist but,

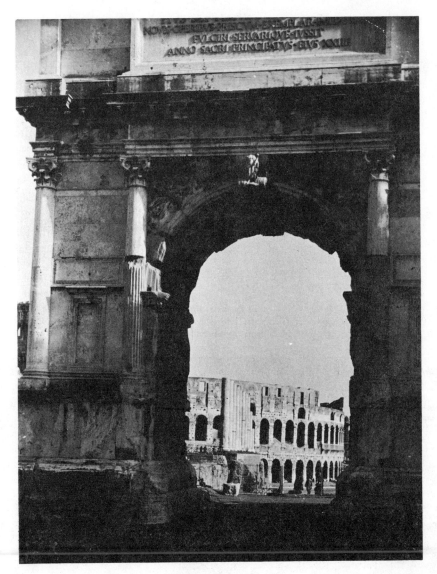

The Arch of Titus in Rome with part of the Colosseum in the background. Titus and his father Vespasian erected this arch in commemoration of the victory over the Jews and the fall of Jerusalem. (Courtesy, Italian State Tourist Office)

after initial success, the Roman contingents were defeated, and the Jews, encouraged by this, rose all over the country. The rebels held several of the strong fortresses built by Herod the Great, such

297

as Herodium, Machaerus, and Masada, but it soon became evident that there was division in their own ranks. The historian Josephus, for example, was sent early to lead the Jews in the Galilee area, but had to compete with a certain John Giscala. When Josephus was captured by the Romans, he became a supporter of the Roman cause and sought to induce his fellows to surrender. Other cases of division in the Jewish ranks are well known.

Emperor Nero sent his general Vespasian to carry out the Roman counter attack, and he was able to subdue the Galilee area by A. D. 67 and then move down into the center and finally overrun Samaria. By A. D. 68 only the area around Jerusalem was still in Jewish hands, apart from a few of the fortresses. Before Vespasian could complete the capture of Jerusalem, Nero had died and Vespasian had been proclaimed emperor by his troops. He did not pursue the subjugation of Palestine till he was secure in his imperial

Inside the Arch of Titus a large panel depicts a triumphal procession of Roman soldiers carrying off the table of shewbread, trumpets, and the seven-branched lampstand from the Temple in Jerusalem. (Courtesy, The Metropolitan Museum of Art)

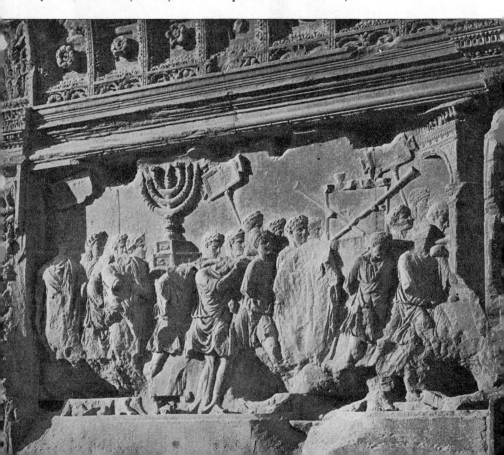

position and then, in A. D. 70, his son Titus took up the task and completed it. He was aided in the latter stages of the war by a considerable amount of quarreling and division among the Jewish leaders in Jerusalem. Once the Holy City fell, this meant the effective end of the struggle and the few remaining outposts were sealed off and finally taken. The stronghold of Masada held out till A. D. 73. Titus commemorated the victory by building an impressive arch in Rome, which is still to be seen. On the inside of this he portrayed his soldiers carrying off sacred vessels from Jerusalem, and the seven-branched candlestick can be easily discerned in the sculptured picture. Jerusalem itself was systematically destroyed and the Temple left in ruins. Archaeological work shows us today just how effective was the destruction of Jewish buildings all over the land.

It was in the wars of these days that the remarkable monastery of the exclusive sect of the Essenes[7] that lived near to the Dead Sea, in the region of the modern village of Qumran, was destroyed. In the panic that attended the approach of the Romans, the members of this community hid their precious documents in caves in the hills about their monastery; and it was here in 1947, and in the following years, that the now famous "Dead Sea Scrolls" were found.

For all practical purposes the Jewish people of Palestine were defeated with the capture of Jerusalem in A. D. 70. But they were a resilient people and were to stage another revolt in the days of Hadrian (A. D. 117-138). Outside Palestine, urged on by some messianic hope, the Jews of Mesopotamia, Cyprus, Egypt, and Cyrene rose in revolt in A. D. 115 in the reign of Emperor Trajan (A. D. 98-117). The uprising was put down with excessive cruelty, and not without much bloodshed on both sides. In Palestine itself, the so-called second Jewish revolt broke out in A. D. 132 and lasted till 135. The leader was a certain Ben Kosebah, formerly known as Bar Kochba, "Son of the Star," who was held by many people to be the Messiah according to Numbers 24:17. Hadrian had issued a decree forbidding circumcision and ordering a temple of Jupiter to be built on the site of the Temple. This was a most grievous offense to the Jews and they rebelled. The revolt was finally quelled, and Hadrian carried out his plan to rebuild Jerusalem as a pagan city, which he called Aelia Capitolina. He forbade the Jews to enter the

---

7. Scholars are more and more inclined to accept the Qumran community as an Essene group, though opinions still vary. Essenes, Zealots, and Pharisees have all been suggested. See above, p. 266.

city at all, on pain of death, and they did not come to Jerusalem again for centuries, at least in any considerable way, although there was a relaxation of the decree sometime later. But in point of fact, the Jews did not again exercise any sort of political control over this land till the setting up of the modern state of Israel in very recent years. Reference has already been made to the valuable documents from the days of Bar Kochba, comprising some actual letters from this leader of the Jews, and some others from his secretaries and scribes.[8] One of the Aramaic contracts was dated "in the third year of the liberation of Israel by the hand of Simeon Ben Kosebah."

Other evidence from the days of the Jewish revolt is to be found on the coins of the Jews. Both in the revolt of A. D. 66-70 and in that of A. D. 132-135, the independent coins that were struck refer to the "Year of Redemption." It was not to be redemption but, rather, defeat and scattering. For the present purpose we must conclude our story at A. D. 135.

8. See above, p. 256

Seventeen:

ARCHAEOLOGY AND
THE ROMAN OCCUPATION OF PALESTINE

T HE NEW TESTAMENT STORY IS SET IN THE CONTEXT OF THE Roman world of the first century A. D. An understanding of that world is necessary for an appreciation of the meaning of the New Testament writings, for these are full of allusions, not only to the history, but also to the customs and culture of the times. The most important influence in our period is the Roman one, and we shall attempt in this chapter to present several important aspects of that culture, especially as it is revealed by the excavations. But there were other influences at work in the first century, some of which had been effective for several centuries, and we should mention these briefly by way of introduction.

SOME CULTURAL ELEMENTS IN THE BACKGROUND OF
NEW TESTAMENT PALESTINE

When the Roman armies entered Palestine in 63 B. C. and introduced Roman rule into the land, they found a people there who had been subjected to a wide variety of influences through the centuries past.

301

Quite basic in the life and outlook of the Jews was their own faith, which by New Testament times found expression in two ways. They were still able to worship in the Temple with the full range of priestly services, sacrifices, and rituals which had long been associated with their religion. Alongside the Temple worship was the worship in the synagogues, which was based rather on the teaching of the law, and where no sacrifice was offered. A Jew with any degree of piety at all was given careful instruction in his faith from boyhood, and the worship of the one true God was fundamental to his whole view of life. Any thought of polytheism or of idol worship was anathema to him, and while some Jews are known to have been careless in their observance of the requirements of the law, the majority were rigid in their ways and were offended by any suggestion of introducing pagan procedures or compromise of any sort.

Roman columns found in Ashkelon have been erected in the Antiquities Park of the present-day town. (Courtesy, Israel Office of Information)

A second element, and in many ways one of the strongest, is the Greek. We have seen in an earlier chapter that Greek influence in Palestine began as early as the fifth century B. C.,[1] and well before the Christian era Greek motifs in architecture and art were widespread in Palestine. With the coming of the Romans this did not die, for they, too, owed much to the Greeks. As we have seen, the days of Herod the Great, a lover of Greek culture, witnessed "the fullest flowering of Hellenistic architecture in Palestine."[2] The remarkable tombs opposite the southern end of the Temple area on the east side of the brook Kedron are now all assigned to the first century B. C., when Greek influence was strong. In addition, the Greek language was well known in the commercial world, and although the ordinary people of Palestine spoke Aramaic, Greek was the *lingua franca* of the East and there would be many in Palestine who knew the language. Greek literature and Greek thought, too, had left their mark on some of the more educated groups.

Reference should also be made in passing to cultural influences from further east. The Persians, and later the Parthians, had made some impact on the culture of Palestine over the years in art, architecture, thought, and religion. The worship of the god Mithras came from lands to the east of Palestine and in due course became popular among the Roman soldiers.

By the first century A. D., however, a culture had emerged that we now distinguish as Graeco-Roman. It took over certain elements from the past and combined these with new tendencies. Building showed points of comparison with Roman architecture while preserving elements of Greek influence. Among these was a fine large building at Jericho which was clearly Roman, as shown by its ruins, although in the structures behind the facade there were discernible some Greek influences. The specifically Roman aspects of this composite culture may be noted in a wide variety of objects used in everyday life such as pottery pieces of various kinds, whether for domestic or for artistic purposes, glass, metal objects, mosaics, coins, and the like. These can be compared with material found in other contexts outside Palestine, and the Roman character demonstrated. In addition to these material items we know that there were influences in law and government, and to some slight extent in language.

1. See above, p. 204.
2. W. F. Albright, *Archaeology of Palestine* (London, 1956), p. 154. See above, pp. 275f.

There are, for example, a goodly number of Latin inscriptions which show that for certain official purposes this language was used.

It is not our purpose in this book to follow up all these cultural influences, but to contentrate on the clearly Roman material, which was so much a part of the daily life of the people in the first century when the Christian Church was born.

COINAGE OF THE PERIOD 4 B.C. TO A.D. 135

Coins play a very important part in dating the material remains that come to light in an excavation, but they tell us a great deal more besides, as we shall see. Today there is a surprising variety of coins available for the student of the New Testament.[3] Commencing with the Maccabaean rulers, we have a range extending through to the second Jewish revolt of A. D. 132 to 135, and including coins of Jewish rulers, procurators, emperors, and even of the free cities in the general area of Palestine.

Roman coinage was introduced into Palestine by Pompey in 63 B. C., but Greek or Hellenistic coinage, which had been in use over the years, persisted. In addition, the Jews themselves minted their own coins, so that the coin picture is a complex one. In the New Testament we have references to coins that were originally Greek and to others that were Roman. The English translation is not always helpful and the same word is used at times for different coins. Some attempt to preserve the Greek or Roman names seems to be warranted.

There are five pieces of money of Greek origin referred to in the Gospels. Two of these, the "talent" and the "pound" or *mina*, were really weights of silver, although golden "talents" and *minas* were known in the world of that time. The talent (Matt. 18:24, 25:15-30) was worth about 960 dollars. The "pound" or *mina*, a silver weight (Luke 19:13f.), was worth about sixteen dollars. The other three pieces were definite coins. One, called the "silver piece" in the New Testament, was really the silver *drachma* and was worth about sixteen cents (Luke 15:8, 9). Then there were the "tribute money" or *didrachma*, a silver coin worth about thirty-two cents (Matt. 17:24), and the "piece of money" or *stater*, the silver *tetradrachm*, worth about sixty-four cents (Matt. 17:27).

---

3. Good reviews are obtainable in Florence A. Banks, *Coins of Bible Days* (New York, 1955); A. Kindler, *Antiquity and Survival* (Jerusalem, 1957), Vol. II, pp. 225f.

Detail of sculpture found in the Roman ruins at Baalbek, Lebanon. This maritime scene apparently is a representation of Neptune and his wife Salacia, deities of the sea. (Courtesy, UNESCO/P.A. Pittet/1961)

In addition to these coins there were others of Roman notation, the "penny" or *denarius*, a silver coin worth about twenty cents (Matt. 18:28; 20:2, 9, 10, 13; etc.), the "farthing" or *quadrans*, a bronze coin worth a fraction of a cent (Matt. 5:26), and another coin called a "farthing" in the English version of the New Testament but known to the Romans as the *as* or *assarion* (Matt. 10:29, Luke 12:6). Its value was about one and one-fourth cent. Finally there was the tiny bronze coin, the "mite" or *lepton* (Mark 12:42), worth only a small fraction of one cent, and originally a non-Roman coin. (These calculations are based on the estimates of G. A. Barrois in Volume I of *The Interpreter's Bible* [pp. 157f.]).

The Romans reserved the right to mine silver coinage but allowed the local mints to make bronze coins. In the excavations we find coins of both types but naturally far more bronze coins than silver ones. There were Roman bronze coins too, but the great majority of the bronze coins found are local.

Strictly, the Roman silver coins constituted Judaea's principal monetary standard, and among these the silver denarius, coined in Rome, was the best known. It was the silver denarius of Tiberius Caesar that Jesus held in His hand on the day when the Herodians sought to trap Him (Matt. 22:19-21). This coin carried the head and superscription of the emperor, which read, "TI. CAESAR DIVI AVG. F. AVGVSTVS" on the side where the head of the emperor was impressed, and on the other side "PONTIF. MAXIM." In translation this means, "Tiberius Caesar, Augustus, Son of Divine Augustus," and "Pontifex Maximus." The Jews were never happy about the emperor worship that the Romans practiced and stubbornly resisted the growing cult of the emperor. For official purposes the Jews were forced, of necessity, to use the coins of Augustus as well as those of Tiberius, his stepson, who was identified as "son of the deified Augustus." So the coin that the Herodians handed to Jesus was full of meaning for them and for Him. "Whose is this image and superscription?" He asked. They replied, "Caesar's." To this He replied, "Render therefore unto Caesar the things which are Caesar's; and unto God the things that are God's," by which He indicated that what was stamped with man's image belonged to man, especially if man made a special claim to it as did Tiberius. This did not, however, prevent men from giving to God the things that were His.

One of the Roman bronze coins was the *dupondius*, which pictured Livia, the wife of Augustus, who was reputed to be a woman of great beauty. She divorced her first husband in order to marry Augustus. She had two sons by her first marriage, one of whom was to become the next emperor. There was something uncanny about the way "fate" disposed of the relatives of Augustus in order to make the succession of Tiberius possible, and many suspected the beautiful Livia without being able to prove anything. We have the picture of this notorious woman today, as well as that of her illustrious husband, on the coins of the time. The handsome head of Augustus reminds us of the Caesar in whose reign "there went out a decree that all the world should be taxed" (Luke 2:1). It was this decree that brought Joseph and Mary to Bethlehem where Jesus was to be born.[4]

The locally minted coins that interest us may be divided into three groups: (a) those of Herod and his descendants, (b) those of

4. See discussion below, pp. 364f.

the procurators, and (c) those from the free cities that evidently held a charter to mint coins.

The coins of Herod the Great were still in use at the beginning of our period. He was the first of the Jewish rulers to drop Hebrew from the inscriptions on the coins and to use Greek. In general, he did not provoke the Jews by using symbols on his coins that would offend them by defying the second commandment, and he confined himself to such symbols as the pomegranate and leaves, the tiara and palm leaves, and the tripod and palm leaves, although on one of his small coins he did make use of an eagle. The normal inscription on the face (obverse) of the coin was "King Herod." His sons Herod Archelaus (4 B. C. to A. D. 6) and Herod Antipas (4 B. C. to A. D. 39) followed the example of their father and used neutral symbols, but Herod Philip (4 B. C. to A. D. 34) minted coins that were completely pagan in character and carried on them the image of the emperor on one side, and such symbols as a temple on the other. His domains were, of course, predominantly Greek, and this would account for his use of pagan symbols.

With the accession of Agrippa I to the throne in A. D. 37 the people of Judaea, after some thirty years of rule by procurators, returned to a king of their own race. He used non-Jewish symbols on the coins, apparently without any embarrassment, and quite freely represented the head of the emperor on the obverse, and on the reverse (the secondary side of the coin) such items as the Greek city goddess, pagan temples, the king and his chariot, a man with a scroll, the king's son and his horse, and the king offering sacrifice. One of his coins carried the words, "King Agrippa the Great, Lover of Caesar" on one side, and on the other, the city goddess holding a cornucopia and leaning on the rudder of a boat. The inscription on the reverse was, "Caesarea on the Sea." Such coins as these must have caused offense to pious Jews. For us their great value lies in the fact that they preserve the picture of Agrippa. In defense of his practice, it should be said that his coins were probably intended for the use of the pagan population in his domains, for he did issue other coins with neutral symbols such as the umbrella and ears of barley, meant to emphasize the dignity of the kingdom and the prosperity of his domains.

Herod Agrippa II (A. D. 50 to about A. D. 100) issued many coins during his long reign of which there are very many in existence today. On some of his early coins he left his portrait as a young man, but on others he placed the bust of a goddess. One of his

In A.D. 79 an unprecedented eruption of Mount Vesu ius buried the two cities Pompeii and Herculaneum under volcanic ashes that attained an average thickness of about twenty feet, although in places they were sixty-five feet deep. Extended excavations have brought many fine Roman buildings and statuary to light. This illustration shows the "house of the deer" in Herculaneum. (Courtesy, Italian State Tourist Office)

coins was a victory coin, issued after the victory of Rome over the Jews in A. D. 70, and shows Agrippa as a vassal king subordinate to the Romans. It had a humiliating intention, no doubt, and was probably issued under instruction from the Romans.

The coins of the procurators from A. D. 6 onwards in Judaea are well represented. In general these men did not offend the Jews and confined themselves to neutral symbols such as the ear of barley, the palm tree, the olive branch and cornucopia, the grape leaf and tendril, and so on. Only the fifth procurator, Pontius Pilate. offended the Jews with pagan symbols on the coins. All these procurators' coins were really imperial coins although they were struck locally, and inscriptions on them referred to the emperor or to his family. No reference to the procurator is made on the coins, and they can be assigned to the year of a given procurator only on the basis of dating material that refers to the emperors. Some of the best known of these coins come from the days of Coponius (A. D. 6-9), Valerius (A. D. 15-26), Pilate (A. D. 26-36), and Felix (A. D. 52-59). Typical of the dating material to be found on the face of these coins is that on a coin of Pilate, a tiny *lepton* in fact, which reads "Tiberius Caesar" on the obverse and carries the symbol of an augur's wand, and on the reverse has a wreath surrounding the date LIZ, which

An excavated house in Pompeii that belonged to the Vetii family, showing the main room and the court. (Courtesy, Italian Information Center)

indicates Year 17 of this emperor, that is, A. D. 30-31.[5] The symbol used in this case was one of those which were offensive to the Jews because augury was forbidden among them (Deut. 18:10f.).

We need not enter into details about the coins from the independent cities. These have been found from a wide variety of places such as Ascalon, Antioch, Tyre, Damascus, Sidon, Byblos, Gadara, Seleucia, Berytus (Beirut), Gaza, Cyprus, and Caesarea.

The tiny coin, the *lepton*, is of special interest to the Bible reader. It was first minted, it seems, in the days of the Maccabees and was worth about one-four-hundredth part of a shekel. Since it was so tiny and worth so little, great care was not taken in stamping it out, and the pattern is quite often incomplete, although there are enough of these coins known to be able to arrive at the typical patterns on them. Some even had an inscription. These tiny coins are known for the reign of Herod the Great, Herod Archelaus, Procurator Valerius, and Procurator Pilate. They must have been made in very great numbers, for even today they are to be found in great quantity in excavations. It was two of these coins that the widow threw into the box in the story in Mark 12:41-44, for which she

5. L=year (Egyptian); I=10 in Greek notation; Z=7 in Greek notation.

earned the praise of the Lord Jesus. The same coin featured also in His remarks to the hypocrites when He made reference to the hard judge who would exact the "very last mite" in his judgment (Luke 12:58f.).

We have referred to the unfortunate translations of the Greek words for coins in the New Testament. Some writers have urged that we ought to translate these terms by English words that bear a close resemblance to the Greek, or even by transliterations. Thus for "penny" we might use *denarius,* for "piece of silver" the correct word, either *stater* or *drachma,* and for "farthing" either *assarion* or *quadrans.* At times, however, there is not much help even in the Greek form of the word, as, for example, in the narrative where we learn of the bribe paid to the Roman soldiers to keep them quiet after the resurrection. This was to be "large money" (Matt. 28:12). Does this mean large in amount, or large in size of the coins? If the latter, then perhaps we should think in terms of one of the big silver coins such as the *tetradrachm.*[6] The thirty pieces of silver that were taken by Judas were of the same kind (Matt. 27:5). Their total value in modern currency could hardly be more than a few pounds, small reward for treachery so base and so far-reaching.

The special coins which the Jews struck at the time of their two revolts in A. D. 66-70 and A. D. 132-135 are of some interest. Fully persuaded that the days of deliverance or redemption had come, they minted shekels and half-shekels in silver, as well as other coins in bronze, which told of their hopes. The symbols were all neutral and included palm trees, citrons, baskets, bundles of twigs, the vine and grape, a chalice, and so on. Typical of the coins issued at the time of the first revolt was the silver shekel that carried on the obverse a chalice and the words in ancient Hebrew script, "Shekel of Israel, I," and on the reverse, "Jerusalem Holy," written around three pomgranates. There was also a bronze coin which bore on its face a

6. Florence A. Banks, *op. cit.,* chap. 8, p. 89f.

Silver "shekel of Israel, Year 1" (obverse), dating from the time of the first Jewish revolt. On the reverse is inscribed, "Jerusalem the Holy." (Courtesy, The British Museum)

bundle of twigs between two citrons and the words, "Year 4," while on the back was a chalice and the words, "For the Redemption of Zion." Four years can be distinguished on these coins, which would be the years A. D. 66 to 70. The Jews were defeated, as we know, and the Romans commemorated their victory by a special series of coins which we now call the *Judaea Capta* coins. They were struck in Rome, as the letters "S. C."("with the consent of the Senate") indicate, and show the head of Emperor Vespasian surrounded by his titles on the obverse, and on the reverse a woman, representing Judaea, sitting under a palm tree with·a Roman soldier on guard over her. The caption reads, *Judaea Capta*. It was a humiliating experience and resulted in the placing of a heavy tax on the Jews for some years. When eventually this was eased in the days of Emperor Nerva (A.D. 96-98), another bronze coin was struck by the Romans.

The second Jewish revolt of A. D. 132-135 produced a second lot of coins rather like those of the first revolt. In the early days of the revolt the leader, Ben Kosebah (Bar Kochba) took Roman coins and over-stamped them with his own markings. Later on he issued what has been described as the "finest set of coins ever issued by any Jewish authority."[7] Among these we may refer to the silver *tetradrachm*, with a star above the Temple and the name "Simon" on the face, and a citron and bundle of twigs, with the words, "For the Liberty of Jerusalem" on the back. The silver *denarius* had a wreath and "Simon" on the front, and a jug and palm with the words, "Year 2 of the Liberty of Israel," on the back. Simon is described as "Prince of Israel" on some of the coins. Another name on these coins is "Eleazar the Priest." Romans commemorated the quelling of the revolt in A.D. 135 with the issue of a special coin depicting the emperor with a pair of oxen ploughing the boundaries of a new town. That town was Jerusalem, renamed Colonia Aelia Capitolina, and thenceforth a pagan Roman colony.

It is evident from this brief study of the coins of these years that there is much to be learned from them about the history of the times. But they have a most important part to play also in the dating of the remains found by the excavator; and since they are found by the hundreds, and even thousands, in Palestine, it is obvious that their discovery in an excavation is hailed with enthusiasm by the archaeologist. There are certain limitations in their value for dating, for they often continued in use for many years after the

7. A. Kindler, "Coins as Documents for Israel's Ancient History," *Antiquity and Survival*, II (1957), p. 235.

death of a king. Again, some coins were struck in considerable numbers and would have a better chance of survival than those which had a limited minting. However, where supplementary evidence is available, they are useful for dating. One or two illustrations of their value in dating ancient remains will now be given.

When the large building in Roman Jericho was excavated in 1951, the question of date naturally arose.[8] Coins found in the debris provided helpful clues and enabled the archaeologists to give a range of years during which the site was in use. The report reads as follows:

> The earliest coins found were those of Herod I of which there were eleven. Twenty-seven bore the stamp of Archelaus; six were Herod Agrippa coins; and five were identified tentatively as belonging to one or another of the Procurators. Two of the Archelaus coins were found directly on major walls of the building. The presence of these forty-nine coins, dating from the century covering the last third of the first century B. C. and the first two-thirds of the second century A. D., with the largest number from the time of Archelaus at the midpoint of this span, would seem to point to a major occupation at the time of Christ and perhaps to the construction of the building within this period.[9]

Coins also give the clue to the period of occupation of the Qumran monastery once occupied by the exclusive Jewish sect that awaited the coming of the Messiah. The coin record starts with John Hyrcanus (135-104 B. C.), and continues without a break till Antigonus (40-37 B. C.). There is only one coin from the days of Herod the Great, but the coin story starts again with Archelaus in 4 B. C., and from then on there is a continuous series of coins till about A. D. 68, including six from Archelaus, three from the procurators under Augustus (A. D. 6-14), seven from the procurators under Tiberius (A. D. 14-37), a coin from Tyre dated A. D. 29, twenty-three from Agrippa I (A.D. 37-44), five from the procurators under Nero (A. D. 54-68), and eleven struck by the Jews during the first two years of the war.[10] The record ends in A. D. 68, although there were

---

8. See pp. 324ff.

9. J. B. Pritchard, "The 1951 Campaign at Herodian Jericho," *BASOR* (Oct., 1951), pp. 14f.

10. F. F. Bruce, *Second Thoughts on the Dead Sea Scrolls* (Grand Rapids, 1956), p. 49.

Marble bust of Emperor Titus (Flavius Sabinus Vespasianus), son of Vespasian, whose armies besieged Jerusalem and destroyed it in A.D. 69-70. During his reign occurred the catastrophic destruction of Herculaneum and Pompeii. (Courtesy, The British Museum)

a few coins which represent the occupation of the site by a Roman garrison from A. D. 70 onwards, say from the end of Nero's reign (A. D. 68) to the reign of Titus (A. D. 79-81). A single coin of Agrippa II found outside the building is not very significant, as it might have been dropped there after the destruction of the building. After a gap there are a few coins from the time of the second Jewish revolt.

From this collection we conclude that the monastery at Qumran was founded sometime before 100 B. C., deserted in the days of Herod the Great, occupied again in the days of Archelaus and then on till the defeat of the Jews in A. D. 70, with a short occupation by a

Roman garrison after that, and finally a brief occupation at the time of the second revolt.

A third illustration comes from the fortress of Masada where recent work brought to light two coins of Year 2 and one of Year 4 near the remains of the wall surrounding the fortress. These coins are typical ones of the first Jewish revolt and bear the words, "Freedom of Zion," and, "For the Redemption of Zion." The years in question would be A. D. 67-68 and 69-70, and the fact that they were found at Masada suggests that this fortress was in contact with Jerusalem till quite late. Masada did not fall till A. D. 73, and the Roman legions were evidently not able to prevent the distribution of such coins. L. Kadman has recently written, "There can be no doubt that the three coins of Masada were found on the spot where they had dropped from the hands of the Jewish defenders of the fortress, nearly 1900 years ago."[11]

INSCRIPTIONS AND WRITTEN RECORDS

One of the most important of these is a Greek inscription found by Clermont Ganneau in 1871 and now housed in the Istanbul Museum.[12] It contains seven lines written in Greek capitals and was evidently once placed in the precincts of the Temple to warn Gentiles to keep away from those areas which were reserved for Jews only. One translation of the text reads:

> No Gentile may enter inside the enclosing screen around the Temple. Whoever is caught is alone responsible for the death which follows.

The inscription was found some fifty meters from the Temple area, but it is agreed that it is ancient and must have come from the Temple. It is of special interest in the light of the statement in Acts 21:28 where Paul was accused by the Jews of bringing Greeks into the "holy place":

> *This is the man that teacheth all men everywhere against the people, and the law, and this place; and further brought Greeks also into the temple, and hath polluted this holy place.*

11. L. Kadman, "A Coin Find at Masada," *IEJ*, Vol. 7, No. 1, pp. 61f.
12. W. F. Albright, *Recent Discoveries in Bible Lands* (New York, 1955), p. 112. See also André Parrot, *Le musée du Louvre et la Bible* (Paris, 1957), pp. 142f.

A second fragmentary example of this inscription was found in 1935 in the course of excavations being conducted by the Department of Antiquities of Palestine not far from St. Stephen's Gate, in the midst of debris.[13]

Another inscription of great interest was found by R. Weill in the excavations at the southern end of Ophel in 1913-1914, but not published till 1920. It is part of a synagogue inscription, the oldest yet known in the whole of Palestine and dating from before A. D. 70.[14] The inscription refers to the building of a synagogue by a certain Theodotus. The complete text reads:

> Theodotus, son of Vettenus, priest and synagogue-president, son of a synagogue-president and grandson of a synagogue-president, has built the synagogue for the reading of the Law and the teaching of the commandments and [he has built] the hostelry and the chambers and the cisterns of water in order to provide lodgings for those from abroad who need them — [the synagogue] which his fathers and the elders and Simonides had founded.[15]

It has been argued that the name Vettenus shows that Theodotus was the son or grandson of a Jewish freedman from Italy who had received his name from the family of the Vetteni (gens Vettena or Vettia), a well-known Roman family. It was a common custom for the freed slave to take the family name of his liberator. The original Jew may have been taken captive to Italy in an earlier day, perhaps in the time of Pompey. Interest in the inscription grows when we read in Acts of a synagogue of the freedmen in the time of Stephen, in whose days "there arose certain of the synagogue which is called the synagogue of the Libertines [Freedmen]" (Acts 6:9).

The men of this synagogue were strongly opposed to Stephen and the new faith, as we learn from the narrative in Acts 6. We may conjecture that the synagogue in question was founded some time early in the first century at the time when Christ lived in Nazareth.

13. André Parrot, *ibid.*, p. 144. Also J. H. Iliffe, "The Thanatos Inscription from Herod's Temple," *Quarterly of the Department of Antiquities of Palestine*, VI (1937), pp. 1-3; and *Museum Catalogue, Palestine Archaeological Museum*, p. 28.

14. W. F. Albright, *Archaeology of Palestine* (London, 1954), pp. 172f.

15. W. F. Albright, *Recent Discoveries in Bible Lands* (New York, 1955), p. 112.

There are a few other inscriptions that date from the first century A. D. which are of no direct interest to the student of the New Testament, although all material of this age from Palestine is of indirect value because it helps build up the total picture. One such inscription scratched in the plaster of a wall at Sebastia (Samaria) reads: "May Martial the learned master and all his friends be remembered by Kore [Persephone]."

The goddess Kore was popular at Samaria in the Roman period and a statue of her, found there some years ago, is on display in the Museum in Jerusalem (Jordan).[16]

Another type of inscription is found on pottery items used in building. A great number of these has been found in Palestine. They are of many kinds, roof tiles, drain pipes, tiles to cover drains, floor tiles, and so on. Some carry the name of the maker of the tile, or the name of the legion or detachment that constructed the building where the object was used. The language on these tiles is regularly Latin. A very common inscription is that of the tenth Roman legion, which was long in Palestine, from the time of Nero till the third century, although other legions feature as well. The complete text on the tiles of the tenth legion reads, *Legio Decima Fretensis.* The adjective *Fretensis* was attached to the tenth legion in memory of some great event in its history, possibly its participation in a battle near the straits between Italy and Sicily in 36 B. C. in the army of Octavian. The word *fretensis* is the genitive of the Latin *fretum,* meaning "sea." It is known that the tenth legion took part in this battle. Quite regularly the tiles bear the words "LEG.X.FRE" or "LEG.X.F." Because this legion made up the garrison of Aelia Capitolina when the pagan colony was founded at Jerusalem by Hadrian after the second Jewish revolt, many of the excavations in Jerusalem have yielded tiles of the tenth legion. One inscription tells a story that must have been repeated many times over. It speaks of a soldier of the tenth legion who died on garrison duty in Palestine. The inscription, which is to be seen today in the Museum in Jerusalem (Jordan), reads: "D M L MAGNIUS FELIX, MIL LEG X FRET, B TRIB MIL ANN XVIII VIX XXXIX." The translation is: "Sacred to the memory of L. Magnius Felix, a soldier of the tenth legion, the Fretensis, who was an orderly to the tribune, served eighteen years, and died aged thrity-nine."[17]

---

16. *Palestine Archaeological Museum Gallery Book,* pp. 55f.
17. A. C. Bouquet, *Everyday Life in New Testament Times* (London, 1956), p. 26.

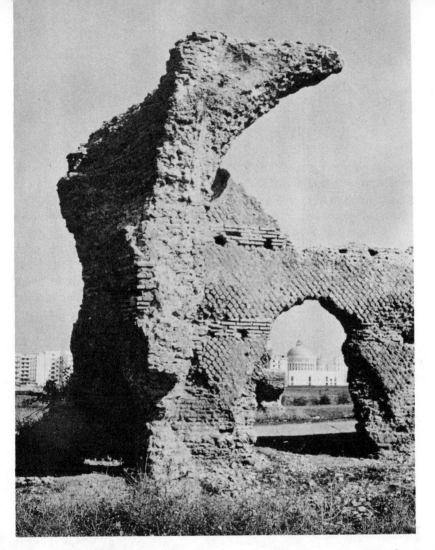

Where modern and ancient times meet — a modern section of Rome (Tuscolano) built a short distance from old Roman ruins. (Courtesy, Italian Information Center)

Finally we should make reference to the Roman milestones left in Palestine by the Roman road makers. These often carry Latin inscriptions.

We have already referred to the remarkable finds of manuscripts in the caves of the Dead Sea area. Some of these come from the later period of the Qumran sect and so fit into our period. There are others which have been found in caves further south which have no connection with the Qumran settlers. Among these were the two letters of Ben Kosebah already mentioned. We shall reserve a fuller discussion of material like this to a chapter on manuscripts.

<h2 style="text-align:center">TOMBS</h2>

Tombs and graves of Roman times have provided some most important material concerning the origins of Christianity. As a general rule in the ancient world, once a grave was sealed up, the likelihood was that it would remain intact through the centuries and objects placed in it would be preserved whole, though there was always the chance of tomb robbers breaking in. In an open city small objects of pottery or glass were likely to be broken as a result of war or earthquake or fire. The grave or the tomb, then, where objects were not normally disturbed, is of particular interest to the excavator. Here he will usually find pottery pieces, glass and metal objects, coins, inscriptions, and graffiti (writing that is scratched on a surface but not cut deeply), and in the case of large tombs, certain architectural features. These larger tombs provided for the burial of a number of people. They were entered by a comparatively small opening which could be closed by rolling a stone in a groove across the entrance. After each burial the large

A typical Palestinian tomb with circular stone door. (Courtesy, École Biblique, Jerusalem; R. de Vaux. O.P., Director)

stone was rolled across the door and the tomb sealed up until the next burial. Some of these stones, which are still to be seen in parts of Palestine, were so big as to require the effort of more than one man to move them. Such a discovery explains the concern of the women who came to the sepulcher where our Lord was buried. Joseph of Arimathaea "rolled a great stone to the door of the sepulchre" (Matt. 27:60), and later the angel came and "rolled back the stone from the door" (Matt. 28:2). Other passages in the Gospels which refer to the rolling of the great stone from the door are Mark 15:46; 16:3f., Luke 24:2; John 11:38, 39, 41; 20:1. Even comparatively small tombs had this rolling stone, but single graves were normally carved out in the rocky hillside and the body interred there.

Inside the larger tombs there were many rooms with shelves on which rested small ossuaries (stone caskets containing the bones of the departed). These ossuaries were normally made of limestone and were beautifully decorated. Quite often they carried a brief inscription naming the departed person. The practice was to collect the bones of the dead person after the flesh had decayed and place these in the ossuary in the family tomb. In this way several generations could be accommodated. Today there are some hundreds of these ossuaries known, and inscriptions in Aramaic and Greek have added a good deal to our knowledge of names and of family and social organization. Thus the typical names of Palestine in the first century A. D. are now well known. Such a name as "Jesus [Jeshua], son of Joseph," is actually known from one of these ossuaries. Other common names are Simon, Judas, Ananias, Lazarus, and among the names of the women are Martha, Elizabeth, Salome, Johanna, Sapphira, Maryam (Mary) and Apphia. It is of real significance to the New Testament scholar to discover that the names of the New Testament are the common names of the day. Even such a title as "Teacher" or "Rabbi" occurs on these ossuaries, for a certain Theodotion is referred to as *didaskalos,* the common name for "teacher" in the Gospels.

One of the most fascinating inscriptions investigated in recent times was evidently associated with a burial, although it had become dissociated from its grave. It read, "Hither were brought the bones of Uzziah, king of Judah — do not open." Supposedly the original tomb contained the bones of this great king, and this inscription was prepared when the tomb was discovered in the first century A. D. Whether this was so or not we cannot now say, but the inscription was in Aramaic of the time of Christ and was neatly inscribed on a slab of stone.[18]

Some of the large tombs in the Kedron valley must be dated to the first century A. D. even though the names that are now attached to them refer to such famous men as Absalom and Jehoshaphat. Other rock-cut tombs are to be found in many places around Jerusalem. One in the Hinnom valley shows early Roman influence in architecture, and is dated to the period before A. D. 70. The impressive Tombs of the Kings, first cleared in 1850 and 1863 by de Saulcy, represent the tomb of Queen Helena of Abilene and her house. She was converted to Judaism in A. D. 48 and migrated to Jerusalem some twenty years before the Jewish revolt. The sarcophagus of the queen and an inscription in Hebrew and Syriac are to be seen in the Louvre in Paris today.[19] This particular tomb was of the catacomb type and contained several rooms underground. It is entered by a small opening which can be closed by rolling a large circular stone, set in a groove, across it.

While there are many Jewish tombs in the ancient cemeteries around Jerusalem, it has been pointed out that after the first Jewish revolt in A. D. 66-70 things were not at all easy for the Jews in the Jerusalem area, and after the second revolt in A. D. 132-135 the Jews were forbidden even to come into the area of the Holy City. Hence it is likely that most of the tombs and ossuaries in the area preceded the fall and destruction of the city and the Temple in A. D. 70.

We have good reason to think that the archaeologists have discovered among the ossuaries in the cemeteries around Jerusalem some of the earliest evidences of Christianity. As early as 1873 the French scholar Clermont Ganneau reported the discovery of a burial chamber on the Mount of Olives containing some thirty ossuaries, on one of which was the name Judah, and a cross with arms of equal length. The name Jesus occurred also, in association with a cross. At the time of the discovery these were taken as being Christian ossuaries of the second century or later, for it was held that Christian Jews would have come under the general ban in the Jerusalem area after A. D. 135, and in any case it was held that the sign of the cross was late. In 1945 the late Professor E. L. Sukenik learned of a tomb that

---

18. W. F. Albright, *Archaeology of Palestine*, pp. 159f.
19. André Parrot, *op. cit.*, pp. 139f.

had been discovered in the Jerusalem suburb of Talpioth.[20] The tomb was carefully excavated by the Museum of Jewish Antiquities and was discovered to be a room some eleven feet square with a courtyard in front. The ossuaries had been placed as usual, in narrow tunnels running off from the main room. Some of them were removed by the workmen who found the room, and eleven others were removed by the archaeologists. Pottery pieces such as lamps, the character of the lettering on the ossuary inscriptions, and a coin of Agrippa I dated A. D. 42-43 found in the tomb, all combine to give a date not later than the middle of the first century A. D. for the final use of the tomb. Of considerable interest to us is the fact that five of the ossuaries carry inscriptions, three in Aramaic, belonging to Simeon Barsaba, Miriam daughter of Simeon, and Mat' (an abbreviation for Mattathias), and two Greek inscriptions which are harder to interpret, although there is no doubt that the name of Jesus appears on each, followed in one case by the word *Iou* and in the other case by the word *Aloth*. One of these was written in charcoal and the other cut into the limestone with a sharp instrument. The two words *Iou* and *Aloth*, according to Sukenik, are typical of exclamations found in other Greek funerary inscriptions and express the idea of misfortune or lamentation. *Iesou Iou* means literally, "Jesus woe," and *Iesou Aloth*, "Jesus Aloth" (probably another word for lamentation).

An alternative explanation sees in the words *Aloth* and *Iou* proper names. *Aloth* stands by itself and *Iou* is taken to mean either Jehu, or an abbreviated form of Judas (Ioudas).

Yet another recent discussion[21] of these words offers the suggestion that "woe" is to be interpreted as a cry to the risen Christ — "Jesus help!" The word *Aloth* is regarded as derived from the Hebrew root "to rise," and is translated, "Jesus, let [him who rests here] arise." If this interpretation is correct, we have here two prayers addressed to Jesus Christ as the living, risen Lord — a remarkable testimony to the early Church's faith in Jesus as the risen Lord. In addition to these words there were crosses on the second of the caskets, drawn in charcoal, in the center of each side. The fact that

---

20. E. L. Sukenik, "The Earliest Christian Records," *American Journal of Archaeology*, Oct.-Dec., 1947. See also A. Parrot, *Golgotha and the Church of the Holy Sepulchre* (English translation, London, 1957), pp. 113-116.
21. Berndt Gustafsson, "The Oldest Graffiti in the History of the Church?", *New Testament Studies*, III, 65-69.

there were two of these side by side in the same tomb, each with the name Jesus, led Sukenik to suggest that here we have Christian burials in which the name of Jesus is invoked in the hour of grief. The crosses he regards as quite deliberate "pictorial expression of the crucifixion tantamount to exclaiming, 'He was crucified.' "

Sukenik even made bold to suggest from the names inscribed on the other ossuaries, namely Simeon Barsabas and Miriam daughter of Simeon, that we may have discovered the burial tomb of a Christian family, and he speculated as to whether it might be the same as the one referred to in Acts 1:23 where "Joseph called Barsabas" was one of the possible candidates of the apostolic band. Again, a certain "Judas named Barsabas" was one of the disciples sent to Antioch with Paul and Barnabas after the great Council of Jerusalem (Acts 15:22). There may be something of speculation in this last suggestion, but it indicates the sort of material that is available for the study of Christian origins. And it could be that Sukenik is correct in his speculations!

Pottery, Glassware, and Metal Objects

We turn now to a brief discussion of the typical pottery, glassware, and metal objects for the years under discussion. The New Testament refers to quite a variety of household vessels, among which we might mention waterpots at Cana (John 2:6), pots and cups to be washed before eating (Mark 7:8), oil vessels and lamps (Matt. 25:4), a vessel for vinegar (John 19:29), platters (Matt. 23:25, Luke 11:39), and so on. Excavations have turned up a great variety of pottery in Palestine, some intact, and a great deal broken in pieces (sherds). A visit to the Palestine Archaeological Museum (in Jordan)[22] or to the Museum in Jerusalem (Israel) will convince the student that there is an abundance of material for study. The ordinary domestic pottery, such as cooking pots, lamps, oil bottles, jugs, juglets, cups, bowls, beakers, dishes, indeed the whole range of household pottery, can be seen and studied quite readily. A great deal of this comes from the tombs of the period and is therefore quite unbroken.

Of special interest is a type of red glazed ware very widely used all over the Roman world, the so-called *terra sigillata* (literally,

22. *Palestine Archaeological Museum Gallery Book,* Persian, Hellenistic, Roman, and Byzantine periods (Jerusalem, 1943), pp. 28-71.

"ornamented earth"). This is not the best name for it, for the name infers that the pottery bears a pattern stamped into it. While this is often so, it is not always so, for much of the pottery is plain, particularly in Palestine. In general this pottery was the "best china" of the Roman world at the time it was in use. It derived originally from Hellenistic pottery and was made in Asia Minor at Pergamum and Samos (hence it is often called Samian ware), as well as in many centers throughout the empire. Some of the potters in Italy exported the ware all over the Roman world, as can be seen from the trademarks and potters' names stamped into the interior of the vessels. The same maker's marks are to be found in places as far apart as Britain and Transjordan. The shapes, the decoration, and the potters are so well dated that it is possible to use this material for a rough dating of a building or a tomb. Among the stamped ware found in Palestine there are pieces from Gaul, from Arretium and Puteoli in Italy, and from kilns in the East.

The typical Roman lamps of the day occur in great numbers and show a gradual change in type as the years advance. Experts in the story of the lamp can give a good estimate of the age of a lamp from its shape.[23] Patterns were quite regularly worked into the lamps, such as animals, human forms, fruit, leaves, geometrical designs, and the like. In the years after the birth of the Christian Church specifically Christian motifs were commonly moulded into the lamp. Among these were the fish, the lamb, the vine and grapes, the cross, and the loaf of bread.

When we come to interpret some of the New Testament references to lamps, we are sometimes at a loss to know what is meant by the Greek word. It is obvious that if we are ever to know what was intended, we shall have to call in the aid of the archaeologist. The Greek word *lampas* is used for "lamp" in Matthew 25:1-8, Acts 20:8, Revelation 4:5 and 8:10, and the word *luchnos*, translated "light," is used in Matthew 6:22, Luke 11:34, 12:35, John 5:35, II Peter 1:19, and Revelation 21:23. Some of these may be torches, and others the small terra cotta lamps so common in the excavations. We await more information on the subject but meanwhile feel that we have in the material from the tombs of Palestine the kind of evidence that will provide the answer.

23. F. W. Robins, *The Story of the Lamp* (London, 1939); H. Menzel, *Antike Lampen.*

Roman glassware is well represented in Palestine.[24] Much of it today has a beautiful multicolored sheen, but this is due to chemical changes that have taken place through the centuries. Glass manufacture came late to Italy from the East, but it then received a certain uniformity of treatment and shape which became known all over the empire. However, each area produced its own glass and developed characteristics of its own.

Various pieces of bronze ware have also been discovered, such as lamps, jars, bowls, cosmetic boxes, cooking pots, buckets, tools of various kinds such as knives, forks, and shovels, ornaments such as pins and brooches, and other items for household use and grooming. It is outside the range of this book to give further detail, but it is now possible for the student of the times of Christ to publish a book in which considerable detail is collected about the ordinary items of everyday life.[25]

Roman Building Remains

When the American Schools of Oriental Research began to excavate among the ruins of Roman Jericho in 1950, they soon discovered evidence of the Roman influence in architecture. The upper layers of the debris that covered what was once a Hellenistic tower, and also the remarkable facade to what may have been a palace in its day, gave evidence of Roman influence. A particular type of construction, made by setting small square stones into plaster so as to give the appearance of a net (called technically *opus reticulatum*), was found in several places. This is a type of construction found quite often in excavations in Italy in such places as Rome, Pompeii, Tivoli, Palestrina, etc., and the excavator, J. L. Kelso, wrote in his report as follows:

> Indeed one might say that here in New Testament Jericho is a section of Rome that has been miraculously transferred on a magic carpet from the banks of the Tiber to the banks of the Wadi Qelt . . . . If this masonry were in Italy, it would not be

24. *Palestine Archaeological Museum Gallery Book*, pp. 47-53. P. P. Kahane, "Some Aspects of Ancient Glass from Israel," *Antiquity and Survival* (1957), pp. 208f.

25. A. C. Bouquet, *op. cit.;* see also G. E. Wright, *Biblical Archaeology* (London, 1957), pp. 239-244.

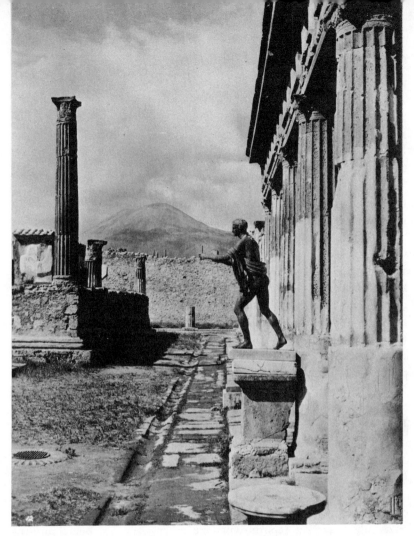

A beautiful view of the temple of Apollo in Pompeii, with Mount Vesuvius in the background. (Courtesy, Italian State Tourist Office)

later than the reign of Tiberius, as there is no brick of any kind used.[26]

In the same area, but slightly to the west, a very large building was unearthed in 1951, whose overall size was some eighty-eight meters long and forty-seven meters deep.[27] Coins suggest that this

26. J. L. Kelso, "The First Campaign of Excavation in New Testament Jericho," *BASOR* (Dec., 1950), p. 19.
27. J. B. Pritchard, "The 1951 Campaign at Herodian Jericho," *BASOR* (Oct., 1951), p. 10. See also *AASOR*, Vols. XXXII and XXXIII.

building was in use in the days of Herod the Great, Archelaus, and Agrippa, which brings it into the time of Christ. It is quite possible that our Lord knew this very building. No doubt it was known to Zacchaeus the taxgatherer (Luke 19). It is evident that the builders of Herod and his successors here were influenced, at least in part, by the Romans.

Other sites where traces of buildings of the first century are to be found include all those where there are still good Herodian remains,[28] as well as important places like Caesarea, the headquarters of the Roman administration. This town was founded in 22 B.C. by Herod the Great at a place called Strato's Tower. Josephus gave a description of the town he knew,[29] but it is evident that there is a great deal of valuable material awaiting excavation in this ancient city. There is already evidence that some of the structures are later than A.D. 100, as, for example, the high-level aqueduct that is dated by inscriptions from the early part of the second century.[30] But the site is a very big one and excavation has only just commenced. The progress of the work here is bound to produce important results for New Testament archaeology.

The Herodian buildings on the fortress of Masada, where the Jews held out for so long in the first Jewish revolt, have a variety of evidences of Roman influence, including building plans and floor mosaics which resemble strongly mosaics excavated in buildings in Italy.[31]

There are a few examples of Roman remains from the first century A.D. which have been found in recent excavations. A closer study of excavation reports will give other examples, but at present there is something of a dearth of evidence of this kind from this period, apart from the Herodian buildings. Of a less spectacular nature are the remains of Roman encampments and siege walls, and these are to be found in various places, some of the best of which are at the foot of Masada[32] and at Bittir,[33] the scene of the last stand by Bar Kosebah in A.D. 135.

---

28. See above, pp. 275-284.
29. Josephus, *Antiquities*, XV, ix, 6.
30. A. Reifenberg, "Caesarea, a Study in the Decline of a Town," *IEJ*, Vol. 1, p. 20.
31. M. Avi-Yonah, *et. al., Masada* (Jerusalem, 1957), pp. 25f.
32. *Ibid.,* p. 8.
33. W. F. Albright, *Archaeology of Palestine*, p. 166.

A fine example of mosaic flooring in one of the Roman villas of the third century, depicting the seasons. (Courtesy, Italian Information Center)

The later period of Roman rule in Palestine provides a good deal more material for our study. These ruins come from a period outside the one to which we have confined ourselves, but in passing we may notice that there are fine ruins at Jerash (old Gerasa), dating from the days of Trajan onwards, that is, from the period of the Roman expansion into the province of Arabia. Trajan erected a great monumental arch here in A. D. 115, and Hadrian likewise in A. D. 130. Other buildings here date from the later second and third centuries. The rest of the towns in the Decapolis region, that famous area where independence was given to ten Greek cities, have likewise Roman remains. We may refer to Scythopolis (Bethshean), Pella, Gadara, Philadelphia (Amman) (see Matt. 4:25, Mark 5:20, 7:31). Samaria, too, has good Roman remains of a later time, including the fine Roman basilica dated about A. D. 180 to 237. A discussion of Jerusalem itself will be taken up in the next chapter, since it will involve our taking notice of a number of important topographical items and seeing them in the light of the New Testament.

ROMAN ROADS IN PALESTINE

The general outline of the road system in Palestine is well known today and maps are available.[34] Inscriptions on milestones have been a great help in determining the roads through the land, although it must be agreed that there may have been more roads than the milestones indicate, since the preservation of a milestone is a matter of chance. We are further assisted in our study by the discovery of the remains of Roman camps and by small pieces of roads, which point to a connection with a larger network.

It seems clear that in the time of Christ the great Roman road system had hardly begun in Palestine. We believe that the earliest road followed the coast, and already in the days of Nero it ran from Antioch to Ptolemais (Acre), as we learn from inscriptions. South of this, although the inscriptions are all later than A. D. 200, it is thought that the road probably ran on to Egypt. Josephus refers to the road surveyors in the Roman army of Vespasian at the time of the first revolt.[35] Such milestones as we have, however, seem to point to a date after A. D. 70 for the Roman expansion of the road system. This would mean that in the time of our Lord the roads were very poor, and passable only in dry seasons.

With the Jewish revolt the situation changed and the Romans, in order to face the new possibility of revolts in Palestine, had to give thought to new roads. The setting up of the tenth legion in Jerusalem seems to have led to the construction of a road to connect Jerusalem with Caesarea, the administrative center. One milestone that can be read was found three miles north of Jerusalem and came from the days of Nerva (A. D. 96-98). Four other milestones, not now decipherable, were found near Gophna on the shortest route between the two towns.

All the evidence points to the fact that the road system of Palestine was not completed till well into the second century. Even

---

34. M. Avi-Yonah, "Map of Roman Palestine," *Quarterly of the Department of Antiquities, Palestine*, V, 139ff. Also F. M. Abel, *Géographie de la Palestine*, (Paris, 1938), II, 222-231.

35. Josephus, *Wars*, III, vi., 2.

A modern-day bitumen road from Beersheba to Sodom. (Courtesy, Israel Office of Information)

the road from Jerusalem to Jericho (Luke 10:30f.), which can be traced today, goes back only to the first Jewish revolt about A. D. 68-70, though no doubt it followed, in large part, the earlier road.[36]

Thus in Jesus' day, although travel was free and constant between all parts of Palestine, it was along the old rough roads which were not passable all the year round.

36. R. Beauvery, "La route romaine de Jérusalem à Jéricho," *RB* (Jan., 1957), pp. 72f.

Eighteen:

THE JERUSALEM THAT JESUS KNEW

Most readers of the New Testament would feel that the pride of place among towns that Jesus knew should be given to Jerusalem. In actual fact Jesus spent far more time away from Jerusalem than He did in it. But it was here that He questioned the doctors when He came up with His parents as a boy (Luke 2:41-50). Here, too, He cleansed the Temple (John 2:13-16), healed the man who had been ill for thirty years (John 5:1-16), spoke to the Jews at the Feast of Tabernacles (John 7), asserted His deity at the Feast of Dedication (John 10:22-30), and finally passed through those tragic days that led up to the cross. It was in Jerusalem that He rose from the dead and appeared to the friends and disciples. Here, too, the Christian Church was born (Acts 1, 2). Hence, though the actual known visits to Jerusalem are few, the impression left by the fourth Gospel is that Jesus was there frequently. These visits were in every case important ones. With tragic irony Jesus told the Pharisees that "it cannot be that a prophet perish out of Jerusalem" (Luke 13:33). With that, He indicated one important feature about

331

the city. Modern archaeology has given us important information about the town of those days, and if it has not solved all our problems, it has pointed the way to a solution of some of them. There must be a great deal of valuable information yet to be taken from the earth under the modern city. It has been occupied through the ages and is today heavily populated in the vital areas so that excavation has been difficult, if not impossible. Rebuilding operations in the old Jewish quarter will now provide opportunity to investigate portions of the area inside the old walled city.

The General Topography of Jerusalem

Through the centuries the disposition of the town of Jerusalem has altered. One feature, however, has remained permanently in the same location since Solomon's day. That is the Temple. At various times the site of the town in relation to the Temple has altered. In the Old Testament period it lay to the south, while in the New Testament period it was largely to the north.

Jerusalem is situated in the central highlands some thirty-three miles from the Mediterranean Sea and fourteen miles west of the north end of the Dead Sea. Immediately to the east of the city is the Kidron valley, which separates the Mount of Olives from the ridge on which Jerusalem proper stands. On the western side of the Temple area in New Testament times was a smaller valley, the Tyropoeon valley, which joined the Kidron valley at the southern end of the Temple ridge. To the west of the Tyropoeon valley is a larger plateau which falls away fairly steeply to the south and west into what was formerly known as the Valley of Hinnom. The small Tyropoeon valley thus divided the Jerusalem area of Jesus' day into two parts, of which the western part was the greater. The Old Testament settlements were on the Temple ridge, which has been variously known as the Jebusite city, the city of David, Zion, and Ophel. Today these sites would be placed to the south of the Temple area. Indeed archaeological work has revealed the exact site where the former city stood on the area south of the present walls.[1] By the time of Christ the city had spread rather to the west, and this southern part of the ridge was little used. At one stage it was cut

1. G. E. Wright and F. V. Filson, *The Westminster Atlas to the Bible* (London, 1957), p. 105.

down by the Hasmonean (Maccabean) rulers so as not to be higher than the Temple site.

The only two springs of any value in the whole area lie on the eastern side. These are Gihon and En-rogel. With the shifting of the city to the west, arrangements had to be made to bring water into the city by aqueduct or to store it in cisterns. Pontius Pilate (A. D. 26-36) constructed an aqueduct for this purpose, although there is some evidence that he may have repaired an old one.

On the north side of the city there were no deep valleys so that the defense of the city called for strong walls on this side. In the course of the centuries there were at least four of these. On the other sides of the city defense was not so difficult because of the deep valleys, although walls were built nevertheless.

HEROD'S JERUSALEM

From the days of the Maccabean revolt on, Jerusalem had suffered a good deal, and even as recently as Pompey's day the walls had been breached. But Herod with his typical massive masonry repaired the walls and erected new buildings. After his extensive building projects there were few changes for many years.

Let us take a quick look around the city of Herod, starting from the west side of the walls at a point overlooking the Valley of Hinnom. Here Herod built a fortified palace at a point where there were gates in the city wall. He erected three towers named Hippicus, Phasael, and Mariamne — after a friend, a brother, and his favorite wife. Part of one of these, probably the tower of Phasael,[2] has survived through the centuries and today forms part of the so-called Tower of David. Excavations by C. N. Johns between 1934 and 1940 established the fact that this tower was built on a foundation of massive stones, weighing up to ten tons, with an average weight of five tons. It was set into a still older wall underneath. At this point the wall curves south, and it is now agreed that we can fix the northwest corner of Herod's city here. It is possible to trace the remains of the so-called first wall of Jerusalem from here in a line running due east to meet the west wall of the Temple enclosure. Josephus described this wall as follows: "That wall began on the north at the tower of Hippicus and extended as far as the Xystus [a court for

---

2. W. F. Albright, *Archaeology of Palestine* (London, 1954), p. 154; G. E. Wright, *Biblical Archaeology* (London, 1957), p. 222.

games] and then, joining to the council house, ended at the west cloister of the Temple."[3]

But there was a second wall, described by Josephus in these words: "The second wall took its beginning from that gate which they called Gennath which belonged to the first wall; it only encompassed the northern quarter of the city and reached as far as the tower of Antonia."[4] This description gives the start and the end of the wall, but does not describe the portion in between. The tower of Antonia can be identified, but the gate of Gennath is not known. Consequently there has been a great deal of discussion about the position of this wall. Its exact location is not merely of academic interest, for our identification of the precise position of Calvary is affected by the decision reached. If the Church of the Holy Sepulcher today

3. Josephus, *Wars*, V, iv, 2.
4. *Ibid.*

Part of the old wall around Jerusalem which dates back to the time of Christ and was probably built by Herod, judging by the masonry of the upper part. (Photo, Philip Gendreau)

occupies a site that was originally outside the city wall, then there may be some reason to accept it as marking the place of Calvary. If, on the other hand, the site was inside the wall in Jesus' day, then the church is not on the site of Calvary. In Jesus' day the second wall was the outside wall of the city. Subsequently there were two other walls outside this one, that is, to the north. There was a wall built by Agrippa in about A. D. 42 of which traces are now known, and later still the wall of Hadrian, built about A. D. 135 in the approximate position of the present north wall of the old city.[5] We shall not discuss these two walls further but shall return in due course to the wall of Jesus' day when we seek to identify the site of Calvary.

Continuing our excursion around the city of Jesus' day, we proceed eastwards from Herod's towers to the Temple area. On the north side of the Temple enclosure Herod rebuilt a fortress that formerly gave protection to the Temple. Extensive excavations in this area by Père L. H. Vincent in recent years have given us the probable outline of the fortress. It evidently had towers at the four corners and was joined to the Temple area by raised roadways. There must have been some space between the fortress, known as Antonia, and the Temple, for the Jews cut away the roads at the time of the first Jewish revolt and engaged in fighting in this area.[6] In our Lord's time there was a Roman garrison here, however, which kept guard over the Temple in case of troubles at the time of the feasts. It was to this "castle" that Paul was taken when he was rescued from the Jewish mob on the day he was accused of bringing a Gentile into the Temple precincts (Acts 21:27-40, esp. v. 34). Some modern scholars think that this is the place of the trial of Jesus before Pontius Pilate.[7] We shall take up the point later in some detail. But it is of interest to note that Père Vincent found here in the excavations a stone pavement which seems to have been the court of Antonia and which he affirms was the "Pavement" of John 19:13.

To the south of Antonia was the great Temple area and the Temple proper. This must be regarded as the highlight of Herod's work.[8] While we do not know precisely how much of the Temple built by the returning exiles in 520-516 B. C. was used again by

---

5. G. E. Wright and F. V. Filson, *op. cit.*, p. 107.
6. Josephus, *op. cit.*, VI, i, 7. See also *Antiquities*, XV, xi, 4.
7. L. H. Vincent, W. F. Albright, among others. See below, pp. 345f.
8. A. Parrot, *The Temple of Jerusalem* (London, 1957), pp. 76-100.

Herod, it seems clear that the various wars had brought the existing Temple to a place where extensive repair was needed, and Herod undertook this. At the same time he enlarged the courts and beautified the whole area. The work began in 20-19 B. C. and although the essential construction was finished in a year and six months,[9] the over-all work of beautification went on till A. D. 64. In Jesus' day the Jews could say, "forty and six years was this temple in building" (John 2:20). These words spoken in A. D. 27 are important in deciding the date of Jesus' ministry.

Josephus again is our chief source of information.[10] He claimed that the court of the Temple was twice the size of the earlier Temple, an arrangement that was made possible by cutting into the rock on the hill Bezetha to the north and building up the embankment to the south. Excavations on the south wall in 1867-68 showed that there was a difference of forty-seven meters between the rock on which the foundation was laid and the level of the inner court at the southeast corner, and thirty meters at the southwest corner where today we have the famous Wailing Wall. Here fourteen courses of the large Herodian masonry are still visible about ground level. Perhaps it was the sight of great blocks of stone like these in some of the buildings that made one of the disciples in the Temple area say to Jesus, "Master, see what manner of stones and what buildings are here!" To which Jesus replied. "Seest thou these great buildings? There shall not be left one stone upon another, that shall not be thrown down" (Mark 13:1f.). In the destruction under Titus, the Temple buildings were in fact destroyed, but these retaining walls were left.

The great courtyard was entered by eight gates, two on the south, four on the west, one on the north, and one on the east. The four gates on the west led to the western city, but passers to and fro had to cross the Tyropoeon valley by bridges or aqueducts. Excavators in recent times have probably found traces of these in the so-called Wilson's arch and Robinson's arch.[11] A gate leading into the Temple area on the west side today, and known as the Gate of the Chain (Bab es-Silsile), probably marks the position of the old Coponius Gate.

9. Josephus, *Antiquities,* XV, xi, 1-6.
10. *Ibid.*
11. A. Parrot, *op. cit.,* p. 38. See also L. H. Vincent and A. M. Steve, *Jérusalem de l'Ancien Testament* (Paris, 1954) , pp. 58-64.

On the east side of the courtyard in the direction of the Kidron valley there was but one gate, probably on the site of the present Golden Gate. In its present form it is Byzantine in origin, although it is thought that its substructure dates from the days of Herod. Both Josephus and the Mishnah know of only one gate in the east side of the city and it is possible that the gate that Jesus entered on Palm Sunday stood at this point, or not far from it (Mark 11:11, Matt. 21:10, Luke 19:28-48). This was the most direct route from Bethany to the Temple.

Josephus had a good deal to say about the porticoes and the courts of Herod's Temple. Within the walls of the Temple area there were rows of pillars, four on the south and two on each of the other sides. As one passed through one of the eight doors, he came into the large open courtyard known as the Court of the Gentiles. On the south was the Royal Porch, and on the east was Solomon's Porch. It was in Solomon's Porch that Jesus walked at the feast of the dedication referred to in John 10:22f. (see also Acts 3:11, 5:12).

The extreme southeastern part of the Temple area is described by Josephus as follows:

> While the valley was very deep and its bottom could not be seen, if you looked from above into the depth, this further vastly high elevation of the cloister stood upon that height, insomuch that if anyone looked down from the top of the battlements, or down both those altitudes, he would be giddy, while his sight could not reach to such an immense depth.[12]

The corner referred to in this passage was probably the "pinnacle of the temple" mentioned in the story of the temptation (Matt. 4:5).

The court of the Gentiles provided a place for non-Jews to gather. Somewhere in this court the moneychangers did their work, and it was probably a thoroughfare for people passing to and fro through the city, from east to west or from north to south. When Jesus cast out those that sold and bought in the Temple area, He forbade that "any man should carry any vessel through the temple" (Mark 11:15f.). Josephus refers to the prohibition against Gentiles passing out of this court behind the balustrade which separated off the area where Jews were permitted. He spoke of "a stone wall for a partition with an inscription which forbade any foreigner to go in

---

12. Josephus, *Antiquities*, XV, xi, 5.

The synagogue inscription of Theodotus (see page 315). (Courtesy, The British Academy)

under pain of death."[13] We have already referred to the discovery of two of these inscriptions.[14]

Finally there was the inner area of the Temple precincts. As one entered through the Gate Beautiful, he would first reach the Women's Court, the furthest point to which women might go. Here the poor widow brought her mites (Mark 12:41-44). After this came the Men's Court, raised somewhat above the Women's Court and entered by seven gates, three on the north, three on the south, and one into the Women's Court. Then came the Priests' Court, where sacrifices were offered on the altar of burnt offering, and finally the Temple proper, with its porch, its Holy Place, and its Most Holy Place. This inner sacred place must have been a most ornate building with its white stone embellished with gold. The people of the day used to swear by the gold of the Temple (Matt. 23:16).

13. *Ibid.*
14. See above, pp. 314f.

It is natural to ask how much of all this remains today for the archaeologist to study. The answer is that very little can be studied at first hand. We gain a lot of information from Josephus, something from the New Testament, and a little from the archaeologist. The difficulty arises because the whole area where the Temple once stood has been sacred down the centuries. After the fall of Jerusalem in A. D. 70 the buildings were destroyed. In the years that followed a variety of structures has appeared on this site, including Christian churches and a mosque, which still stands today. The whole area is a sacred site to the Moslems nowadays, and although a good deal of valuable information surely lies buried beneath the surface, we are unable to excavate. For the present at least we must be content to remain in comparative ignorance about what lies beneath the present ground level.

The visitor to Jerusalem in Herod's day would see other items of interest, among which would be a theater, an amphitheater, and a hippodrome. These catered to the dramatic and athletic interests of the people. Other buildings are mentioned by Josephus, such as the palace of the Hasmoneans and the meeting place of the Sanhedrin. Then there were impressive tombs to be seen on the east side of the Kidron valley. In the valley itself were the springs of Gihon and En-rogel. Other important pools of water were to be seen in the city, such as the pool of Bethesda. To complete the picture, the houses of the ordinary people were scattered throughout the city and its environs. This was the town that Jesus knew so well.

JESUS IN JERUSALEM

It is a well-known fact that John, of all the Gospel writers, emphasized the ministry of Jesus in Jerusalem. Indeed, John says very little about the ministry in Galilee, although he does not altogether neglect this. We are concerned to indicate where modern archaeology has given some light on the Gospel narratives.

A good deal of the material in the Gospels is concerned with happenings in the Temple. With the aid of Josephus and modern interpretations of his descriptions, we can picture many of the incidents reported. Thus the presentation of the baby Jesus (Luke 2:22) probably took place at the door leading from the Women's Court into the Men's Court. It is not easy to decide where Jesus as a boy of twelve sat and asked questions of the doctors (Luke 2:46-50), but it was probably somewhere in the Outer Court, the place where

339

JERUSALEM in the NEW TESTAMENT ERA

Third Wall

BEZETHA

Pool of Bethesda

Second Wall

TOWER OF ANTONIA

Sheep Gate

Church of the Holy Sepulcher

TEMPLE

MOUNT OF OLIVES

Amygdalon Pool

Wilson's Bridge

Water Gate

Gennath Gate

Xystus

Huldah Gates

Phasael

Hippicus Mariamne

Hasmonaean Palace

Robinson's Arch Bridge

Palace of Herod

Palace of Helena

OPHEL

Gihon (spring)

UPPER CITY

VALLEY

OF KIDRON

LOWER CITY

Serpent's Pool

TYROPOEON VALLEY

Pool of Siloam

VALLEY OF

Essene Gate

GEHENNA or VALLEY OF HINNOM

Well of Job

(En Rog

public instruction was often given. The Temple features in the temptation story, and we have already referred to the pinnacle (Matt. 4:5, Luke 4:9).[15] The cleansing of the Temple took place out in the Court of the Gentiles (Matt. 21:12f.; Mark 11:5; Luke 19:45f., John 2:14-16). Perhaps trading and business were carried on in the Royal Porch at the south end of the great enclosure. On one of these occasions Jesus forbade people to make the courtyard a thoroughfare (Mark 11:16).

After the early ministry in Jerusalem Jesus went to Galilee, but returned to Jerusalem for a "feast" of the Jews, probably the Passover. It was on this occasion that He was present at the Sheep Gate near the pool of Bethesda and healed a man who had been sick for thirty-eight years (John 5:1-15). Some writers argue that we have some archaeological information on this site today. Some ancient manuscripts read Bethzetha instead of Bethesda. The word Bethzetha recalls the name of the district of Bethzatha to the north of the second wall.[16] There is some reason to believe that the pools in the property of the monastery of St. Anne, in the area of old Bezetha, represent the waters in question. Painstaking work has been done here by the White Fathers in ancient pools now many feet below ground level. The remains of pillars around the area point to the "porches" of John 5:2. Père L. H. Vincent and N. van der Vliet agree with the identification.[17] More recently R. de Vaux and P. Rouseé have extended these excavations into other Byzantine and Roman remains.

As we move along in the chronological order of our Lord's life,[18] we come to the later Judaean ministry where Jesus had many contacts with the Temple. He was there at the Feast of Tabernacles (John 7:10-52) and appeared first on the fourth day (v. 14) and again on the last day, making a special appeal to the people. This was the occasion of the ceremony of offering up the golden vessel of water brought from the pool of Siloam. He declared that in Himself alone there was a source of living water. The pool of Siloam is quite well known today. It is the termination of an important conduit that brought water from the spring Gihon (the Virgin's Spring)

15. See p. 337.
16. There is a textual problem here and the strength of this argument depends on the choice of Bethzatha as the true reading.
17. N. van der Vliet, *Sainte Marie, où elle est née, et la piscine probatique* (Paris). E. G. Kraeling, *Bible Atlas* (New York, 1956), pp. 392f. Cf. *RB* (1957), pp. 226-228.
18. We follow A. T. Robertson, *A Harmony of the Gospels* (London, 1922).

Aerial view of Jerusalem from the south. The city is seen under floating clouds. To identify the points of interest, compare this photograph with the map on page 340. Note how easily the walls can be traced. (The Matson Photo Service)

into the heart of the city of David. Probably the conduit that still exists was cut by King Hezekiah (II Kings 20:20). It was in this tunnel that the famous Siloam inscription was found in 1880.[19] The man born blind whom Jesus healed was sent to wash in this same pool of Siloam (John 9:7).

Jesus was in the Temple again at the Feast of Dedication, walking in Solomon's Porch (John 10:23). It was winter according to John, and perhaps Jesus joined the people on the eastern side of the great courtyard in order to seek some sunshine and shelter from the winds. In any case, He spoke concerning His oneness with the Father and offended the Jews greatly. After His Peraean ministry, He returned to Jerusalem for the last time. It was on this occasion

19. J. B. Pritchard, *ANET* (Princeton, 1955), p. 321.

that He made His triumphal entry into the city (Matt. 21, Mark 11). We have suggested that He entered the city by the eastern gate which stood at the site of the present Golden Gate.[20] There followed the second cleansing of the Temple, which, we hold, followed the pattern of the first (Matt. 21:12f.; Mark 11:12-18; Luke 19:45-48). It was at this last period of His life that the Pharisees and the Herodians tried to involve Him in criticism of Caesar in the matter of tribute money.[21] During these days, too, He commended the poor woman in the Temple as she offered her mites (*lepton*),[22] placing them in the offering box in the Women's Court (Mark 12:41-44).

The day of our Lord's crucifixion drew on apace. He spoke of His coming death and of the destruction of Jerusalem and the Temple. He was going out of the Temple when one of His disciples drew attention to the great stones of the building. It was then that He

20. See above, p. 337.
21. See above, p. 306.
22. See above, pp. 305, 308.

There is a marked contrast between the modern section of Jerusalem and the historical old city. This illustration shows King George Street and part of the Municipal Park. (Courtesy, Israel Office of Information)

prophesied that there would not be left one stone standing upon another (Mark 13:1f.).[23]

Then came Gethsemane. The site of the final hours of prayer is not known with certainty, although it was across the Kidron valley on the side of the Mount of Olives. There are today several rival sites for the place. The confused visitor will be shown the scene by the Roman Catholics, the Greeks, the Armenians, and the Russians. The oldest tradition places the scene on the ground now occupied by the Tomb of the Virgin. But the fact is that we have no clear information, archaeological or historical, which will allow precise identification.

It is not any easier to identify the scenes of the last hours of Jesus on earth although the visitor to Palestine will be shown a bewildering variety of places. There is more than one proposed site for the prison of our Lord (the house of Caiaphas), the place of the trial, Calvary, and the "garden tomb." For some of these sites there is some archaeological information that may finally prove to be of value.

The first place for which some scholars appear to have some solid grounds is the site of the Praetorium where Jesus was tried. After the arrest in the garden of Gethsemane, Jesus was examined by the high priest Annas (John 18:13), then by Caiaphas and the Sanhedrin (Matt. 26:57-68, Mark 14:53-56, Luke 22:54-71, John 18:24). Finally in a formal way, after dawn, the Sanhedrin condemned Him (Matt. 27:1f.; Mark 15:1, Luke 22:66-71). In this context Peter's denial and the remorse of Judas are set. Then came the first appearance before Pilate (Matt. 27:2, 11-14; Mark 15:1-5; Luke 23:1-5; John 18:28-38) who called in Herod Antipas,[24] the ruler of Galilee where Jesus belonged (Luke 23:6-12). A second time Jesus was sent to Pilate, who slowly, reluctantly, and in fear, surrendered Him to be crucified.

It is in connection with this trial before Pilate that important statements are made in the New Testament text, especially in John's Gospel. After surrendering Jesus to the Jews, Pilate "brought Jesus

23. See above p. 336.
24. See above, pp. 290, 292f.

Pontius Pilate issued this bronze coin dating from A.D. 29/30. The obverse has three ears of wheat (the middle one upright, the others bending sideways). (Courtesy, The British Museum)

Pavement of the court in Antonia. (Courtesy, Librarie Le Coffre, J. Gabalda et Cie, Paris)

forth, and sat down in the judgment seat [Greek *bema*] in a place that is called the Pavement [Greek *Lithostrotos*], but in the Hebrew, *Gabbatha*" (John 19:13). The Hebrew word means literally, "ridge or elevated terrain."[25] Hence a search has been made for a rocky pavement that might be associated with some of the buildings where Pilate would be likely to be at the time. For a considerable time there has been a debate about the location of the Praetorium referred to in Mark 15:16, to which Jesus was led after Pilate had condemned Him. Some argue that the Praetorium was the place where Jesus stood, and feel that it was more likely the palace of Herod than the barracks of Antonia.[26] The argument has taken on new interest following the work of the Dames de Sion and the Franciscans of the Convent of the Flagellation in the area just to the northwest of the present Temple area.[27] Here, in the position of the former tower of Antonia, a large Roman pavement has been discovered under the so-

25. W. F. Albright, *Archaeology of Palestine* (London, 1956), p. 245.
26. G. E. Wright and F. V. Filson, *op. cit.*, p. 106.
27. *Le Lithostrotos,* with a foreword by L. H. Vincent, 1933.

called Ecce Homo arch, occcupying not less than twenty-five hundred square meters. This pavement was the court of the tower of Antonia and stood on the rocky elevation which rose above the surrounding terrain. It might well be called *Gabbatha*. It is worth mentioning that the Ecce Homo arch in the vicinity was built over this pavement long after it had been buried under the ruins of Antonia, in the time of Aelia Capitolina. The arch does not therefore belong to the pavement. According to W. F. Albright, "the location of the Litho-strotos has been settled by the brilliant investigations of L. H. Vincent, utilizing both the outcroppings of rock in the region of the Tower of Antonia [at the northwestern end of the Temple enclosure] and the excavations carried on quietly for many years by the Dames de Sion and the Franciscans of the Convent of Flagella-tion."[28] Of passing interest are the patterns scratched in the stones of the pavement in more than one place. These represent the play board for a popular game played by the Roman soldiers on duty.

While this evidence seems convincing, there are those who feel that it is not final. It is argued that while no pavement has been found in the area of Herod's palace, there may well have been one there. When Pilate came from Caesarea to Jerusalem at the time of the Passover, he would be more likely to stay at the palace of Herod than in Antonia. Josephus tells us of a later occasion when the procurator Florus sat in judgment before Herod's palace.[29] There was evidently a judgment seat (*bema*) set up there for Herod to carry out his own ordinary judicial functions. Hence the entrance to the palace could well have been the Praetorium on that occasion. In this opinion the Roman Catholic scholar R. P. P. Benoit shares, against some of his colleagues.[30] Other competent scholars agree, among whom are E. G. Kraeling[31] and G. E. Wright.[32] If this latter opinion is correct, then the traditional *Via Dolorosa* cannot be the path taken by Jesus from Pilate's residence to the cross. When Jesus went to Herod Antipas (Luke 23:7), He would then have gone in the opposite direction, moving from Herod's palace towards Antonia, but stopping perhaps at the place of the Hasmoneans. L. H. Vincent's reply to all this is that Antonia may well have been Herod's

28. W. F. Albright, *op. cit.,* p. 245.
29. Josephus, *Wars,* II, xiv, 8.
30. R. P. P. Benoit, "Prétoire, Lithostroton et Gabbatha," *RB* (Oct., 1952), pp. 531f.
31. E. G. Kraeling, *op. cit.,* pp. 405f.
32. G. E. Wright and F. V. Filson, *op. cit.,* p. 107.

early palace that kept its name.[33] It is evident that no final conclusion is yet possible, but in the discussion we have looked at important material which will surely help in the final solution, even if it only helps to eliminate unsound suggestions.

The site of Calvary and the tomb where Jesus was buried present us with another difficult problem. A great deal turns on the position of the second wall of the city, for the crucifixion took place outside this wall. Traditionally, the present position of the Church of the Holy Sepulcher marks the site of Calvary, and the tomb must be close by. If this tradition is correct, then the wall of the city must have passed to the east of the church so as to allow it to be outside in the days of our Lord.

As we have seen, the start and finish of the second wall are defined by Josephus.[34] The end of the wall was at the tower of Antonia. This is well marked. But the start of the wall at the gate Gennath is not known. According to some writers, this gate was between the towers of Hippicus and Phasael. But, in fact, four courses have been proposed for this second wall, and none of them is finally acceptable to all scholars.

In our discussion, the map on page 340 should be followed.[35] The shortest wall suggested leads west from Antonia and turns south to meet the first wall halfway between Herod's Temple and the palace (AEFH). This would allow the Church of the Holy Sepulcher to be outside the wall. There are traces of Herodian masonry along this course, but their meaning is not clear, and in any case the area enclosed seems to be very small and leaves outside the wall the small hill on which the Church of the Holy Sepulcher stands. This would be a strange arrangement for fortification purposes, which was the reason for building the wall in the first place. An enemy on this small hill would have a distinct advantage in siege warfare.

A second proposal is to follow this same line to a point just south of the church, and then to assume a turn to the west. Finally the wall turned south to meet the first wall near Herod's palace (AEFGP). This suggestion has the weakness of the first one in regard to defense, and is rejected by many writers.

The third proposal allows for the wall to swing to the north from Antonia and then to circle south to Herod's palace. The

33. L. H. Vincent, "Le lithostrotos évangélique," *RB* (Oct., 1952), pp. 513f.
34. See above, p. 334.
35. We follow the notation in G. E. Wright and F. V. Filson, *op. cit.*, Pl. XVII C.

difficulty here is that there is some evidence that the wall did, in fact, start in a westerly direction from Antonia, rather than towards the north. But such a wall would include the church and thus bring the traditional site of Calvary inside the walls (ABCDP).

The fourth suggestion for this second wall follows a line west from Antonia and then swings in a half-circle to include the Church of the Holy Sepulcher before it meets the first wall at the palace of Herod (AEGP).

Opinion is still sharply divided. There are traces of Herodian walls or of other ancient walls along all of these lines, and each suggestion has its advocates. For the most part, the Roman Catholic writers seek to exclude the church from the area marked out by the wall, whether they follow the first or the second proposal.[36] The serious difficulty for these suggestions is the peculiar weakness thus created for a defensive wall that had a hill overlooking it at a vital point. Protestant scholars have not been greatly interested to preserve the reputation of the traditional site of Calvary and have tended to follow the third or the fourth suggestion. Perhaps the most favored of these is the latter. This view appears to be favored by W. F. Albright[37] and G. E. Wright.[38] However, E. G. Kraeling in his *Bible Atlas* follows the second proposal.[39] The conclusion we reach finally is that the site of Calvary cannot be identified with certainty today.

As to the site of the tomb, it was evidently close to the place of the crucifixion according to John, who wrote, "Now in the place where he was crucified there was a garden; and in the garden a new sepulchre, wherein was never man yet laid" (John 19:41). Those who contend that the Church of the Holy Sepulcher gives us the site will show a tomb within the precincts of the church. But this lies under the same kind of doubt that attaches to the site of Calvary.

A popular alternative site for Calvary and the tomb was taken up by General Gordon in 1883 when he saw a peculiar skull-like formation in the rocks to the north of the present wall. The rocky hill above was identified with Calvary and a tomb in the vicinity

---

36. A. Parrot, *Golgotha* (London, 1957), pp. 49ff., gives a simple summary of the arguments advanced by these writers.
37. W. F. Albright *op. cit.*, pp. 154f.
38. G. E. Wright and F. V. Filson, *op. cit.*, p. 107.
39. E. G. Kraeling, *op. cit.*, Map XVIII.

was taken as the garden tomb. More careful archaeological investigation shows that there are other tombs in the area which are Byzantine (fifth and sixth centuries). But there is no convincing evidence at all that Gordon's Calvary and the tomb have authentic value. The tomb may indeed be as late as the third or fourth century A. D.[40] The setting is, however, a beautiful one and has often been an inspiration to the casual visitor. But in archaeological matters we cannot be moved by mere sentiment.

We feel that the ancient city of Jerusalem has many secrets yet to be given up to the archaeologist and the scholar. It is tantalizing to the New Testament scholar to think of the many problems whose solution lies beneath the soil of old Jerusalem. With the progress of the years and the need to rebuild parts of the old city, we may expect valuable information to come to light. Meanwhile we are grateful for the light we have.[41]

40. J. Finegan, *Light from the Ancient Past* (Princeton, 1947), p. 240.
41. In recent years two important works have been written that present to the student a wealth of valuable information about the city where Jesus gave much of His teaching and where He died and rose again. J. Simons, *Jerusalem and the Old Testament* (Leiden, 1952); H. Vincent and A. M. Steve, *Jérusalem de l'Ancien Testament* (Paris, 1954).

Nineteen:

FIRST-CENTURY TOWNS IN
PALESTINE AND SYRIA

T HOUGH JERUSALEM OCCUPIED PRIDE OF PLACE AMONG THE TOWNS
of Palestine in Jesus' days, we must remember that the events of
the New Testament took place in a wide variety of towns stretching
from Palestine to Italy. In Palestine itself many towns are mentioned.
For many of these we have information from excavations, although
there is a vast field of research still open for the archaeologist in
this regard. Considerable uncertainty still obtains in numerous areas,
but the combined results of excavations and literary records provide
the student with valuable insights. We shall confine our attention in
this chapter to the towns of Palestine and Syria.

TOWNS IN PHOENICIA AND IN THE DOMAINS OF HEROD PHILIP

Phoenicia was ruled by the Roman governor of Syria. Three of
its towns are of interest to the New Testament student, Tyre, Sidon,
and Ptolemais (Acre).

There are several references to Tyre in the New Testament.
Jesus Himself was once in "the coasts of Tyre and Sidon" (Matt.

351

stration on page 350: A covered market street in Damascus, Syria. (Courtesy,
ESCO/P.A. Pittet/1961)

15:21-28, Mark 7:24-30), and the people of the region came to see Him (Mark 3:8, Luke 6:17). It is not clear that He Himself was in the town, though it is not impossible. A woman from this area, the Syro-Phoenician woman, received kindly treatment at His hand when her daughter was healed. Tyre itself was an ancient town. For some years now systematic excavation has been going on here. Formerly the town was divided between the island and the mainland, but following the attack of Alexander the Great in which two causeways were built out to the island, the two areas became joined. Excavation has taken the story of the town back to very early times. Of special interest to us is the fact that in Roman times there was a sizable town here.

Just to the north of Tyre lies the town of Sidon. Here, too, remains of Roman times have been found. A considerable range of tombs and sarcophagi has been found in the area behind the modern town which provides valuable information about Roman times.

The town of Ptolemais (Acco) features only in the story of Paul's journeys (Acts 21:7). It was the end point of the Roman road from the north in the days of Nero, as we have already seen.[1] It, too, had a long history. Excavation in the area has shown a range of occupation from early Canaanite times through Roman times up to the modern period.

In the domains of Herod Philip we have the important towns of Caesarea Philippi and Bethsaida. The former of these was the scene of Peter's great confession (Matt. 16:13-20, Mark 8:27-30). The town was formerly known as Panias, but in 3 B.C. Herod Philip named it Caesarea Philippi (Philip's Caesarea), in honor of Augustus. After the defeat of the Jews in A.D. 70, the name reverted to Panias, which eventually became Banias, its name today. There are ruins in the area, but the most spectacular of them date from the Middle Ages when Crusaders and Moslems fought in the region round about. Medieval walls and towers are to be seen today on the heights above the modern village, but it is thought that they are built over the site of the ancient acropolis of Roman times. Herod Philip permitted the presence of pagan shrines in the area for his predominantly Greek population. There are still to be seen the remains of a grotto carved out of solid rock in honor of Augustus — a shrine to Pan, the Roman nature god. Greek inscriptions in the area dating to the days of Agrippa tell of an altar dedicated to the Nymphs. But there has been little

---

1. See above, p. 328.

serious archaeological work in the place, though it appears to be full of promise.

There is a problem associated with the town of Bethsaida. It seems likely that Philip built his capital a short distance to the north of the old town and called it Julias, in honor of the daughter of Augustus. No excavation has been done in the area which probably marks the site of Julias, but we feel fairly certain that the old town of Bethsaida is represented by an area known as Khirbet el 'Araj. E. G. Kraeling, in his *Bible Atlas*, writes about the place as follows:

> [A traveller at the site] had an unusual opportunity to examine the stratification there when the wall of a cistern that workmen were constructing for his host, collapsed. There was an upper layer of about twenty inches composed of alluvial sand; below that was a layer of about six inches with sherds of the Roman period down to about 250 A.D. He mentions the typical red-coloured ones and the painted jar-handles. Another layer of alluvial sand of twelve to fourteen inches lay above the next lower stratum of twelve inches. This last layer he confidently assigned to the time of Christ, for from it he was able to extract four lamps and eleven small coins showing three ears

Catacombs at ancient Atlit, near Mount Carmel. (Courtesy, Israel Office of Information)

of grain on one side; these he asserts were minted in the time of Pilate (26-36 A. D.). He notes that the stratum in question was destroyed by fire, and finds therein a remarkable vindication of Jesus' woe over Bethsaida (Matt. 11:21). In any case the situation observed here warrants further investigation.[2]

Towns in Galilee and Peraea, the Domains of Herod Antipas

Archaeologically we are not much better off here than in the case of the towns already mentioned. The most important cities were in the area to the west of Jordan. There was little of importance in Peraea.

Capernaum (literally "Village of Nahum") features a good deal in the Gospels. Jesus began His ministry here after the temptation

2. E. G. Kraeling, *Bible Atlas* (New York, 1956), pp. 388f.

The magnificent ruins of the second-century synagogue at Capernaum attract many visitors. It is not, however, as was formerly thought, the synagogue in which Jesus taught (Mark 1:21). (Courtesy, Israel Office of Information)

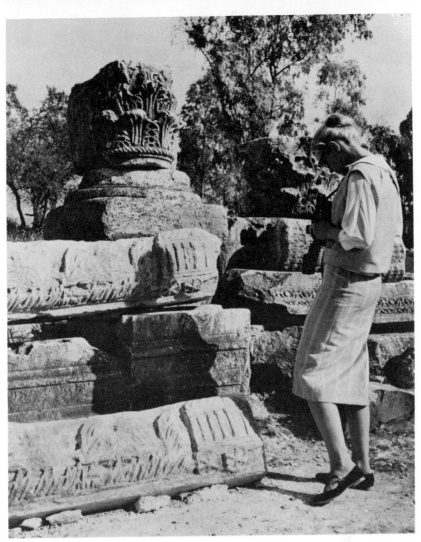

Many stones of the ruins of the synagogue at Capernaum are decorated with symbolic motifs, purely geometric designs, and flowers and leaves cut into the stone. (Courtesy, Israel Office of Information)

(Matt. 4:13-16). Here, too, He healed many, including the centurion's servant and Peter's wife's mother (Matt. 8:5-17, Mark 1:21-34, 2:1-12); and here the incident of the fish and the tribute money took place (Matt. 17:24ff.). It was on the way to Capernaum that the dispute as to who should be the greatest took place (Mark 9:33-37), and nearby Jesus walked on the water (John 6:16-21). Here He gave some of His most profound teaching, as, for example, the instruction about the bread of life (John 6:32-35), but He also delivered woes against the same proud city (Luke 10:15).

For a number of years there has been a dispute about the exact location of the town, and more than one site has been suggested,[3] but the area of Tell Hum (an Arabic form of a Jewish name Tanhum) is now widely accepted. The original name Capernaum has now been confirmed by an Aramaic inscription found by the late Professor Sukenik in excavations in an old synagogue at Hamath Geder near the mouth of the Yarmuk river, where persons who presented gifts are recorded, among them, one Dositheus of Capernaum (Kephar Nahum).[4] The ruins of Capernaum are spread over an area of about a mile along the shore of the lake. Up to the present there has been little in the way of excavation at the site except in the case of the fine, partly ruined structure that represents an ancient synagogue. It has been for many years in the custody of the Franciscan monks and has been preserved by them and in part restored. This ancient synagogue was formerly thought to be the building referred to in Luke 7:5, but more mature judgment has led to the conclusion that the present ruins are later than the time of Christ. Very likely they were built on the site of the earlier synagogue, but no excavation has been done under the present remains, and indeed none is likely to be done, since no one would wish to destroy the present magnificent ruins in order to find the foundations underneath.

The first work was done here as early as 1905 by the German archaeologists Kohl and Watzinger. Since then the Franciscan monks have carried on the work. It is now clear that the structure is a third-century building, made of white limestone, which must have been brought into the area, for the native stone here is black basalt. The present ruins reveal a building of the basilica type. Originally it had a stairway leading up to the four-columned front where there were a large central door and two smaller side doors. Inside there were nine columns on each side, and five at the rear. The main hall was more than seventy feet long and fifty feet wide. There were galleries for women at the back, and a courtyard on the east side. The carved stone work scattered about the area gives a good idea of the decoration of the typical synagogue of the day, with ornamentation showing seven-branched candlesticks, vine leaves and grapes, palm trees, eagles, doves, all sorts of animals, especially lions, and a wide variety of geometrical patterns. Among the items scattered about were some that carried inscriptions to show that they had

---

3. S. L. Caiger, *Archaeology and the New Testament* (London, 1948), p. 83.
4. E. G. Kraeling, *op. cit.*, p. 377.

A close-up view of one of the symbolic motifs (possibly of the holy arc) visible on the picture on page 355. (Courtesy, Israel Office of Information)

been presented by individuals. One such fragment of a pillar carried the name of Zebida bar Jochanan (Zebedee the son of John).[5] This was quite a regular practice among the Jews and some valuable information has come from such inscribed items donated to synagogues.

We notice in passing that the existing ruins of synagogues in Palestine are all later than the first Jewish revolt. It would seem that the destruction of the synagogues was carried out systematically by the Romans. The oldest trace of such a building seems to be the inscription found in Jerusalem referring probably to the synagogue of the Freedmen.[6] There are several in Galilee but none of them can be dated earlier than the end of the second century A. D. To this earlier period belong the synagogues at Capernaum, Chorazin, and Kefr Bir'im.

5. J. Finegan, *Light from the Ancient Past* (Princeton, 1946), p. 227.
6. See above, p. 315.

357

Not far from Capernaum was Chorazin which was associated with Bethsaida in our Lord's warning of judgment (Matt. 11:21-23, Luke 10:13-15). The position of Chorazin is marked today by Keraze, two miles to the north of Capernaum. Here, too, we may see the impressive remains of a synagogue but, unlike the one at Capernaum, this is built of the black basalt which abounds in the area. It dates like its neighbor from the late second or early third century A. D., and shows the same rich ornamentation. There was evidently a new and more liberal attitude towards art by the third century, for these synagogues depict animals and human beings, motifs forbidden by the second commandment.

One of the very interesting features of this synagogue is the seat of honor set in the end of the building, facing the congregation. Here sat honored visitors or elders who might minister to the people. It is thought that we have in this an example of the "seat of Moses" referred to in Matthew 23:2.[7] It was cut into solid basalt and was provided with a back rest and decorated arm rests, and carried an inscription which read, "May Judan son of Ishmael be remembered for good, who made this portico and its staircase. As his reward may he have a share with the righteous."[8] The man referred to here was the donor of the seat. One other such seat is known from Hammath, south of Tiberias.[9] Perhaps the synagogue that Jesus knew at Capernaum had such a "seat of Moses" and carried the name of the centurion who built it!

The area of Capernaum and Chorazin brings to mind the story of the feeding of the five thousand. While it is outside our period, it is of some interest to note that an ancient Christian church, excavated at Tabghah on the lakeside between Capernaum and Tiberias, has a very fine floor mosaic on which is represented a basket full of loaves and two fishes beside it, illustrating no doubt the famous miracle. One tradition is that Jesus preached the Sermon on the Mount to the people on the little hillside nearby. We cannot be sure of this, but the whole area is full of rich association, and almost any place in the region might have witnessed the ministry of our Lord.

---

7. G. E. Wright and F. V. Filson, *Westminster Historical Atlas* (London, 1958), p. 60. See also I. Renov, "The Seat of Moses," *IEJ* (1955), p. 262f.
8. E. G. Kraeling, *op. cit.*, p. 378.
9. G. E. Wright and F. V. Filson, *op. cit.*, p. 60.
10. See p. 293.

The town of Tiberias lay further south along the lake. In its day it was an important town,[10] and no doubt much lies buried here for our investigation. Since 1955 excavations in some ancient baths produced evidence from the days of Herod Antipas, whose capital was here.[11] The region has remains extending through to the tenth century A. D., and it is felt that even if the town has today little of the glory of the past, there may well be a story awaiting the excavator. Tiberias is mentioned only once in the New Testament (John 6:23).

To the west of Galilee lay the towns of Nazareth, Cana, and Nain. The geographical position of these can be determined today fairly easily although our archaeological knowledge of them is limited. In a more general connection G. E. Wright and F. V. Filson have remarked that "it is gratifying to find that we can identify the main sites of Jesus' life and ministry. The birthplace, Bethlehem, and the childhood residence, Nazareth, are certainly known. Concerning the Sea of Galilee, Cana, Nain, Capernaum, and Chorazin, there can be no reasonable doubt."[12]

While this statement is true in regard to geographical position, we are in difficulty about the identification of the details of the towns. Thus Nazareth is a town that is full of traditional churches and other sites. The visitor is shown the Church of the Annunciation, the workshop of Joseph, the table of Christ, and so on. There is no solid evidence for any of these. Perhaps the one authentic item is the village well where Mary drew water, for it is the only well in the area. An ancient synagogue, now restored as a church, may possibly provide a link with early times. But the simple fact is that Nazareth has little of a reliable nature to offer us today. Indeed, some writers suggest that the Nazareth of the New Testament may actually have been some little distance from the modern town.[13]

Cana is to be identified with the modern Khirbet [ruin] Qana (John 2:1, 11; 4:46). There are remains of the third century A. D. here, but on the hill behind the village, potsherds of the time of Christ and of the early Christian period are scattered about.[14]

Nain likewise may be identified today with a village that carries the same name. There is some evidence that excavation for the

11. Articles in *RB* (Jan. 1956), p. 97, (Apr. 1957), p. 258.
12. G. E. Wright and F. V. Filson, *op. cit.,* p. 94.
13. E. G. Kraeling, *op. cit.,* pp. 358-360.
14. F. M. Abel *Géographie de la Palestine* (Paris, 1938), II, 413.

Nazareth was the place where Jesus grew up and lived until His public ministry. This charming scene of the city must contain many places where He walked. (Courtesy, Israel Office of Information)

foundation of houses being built here disturbed ancient Roman remains.[15]

The other part of the domains of Herod Antipas lay in Trans-Jordan. At the extreme south of the area, on the edge of the Nabataean kingdom, was the fortress of Machaerus, situated on an isolated hill and surrounded by a wall. It was first built by Alexander Jannaeus, but was razed by the Romans in 63 B. C. Herod the Great rebuilt it between 25 and 13 B. C. Later it came into the territory of Antipas, and here, according to Josephus, John the Baptist met his death.[16] The town is not mentioned in the New Testament. Today there is a considerable area of ruins awaiting serious excavation.

15. E. G. Kraeling, *op. cit.,* p. 380.
16. Josephus, *Antiquities,* XVIII, v, 2.

TOWNS IN THE PROCURATORIAL PROVINCE OF JUDAEA

At the time of Christ this province included Samaria and extended from north of Caesarea on the coast to below Hebron. It included important towns, such as Samaria, Shechem (Sychem or Sychar), Jericho, Bethlehem, Jerusalem, Samaria, and a number of smaller places like Joppa, Lydda, and Bethany.

Caesarea on the Mediterranean was the administrative center of the Roman government. Philip preached here (Acts 8:40), and Paul was imprisoned here. Here, too, Cornelius lived (Acts 10), and Peter preached (Acts 11:11, 12:19). The town remained important into the Middle Ages and is mentioned in several writings of that time.[17] Until very recent times this important site was neglected, but now a new interest is being taken in the old town. Certain parts of it

17. A. Reifenberg, "A study in the Decline of a Town," *IEJ*, Vol. I, No. 1, pp. 20ff.

Remnants of Roman columns near the sea wall of the ancient fort of Caesarea on the Mediterranean coast. (Courtesy, Israel Office of Information)

The great stairway to the temple Herod built for Augustus in the city of Samaria. (Courtesy,
J. Eijckeler, Druten, the Netherlands)

have been excavated by the government of Israel.[18] Already buildings
of Roman times and from later periods are coming to light and
inscriptions and coins[19] are adding their part to the story that is
unfolding. During 1961 an inscription bearing the name of Pontius
Pilate was discovered in the ruins of the Roman theater.[20] The whole
neighborhood offers scope for excavation, and even the sea bed off
the coast has been investigated in order to test out the extent of the
remains of the harbor installations built originally by Herod the
Great.

18. Preliminary reports in *RB* (April, 1957), p. 259. C. T. Fritsch and I. Ben-
Dor, "The Link Expedition to Israel, 1960," *BA* (May, 1961), pp. 50-59.
19. H. Hamburger, "Minute Coins from Caesarea," *Atiqot* (Jerusalem, 1955),
pp. 115-138.
20. See J. Vardaman, "A New Inscription Which Mentions Pilate as 'Prefect,'"
JBL (March, 1962), pp. 70f.

Samaria is a town that has been excavated in some detail in recent times.[21] In the New Testament it does not feature a great deal, although the district is important. Philip preached here (Acts 8:5), and Simon the sorcerer came under the sound of the gospel. God blessed the ministry of Philip so that many believed. A woman from the same district met Jesus at the well (John 4), and early Christians preached here with some success (Acts 1:8, 8:4-6). Paul's conversion brought peace to the new churches in the area (Acts 9:31). There is no indication that Jesus Himself was ever there. It was a strongly Hellenized city, and Jesus' work lay chiefly among the Jews.

The nature of the city in the days when Herod the Great sponsored a building program is now well understood. As we have seen,[22] he built a temple for Augustus over the site of the palace of the earlier kings of Israel, and erected a stadium and forum in the town. The city was extended again towards the close of the second century and in the early third century A. D. A great basilica here later became a Christian church. But there are not the same sacred memories attaching to Samaria as there are to many other towns.

The town of Shechem, with a history reaching back into the pre-patriarchal times, has more recently been suggested as the town referred to in John's Gospel as Sychar. It is called Shechem in the old Syriac Gospels, and this points to a corruption of an original *Sycem* to *Sychar*. But the identification is not finally secure despite the suggestion of W. F. Albright.[23] The most recent excavations at this site indicate that this town came to an end somewhere about 100 B.C.[24] The coin record for the Hellenistic city is quite strong up to about that point. If the indications are supported by subsequent excavations, then the old site known today as Tell Balatah ceased to be occupied before Roman times, and we shall need to look elsewhere for the *Sychar* of the New Testament times. G. E. Wright, the present excavator, says that there are occasional Roman coins in the debris but thinks these are probably from a Roman village near the spring below the present village of Balatah.[25] It seems therefore that we must await further evidence about the village known to Jesus.

21. The complete report has been published by the Palestine Exploration Fund (1958), as *Samaria-Sebaste, Vol. III.*
22. See above, pp. 280f.
23. W. F. Albright, *Archaeology of Palestine* (London, 1956), p. 247.
24. G. E. Wright, "The Second Campaign at Tell Balatah (Shechem)," *BASOR* (Dec., 1957), p. 28.
25. *Ibid.,* p. 26.

A great deal of work on the Roman town of Jericho still needs to be done. Reference has already been made to excavations done in this area in 1950-1951.[26] A fortress of pre-Herodian times was discovered as well as quite an amount of building remains from the days of Herod and his immediate successors. In the neighborhood of these excavations surface investigation revealed the presence of a considerable number of buildings both north and south of the Wadi Qelt which issues into the plain at this point. There is evidently much material awaiting excavation.[27] The site of Roman Jericho, built largely by Herod and his friends, is to be found here. This town was the scene of several New Testament incidents, such as the healing of the two blind men (Matt. 20:29ff.), the healing of blind Bartimaeus (Mark 10:46ff.), and the incident in which Zacchaeus the taxgatherer was converted (Luke 19:1-10).

There is strong circumstantial evidence that the modern village of Bethlehem represents the birthplace of Jesus. There are very early traditions attaching to the town and there are ancient building remains as well. As early as the time of Justin Martyr (about A. D. 150), the tradition that a certain cave was the place where Jesus was born seems to have been established. Other writers of antiquity state that the cave of the nativity was desecrated by Hadrian and was used by a cult of the god Adonis about A. D. 140. Jerome, the early Christian writer and translator of the Bible, who lived towards the close of the fourth century, is believed to have done some of his work here. In any case, he spoke of the restoration of the sacred place by the Emperor Constantine (A. D. 323-337), who cleared away the last traces of paganism and built a church over the cave.[28]

The present Church of the Nativity built on this site has undergone considerable rebuilding, notably in the sixth century. The original church was built by Constantine though little remains of the original structures within the later buildings still standing.[29] One enters the cave by a set of steps leading down below floor level to a grotto some thirty-three feet long and thirteen feet wide. There is little doubt that this is the cave known to the Christians in the fourth century, and no doubt the tradition goes back further. But we have no archaeo-

26. See above, pp. 324ff.
27. L. Mowry, "Settlements in the Jericho Valley During the Roman Period," *BA* (May, 1952), pp. 26ff.
28. E. G. Kraeling, *op. cit.*, pp. 361f.
29. R. W. Hamilton, *The Church of the Nativity, Bethlehem* (Jerusalem, 1947), pp. 91-96.

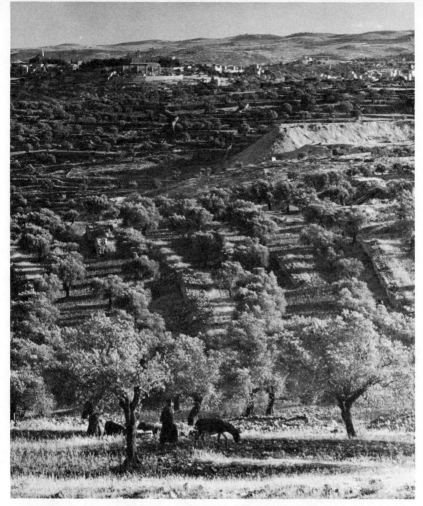

A peaceful scene near Bethlehem, with part of the city in the background. (Courtesy, Trans World Airlines)

logical evidence before about A. D. 325. Tradition is not always wrong, and we have come to look behind tradition for elements of truth. But we still lack clear evidence that here we have the authentic birthplace of Christ. Nearby is a "shepherd's field" that lends an air of verisimilitude to the picture, but even here the tourist is shown at least two such fields, so that we have to rest content that Christ was born somewhere in the area, without knowing exactly where.[30]

Bethany was a village known to our Lord. It lay a little to the southeast of Jerusalem and was the village where Jesus was

30. S. L. Caiger, *op. cit.*, pp. 77f.

anointed by the woman with the alabaster box of ointment and where He raised Lazarus from the dead (John 11). It is mentioned in the Passion narratives (Mark 11:1, 14:3.) and is described by John as "fifteen furlongs" (literally, *stadia*), or half an hour's walk, from Jerusalem. In the Syriac version of the New Testament it is written as Beth 'Anya which may be the short form of Beth Ananiah (Neh. 11:32). Today there is a little village called El Azariyeh ("place of Lazarus"), and just to the west of this is a small hill where cisterns and Jewish tombs have been discovered.[31] Close to the present village there is the traditional tomb of Lazarus and even though a church was built here about A. D. 380, looking back perhaps to an earlier

31. E. G. Kraeling, *op. cit.,* pp. 393f.

The traditional "tomb of Lazarus" close to the present village of Bethany. (Religious News Service Photo)

tradition about the burial place of Lazarus, there is no clear evidence that we have here the authentic site of Lazarus' tomb. The church has been excavated in recent times. All we can allow is that we probably have here the general position of the village of Bethany. Bethphage was not far away, most likely to the northwest, but there is no certainty about its position either.

Other towns of interest in the area of Judaea, such as Joppa, Lydda, Emmaus, Hebron, Gaza, Ascalon, Azotus, have their interest but must be studied in a fuller work than this.

The Population of Palestine in the Time of Jesus

Various peoples were to be found in the Holy Land in our Lord's day: Jews, Greeks, Phoenician-Canaanites, and smaller numbers of other peoples. The Jews, or, to speak more correctly, the descendants of the Israelites, were well scattered through many areas. The Greeks, who had been brought to Palestine following the conquest of Alexander the Great, had established colonies in many places but chiefly in the center and in the areas around Galilee. In the south were the Idumaeans, the old Edomites, now partly mixed by intermarriage. Herod and his father and grandfather were of this stock. Across the Jordan, in addition to the Greek population and the admixture of Arabs, there was the important, and now strong, kingdom of the Nabataeans, who occupied the areas south of Peraea. Their capital was at Petra.

We have seen that Herod Philip ruled a largely Greek population and that even in Galilee and in Samaria there were many Greeks. The most interesting area is that of the Decapolis (ten cities). The name occurs in the New Testament in Mark 5:20. Its origin goes back to the early days of the Romans in Palestine. Following the expansion of the Seleucid (Greek) rulers and their tremendous building program, the area to the east of Jordan became dotted with cities. With the restoration of the Jewish state under the Maccabees, the independence of these towns was threatened. When Pompey came in 63 B. C., he saw that these Greek towns could be useful to Rome. He therefore confined the Jews in Trans-Jordan to a narrow strip along the Jordan and gave to the Greek cities their independence. Towns like Jerash, Gadara, Philadelphia, Scythopolis (Bethshean), Hippos, Abila, and some to the north, including Damascus, were numbered among the cities of the Decapolis. Roman remains exist in some of these, and a place like Jerash has even

PALESTINE
in the
TIME OF CHRIST

EGYPT

today a magnificent amount of material for the archaeologist.[32] A good deal of work has been done here, as we have seen.

To the northwest of Palestine lived the Canaanite-Phoenician population, the traders of the day. Many of them came into Palestine, and some at least had dealings with Jesus. In religion they were still polytheists as they had been for centuries. They provided a splendid mission field for the early preachers of the gospel who went to their lands and established the Christian Church.

Finally we refer to the Nabataeans who defied all conquerors till the Romans finally overcame them in A.D. 106.[33] Their greatest king was Aretas IV (9 B.C.–A.D. 40), who at the time of our Lord held places like Damascus under his sway. Paul in Damascus had an adventure with the "governor under Aretas," who sought to take him, and Paul had to escape over the wall in a basket (II Cor. 11:32,

32. W. F. Albright, *op. cit.*, pp. 168-170.
33. Jean Starcky, "The Nabataeans, a Historical Sketch," *BA* (Dec., 1955).

A general view of the city of Damascus, Syria. The central building is the Omayyad mosque, which was originally the Christian church of St. John the Baptist until c. 700. It was destroyed by fire in 1893 and subsequently rebuilt. (Courtesy, UNESCO/P.A. Pittet/1961)

33). The Nabataeans chose as their capital the mountain retreat of Petra[34] and carved out of the rock magnificent buildings of all kinds — temples, houses, shops, tombs, and so on. Their architecture shows Greek and Roman influence. Excavation here and in other sites has given us a good picture of their culture. They were polytheists, manufactured splendid pottery, and were good builders. They controlled and exploited the trade routes leading from the Arabian peninsula to the lands along the Mediterranean Sea. It was a Nabataean princess who was the first wife of Herod Antipas. His divorce of this woman in favor of the notorious Herodias caused a war with the king of the Nabataeans. The fortress of Machaerus stood at the southern boundary of the domains of Antipas as a protection against the Nabataeans.[35]

As we leave our brief survey of the towns and peoples of the Palestine that Jesus knew, we have the impression that we are still comparatively ignorant of much of the detail about them. There is strong hope that the picture will be enlarged in the future. Active excavation is going on in many sites in Palestine and in the very places mentioned in the New Testament narratives. The subject is by no means exhausted and holds out much promise for future study.

34. W. F. Albright, *op. cit.*, pp. 160-165.
35. See above, p. 360.

Twenty:

LUKE THE HISTORIAN

AT THE CLOSE OF THE NINETEENTH CENTURY EXTREME CRITICS LIKE F. C. Bauer could argue that statements in Acts "can only be looked upon as intentional deviations from historic truth in the interest of the special tendency which they possess."[1] Such extremists compelled special study of Acts, with the result that it is widely agreed today that in this book we can see the hand of a historian of the first rank. Much of the credit for this change is due to the work of Sir W. M. Ramsay whose patient work proved that F. C. Bauer and his school were wrong. Ramsay wrote a series of volumes to establish his point, among which *St. Paul the Traveller and the Roman Citizen* and *The Bearing of Recent Discovery on the Trustworthiness of the New Testament* are the best known. In the former of these books Ramsay made the following statement:

I may fairly claim to have entered on this investigation without prejudice in favour of the conclusion which I shall now

1. Quoted by A. T. Robertson in *Luke the Historian in the Light of Research* (Edinburgh, 1920), p. 1.

373

attempt to justify to the reader. On the contrary, I began with a mind unfavourable to it, for the ingenuity and apparent completeness of the Tübingen theory had at one time quite convinced me. It did not then lie in my line of life to investigate the subject minutely; but more recently I found myself brought in contact with the book of Acts as an authority for the topography, antiquities and society of Asia Minor. It was gradually borne in upon me that in various details the narrative showed marvellous truth. In fact, beginning with the fixed idea that the work was essentially a second-century composition and never relying on its evidence as trustworthy for first-century conditions, I gradually came to find it a useful ally in some obscure and difficult investigations.[2]

If we ask what it was that produced this radical change of opinion in Ramsay, the answer is largely that archaeological investigation demonstrated that the historical, geographical, topographical, and political atmosphere of the books Luke and Acts as a whole, and of Acts in particular, suggests a close knowledge of the first century A. D. On many of the pages of his writings Ramsay pays glowing tribute to the sound historical sense of Luke, whom he describes as "among the historians of the first rank."[3]

SOME MATERIAL FROM LUKE'S GOSPEL

It is evident that the writer of this Gospel is interested in placing events he narrates in the context of history, because he keeps on giving historical landmarks. It was in the "days of Herod, the king of Judaea," that Zacharias the priest learned from the angel about the birth of a son (Luke 1:5). It was in the days of "Caesar Augustus, that all the world should be taxed; and this taxing was first made when Cyrenius was governor of Syria" (Luke 2:1f.). "In the fifteenth year of the reign of Tiberius Caesar, Pontius Pilate being governor of Judaea, and Herod being tetrarch of Galilee, and his brother Philip tetrarch of Ituraea and of the region of Trachonitis, and Lysanias the tetrarch of Abilene, Annas and Caiaphas being the high priests," John the Baptist began to preach (Luke 3:1f.).

2. W. M. Ramsay, *St. Paul the Traveller and the Roman Citizen* (London, 1897), pp. 7f.
3. *Ibid.*, p. 4.

Greek marble bust of Augustus Caesar (29 B.C. - A.D. 14) who was emperor at the time of Jesus' birth, and who issued the decree "that all the world should be taxed." (Courtesy, The British Museum)

Such statements as these are open to archaeological and historical investigation. Herod reigned from 37 B. C. to 4 B. C. This gives a date before 4 B. C. for the birth of John the Baptist and Jesus Christ. There is no difficulty about these facts, but some interesting points are raised in Luke 2:1f. where reference is made to the census of Augustus, and to Cyrenius. First of all, "all the world" in verse 1 is not meant to be taken literally. It refers to the Roman world of those times. Nor does the passage require that a single census was to be held at one time, but rather that the world "should be enrolled." Ramsay pointed out that Luke used the present tense deliberately and meant "that Augustus ordered enrollments to be regularly taken."[4] This interpretation is according to the strict and proper usage of the present tense. What Augustus did was to lay down the principle of systematic "enrollment" in the Roman world, not to arrange for the taking of one single census.

This enrollment was the "first enrollment when Quirinius was governor," and is thus to be distinguished from the later census referred

4. W. M. Ramsay, *Was Christ Born at Bethlehem?* (London, 1898), pp. 123f.

375

to in Acts 5:37. The point may be raised as to whether there is evidence that Augustus did in fact have an arrangement for such a system of enrollment. Here we have a good deal of material on hand. Clement of Alexandria (A. D. 155-220) spoke as though he knew of such a system and said that it began with the census at the time of the birth of Christ. It is established that in the later empire there was a cycle of fourteen years between enrollments; and in Egypt, at any rate, there is documentary evidence, in the form of actual census papers, for enrollments in A. D. 90, 104, 118, 132, and on till 230.[5] Ramsay speaks of census records for A. D. 34 and 62, and of indirect references to the census of A. D. 20 and 48. There is no reference extant to a census in A. D. 6, which would be the one in Acts 5:37, but presumably it took place. The one before this would be 8 B. C. E. M. Blaiklock in his *Pathway* book quotes a notice from A. D. 104, which reads as follows:

> Gaius Vibius, chief prefect of Egypt. Because of the approaching census it is necessary for all those residing for any cause away from their own districts to prepare to return at once to their own governments, in order that they may complete the family administration of the enrollment, and that the tilled lands may retain those belonging to them. Knowing that your city has need of provisioning, I desire . . . ."[6]

This document shows that the enrollment was by households. It is evident that, even if there is no direct evidence of such an enrollment in Palestine, the picture from Egypt provides a good deal of circumstantial support that this kind of thing went on in the Roman world. If it happened in Egypt, we might expect that the same thing would occur in Palestine. Professor Blaiklock, in the same chapter, adds other illustrations of documents found in Egypt, one being lodged by a woman in Egypt on the occasion of the census in A. D. 48.

The question of the exact date of the decree in Luke 2 is raised because on several grounds the birth of Christ seems to be about 7-6 B. C.[7] The census cycle would give a date of 8-7 B. C.

5. A. T. Robertson, *op. cit.*, pp. 123ff., summarizes the data in a handy form.
6. E. M. Blaiklock, *Out of the Earth* (Grand Rapids, 1957), p. 14.
7. A. J. Maclean, "Chronology of the New Testament," *Hastings Dictionary of the Bible* (Edinburgh, 1954), pp. 133ff., gives five converging lines of evidence for this date.

Ramsay argued that the situation in Palestine and Syria at the time may well have caused some delay in Herod's kingdom.[8]

We raise finally a question about Quirinius (Cyrenius). According to Josephus, this man was governor of Syria in A. D. 6 when a census that angered the Jews was taken. The Greek word translated "governor" in Luke 2:1 may not, however, carry precisely the same idea as our word. Its basic idea is that of "oversight," and this may take on various forms. It is now clear from inscriptions that Quirinius had authority of some kind on two occasions in Syria, though the office was not the same. One inscription tells us that *P. Sulpicius Quirinius duumvir* was engaged in war in Syria sometime before 6 B. C.[9] F. F. Bruce believes that "there is substantial evidence that Quirinius held such a post at an earlier time, probably between 10 B. C. and 7 B. C. when, as extraordinary imperial legate in the province of Syro-Cilicia for military purposes, he commanded an expedition against the Homanadenses, a mountain tribe of Asia Minor."[10] Ramsay found an inscription to this effect at Antioch of Pisidia. Luke does not say that Quirinius himself held the census which took place at the time of our Lord's birth, but only that it was while he was governor. He was actually fulfilling an extraordinary function alongside the regular governor, who at that time was Sentius Saturnius (8-6 B. C.).

The third reference we have noticed in Luke 3:1 gives yet another attempt to date an event by reference to persons who lived at the time. Ancient historians used different methods to fix their dates and quite often made no attempt to be as exact as we are today. Here in Luke 3:1 seven synchronisms are given to establish the time when the ministry of John the Baptist began. A difficulty has been imagined in the mention of Lysanius, who is here named as tetrarch of Abilene (west of Damascus), in the fifteenth year of Tiberius (A. D. 27-28). The only Lysanias of Abilene known from ancient history died in 34 B. C. Josephus refers to his father Ptolemais as ruler of a state, which included Abilene and whose capital was Chalcis. He supported Jewish nationalists against the Romans in 49 B. C. Lysanias, the son, followed his father's policy, but was finally put to death by Antonius in 34 B. C. After this there is little

8. W. M. Ramsay, *op. cit.*, pp. 174f.
9. A. T. Robertson, *op. cit.*, p. 128.
10. F. F. Bruce, *Are the New Testament Documents Reliable?* (Grand Rapids, 1946), p. 85.

known about Abilene till A. D. 53.[11] Josephus tells us that this area was added to the kingdom of Agrippa II by the emperor Claudius. In this later reference there is a mention of Lysanias. Josephus says concerning Abilene that "this had been the tetrarchy of Lysanias."[12] A second and later Lysanias was postulated for a time, but there are now two inscriptions which refer to such a man so that his existence is no longer a matter of speculation. In one of these he is coupled with a certain Zenodorus and is called "tetrarch." In the other we have a record of the dedication of a temple "for the salvation of the Lords Imperial and their whole household, by Nymphaeus a freedman of Lysanias the tetrarch."[13] The "Lords Imperial" was a joint title given to the emperor Tiberius and his mother Livia, the widow of Augustus, so that the date of the inscription may be fixed between A.D. 14, the year of Tiberius' accession, and A. D. 29 the year of Livia's death. Luke's reference to Lysanias in Luke 2:1 is therefore strongly supported by archaeological evidence.

Alfred Plummer, whose commentary on Luke was written in 1913 when much of this evidence was unavailable, remarked then that "the accuracy of Luke is such that we ought to require very strong evidence before rejecting any statement of his as an unquestionable blunder."[14] This statement is in strong contrast with the statements of numerous New Testament scholars of the last part of the nineteenth century, thanks to the discoveries of the archaeologists and the careful research of scholars such as Sir William Ramsay.

ACTS IN THE LIGHT OF ARCHAEOLOGY — PAUL'S FIRST MISSIONARY JOURNEY

The accuracy of Luke shows up particularly well in the book of Acts. Ramsay's *St. Luke the Traveller and the Roman Citizen* is devoted largely to an account of the journeys of Paul and the archaeological material bearing on them. Since Ramsay's day we have additional information from excavations and documents unknown to him. There is more reason than ever to conclude with Ramsay that

---

11. J. M. Creed, *The Gospel According to St. Luke* (London, 1950), p. 308.
12. Josephus, *Wars*, XX, vii, 1.
13. J. M. Creed, *op. cit.*, p. 309.
14. A. Plummer, *St. Luke*, ICC (Edinburgh, 1913), p. 50.

Luke is a historian of the first rank; not merely are his statements of fact trustworthy; he is possessed of the true historic sense; he fixes his mind on the idea and plan that rules in the evolution of history, and proportions the scale of his treatment to the importance of each incident. He seizes the important and critical events and shows their true nature at greater length, while he touches lightly, or omits entirely, much that was valueless for his purpose. In short, this author should be placed along with the very greatest of historians.[15]

Our method of treatment will be a chronological one. We shall proceed through the book of Acts in order, commenting on the narrative with archaeological material as we go.

We commence with Acts 11:27-30 where there is a reference to "great dearth throughout all the world" which came in the days of Claudius Caesar. Ramsay collected evidence to show that this famine is "singularly well attested."[16] Suetonius speaks of *assiduae sterilitates*, causing famine prices under Claudius; and Dion Cassius and Tacitus refer to two famines in Rome, which imply famines in the Mediterranean area, for Rome received her grain from overseas. Eusebius speaks of famine in Greece, and an inscription points to famine in Asia Minor. It seems clear that the reign of Claudius (A. D. 41-54) was marked by a succession of bad harvests which caused serious famines in various parts of the empire.[17] It was this famine that stirred up Christians in Antioch to send help to the poor Christians in Jerusalem, and Paul went on his second visit to this great city about A. D. 46, bearing a gift. It is known that others helped the poor of Jerusalem at this time as, for example, Queen Helena of Abilene, who bought corn in Egypt and figs in Cyprus, and sent them to Jerusalem. Josephus dates this event in the days of Cuspius Fadus (A. D. 44-46) and Tiberius Julius Alexander (46-48), procurators of the time.[18] This visit of Paul is probably the same as that referred to in Galatians 2:1ff. It was by revelation (cf. Acts 11:28 and Gal. 2:2), and the friends of Jerusalem asked that they go on remembering the poor (Gal. 2:10).

15. W. M. Ramsay, *The Bearing of Recent Discovery on the Trustworthiness of the New Testament* (London, 1915), p. 222.
16. W. M. Ramsay, *St. Luke the Traveller and the Roman Citizen* (London, 1897), pp. 48f.
17. F. F. Bruce, *The Book of Acts* (Grand Rapids, 1954), p. 243.
18. Josephus, *Antiquities*, XX. ii, 5 and v, 2.

With chapter 13 we come to that portion of Acts that concentrates on the life and work of Paul. It must have been in about A. D. 46 that the church of Antioch "separated Paul and Barnabas for the work" and sent them off on the first missionary journey. They left Seleucia by boat to go to Cyprus. Today the ruins of the old port of Seleucia, founded originally by Seleucus, the first Seleucid king, in 301 B. C., lie scattered along the shore and for some distance inland. Very little excavation has been done here, but there is a splendid opportunity for someone to undertake this task. The travelers landed in Cyprus, an

Another view of the Roman ruins at Baalbek, Lebanon, (see pages 288 and 305). Note the position of the only tier of heavy stones that remains of the roof that originally covered the dome. (Courtesy, UNESCO/P.A. Pittet/1961)

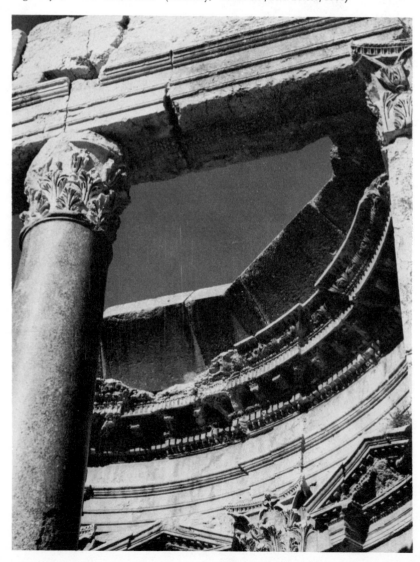

island of great importance for many centuries past, but annexed by Rome in 57 B. C., and attached to the province of Cilicia in Asia Minor in 55 B. C. In 27 B. C. it became a separate province governed by a legate. Then, in 22 B. C., Augustus handed it over to the Senate and it was administered by a proconsul. Thus, in the course of thirty-five years, it had four types of Roman government. Unless Luke were well acquainted with the facts there was plenty of occasion to make a mistake. However, in verse 7 he gives to the ruler of those times the correct title of "deputy" (Greek *anthupatos* translates the Latin *proconsul*).

Salamis and Paphos, mentioned in the narrative, are both places in which, although some excavation has already been undertaken, there is an excellent opportunity for further work.

In Paphos the missionaries met the proconsul Sergius Paulus. There is a good possibility that the name of this man has been found on an inscription in Cyprus. Ramsay refers to such an inscription found at Soloi on the north coast dated "in the proconsulship of Paullus."[19] One of the officers of Claudius in Rome, the "curator of the Tiber," was a man named Lucius Sergius Paullus,[20] and it is quite possible that he went afterwards to Cyprus as a proconsul.

One of the interesting suggestions of Ramsay is that some of the family of this Sergius Paullus later became Christians. He advanced epigraphic evidence for this suggestion.[21] Another item in this passage which possibly follows Roman usage is the reference to Paul's names in verse 9. Roman citizens had three names, a praenomen, a nomen, and a cognomen. Luke here gives only one of these names, Paulus, the cognomen. Luke, being a Greek, probably did not bother with other names. On the other hand, we may have here an example of the Jewish custom of an alternative Jewish name.

Leaving Cyprus, Paul and Barnabas went to Pamphylia in Asia Minor and then struck inland to the southern parts of the large Roman province of Galatia, which had been formed in 25 B. C. It was divided into a number of regions such as Pisidia, Isauria, Phrygia, and Lycaonia.[22] It seems that there were two regions known as Lycaonia, one in Galatia (Lycaonia Galatica) and one further east belonging

19. W. M. Ramsay, *St. Paul the Traveller and the Roman Citizen*, p. 74.
20. F. F. Bruce, *op. cit.*, p. 264.
21. W. M. Ramsay, *The Bearing of Recent Discovery on the Trustworthiness of the New Testament*, pp. 150f.
22. W. M. Ramsay, *St. Paul the Traveller and the Roman Citizen*, p. 104.

to an independent kingdom (Lycaonia Antiochiana). The town of Antioch mentioned in verse 14 is called by Strabo "Antioch near [or towards] Pisidia." It was the center of the region known as Galatic Phrygia and was the chief civil and military center of that part. An inscription found here some years ago speaks of a "regionary centurion," evidently a military officer charged with special duties in the area.[23] Hence Luke in Acts 13:49 quite accurately refers to preaching taking place in all the "region" round about.

The result of the preaching of the Word in the synagogue was that "almost the whole city" returned on the next Sabbath to hear. The local Jews stirred up strife. Luke mentions that the women had a share in this, and Ramsay points out that whereas this kind of thing would be unthinkable in Athens or an Ionian city, it was in accord with the custom in these inland cities.[24] So the missionaries moved on to Iconium, a town in the same region politically, but on the eastern edge of Galatic Phrygia. Actually the boundary here was a little artificial, and Iconium was quite near to Lystra, so that the two towns had close commercial relations. This fact is evident from Luke's comment in Acts 16:2. After more troubles in Iconium, Paul and Barnabas moved on to another "region," crossing over the boundary between Phrygia Galatica and Lycaonia Galatica. Ramsay confessed that it was the discovery of this fact of geography that led to his "first change in judgment" about the book of Acts, which he had hitherto regarded as of uncertain value.[25] The Greek writer Xenophon in 401 B. C. referred to Iconium as a Phrygian city, and there is both literary and epigraphic evidence to show that it remained a Phrygian city till A. D. 295.[26] So that while it was linked with Lystra and the towns of Lycaonia for commerce, it was in fact politically in Phrygia. This fact appealed greatly to Ramsay since it showed that Luke was accurately informed on such a precise detail.

The description in Acts 14:6 is entirely correct. There was a region here consisting of two large towns, Lystra and Derbe, and the area round about. Both towns lay in Lycaonia Galatica. To these strategic cities Paul and Barnabas came to preach. Lystra had become a Roman colony in the time of Augustus in A. D. 6,

23. W. M. Ramsay, *ibid.*, p. 103.
24. *Ibid.*, p. 102.
25. W. M. Ramsay, *The Bearing of Recent Discovery on the Trustworthiness of the New Testament*, pp. 35f.
26. F. F. Bruce, *op. cit.*, p. 288.

and lay eighteen miles from Iconium which was in Phrygian Galatia Paul healed a crippled man here and won the admiration and worship of the local population who came out with offerings and garlands as to gods, and cried out in the local dialect. Inscriptions show that Latin was the language of the colonists, but evidently the local people still spoke their own dialect, especially when they were excited.[27] There do not seem to be inscriptions in this local dialect so perhaps there was no written language.

The mention of the two gods, Mercurius and Jupiter, leads us to ask why these two were chosen out of all the possible gods in the pantheon. The names in the authorized version of the Bible are Latin and differ from the Greek form of the names, Hermes and Zeus, which occur in the Greek New Testament. At Sedasa, near Lystra, two inscriptions have been found.[28] One, dating from the middle of the third century A. D., records the dedication to Zeus of a statue of Hermes by men with Lycaonian names. The other mentions the "priests of Zeus." A stone altar, also found near Lystra in 1926, and dedicated to the "Hearer of Prayer [presumably Zeus] and Hermes," makes it clear that these two gods were linked in the worship of the people in this area.[29] Zeus was the head of the pantheon and Hermes was his herald. It is evident that when Paul and Barnabas came to Lystra, Paul was the active one and was thought to be Hermes the messenger, while Barnabas appeared more like Zeus who sent Hermes about his affairs.

Paul and Barnabas then moved on to Derbe and finally retraced their tracks to Antioch in Syria to report to the Church. So ended the first missionary journey.

PAUL'S SECOND MISSIONARY JOURNEY

The great Council of Jerusalem met in the period between Paul's first two journeys. In the years between, Paul wrote his letter to the Galatians whom he had visited.[30] It was the remarkable events of the first journey, and the conversion of the many Gentiles, that required the Church to state its policy. This was done at the

27. F. F. Bruce, *op. cit.*, p. 291.
28. *Ibid.*
29. *Ibid.*, p. 292.
30. New Testament scholars still argue as to whether Paul's letter to the Galatians was written to the churches around Antioch in the south, or to churches further north. English scholars on the whole accept the "South Galatian" theory, which is accepted by the present writer.

Council of Jerusalem. Then Paul and Barnabas were ready to set off again to visit the churches they had founded in Galatia. As things turned out, Paul took Silas, and Mark accompanied Barnabas (Acts 15:36-40). This must have been in A. D. 49 after an interval of teaching at Antioch.

Traveling this time overland, Paul and Silas passed through the province of Syria and Cilicia, a single Roman province (15:41), and then came to the province of Galatia. The book of Acts does not refer to this as such, but merely to the region of Derbe and Lystra. There is a precise touch here in chapter 16, verse 2, where Timothy is spoken of as "well reported of by the brethren that were at Lystra and Iconium." These two towns were, as we have seen, in different regions politically, but closely related economically, and it would be more likely that a man would be better known in them than in Lystra and Derbe. Ramsay notes that "this is true to the facts of commerce and intercourse."[31]

The geographical information is continued in 16:6, which refers to the crossing over of the boundary of a new region. The Greek text describes it as "Phrygia and the Galatian territory" (or possibly, "the Phrygian and Galatian territory"). This is a composite phrase for a single district. Actually old Phrygia was now divided by the Romans into a Galatian and an Asian portion (see map, p. 399). Mysia (v. 7) was a region of Asia, Bithynia (v. 7) a province, and Macedonia (v. 9) the first province of Europe to be visited by the missionaries. In all of this, Luke's information is quite consistent with what we know about the geography of this part of the Roman empire in the first century A. D. from a study of ancient documents. And so to Philippi and the evangelization of Europe!

Archaeological work has made an important contribution to our understanding of the story of Paul's visit to Philippi (Acts 16:12-40). Philippi came under Roman control in 168 B. C. After a battle in which Antony and Octavian defeated Brutus and Cassius in 42 B. C., veterans of the battle were allowed to settle here and to form a Roman colony, and other Roman citizens came later. The Greek text refers to it as a *kolonia*, which is correct. One other feature about this city is that it is described here as "first." There are inscriptions extant which show that some cities in Asia, Bithynia, and Macedonia had such a title. Acts 16:12 is a much discussed text, but it is evidently based on fact.[32] The point of discussion turns on

---

31. W. M. Ramsay, *St. Paul the Traveller and the Roman Citizen*, p. 179.
32. F. F. Bruce, *op. cit.*, p. 330.

the exact meaning of "first," but while scholars decide the true interpretation, the fact remains that this title "first" was used.

The A.V. in verse 13 should be changed to read, "we went forth without the gate by a river side," which is in close accord with the facts of archaeology. From 1914 to 1938 French archaeologists worked in Philippi. In the course of uncovering the old Roman road that ran through the town, they discovered the foundations of a great arched gateway at the northwest edge of the town through which the old road passed.[33] The only watercourse in

33. W. A. McDonald, "Archaeology and St. Paul's Journeys in Greek Lands," *BA* (May, 1940), p. 20.

Ruins of the villa of Emperor Hadrian (A.D. 117-138) near Tivoli (ancient Tibur), about eighteen miles east of Rome. Hadrian's villa was situated on low ground that covered an area of about 160 acres. Many statues, as well as costly foreign marbles and fine mosaics, have been found in the villa. (Courtesy, Italian State Tourist Office)

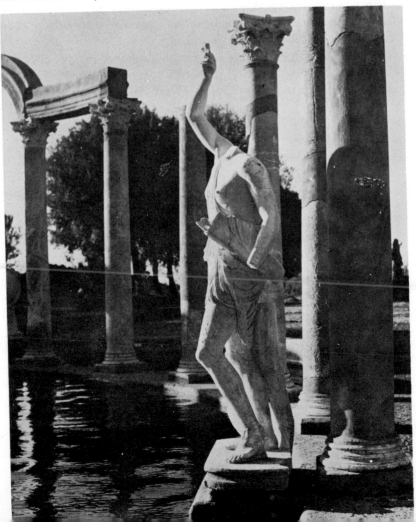

the region that is worthy of the name of river adjoins this road at only one place, a little more than a mile to the west of the city limits. The topography of Acts is thus quite accurate. The missionaries would in fact have gone "without the gate to the river side." We judge that we have here the exact spot where the gospel was first proclaimed in Europe.

A woman named Lydia, a seller of purple dye, was converted here, and a damsel was delivered of a demon. This caused an uproar and Paul and Silas were dragged into the market place (Greek *agora*). This site has been exposed by the excavations.[34] It followed the usual pattern of a Roman forum with a platform to the north, where cases were heard, and a large open square surrounded by important buildings. Paul and Silas appeared before the "magistrates" (Greek *strategoi*, v. 20). There were various kinds of magistrates and the Greek term here is normally used for the Latin magistrate, the *praetor*. In Roman colonies the magistrates were normally not *praetors* but *duumvirs*. We need not conclude that Luke has erred here, for these officers often took the more dignified title *praetor*, according to Cicero, one of the writers of the time.[35] This is no doubt what happened here. In any case Paul and Silas were beaten with the attendants' (*lictors'*) rods and cast into prison, where the jailor was converted in the night. Next day the magistrates sent to the "sergeants" (Greek *rabdouchoi;* literally, "rod bearers," the equivalent of *lictor*), to release them. Learning that Paul and Silas were Roman citizens, who were exempted from flogging and all degrading forms of punishment, the Roman magistrates were full of confusion and urged them to leave, which they did, passing through the city gate and traveling westward along the Egnatian Way, of which remains have now been discovered.

The next town for which we have some information is Thessalonica (Acts 17:1-9). Little in the way of excavation has been done here, for modern buildings cover the site of this ancient town. There are, however, a number of monuments of late Roman and early Christian times still standing. One important item bears on the days of Paul, and is connected with the reference to the "rulers" (v. 6) before whom Jason and the brethren were brought after the uproar. Jason had received Paul and earned the wrath of the Jews. The

---

34. *Ibid.*
35. F. F. Bruce, *op. cit.,* p. 335.

386

A Greek inscription, once part of the Gate of Vardar at Thessalonica, listing six "rulers of the city," the Greek designation for whom was "politarchs." Luke, in Acts 17:6, correctly calls such officials by that name. (Courtesy, The British Museum)

Greek word for "ruler" here is *politarchos*. It is now known to have been used particularly in Macedonian towns, although it is not yet known elsewhere in Greek literature. There are extant today some nineteen inscriptions ranging from the second century B. C. to the third century A. D. where the title is used, and in the majority of cases the reference is to magistrates of the Macedonian cities, although a few refer to other cities. Of the Macedonian examples five refer specifically to Thessalonica, which seems to have had five politarchs at the beginning of the first century B. C. and six in the following century.[36]

Paul left Silas and Timothy in Macedonia and went on alone to the province of Achaia in which lay the important towns of Athens and Corinth. There have been excavations in both of these towns and the archaeologist's spade has again produced considerable material for the student of the New Testament.

While Paul waited in Athens for his friends (they joined him after a few weeks in Corinth, Acts 18:5), he was able to look around this famous city with all its beauty of architecture and sculpture.

36. F. F. Bruce, *op. cit.*, p. 344.

The Acropolis at Athens, Greece, with its temples atop the hill and the Odeon of Herodes Atticus, a wealthy Roman resident, at its base, makes the most wonderful, impressive scene in Greece. Many of he large buildings, including the Parthenon, were built during the Golden Age of Pericles in the fifth century B.C. (Photo, Ewing Galloway)

Although the heyday of Athens in sculpture, literature, philosophy, and oratory had been the fifth and fourth centuries B. C., she was still unsurpassed, and the Romans, who had a considerable respect for its culture, gave Athens a certain freedom. Much of the beautiful sculpture and architecture, however, was for the honor of the gods, and this offended Paul. He "disputed in the synagogue with the Jews, and with the devout persons, and in the market daily" (v. 17).

In this statement there are two items of interest. First, excavations have brought the market place (Greek *agora*) to light, and it is possible today to draw a fairly complete plan of it.[37] Secondly, there is a keen observation hidden away here that reveals close knowledge of local customs. Ramsay pointed out that "in Ephesus, Paul taught 'in the school of Tyrannus'; in the city of Socrates he discussed moral questions in the market place. How incongruous it would seem if the methods were transposed."[38]

The Areopagus mentioned in verse 19 was where Paul was taken by the philosophers. This was an ancient court which met on a small rocky hill just at the foot of the great Acropolis and almost due west. The Acropolis itself was formerly the site of the fortress which protected the town. It was a striking, rocky hill which rose high behind Athens. According to tradition this little hill was the place where Ares, the god of war, stood trial for slaying the son of the sea god, and thereafter this rocky eminence served as the meeting place of the most ancient court and council of Athens. There were two white stones here, on one of which the defendant stood and on the other the prosecutor. In Paul's time the Areopagus had control over teachers like Paul who were expounding a new philosophy. By then, however, much, if not all, of the judicial authority had been lost, and its power lay chiefly in matters of religion and morals. Ramsay refers to the occasion when the Roman Cicero persuaded the Areopagus to invite a certain Cratippus, a philosopher, to lecture in Athens.[39] Paul was invited by this august body to come to the little hill to expound his philosophy, and in verses 22 to 31 we have a summary of his address.

Archaeological comment may be made on two items in Paul's address. The reference to the Athenians being "too superstitious," or preferably, "very religious," is better understood in the light of our knowledge of the very great number of temples and religious statues and images that were to be seen in the city. Other writers, like Sophocles, Pausanias, and Josephus, were similarly impressed.[40] The extant remains of temples and religious sculptures certainly support Paul's remark. The great Acropolis, on which stood the Parthenon,

37. Oscar Broneer, "Athens, City of Idol Worship," *BA* (Feb., 1958), p. 17.
38. W. M. Ramsay, *op. cit.*, p. 238.
39. *Ibid.*, p. 247.
40. F. F. Bruce, *op. cit.*, p. 355.

was covered with a variety of temples and shrines, many of which can still be seen even though they are in a state of ruin.[41]

The other item on which we should comment is the reference to the altar with an inscription, "To the Unknown God." That such altars were known in Greece, and in particular in Athens, is borne out by two writers of ancient times. Pausanias, who lived in the second century A. D. and traveled widely, observed in his description of Greece that at Athens there were altars of gods called "unknown." Again Philostratus in the early third century spoke of Athens "where even unknown divinities have altars erected to them."[42]

As a result of Paul's preaching some believed, including a woman called Damaris. Ramsay suggests that this woman may have been foreign, perhaps one of the educated foreigners, who were common in Athens. "It was impossible in Athenian society for a woman of respectable position and family to have opportunity of hearing Paul."[43] This may be true, though it is not entirely clear, for she may have been one of the "God-fearers who heard him in the synagogue."

The last great town Paul visited on this journey was Corinth (18:1-17). He stayed here a year and six months "teaching the word of God among them." This was probably about A. D. 51. At that time Corinth was the commercial and political center of the Roman province of Achaia and therefore a strategic center from Paul's point of view. A strange occurrence made it possible for the archaeologists to work in old Corinth. In 1858 an earthquake in the region caused most of the survivors to abandon the old site and move three or four miles away. In 1896 the Greek government gave a permit to the American School of Classical Studies to excavate, and since that day an enormous amount of information has been accumulated.

The city of Corinth had been badly damaged by the Romans in 146 B. C., though not completely obliterated. Remains of the earlier city, such as the great columns of the temple of Apollo, have been discovered. Julius Caesar refounded the city as a Roman colony, and it made rapid strides in prosperity. It became the capital of the Roman province of Achaia in 27 B. C.

---

41. W. A. McDonald, "Archaeology and St. Paul's Journeys in Greek Lands, Part II, Athens," *BA* (Feb., 1941). See also Oscar Broneer, *op. cit.*
42. F. F. Bruce, *op. cit.*, p. 355.
43. W. M. Ramsay, *op. cit.*, p. 252.

Remains of the ancient market place (agora) and of the old city of Corinth, Greece. Corinth had been badly damaged by the Romans in 146 B.C., so when Paul visited the city about A.D. 51, he may have seen these very ruins in an earlier stage. (Photo, Ewing Galloway)

Paul met a Jewish couple, Aquila and Priscilla, shortly after his arrival and discovered them to be of the same trade as himself. They became friends. These two had come from Rome on the occasion of the expulsion of the Jews from that city by Emperor Claudius. We have referred to this event already and to the uncertainty attaching to the name *Chrestus* in the account of Suetonius.[44]

44. See above, p. 295.

It is quite possible that we have here a reference to troubles caused by the Jews at the time of the introduction of Christianity to Rome. The passage in Suetonius reads: "Because the Jews at Rome caused continuous disturbances at the instigation of Chrestus, he [Claudius] expelled them from the city."[45]

Paul, as usual, preached to the Jews, whose synagogue is mentioned in verse 4. That there was a synagogue somewhere in the city is evidenced by the discovery of a long block of stone which was evidently the lintel of a doorway. Seven Greek letters were still visible, "GOGEEBR." An attempted restoration is "[SUNA]GOGE EBR[AION]," which means, "Synagogue of the Jews."[46] This piece was dated by Deissmann at between 100 B. C. and A. D. 200, although some writers do not allow that it is pre-Christian. W. A. McDonald argues that it was actually after Paul's time. "The careless style of lettering indicates that the inscription,

45. Suetonius, *The Twelve Caesars* (Penguin, 1958), p. 197.
46. A. Deissmann, *Light from the Ancient East* (London, 1927), p. 16.

An imposing aerial view of the Colosseum in Rome, built by Emperor Titus, c. A.D. 80. The Arch of Constantine is in the foreground. (Courtesy, Italian State Tourist Office)

and presumably the synagogue to which it belonged, is considerably later than the time of St. Paul. But it is reasonable to conclude that both this and the earlier one, in which the Apostle 'reasoned every sabbath, and persuaded the Jews and the Greeks' (Acts 18:4), were located in this area. No existing foundation has yet been convincingly associated with this lintel."[47]

Paul's two friends Titus and Timothy (v. 5) now joined him, and the work of preaching went on. In time, however, trouble began

47. W. A. McDonald, "Archaeology and St. Paul's Journeys in Greek Lands, Part III, Corinth," *BA* (Sept., 1942), p. 41.

Another view of the Colosseum, looking down into the arena. The flooring having deteriorated during the centuries, its absence affords a comprehensive view of the cellars and chambers below where wild beasts and human victims were kept until the hour of performance. (Courtesy, Italian State Tourist Office)

according to the usual pattern, and Paul was brought before Gallio, the "deputy of Achaia" (v. 12). The date of spring A. D. 52 can be given with considerable accuracy from the reference to Gallio. Paul was thus in Corinth from autumn A. D. 50 to spring A. D. 52. Certain pieces of information link together very neatly in this connection.

Gallio is described as the "deputy" (Greek *anthupatos*), that is, *proconsul*, in Latin. The first question we ask concerns the precise nature of the governor of Achaia. Ramsay gives the facts as follows: "Achaia was governed by a proconsul from 27 B. C. to A. D. 15 and from A. D. 44 onwards. It was a province of the second rank and was administered by Roman officials after holding the praetorship, and generally before the consulship."[48] So Paul gives the correct title for Gallio.

Next, what can be discovered about this Gallio? There was a Gallio, son of the elder Seneca (about 50 B. C. to A. D. 40) and brother of the younger Seneca the philosopher (about 3 B. C. to A. D. 65). He was adopted by the rhetorician Lucius Junius Gallio, and took his name. He was renowned for his amiable character and his wit. An inscription, found at Delphi in central Greece, records a proclamation of the emperor Claudius sometime early in A. D. 52, which mentions that Gallio was proconsul of Achaia[49] and suggests that he had been appointed to the office earlier, perhaps in A. D. 51. Seneca mentions that Gallio caught fever in Achaia and took a cruise. He was later in Rome, but perished finally with Seneca and other members of his family in the days of Nero's purges.[50] All of which shows again that Luke was well acquainted with the facts of the case.

Paul was taken to the "judgment seat" (Greek *bema*). The position of this in the market place in Corinth is now known. It was situated near the center of the Agora, along a magnificent terrace dividing the lower area on the north from the upper area on the south. There was a structure here which was really an outdoor speaker's stand. It originally had an outer coat of marble, traces of which remain and indicate the richness of its decoration. Flanking the *bema* at the level of the lower Agora were waiting rooms with mosaic floors and marble benches on each side.[51]

48. W. M. Ramsay, *op. cit.*, p. 258.
49. A. Deissmann, *Paul* (London, 1926), pp. 261ff., note p. 272.
50. F. F. Bruce, *op. cit.*, pp. 373f.
51. Oscar Broneer, "Corinth," *BA* (Dec., 1951), pp. 91f.

Gallio quickly decided that the matter was purely one of a difference in interpretation between groups of Jews and dismissed the case. The mob, sensing the insult to the Jews, took occasion to beat up their leader in a sort of anti-Jewish demonstration. Gallio ignored this (v. 17), and Paul rejoiced in the "freedom of speech which the imperial policy as declared by Gallio seemed inclined to permit." So says Ramsay, and adds, "The action of Gallio, as we understand it, seems to pave the way for Paul's appeal a few years later from the petty outlying court of the procurator of Judaea, who was always much under the influence of the ruling party in Jerusalem, to the supreme tribunal of the Empire."[52]

We have a gleam of light today about the meat market of I Corinthians 10:25. The Christians in Corinth were concerned about purchasing meat sold in the "shambles" (Greek *makellon*) because it had first been offered to idols. An inscription found in the course of the American excavations was identified as belonging to the meat market and it may have come from a large commercial building on the northern side of the agora.[53] Several ruined temples are to be found in the general area of the market place, among them being the temple of Apollo, which lies quite close to the area suspected of being the meat market.

Paul tarried in Corinth "yet a good while" (v. 18) and then passed on to Ephesus, taking with him Priscilla and Aquila. His visit to Ephesus on this occasion was brief, for he was pressing on to Jerusalem to keep the feast (v. 21). He was to return for an extended ministry on his third missionary journey in A. D. 53.

PAUL'S THIRD MISSIONARY JOURNEY AND HIS LAST YEARS

After his return to Jerusalem from his second journey (18:21f.), Paul had hurried on to Antioch. The Greek text in verses 22 and 23 gives an impression of haste with its succession of participles. Paul set out by land again and traversed the "Galatic region" (literal Greek), that is the Galatic Lycaonia and "Phrygia" (probably the whole area including both the Galatic and the Asian). As there was no bar to the way (cf. 16:6), he pressed on into Asia and, having visited his old friends of southern Galatia, he was now ready to

---

52. W. M. Ramsay, *op. cit.*, p. 260.
53. W. F. Albright, *Recent Discoveries in Bible Lands*, p. 119; Oscar Broneer, *op. cit.*, pp. 79, 89f.

View across the theater and esplanade of ancient Ephesus in Phrygia, Asia Minor, towards the Aegean Sea and Smyrna. (Photo, Ewing Galloway)

conquer new fields. He came to Ephesus where his friends Priscilla and Aquila had instructed a well-informed Jew, named Apollos, about Jesus the Messiah. This man returned to Corinth from whence he had come and taught in the synagogue, "shewing by the scriptures that Jesus was Christ" (18:28).

Paul, as usual, ministered in the synagogue in Ephesus, but after three months he had to move to the school of Tyrannus. It was quite usual in Ephesus for discussions to take place in a school and not in the market place as in Athens.[54] Paul's ministry continued for two years, during which time he healed many who were ill, in the name of Jesus. Jewish exorcists then tried to cure those possessed by demons by using the same name. It is a fact that there were Jews who did this kind of thing in those days. There are in existence still several magical papyri in which the sacred name of God, variously pronounced as *Iao, Iae, Iaoue,* and so on, was used,

54. See above, p. 389.

along with other expressions, in magic spells.[55] Ephesus in particular was renowned for its devotion to magic. The word "deeds" (19:18) is used in a technical sense and seems to refer to such magic spells.

Another word, here translated "curious arts," also had a technical meaning. These magical formulae were destroyed when the practitioners were converted (v. 19). Examples of such documents can still be seen in the British Museum or the Louvre.[56]

Paul's heart was set on visiting Rome. His plan was to pay a quick visit to Macedonia, then Jerusalem, and after that, Rome. He sent Timothy and Erastus ahead of him into Macedonia (19:22) as a first step in the working out of what were to be his final plans. The mention of Erastus here has led to a discussion as to whether this might be the Erastus who was the city treasurer of Corinth, referred to in Romans 16:23 as Erastus the "chamberlain" (Greek *oikonomos*). We are not certain that it is the same person, but there was certainly an Erastus of some importance in Corinth. Paul, who was almost certainly in Corinth when he wrote his letter to the Romans,[57] refers to the "chamberlain" of the city as a man he knew there. There is another reference to Erastus in II Timothy 4:20, where we learn that Erastus abode in Corinth. This is no doubt the same man that we meet in Paul's letter to the Romans. In the course of excavations in Corinth in 1929 Professor T. L. Shear found a pavement bearing the inscription ERASTVS PRO: AED: S: P: STRAVIT, which in translation reads, "Erastus, procurator and aedile, laid this pavement at his own expense." An article was later written in the *Journal of Hellenic Studies* by A. W. Woodward, who remarked, "The evidence indicates that this pavement existed in the first century A. D. and it is most probable that the donor is identical with Erastus the friend of Paul who is mentioned in the Epistle to the Romans."[58] The inscription was found in the little square at the north end of the street leading past the theater. The letters are rather deeply hollowed out and were once filled with bronze held in place by lead.[59]

The question may be asked whether the Greek word *oikonomos* could represent the Latin *aedile*. We discover that these officials,

---

55. A. Deissmann, *Bible Studies* (English transl., Edinburgh, 1909), pp. 322ff.
56. Adolf Deissmann gives a number of excellent examples in his remarkable book, *Light from the Ancient East*, pp. 254ff., 302ff., 453ff.
57. A. M. Hunter, *Introducing the New Testament* (London, 1955), p. 69, etc.
58. F. F. Bruce, *Are the New Testament Documents Reliable?*, p. 92.
59. W. A. McDonald, "Archaeology and St. Paul's Journeys in Greek Lands, Part III, Corinth," *BA* (Sept., 1942), p. 46.

whether Greek or Roman, included in their functions the charge of the financial affairs of the city, and thus the identification seems very probable. Most scholars today are agreed that there is no good reason why the man who prepared the pavement inscription should not be the same as Erastus the chamberlain.

Before Paul could join his friends, a serious riot broke out. It was apparently provoked because the gospel Paul preached was presenting a serious threat to the cult of Diana (Greek, Artemis). In the account in Acts 19:23-41 there is a good deal of local color, and archaeological research has shown that in these details Luke has given a faithful picture.

Ephesus was the center of the Artemis cult in the East. The goddess Artemis (called Diana by the Romans) was, in a special sense, "Diana of the Ephesians" (v. 28). Her temple was one of the seven wonders of the world. It was considered so sacred and inviolable that not only the Ephesians, but also foreign individuals, kings, and peoples deposited money there for safekeeping. So the temple was a sort of bank. In addition, great gifts were made to the goddess, which added to the wealth of her temple. One inscription tells of the gift of a certain Vibius Salutaris of twenty-nine statues of silver and gold, to be carried in a public procession to the temple. In the light of all this we begin to appreciate the concern of "Demetrius, a silversmith, which made silver shrines for Diana" (v. 24), when the preaching of Paul began to produce a stream of converts to Christ. Demetrius "called together the workmen of like occupation" and pointed out that Paul had "persuaded and turned away much people, saying that they be no gods, which are made with hands" (vv. 24-26). No doubt at every center of sight-seeing to which pilgrims came in the month of Artemison (March-April) to pay their homage to Artemis, a brisk trade was done in souvenirs and objects of devotion. No silver shrines have been found in excavations, although small pottery ones have, along with a great variety of votive gifts.

Artemis, according to tradition, fell down from heaven, and her image was enshrined in her temple. Possibly the origin of the belief was that a meteorite, resembling a many-breasted female, once fell in the region. Despite its former glory, the temple was lost for many centuries but it was found at the end of the last century to the northeast of the city in the low ground at the base of the hill of Ayassoluk, on which later a Christian church was built. Today a

PAUL'S MISSIONARY JOURNEYS and the CHURCHES of ASIA and EUROPE

MEDITERRANEAN SEA

BLACK SEA

ADRIATIC SEA

Rome

ITALY

SICILY

MALTA

MACEDONIA

Beroea

Thessalonica

Philippi

ACHAIA

Corinth

Athens

CRETE

FAIR HAVENS

BITHYNIA

GALATIA

Pergamum

Thyatira

Sardis

Philadelphia

Antioch

PHRYGIA

Smyrna

Ephesus

Laodicea

Colossae

Miletus

PAMPHYLIA

LYCAONIA

Iconium

Lystra

Derbe

CILICIA

Tarsus

Paphos

CYPRUS

Salamis

Antioch

Seleucia

SYRIA

Damascus

Sidon

Tyre

Ptolemais

Caesarea

Jerusalem

First Journey
Second
Third

plan can be drawn, showing a platform 418 feet long and 239 feet wide, from which a flight of ten steps led up to a pavement, and three more steps led up to the temple platform.[60] The temple itself was about 343 feet long and 164 feet wide, and contained one hundred columns just over six feet in diameter. Some of these were sculptured. The sanctuary was seventy feet wide and the altar twenty feet square. The statue is thought to have been behind the altar. Fragments found in the excavation prove that brilliant color, as well as gold, was used in the temple decoration.

It was this temple and all that it stood for that was in danger of being "despised" (v. 27), so the excited crowd cried out, "Great Artemis of the Ephesians!" Ramsay points out that this was "a common formula of devotion and prayer as is attested by several inscriptions."[61]

In the uproar, the crowd seized two of Paul's companions and "rushed with one accord into the theater" (v. 29). This is the structure to be seen today by the tourist on the western slope of Mount Pion. It was 495 feet in diameter and would hold about 24,500 people in its heyday. It was connected to the harbor of Ephesus by a fine marble paved street, the so-called Arkadiane, which was thirty-six feet wide, 1735 feet long, and lined with a colonnade on each side, behind which were shops and stores.

The town clerk (Greek *grammateus*) was alarmed at the riot, fearing the consequences of an inquiry; for he, as the executive officer, was responsible to the Roman provincial administration. He urged the people not to be alarmed for the honor of the great goddess, for everyone knew of her fame and her heavenly origin. Indeed, she had so honored the city as to give it a special title, "Warden of the Temple of Artemis" (Greek *neokoros*, literally, "temple sweeper"). The A.V. misses the point by translating, "the city of the Ephesians is a worshipper of the great goddess Diana, and of the image which fell down from Jupiter" (v. 35). This very title, *neokoros*, once used of very menial temple services, came to be used as a title of honor, and is attested in many inscriptions.[62] It was in fact used very widely of individuals in Egypt and Asia Minor, and sometimes for a people as a whole group. Josephus speaks

---

60. M. M. Parvis, "Archaeology and St. Paul's Journeys in Greek Lands, Part IV, Ephesus," *BA* (Sept., 1945), pp. 67ff.

61. W. M. Ramsay, *op. cit.*, p. 279.

62. M. M. Parvis, *op. cit.*, p. 80.

The Artimision in ancient Ephesus, the temple of Artemis, or Diana, as this goddess was called there, was one of the seven wonders of the ancient world. The temple was of immense dimensions and was supported by one hundred columns, some of which were sculptured. This illustration shows the drum of one of the eight pillars that supported the pediment. (Courtesy, The British Museum)

of Israel as "temple keeper of God," for example.[63] For our purpose it is important to know that the term was in fact used of Ephesus.

One final point comes out of our study of this chapter. It is the reference to "Asiarchs" in verse 31, or as the A.V. has it, the "chiefs of Asia." These Asiarchs, or high priests of Asia, were the heads of the provincial cult of "Rome and Emperor." Augustus permitted Ephesus, among others, to dedicate a sacred area to Rome and the Caesar. The Asiarchs are mentioned often in inscriptions and seem to have been chosen from families of position and means to care for the rites of the imperial cult, observed by the league of cities in the Roman province of Asia.

The office was held for one year, but the title was used after the individual retired from office. There could thus be several Asiarchs at once in Ephesus who represented rather public honor than narrow religious fanaticism. Their tolerance of Paul (v. 31) was thus quite in keeping with their general attitude in such cases.[64]

Shortly after, Paul left for Macedonia. Very quickly he visited Greece again, returned to Macedonia, and then set sail for home. He was able to see the Ephesian elders en route (Acts 20:17-38), but proceeded on his way and landed at Caesarea. Nothing could dissuade him from going to Jerusalem, but as it happened, it led to his imprisonment, his detention in Caesarea under the procurators Felix and Festus, and his final journey to Rome.

Three archaeological notes will complete our account. We have already referred to the Temple inscription implied in Acts 21:28,[65] and to the "castle" or "fortress" in Acts 21:34 being Antonia.[66] The final item concerns the exact title of the "chief man" of Malta where Paul was shipwrecked (Acts 28:7). This title appears on two Maltese inscriptions, one in Greek and one in Latin.[67] The "first man," or *protos*, in this case was Publius. Luke's title is the correct designation of the Roman governor of Malta.

Our discussion has been a lengthy one, but it will have served to show the tremendous value of archaeological research for our understanding of such a book as Acts. Luke is shown to be a most careful recorder of information, whether it be matters of geography

63. Josephus, *Wars*, V, ix, 4.
64. M. M. Parvis, *op. cit.*, p. 80.
65. See above, pp. 314f.
66. See above, pp. 345f.
67. F. F. Bruce, *The Book of Acts* (Grand Rapids, 1954), p. 523.

and political boundaries, local customs, titles of local officers, local religious practices, details of local topography, or the disposition of buildings in Greek or Roman, Asian or European towns. Most of our information has come from archaeological research, which has only just begun its enormous task.

Twenty-one:

ARCHAEOLOGY, JOHN'S GOSPEL, AND THE BOOK OF REVELATION

Among the difficult problems of New Testament study are those of the date and authorship of the books. The writings that appear under the name of John in the New Testament have been the subject of a great deal of discussion, both as to date of writing and as to authorship. Perhaps it is true to say that the world of scholars has not yet entirely made up its mind about these questions. It is not our intention here to raise the issue but only to show how the discoveries of the archaeologists have thrown light on two of these books, the Gospel of John and the book of Revelation. Archaeological discovery has brought to bear on the problems connected with these books some solid material evidence. This is refreshing because a great deal of the thinking in the past has been based largely on internal evidence only and has lacked the control provided by external points of reference.

Archaeology and the Gospel of John

At the end of the nineteenth century and in the earlier part of the present century radical scholars placed this Gospel in the

Illustration on page 404: Fishing scene near Elath, the southernmost place in the modern *state of Israel, near the old town of Ezion Geber, on the Gulf of Aqaba, which is part f the Red Sea*. (Courtesy, Israel Office of Information)

second century A. D. and insisted that it showed Gnostic influences. One Gnostic sect in particular, the Mandeans, was said to have influenced the writer of this Gospel greatly. The dualistic thought of these people was said to be clearly evident in the Gospel, and for this reason it was placed late in the second century.

More conservative scholars were not slow to point out that the external evidence was at the least fragmentary and the internal evidence lacked external controls. Then came the discoveries of the past half-century, and the subsequent mature consideration of their significance. These have seriously affected the discussion.

In some ways the most interesting of all of these discoveries is a small papyrus scrap of John's Gospel found in Egypt and dated no later than A. D. 150.[1] This showed that the Gospel had already been circulated in a provincial area of Egypt, and hence its date of composition must have been earlier in the century at the very least.

1. Discussed in detail on p. 437.

Dam in the Beit Netufa Valley in Galilee; it is part of the irrigation system which the Israel Government has developed to make large areas tillable. (Courtesy, Israel Office of Information)

Reference has already been made to the topographical references in John's Gospel which have led W. F. Albright to conclude that the author was well acquainted with features of Palestine that were obliterated after the Roman campaign of A. D. 70.[2] We have also noted that there are practically no Jewish remains in Palestine that can be dated to the last quarter of the first century A. D.[3] Jews were driven out after A. D. 70, and such tombs as we have are all before this date. Practically all traces of synagogues have gone, and synagogue remains left today are all from late in the second century. Christians were gathered up in this ruthless destruction by the Romans so that there was an almost complete break in Christian tradition as well. In this connection W. F. Albright has written:

> Any reminiscences of the life of Jesus or of conditions in Palestine in His time must have been carried into the Diaspora by Christian refugees, either voluntarily or otherwise. This means that if there are correct data in the Gospels or Acts of the Apostles which can be validated archaeologically or topographically, they must have been carried from Palestine in oral form by Christians who left that land before or during the first Jewish revolt.[4]

What are some of these first-century items listed by Albright? We have in fact referred to most of them. Thus he pointed out that the names Rabbi (my master), and the equivalent Greek term *didaskalos* (literally "teacher") were both used in a number of places in John's Gospel. But whereas it was once argued that the use of these terms pointed to a late date for John, who used the words far more than the Synoptics, it is now evident that both words were in common use in the days of Christ. The data point rather to an early than to a late date for John.[5]

The names on the ossuaries show that the range of names in John is quite consistent with the names in common use in Palestine in the first century. Thus the name Laz'ar, an abbreviated form

---

2. See above, p. 363; and cf. W. F. Albright, *The Archaeology of Palestine* (London, 1954), pp. 247f.; also W. F. Albright, "Recent Discoveries in Palestine and the Gospel of St. John" in *The Background of the New Testament and Its Eschatology* (Cambridge, 1956), pp. 153ff.

3. See above, pp. 320, 357.

4. W. F. Albright, *The Background of the New Testament and Its Eschatology*, p. 156.

5. *Ibid.*, pp. 157f.

A close-up view of the city of Nazareth with the Church of the Annunciation in the background to the right. (Courtesy, Trans World Airlines)

for Eleazar, is common on the ossuaries, as are female names like Maryam (Mary), Marta (Martha), Elisheba (Elisabeth), Shalom (Salome). All of these names are in good first-century tradition.[6]

We have already discussed the topographical reference to the "Pavement" (Greek *Lithostrotos,* and Aramaic *Gabbatha*).[7] And even if there remains some doubt about the exact identity of the site, the reference has the ring of authenticity about it.

Albright also drew attention to a topographical note in John 3:23, where we learn that John the Baptist was baptizing at "Aenon near Salim, because there was much water there."[8] This description suits the area close to Shechem and Nablus where there is still a

6. *Ibid.*
7. See above, pp. 345f.; and cf. W. F. Albright, *ibid.,* pp. 158f.
8. *Ibid.,* p. 159.

village of Salim and, close by, the village of 'Ainun. These two lie near the head waters of the Wadi Far'ah, with many springs in the vicinity. Later Christian tradition which identified Salim with Salumias in the Jordan valley was wrong. If John were really baptizing near the Jordan, there would be no need to comment on the fact that there was much water there. Recent study of these names points to the accuracy of the topographical information in John's Gospel at this point and provides a note of authenticity.

Another of Albright's suggestions needs some modification. He argued that Sychar in John 4 is to be identified with old Shechem (or Sychem) which, according to information available in 1956, was not destroyed till the time of the Jewish revolt and was therefore still in existence in Jesus' day.[9] But, according to the latest excavations, Shechem ceased to exist about 100 B. C., so that Albright's point is not valid at present unless, of course, further excavation at old Shechem reveals an area of the town that was occupied during the first part of the first century A. D.[10]

9. *Ibid.,* p. 160.
10. See discussion on p. 363.

Mount Gilboah, bordering the Valley of Jezreel. In the foreground is a present-day Jewish settlement. (Courtesy, Israel Office of Information)

Evidence of the possible early date of John's Gospel has come recently from two most unusual sources; first, from the discovery of some early Gnostic documents from Egypt and, secondly, from the manuscripts found in caves near the Dead Sea. The argument regularly advanced by critical scholars was, as we have seen, that John's Gospel was heavily overlaid with dualistic thought. Now and again a writer would protest.[11] Thus E. R. Goodenough held that the thought of John's Gospel expressed in the prologue presents a view of the Logos doctrine that was more primitive in its philosophy than was the doctrine of Philo (about 20 B.C. to A.D. 50). He accordingly suggested that both Philo and John drew on earlier material. C. H. Dodd also sought to deny the direct influence of the Gnostics. Now, due to archaeological discovery, we are able to approach the problem from two angles. First, we have opportunity to study in some detail and at first hand a set of Gnostic documents from Egypt and, secondly, we are able to study the type of thinking of one of the religious communities in Palestine at, and before, the time of Christ, and this community was not in any way a Gnostic community.

The Gnostic material from Egypt comes from Chenoboskion in upper Egypt and includes nearly forty lost treatises.[12] The date, judged from a study of the style of writing (paleography), is the late third or early fourth century. Up to recent times our knowledge of the Gnostics had come at second hand, largely from the Church Fathers. Whereas we had only three original codices and seven different writings a few years ago, we now have thirteen codices and forty-four different writings. Of all the various Gnostic works mentioned by the Fathers, only a few are now missing. It becomes clear that the picture the Fathers drew was a true one. Indeed, on the evidence of the new material, the early Gnostics were even worse heretics than the Fathers indicated. The supposed form of mild Gnosticism that is said to have influenced John was simply non-existent in the second century when the Gospel of John was supposed to have been written and when John supposedly came under their influence. By that date the Gnostics were already outrageously heretical. Whence then came the simple dualism so clearly expressed in John's Gospel? It did not come from the Gnostics, for

---

11. W. F. Albright, *op. cit.*, p. 161.
12. V. R. Gold, "The Gnostic Library of Chenoboskion," *BA* (Dec., 1952), pp. 70ff.

they had a strongly developed and quite non-Jewish dualism. In any case, their whole approach was quite out of keeping with the sublime teaching of John's Gospel.

A study of the Qumran materials reveals that the Messianic sect that produced these documents had a theological system that was characterized by a far-reaching dualism. Perhaps these people were originally influenced by the Persians, but if they were, the system had been greatly modified. If the Persian thinkers spoke of two opposed principles at work in the world, good and evil, both independent of one another, the Qumran secretaries thought rather of two opposing spirits, both created by God at the beginning of time. The dualism is therefore monotheistic, as well as being strongly ethical. Indeed we have here an ethical dualism not unlike what we find in the New Testament, and very strongly expressed in both John and Paul. Both John and the Essene sect of Qumran speak of truth and perversity (or lying), light and darkness, and so on.

Concerning the dualism of the Qumran sect, W. F. Albright has written:

> . . . their theology was characterized by a simple dualism, derived from Iranian sources, but thoroughly Judaized in the process of adaptation. There is a Spirit of Truth and a Spirit of Falsehood, both created by God; it is man's duty to choose between them. The Spirit of Truth is substantially the Christian Holy Spirit, but lacks all specifically Christian overtones. This simple dualism, contrasting good and evil, truth and falsehood, light and darkness, appears in the Gospel of John; there is nothing Gnostic about it, and those many N. T. scholars who date the Gospel after the rise of Gnosticism are now proved wrong. The Gospel of John is saturated with phraseology and conceptual imagery reminding us of the Dead Sea Scrolls.[13]

In the light of this study it is clear that John's Gospel is far closer to the ethical dualism of the Qumran sect than it is to the material dualism of the Gnostics. Even so, it is by no means exactly parallel. This much is clear, however, that there is no compelling reason why John's Gospel should not be dated in the first century A. D., for the Qumran documents can be dated from the period approximately 100 B. C. to A. D. 70.

13. W. F. Albright, *Recent Discoveries in Bible Lands* (New York, 1955), p. 131.

To sum up, then, there is a good deal of interest for us in the archaeological discoveries which bear on John's Gospel. The items we have mentioned all tend to support an early date as well as the authenticity of the book. It would seem, therefore, that we have reached a point in the study of John's Gospel where archaeological evidence practically compels us to agree to a first-century date for its original composition. There is nothing which requires a second-century date and much that suits the first century.

Remains of an ancient Greek temple near Agrigentum, Sicily. Note the Doric style of the columns. (Courtesy, Italian Information Center)

The temple of Concordia is the best preserved of those found at Agrigentum, Sicily. It was built by the Greeks between 440 and 420 B.C. The Doric columns are twenty-two feet high and at the bottom have a diameter of four and a half feet. (Courtesy, Italian Information Center)

ARCHAEOLOGY AND THE BOOK OF REVELATION

Some years ago Sir William Ramsay wrote a book called *The Letters to the Seven Churches of Asia*.[14] He took up the seven churches mentioned in Revelation 2 and 3, and sought to describe their origin and their relationship to one another. He was able to gather important archaeological material about them as well. It was his idea that the seven churches represented seven postal centers studded along a circular route, each on the center of a Christian circuit.[15]

Archaeology can provide a description of the towns as they stood at the close of the first century A. D. This may contribute something to our understanding of the peculiar problems that faced each of the churches. It cannot, of course, give us any information about the inner faith of the members of these churches.

14. (London, 1904). Cf. the more recent book, Wm. Barclay, *Letters to the Seven Churches* (London, 1957).
15. *Ibid.*, p. 191.

Details of the town of *Ephesus* have already been given.[16] As we have seen, the town was a center for the worship of Artemis, the great Diana. Emperor worship, too, was practiced here, as well as all kinds of magical arts. Later it became the home of various Gnostic sects. Paul founded the Christian Church here and came into conflict with vested interests (Acts 19). The Church received some commendation in the book of Revelation.

Smyrna was originally founded as a Greek colony more than a thousand years before Christ. It lay on a deep gulf, thirty-five miles north of Ephesus at the end of a great road. It had a good outlet to the sea a few miles away, and was actually a maritime city that became a close associate of Rome. The people of Smyrna were proud of this fact and regarded themselves as the "first of Asia," a title carried on their coins. Ancient writers often refer to the "crown of Smyrna," which seems to have been a reference to the garland of flowers worn by the worshippers of the goddess Cybele. The foundress of the city in mythology was the Amazon Smyrna,[17] who is depicted on coins and elsewhere armed with the double-headed axe of the Amazons and wearing the short tunic and high boots of the huntress and warrior. A high crown rests on her head.[18]

Perhaps the reference to the "crown of life" (Rev. 2:10) had special significance for these people who had heard from childhood about the crown of Smyrna. The true Smyrna would wear a crown suited to the servant of the living God. Ramsay sees in the reference to "faithful" (v. 10) a reminder of the faithfulness that the worldly city had shown to Rome. This constituted a call to the Christians to show like faithfulness to Christ. No excavations of any extent have been made at Smyrna up to the present, but visitors can still make out the plan of the ancient stadium and a few other ruins. The modern city unfortunately covers most of the old site and we are almost entirely dependent on literary material.

Pergamum, capital of the province, was sixteen miles inland and fifty miles north of Smyrna. It was a center for several religious cults. Asklepios, the god of healing, was greatly honored here. His symbol, the serpent, is found often on coins. Pergamum was also a

16. See above, pp. 396-402.
17. The Amazons were a mythical race of warlike females.
18. W. M. Ramsay, *op. cit.,* pp. 266f.

center for emperor worship and there had been a temple here for that purpose since the days of Augustus in 29 B. C. Traditional Greek gods like Zeus, Athene the goddess of poetry and learning, and Dionysius the god of wine were likewise worshipped, and these, together with Asklepios, were worshipped in times of national disaster.[19] The city had a certain pride in its religious significance. It was the first, and for a time the only, provincial town to have a temple dedicated to the imperial cult. By the end of the second century it had three, the original one created by Augustus, a second built in the days of Trajan (A. D. 98-117), and a third in the days of Severus (A. D. 193-211). The Augustan temple is represented on coins.

19. *Ibid.,* p. 284.

General view of the remains of a fourth-century Christian church at Shavei Zion. Note the mosaic flooring on different levels. (Courtesy, Israel Office of Information)

One of the mosaic patterns on the third level carries an inscription, partly damaged, that has reference to Luke 2:2 (Courtesy, Israel Office of Information)

Probably the reference to "Satan's seat" in Revelation 2:13 is to the emperor worship. Christians were in danger of showing tolerance to these cults and of compromising their stand for Christ, so as to follow "the doctrine of Balaam" and "the doctrine of the Nicolaitanes" (vv. 14f.). On the other hand, if a Christian resisted the pressure of the society in which he lived, he ran the risk of persecution. Already there had been at least one martyr when Revelation was written (v. 13).

Excavations have been carried out in Pergamum since 1878 and these have revealed much of the glory of the city, notably its

General mosaic flooring of the northern aisle of the same church. Note the fine motif, which has been adapted for the design of the symbols at the head of the chapters of Part III of this book. (Courtesy, Israel Office of Information)

acropolis.[20] One of the important discoveries was the remains of the gigantic altar of Zeus, which was adorned with marvelous sculptures portraying the battle of Zeus against the primeval giants. This altar was restored and reconstructed for display in the Berlin Museum.[21] Another large temple dedicated to the worship of Trajan and Hadrian has been exposed. There is much more yet to be discovered about the story of Pergamum.

20. C. M. Cobern, *The New Archaeological Discoveries* (New York, 1918), pp. 563f.

21. More recently it has been removed to Russia.

417

Thyatira was a small town between Pergamum and Sardis but lay inland on a main road. It was likewise the center of several cults, among them being those of Apollo and Sibyl, the female diviner. Apollo, the sun god, was the tutelary or guardian deity here, and his worship was coupled with that of the emperors.

The town was founded by Seleucus I about 300 B.C. as a garrison city even though it had no natural defense advantages. It lay on a plain and was an important trading center whose great period of prosperity was only just beginning at the time Revelation was written. Numerous inscriptions from Thyatira mention all sorts of trades in the city and speak of workers in wool, linen, and garments, dyers, leather workers, tanners, potters, bakers, and bronze smiths.[22] We are reminded of Lydia, the woman of Thyatira, a seller of purple (Acts 16:14).

The letter to Thyatira comes from "the Son of God, who hath his eyes like unto a flame of fire, and his feet are like fine brass" (v. 18). The celestial Christ is thus contrasted with Apollo, the son of Zeus, and the emperor, his incarnation. The church at Thyatira is castigated because she lacked fortitude to resist the insidiousness of these cults. Actually the false teaching of Montanism[23] flourished here after about A.D. 150.

Sardis lay thirty-five miles to the south of Thyatira in the center of numerous trade routes. It was a big city and was formerly the capital of the rich kingdom of Lydia. The original Sardis was an almost impregnable fortress perched on a hill, but later the town spread to the plain below and the old city became an acropolis. Cyrus, the Persian conqueror, took the city from Croesus in 546 B.C., but later it was recaptured by the Seleucid king Antiochus the Great. The patron goddess of the city was the native Cybele who was identified with Artemis. The ruins of her temple are still standing. Several of the broken columns and two full columns still stand on an area 327 feet long and 163 feet across, and on the sacred way leading to the temple the visitor can see some of the flanking lions.

In A.D. 17 Sardis suffered greatly from an earthquake, but the town was rebuilt with help from Emperor Hadrian, who appears on coins extending his bounty to a kneeling figure. In the writers of

22. W. M. Ramsay, *op. cit.*, p. 325.
23. This teaching commenced with Montanus, who was regarded as the incarnation of the Spirit of God. It placed great emphasis on the gifts of the Spirit and held to strict discipline in the Church.

that age the town had a bad name for luxury and loose living, and the letter of Revelation 3:1-6 urges the church to watch lest the Lord come in judgment. In later days there was a Christian church there. Excavations by an American expedition in Sardis began in 1910 and revealed the temple of Cybele-Artemis.[24] It was evident that this temple had been taken over by Christians, for the sign of the cross was engraved into the stone in many places, indicating the new use to which the building had been put. One of the most famous bishops here was Melito, who died about A. D. 190. A mortgage deed dating to 300 B. C., found in the ruins of the building, proved that it had originally been dedicated to Artemis. The area was rich in inscriptions, the most famous of which was probably a bilingual text in Lydian and Aramaic, dating from the tenth year of the Persian king Artaxerxes.

Quite recently excavation has been commenced here again and important material is being produced.[25]

Philadelphia was twenty-eight miles to the southeast of Sardis. It was the center of a wine industry and its chief deity was Dionysius. Its position was strategic for defense and for entry into the heart of Phrygia, so that it was a "doorway." It was to be an "open door" (v. 8) now in a new mission, as formerly it had been the center from which Hellenistic culture had spread. Little has been done in the way of excavation, hence our knowledge rests on literary references, a few inscriptions, and some coins.

Finally *Laodicea*, situated on a spur of hills some forty-three miles southeast of Philadelphia, was a very wealthy center, trading garments and cloth made from the glossy black wool of the local sheep. Today the ruins of this ancient town lie over many acres, but no thorough examination of the site has been undertaken. There was more to be seen a hundred years ago, but since then the local inhabitants have removed a great deal of the remains of ancient buildings in order to build other towns nearby; and, alas, this has been going on ever since the eleventh century.

The letter in Revelation 3:14-22 draws a contrast between the wealth of the city as represented by its woolen cloth, its medical work, and perhaps the eye salve made there on the one hand, and the depth of its spiritual poverty on the other. Sir William Ramsay saw in these

24. C. M. Cobern, *op. cit.*, pp. 565ff.
25. G. M. A. Hanfman, "Excavations at Sardis, 1958," *BASOR* (April, 1959).

verses references to the actual source of Laodicea's wealth.[26] Until serious excavation is done, however, we must remain in ignorance about the full significance of the references to the city.

It is evident that a great deal still needs to be done in the way of excavation in these cities. Indeed, only Ephesus, Pergamum, and Sardis have been excavated at all, although some surface surveys have been carried out in all these towns. Yet these places were vital centers of Christian worship in the first century A.D., and the book of Revelation, being a document of early Church history, will yield its primary meaning much more clearly when the archaeologist has unraveled the underlying thought and culture of the society represented in this book.[27]

26. W. M. Ramsay, *op. cit.,* pp. 416-419.
27. E. M. Blaiklock, *Out of the Earth* (Grand Rapids, 1957), chap. 6, p. 54, and W. M. Ramsay, *op. cit.,* give useful material of this kind.

A present-day Jewish agricultural colony, Nahalal, on the Plain of Armageddon, showing that with proper care and irrigation the country can be turned into a "land flowing with milk and honey" once more. (Courtesy, Israel Office of Information)

Twenty-two:

THE NEW TESTAMENT AND THE PAPYRI

O NE OF THE GREATEST CHAPTERS IN THE ANNALS OF NEW TESTAMENT archaeology is the remarkable story of the discovery and interpretation of the papyri of the centuries surrounding the life of our Lord.[1] As early as the end of the sixteenth century a few scattered examples of papyri were brought to Europe. In 1752 some more were found in Herculaneum, the ruins of which lay beneath the ash thrown out by Mount Vesuvius in A. D. 79. By the close of the eighteenth century some papyri were coming to Europe from Egypt. Though tragic stories are told of peasants burning papyri in order to enjoy the odor of the smoke, it was during the nineteenth century that increasing numbers of these precious documents began to find their way into Europe and their significance became clear even to the peasants of Egypt. The great Fayum depression some fifty or sixty miles southwest of Cairo became a veritable quarry of papyri. In 1877 great masses of these valuable documents were found at the

1. J. Finegan, *Light from the Ancient Past* (Princeton, 1947), pp. 321f., gives a good summary.

ancient site of Crocodopolis in the Fayum and were sent to Vienna. Then in 1889-1890 Sir Flinders Petrie began scientific excavation at the site of Gurob and found many papyri wrapped around mummies. These he carefully recovered and passed on to other scholars. His work was supplemented by the discoveries of B. P. Grenfell, A. S. Hunt, and D. G. Hogarth, who carried out a systematic search for papyri in Egypt and over several years had remarkable success, notably at Oxyrhynchus. One of the first pieces to come to light bore the familiar noun for "mote" known from Matthew 7:3-5. When eventually the piece was cleaned, it turned out to be a collection of sayings of Jesus, dating probably from the third century A. D.

It can readily be seen that such material is likely to provide evidence of a most intimate kind for the life of the people in Egypt and elsewhere, for a piece of papyrus then was as important as a sheet of writing paper now. Letters, receipts, official documents, licenses of all kinds, permits, summonses, title deeds, in fact, written documents of every kind, whether personal or official, feature among the papyri. The documents themselves also provide valuable information about the language of the common people of the time, and this discovery is of tremendous significance for the study of New Testament language.

Another view of the ruins near the sea wall at Caesarea that for centuries have been pounded by the waves of the Mediterranean Sea. (Courtesy, Israel Office of Information)

THE NATURE AND USE OF PAPYRUS

Papyrus is really a swamp plant which grows in great profusion in Egypt. Quite early, perhaps as early as 2500 B. C.,[2] the stem of the papyrus plant was cut into long thin strips which were laid out on a flat surface and soaked in water. A second layer was then placed crosswise on top of the first and the two layers were pressed together to form a single sheet. This was dried in the sun, scraped with a shell or a bone to remove roughness, and then used for writing. The size of the sheets varied according to the need. An average size would be nine to eleven inches long and six to nine inches wide. Sheets could be joined together so as to form a long roll, one such roll being 140 feet in length. The side on which the fibre ran horizontally, and which was normally used for writing, is known as *recto*. The back of the sheet, with the fibres running vertically and not normally used for writing because of its roughness, is called *verso*. Perhaps we see here some explanation of such references in the Bible as Revelation 5:1 where we read of writing "within and on the backside" (cf. Ezek. 2:10).

2. J. Finegan, *op. cit.*, p. 307. See also Sir Frederick Kenyon, *Our Bible and the Ancient Manuscripts* (London, 1958), p. 38.

Caesarea was captured by the Crusaders in 1102 from the Moslems who had held the city since 638. Saladin recaptured it in 1187; the Crusaders took it once more in 1191 and held it until 1265. Remains of the Crusader walls have recently been excavated by the State of Israel and are shown here. (Courtesy, Israel Office of Information)

The oldest piece of papyrus in existence today dates from the fifth Egyptian dynasty (about 2500 to 2350 B. C.). From then on papyrus continued in regular use till long after the time of Christ. From Egypt the use of papyrus spread to other lands, and there was a regular trade between Egypt and Phoenicia and Greece at an early period. One story from about 1100 B. C. tells of a certain Wen-amon who went from Egypt to Byblos in Phoenicia.[3] Among many interesting facts in this story we find a reference to the trade in papyrus. An account of the process of making papyrus comes from the Roman writer Pliny who lived in the first century A. D.[4]

For ordinary purposes the small sheets of papyrus were used, the long roll being used for literary purposes. Some of the longer books in the New Testament provide a good illustration. Thus Luke's Gospel would require a roll just over thirty feet long. Perhaps one such roll was as much as could be handled conveniently by the reader, and therefore Luke divided his story into two rolls. Paul would have written his letters on papyrus rolls. In fact, in one passage in Timothy he asked his friend to bring with him "the books, but especially the parchments" (II Tim. 4:13). These "books" were very likely rolls of papyrus.

It sometimes happened that when a piece of papyrus was needed in a hurry, or when nothing else was available, an old piece would be reused. The original writing was erased as far as possible and the papyrus given a second application of writing. Such a rewritten piece of papyrus is known as a *palimpsest.*

Writing was done with a reed pen, and ink made either from lampblack, gum, and water, or from nut galls, green vitriol, and water. There are references to pens and ink in the New Testament (II Cor. 3:3, II John 12, III John 13).

In the first century A. D. papyrus was the normal writing material, though other media were also used. We can think of the New Testament books as being written on papyrus. It is of some interest to note that the Greek word *biblos* means "the pith of the papyrus stalk." From this came the word *biblion* for the papyrus roll. Hence the early Christians referred to the sacred books used among them as *ta biblia* (plural of *biblion*), "the books." In Latin this became *biblia* and hence our English word, Bible.

Recent research has made it fairly clear that it was the Christians who popularized the leaf-book (codex), and abandoned the rolls

---

3. J. B. Pritchard, *ANET* (Princeton, 1955), pp. 25-29.
4. Pliny, *Natural History,* XIII, 11f.

for church use. It was necessary for the early Christians both to be able to make rapid reference to texts in order to justify their interpretation of the Old Testament and to see what Jesus, Paul, and others had said,[5] and to have a number of different writings conveniently accessible at one time. The page-type of "book" was of more use. A study of the existing manuscripts of the third and fourth centuries A. D. shows that for the third century A. D. Christian papyri are nearly eighty-four percent codex type, whereas for non-Christian writings which still used the roll form there are only just over six percent codex form. By the next century Christian books show a ninety-seven percent preference for the codex, while the non-Christian show sixty-five percent. The Christians on this evidence gave the lead in the use of the codex or leaf book.

Passing reference should be made to the very valuable documents known as *ostraca*.[6] These were pieces of broken pottery on which letters, receipts, notes, and the like were written in ink. Early excavators threw these away so that they are often found in rubbish heaps, but they are now carefully collected and allowed to make

5. C. C. McCown, "The Earliest Christian Books," *BA* (May, 1943) .

6. A. Deissmann, *Light from the Ancient East* (English trans. London, 1927) , pp. 50ff.

Ancient ruins extending into the sea at Atlit, in the area of Mount Carmel. (Courtesy, Israel Office of Information)

their contribution to the study of the language used in the New Testament. The scantiness of our treatment must not be considered a measure of the very great importance of these precious documents.

The Language of the Papyri

The language of the papyri was Greek for the most part, but it has been clear for many centuries that it was not the Greek of the great classical writers. It was rather like the Greek of the New Testament, which had been something of a puzzle· to the scholars, who regarded it as a sort of Judaic or Hebraic Greek. Some scholars actually suspected that there was a special dialect of Greek lying behind the New Testament, and there are some interesting anticipations of the modern view in the writings of such scholars as Professor Lightfoot and Dean Farrar.[7]

The discovery of the papyri added greatly to our knowledge of a type of Greek which hitherto seemed so strange. New Testament scholars had actually compiled lists of words which they assigned to a so-called Biblical or ecclesiastical Greek. But whereas this list once consisted of some five hundred words, it could be very greatly reduced in the light of this new information. The papyri, along with inscriptions and ostraca, had revealed a vocabulary that seemed to be quite well known in the first century A. D. What was the meaning of this discovery? This task was taken up by a German pastor in Marburg, who later became the famous Professor Adolf Deissmann and held the chair of New Testament exegesis in Berlin. He was suddenly struck by the likeness of the language of the papyri to that of the New Testament, and he realized that the key to many of the problems of the language of the New Testament lay here.[8] It seemed to him that the papyri gave the vernacular Greek of considerable parts of the East, Greek as it was spoken and written by the ordinary men and women of the day. It was the common (or *koine*) Greek, and this was the language to be found in the New Testament.

The idea was taken up by other scholars such as J. H. Moulton, and although in their first zeal these early workers arrived at some conclusions that were later modified, their researches gave the correct

7. George Milligan, *Here and There Among the Papyri* (London, 1923), pp. 59-62.
8. Adolf Deissmann, *op. cit.,* outlines the story.

general interpretation of the language of the New Testament. The subsequent study of many thousands of documents has placed scholars in a position where they know the grammar of Koine Greek, and new lexicons have been written to include this latest vocabulary material. One of the most famous of these is *The Vocabulary of the Greek New Testament,* illustrated from the papyri and other non-literary sources, by J. H. Moulton and George Milligan. It is now accepted that the New Testament language was under heavy debt to the lingua franca of the day, itself a descendant of Attic Greek of the fifth century B. C. in which the classical Greek literature was written. It had, however, gained from admixture with other kinds of Greek. Even if the problem is a little more complex than we have indicated, it remains true that with the discovery of the papyri the first known examples of a kind of Greek hitherto known only in the Bible came to light. In the absence of such material it is no wonder that the scholars thought that the New Testament was written in the special language of the Greek-speaking Jews and early Christians. Only when the archaeologists produced from the dry sands of Egypt documents that had lain for centuries wrapped around mummies, stuffed into odd corners of collapsed buildings, or cast out into rubbish heaps, did the picture become clear. It was then the task of the linguist to interpret and to translate these documents.

The Letters of the First Century A. D.

A great variety of private letters from the days when the New Testament was being written is now available for study. Deissmann has presented a selection of these coming from the centuries ranging from the time of Alexander the Great to Mohammed. He began with the oldest Greek letter then in existence and included letters of Egyptian Christians in the years just before the Moslem invasion of Egypt.[9] This collection makes the nature of the letter form in antiquity very clear.

Letters were written on separate papyrus rolls which, when completed, would be rolled up, fastened with a string, sealed, and addressed on the outside. The postal system of the day was reserved for official messages and ordinary individuals depended on friends to carry their "mail." Paul's letters were delivered in this way. They

9. Adolf Deissmann, *op. cit.,* pp. 146ff.

A typical letter, written in a large, semi-cursive hand, from the first century. In it, a certain Procleius requests Pecusis to have Sotas, his friend, bring along some drugs to Alexandria. This letter, about four by seven and a half inches in size, is typical of the many that have come to light. (Courtesy, The British Museum)

428

were never designed to be read as literary treatises but were addressed to personal friends or to groups of Christians and dealt with some of the practical problems that arose in a church or in the life of an individual. Sir William Ramsay stated some years ago that "in the individual case they discover the universal principle, and state it in such a way as to reach the heart of every man similarly situated, and yet they state this, not in the way of formal exposition, but in the way of direct personal converse, written in place of spoken."[10]

The personal note struck by Paul is closely in agreement with the general procedure of other letter writers of his day. It is usual to have opening and closing salutations, and a wide range of regular niceties of expression. Samples of these letters are readily available for the student,[11] but we shall choose two to illustrate.

A good example of a letter of commendation comes from Oxyrhynchus and has been dated A. D. 16. A certain Theon recommended the bearer of the letter, Hermophilus, to his brother Heraclides in the following words:

> Theon to Heraclides his brother, many greetings and wishes for good health. Hermophilus the bearer of this letter is friend . . . and asked me to write to you. Hermophilus declares that he has business at Kerkemounis. Please therefore further him in this matter, as is just. For the rest take care of yourself that you may remain in good health. Good-bye. The third year of Tiberius Caesar Augustus.[12]

The address was written on the verso (back).

We notice in this letter that the writer's name is first, then the name of the person to whom the letter is addressed, and a greeting. At the end of the letter is a parting greeting and a wish. These features are to be found quite regularly in Paul's letters. Indeed Paul also spoke of "letters of commendation" (II Cor. 3:1).

Some of these non-Christian epistles contained, in addition to the usual introductory material, a "prayer" and "thanksgiving" very much like what we find in Paul's letters. Thus in the second century A. D. a young man named Apion, serving with his regiment in Italy, wrote to his father, telling of his stormy trip and giving some details of his present life:

---

10. W. M. Ramsay, *Letters to the Seven Churches* (London, 1908), p. 25.
11. Adolf Deissmann, *op. cit.;* J. Finegan, *op. cit.;* George Milligan, *op. cit.*
12. George Milligan, *op. cit.,* pp. 33f.

A present-day scene near the Sea of Galilee — tomatoes being grown near the town of Migdal, north of Tiberias. (Courtesy, Israel Office of Information)

Apion, to Epimachus his father and lord, many greetings. Before all things I pray you are in health and that you prosper and fare well continually together with my sister and her daughter and my brother. I thank the Lord Serapis that, when I was in peril in the sea, he saved me immediately. When I came to Miseni, I received as journey-money from the Caesar three pieces of gold. And it is well with me. I beseech you therefore, my lord father, to write me a little letter, firstly of your health, secondly of that of my brother and sister, thirdly that I may look upon your handwriting with reverence, because you have taught me well and I therefore hope to advance rapidly, if the gods will. Salute Capito much, and my brother and sister Serenilla and my friends. I am sending you by Eucetemon a little picture of me. Moreover my name is Antonis Maximus. Fare you well I pray.[13]

13. J. Finegan, *op. cit.*, pp. 327f.

General view of the modern city of Haifa seen from Mount Carmel, at whose foot the city is situated. It represents the classical Sycaminum (Sykaminos), but since about 1890 it has developed into an important port, having the best natural harbor on the Palestinian coast. (Courtesy, Israel Office of Information)

In the margin alongside the letter the following words are found:

> There salute you Serenus the son of Agathus Daemon, and . . .
> Turbo the son of Gallonius . . . .

There are similarities of expression and technique between this letter and those of Paul, Peter, and John. Thus the phrase, "I pray that you are in health," compares with III John, verse 2. The acknowledgement of the help of the gods is very like the expression of Paul's gratitude to God which we often find in the introduction to his letters (Rom. 1:8, I Cor. 1:4, Phil. 1:3, Col. 1:3, I Thess. 1:2, II Thess. 1:3, etc.). The phrase "Salute Capito" is to be compared with such a greeting as that in I Corinthians 16:19, and the salutations from friends can be compared with salutations at the end of several of Paul's letters. Altogether, in the construction of the sentences, in the general absence of connecting particles, and in the whole mold of the letter with its greeting, prayer of thanksgiving, general contents, salutations, and closing valediction, we have much to remind us of Paul and of the others who wrote the letters in the New Testament. Our Biblical letters are typical of the correspondence of the day.

THE COMMON DOCUMENTS OF EVERYDAY LIFE

There is a great variety of these, and they give detailed information about all aspects of life, family relationships, education, taxation, religion, slavery, petitions of one kind and another, sickness and death, food and dress, and so on. The great value for us is that they give us the typical vocabulary of the common people as well as parallel information to what we find in the New Testament.

Reference has already been made to the official documents summoning people to their home town for the census in the days of Augustus and later.[14] These were found in Egyptian rubbish heaps. We have also mentioned the magical papyri and the incantation texts which have been recovered in great numbers.[15] Many of the letters give interesting details about the relationships inside the family. One letter instructs a wife to "expose" a child about to be born if it is a girl.[16] Another letter from a wife expresses concern for her husband in a time of danger.[17] Other letters from children to parents tell us a great deal about family relationships. Letters referring to bereavements manifest, as we might have expected, deep feelings. Sometimes they are poignantly beautiful. But the Christian cannot help being impressed by their general air of despair in marked contrast with the Christian hope.

At times we have a glimpse into the education of the day, as, for example, in the case of a mother who wrote to a son whose teacher had left him:

> I took care to send and ask about your health and learn what you are reading; he said that it was the sixth book [of Homer] and testified at length regarding your pedagogue. So,

14. See above, p. 376.
15. See above, pp. 396f.
16. George Milligan, *op. cit.*, p. 93. Unwanted children were left unattended in the open fields or by the roadside to perish; that is, they were "exposed."
17. *Ibid.*, p. 91.

my son, I urge both you and your pedagogue to take care that you go to a suitable teacher.[18]

This shows that it was the task of the pedagogue to take the boy to school and to act as his guardian until he reached maturity. We here meet the word Paul used in Galatians 3:24, where he says that the law was a pedagogue (schoolmaster) to bring us to Christ.

Slavery was part of the social structure of those days and the papyri tell us much about this institution. The pedagogue, for example, was often a slave, but generally a greatly honored one. Even if the slave system was evil in many ways, we have many instances of deep concern for the welfare of the slaves. The manumission (setting free) of slaves was used in Christian writings as a picture of freeing men from the bondage of sin to become Christ's bondslaves. Deissmann has an interesting section on such documents and points out many parallels in phraseology between the common and the Pauline usage of this vocabulary.[19]

Some of the expressions that refer to slavery are found in the New Testament, and we may study the everyday usage of such words as "slave," "redemption," "ransom" in these documents. In this connection the papyri help us sometimes to translate difficult passages in the New Testament. In Romans 8:23, for example, there is a Greek word *aparche*, translated in the A.V. as "firstfruits." In classical Greek it was used for the first fruits or the first offerings made to the gods. One papyrus, however, renders it "legacy duty," another uses it for the "entrance fee" paid by Alexandrian men who became citizens. Sometimes it is used for a "gift" to a god.[20] One special use is where it refers to the "birth certificate" of a free person. This latter meaning has been suggested as the correct one for Romans 8:23. The point is that children of God have the *birth certificate* of the Spirit, which makes them free men even if they still await formal release from the bondage of the flesh.[21]

Other papyri give information about social life. Here, for example, is an invitation to a man to be present at some ceremonial occasion:

18. *Ibid.,* p. 97.
19. A. Deissmann, *op. cit.,* pp. 320f.
20. J. H. Moulton and George Milligan, *Vocabulary of the Greek New Testament* (London, 1957), p. 54.
21. George Milligan, *op. cit.,* pp. 99f.

Antonius, son of Ptolemaeus, invites you to dine with him at the table of the Lord Serapis in the house of Claudius Serapion on the 16th at 9 o'clock.[22]

The word for "invite," "request," or "beseech," is regularly used in the New Testament (e.g., Luke 11:37, I Thess. 4:1), and the word "lord" (Greek *kurios*), is regularly used as a divine title. For Paul there is but one Lord, Jesus Christ, despite the claims of others "deities" to be lord. Again, in the phrase, "in the house of Claudius," the word "house" does not occur in the text, but must be supplied. This usage is also found in the New Testament, for example, in Luke 2:49, R.V., where the words of Jesus are reported, "Wist ye not that I must be in my Father's house?"[23]

SOME EXAMPLES OF NEW TESTAMENT VOCABULARY FOUND IN THE PAPYRI AND THE OSTRACA

The papyri and the ostraca enable us to study at first hand the everyday use to which numbers of words in the New Testament were put. Even where classical Greek used certain words, we discover that Koine Greek sometimes had a different shade of meaning and a breadth of common usage which would not have been suspected. In many cases the popular usage is taken over into the New Testament as a metaphor to describe some spiritual experience. We shall take a few examples to show the value of this new material for our understanding of the meaning and usage of such words.

The word "earnest" (Greek *arrabon*) in the New Testament occurs in II Corinthians 1:22, 5:5, and Ephesians 1:14 and seems to indicate an advance payment in expectation of the full payment at a later date. The papyri use the word in precisely this sense. One example comes from Egypt where a woman who sold a cow received an *arrabon* of one thousand drachma in advance. Another document refers to some dancing girls who received money as an *arrabon* on their promised salary.[24] This particular word is in fact used by some classical writers, but it is a direct borrowing from Semitic languages.

---

22. *Ibid.*, pp. 101f.
23. The reasons for this translation are given in the standard commentaries, e.g., A. Plummer, *Gospel According to St. Luke*, (*ICC*), (Edinburgh, 1913), pp. 77f.
24. J. H. Moulton and G. Milligan, *op. cit.*, p. 79.

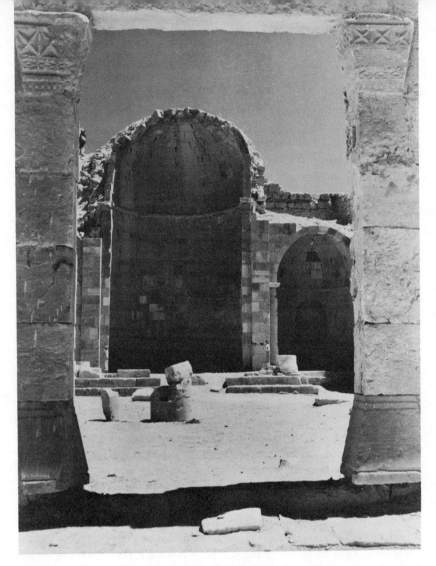

View of the triple apse of the central cathedral of the Byzantine Negev city of Shivta (Subeita), after clearing of the debris and restoration of the ruins. (Courtesy, Israel Office of Information)

The verb rendered "have" in Matthew 6:16 (Greek *apecho*), in the phrase concerning the hypocrites, "they have their reward," is a regular technical word in the papyri for the granting of a receipt. It is also found on many ostraca which were commonly used for the issuing of receipts. This word is found in the classics, although there it has other meanings too. Deissmann, commenting on its use in Matthew, says that "it is as though they [the hypocrites] had already given a receipt, and they have absolutely no further claim to reward. This added touch of quiet irony makes the text more lifelike and pointed."[25] In other words, when the hypocrites had won the applause of men by disfiguring their faces, their right to receive a reward had been realized, and it was as though the receipt had been issued. Here the matter ended.

There is another use of the word in Philippians 4:18, where Paul, expressing gratitude to the church at Philippi for their help, said, "I have [Greek *apecho*] all, and abound," that is, "I give you a receipt in full." Again, in Philemon 15, Paul, writing to Philemon concerning the slave Onesimus who had departed, suggested that this had been but for a time so that "thou shouldest *receive* him [as one for whom he had signed a receipt] for ever."

The word for "seal" in Romans 15:28 (Greek *sphragizo*) was regularly used in commerce, according to the papyri. Paul had remarked that the Gentiles, having shared in the spiritual blessings of the poor saints in Jerusalem, should now share with them the things needed to sustain their bodies. He promised to "secure [or seal] this fruit" for the saints in Jerusalem, and after that to go on to Spain. What does the phrase mean? The verb *sphragizo* occurs in a specialized commercial sense in the papyri, where it is used for sealing up bags of wheat and barley.[26] The sealing was the proof that everything was in order for delivery. So Paul, like an honest merchant, would see to it that the gift entrusted to his care would be properly secured for those to whom it was consigned. In classical Greek the word also meant "to seal," though its connotation was wider.

The phrase "in a disorderly manner" (Greek *ataktos*), to be found in II Thessalonians 3:11, is known in the papyri, from which we discover an interesting usage. One contract from A. D. 66 deals with the apprenticeship of a boy to a master. The boy is to be supported with food and clothing by his father, and the master is to give the boy a monthly allowance. If there are days when the boy "fails to attend work" or "plays truant," the father has to arrange for an equivalent number of days at the conclusion of the contract.[27] The adverb used in II Thessalonians is from the same root as that used here for "play truant" or "fail to attend" and

25. A. Deissmann, *op. cit.*, pp. 110f.
26. George Milligan, *op. cit.*, pp. 72ff.
27. *Ibid.*, pp. 74f.

denotes culpable idleness. In Thessalonica there were those who were *ataktos*, "working not at all," that is, they were idlers. Paul deplored this and indicated that even if these people thought that the Lord was coming, the best way to prepare was to be busy at profitable occupation when He came. Those who played truant were behaving "in a disorderly manner" (Greek *ataktos*).[28]

These examples will show the kind of information that is now available from the papyri and the ostraca. And the exciting thing is that the task has only just begun.

The Earliest New Testament Documents

The question is often asked whether we have copies of the New Testament books reaching back to the first century A. D. We must admit that we have no such material. The earliest extant manuscript falls just inside the period covered by this book. In 1935, C. H. Roberts noticed in the John Rylands Library in Manchester a scrap of John's Gospel which had been acquired in 1920 by Dr. B. P. Grenfell, but was unnoticed till Roberts examined it.[29] It was a small piece of papyrus, only three and a half by two and a half inches, containing fragments of John's Gospel, chapter 18, verses 31 to 33 and 37 and 38. The style of writing enabled it to be assigned to the first half of the second century. As we have seen,[30] the fact that it was not only written in Egypt but that it had been used in a provincial town in Egypt at this early date points to the fact that John's Gospel, far from being a late second-century production as some had maintained, was in fact far earlier, and more likely to have been written in the first century, or at least very early in the second. Up to the present this is our earliest piece of the New Testament.

There are other second-century papyri, however, including one at Manchester containing Titus 1:11-15 and 2:4-8, and another at Oxford containing fragments of Matthew 26.[31] But the great manuscripts of the New Testament come from the third and the following

---

28. L. L. Morris, *The Epistles of Paul to the Thessalonians* (Grand Rapids, 1958), p. 100.

29. C. H. Roberts, *An Unpublished Fragment of the Fourth Gospel* (Manchester, 1935).

30. See above, p. 406.

31. See Nestle's *Greek New Testament*, British and Foreign Bible Society, for a convenient list.

The scrap of the Gospel of John, detected in the John Rylands Library, Manchester, dating from the early second century (Rylands Greek Pap. 457). (Courtesy, The John Rylands Library)

centuries and lie outside the scope of this book. It is by no means unlikely that yet other manuscripts of the New Testament dating from the second century will be discovered, for archaeological work is going on all the time.

GENERAL CONCLUSION

There is something exciting about supplementing the Biblical records with information from non-Biblical historians and from the thrilling discoveries of modern archaeology. It is very evident that the Biblical records have their roots firmly in general world history. Archaeological discovery supplements, explains, and at times corroborates the Biblical story. The happy combination of the Biblical records, the non-Biblical histories, and the discoveries of the archaeologists has produced such splendid results to date that we are full of optimism about the future. There is work for many centuries yet to be done. Many sites have yet to be excavated thoroughly and many others remain whose excavation has not yet commenced. If the achievements of the excavator up to the present have yielded such important results, what may not the future hold for us?

APPENDIXES

KINGS OF JUDAH   PROPHETS   KINGS OF ISRAEL

KINGS OF JUDAH		PROPHETS	KINGS OF ISRAEL	
Rehoboam	922-915		Jeroboam I	922-901
Abijah	915-913			
Asa	913-873		Nadab	901-900
(9th)			Baasha	900-877
			Elah	877-876
		E	Zimri	876
		L	Omri	876-869
		I		
Jehoshaphat	873-849	I	Ahab	869-850
Joram	849-842	J E	Ahaziah	850-849
Ahaziah	842	A L	Joram	849-842
Athaliah	842-837	H I		
Joash	837-800	S	Jehu	842-815
		H		
		A	Jehoahaz	815-801
			Joash	801-786
(8th) Amaziah	800-783	A		
		M	Jeroboam II	786-746
Uzziah	783-742	) I H O S		
		) S O		
		) A S	Zechariah	746-745
		) I) E	Shallum	745
Jotham	742-735	) A) A	Menahem	745-738
Ahaz	735-715	) H)	Pekahiah	738-737
		)) M	Pekah	737-732
		)) I	Hoshea	732-724
		)) C		
Hezekiah	715-687	)) A	ISRAEL FALLS TO ASSYRIA 722/721	
(7th)		)) H		
Manasseh	687-642	))		
Amon	642-640			
Josiah	640-609			
		) J		
		) E NAHUM		
		) R ZEPHANIAH		
		) E		
Jehoahaz	609	) M		
Jehoiakim	609-598	)		
(6th) Jehoiakin	598	) I HABAKKUK		
Zedekiah	598-587	) A		
JUDAH FALLS TO BABYLONIA		) H		

**Left margin century markers:**
9th CENTURY B.C.
8th CENTURY B.C.
7th CENTURY B.C.
6th CENTURY B.C.

	BABYLONIAN, PERSIAN AND GREEK KINGS	THE JEWS
600	**BABYLONIAN KINGS** Nebuchadnezzar 605-562 Amel Marduk 562-560 Neriglissar 560-556 Nabonidus 556-539	586 Fall of Jerusalem
550	**PERSIAN KINGS** Cyrus 539-530 Cambyses 530-522 Darius 522-486	538 Edict of Cyrus 520 Haggai and Zechariah 516 Temple completed
500	Xerxes 486-465 Artaxerxes I 465-424	Esther 458 Ezra Malachi
450	Xerxes II 424-423 Darius II 423-404	445 Nehemiah 432 Nehemiah recalled 407 Elephantine Letter
400	Artaxerxes II 404-358 Artaxerxes III 358-338 Arses 338-336 Darius III 336-331	
350	**GREEK KINGS** Ptolemies Seleucids Ptolemy I 323-283	332 Jews fall under Greeks 320 Ptolemies take control
300	Ptolemy II 283-246 Early Ptolemy III 246-221 Seleucid Kings Ptolemy IV 221-203 Ptolemy V 203-181 Antiochus III 223-187	Ptolemies in Palestine
250		
200	Later Ptolemaic Kings	198 Seleucids take Palestine
	Seleucus IV 187-175 Antiochus IV 175-163	167 Pollution of Temple 166-160 Judas
	Antiochus V 163-162 Demetrius I 162-150	164 Temple cleansed 160-142 Jonathan 152 Jonathan high priest
150	Balas 150-145 Antiochus VI 145-142 Demetrius II 145-139	142-134 Simon
	Antiochus VII 139-129	134-104 John Hyrcanus 104-103 Aristobulus I
100	Seleucids continue with internal troubles till Roman conquest in 63 B.C.	103-76 Alexander Jannaeus 76-67 Alexandra 67-63 Aristobulus II 63 Pompey takes Jerusalem 63-40 Hyrcanus II
50		40-37 Antigonus Mattathias 37- 4 Herod
0		

442

LIST OF EMPERORS

Emperor	Date	New Testament Reference
Augustus	B.C. 30-A.D. 14	Luke 2:1
Tiberius	A.D. 14-37	Luke 3:1
Caligula	A.D. 37-41	
Claudius	A.D. 41-54	Acts 11:28, 18:2
Nero	A.D. 54-68	Acts 25:10-12, 27:24 II Tim. 4:16, 17
Galba	A.D. 68-69	
Otho	A.D. 69 (3 months)	
Vitellus	A.D. 69 (1 month)	
Vespasian	A.D. 69-79	
Titus	A.D. 79-81	
Domitian	A.D. 81-96	
Nerva	A.D. 96-98	
Trajan	A.D. 98-117	
Hadrian	A.D. 117-138	

LIST OF PROCURATORS

Procurator	Date	New Testament Reference
Coponius	A.D. 6-10	
M. Ambivius	A.D. 10-13	
Annius Rufus	A.D. 13-15	
Valerius Gratus	A.D. 15-26	
Pontius Pilate	A.D. 26-36	Matt. 27, Mark 15:1-5, John 18:28-38
Marcellus	A.D. 36-38	
Maryllus	A.D. 38-44	
Cuspius Fadus	A.D. 44- ?	
Alexander	A.D. ?-48	
Cumanus	A.D. 48-52	
Felix	A.D. 52-59(?)	Acts 23, 24
Porcius Festus	A.D. 59(?)-62	Acts 25, 26
Albinus	A.D. 62-64	
Gessius Florus		
(Siege of Jerusalem)	A.D. 64-66	

THE FAMILY OF HEROD THE GREAT

Father

HEROD THE GREAT
King of Judaea 37 – 4 B.C.
Matt. 2:1-19   Luke 1:5

Sons

Son of DORIS: ANTIPATER

Sons of first MARIAMNE: ALEXANDER, ARISTOBOLUS

Son of second MARIAMNE: HEROD PHILIP I (first husband of HERODIAS, Mark 6:17)

Sons of MALTHACE:
- HEROD ANTIPAS — Tetrarch of Galilee 4 B.C.-A.D. 39 (Luke 3:1, 19; 9:7-9; 23:7-12)
- HEROD ARCHELAUS — Ethnarch of Judaea, 4 B.C.-A.D. 6 (Matt. 2:22)

Son of CLEOPATRA: HEROD PHILIP II — Tetrarch of Ituraea, etc., 4 B.C.-A.D. 34, married SALOME, daughter of HEROD PHILIP I and HERODIAS (Luke 3:1)

Grandchildren

- HEROD of CHALCIS
- HEROD AGRIPPA I — King of Judaea A.D. 37-44 (Acts 12:1-24)
- HERODIAS — Consort of HEROD ANTIPAS (Matt. 14:6f., Mark 6:17f.)

Great-grandchildren

- BERNICE — Consort of her brother (Acts 25:13)
- HEROD AGRIPPA II — (Acts 25:13-26:32)
- DRUSILLA — Wife of FELIX, procurator of Judaea (Acts 24:24)
- SALOME — Wife of HEROD PHILIP II

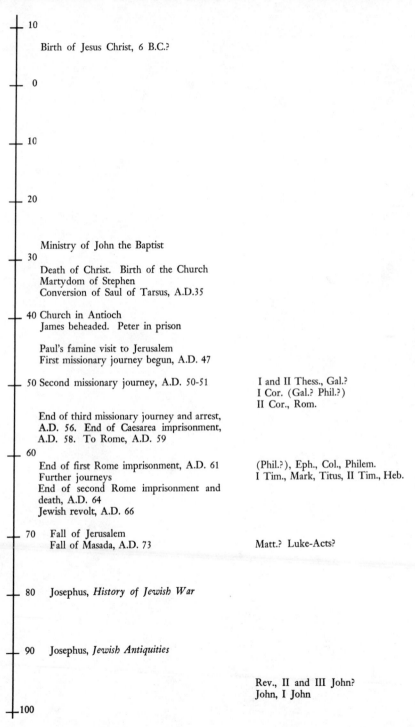

10

Birth of Jesus Christ, 6 B.C.?

0

10

20

Ministry of John the Baptist
30
Death of Christ. Birth of the Church
Martydom of Stephen
Conversion of Saul of Tarsus, A.D.35

40 Church in Antioch
James beheaded. Peter in prison

Paul's famine visit to Jerusalem
First missionary journey begun, A.D. 47

50 Second missionary journey, A.D. 50-51   I and II Thess., Gal.?
     I Cor. (Gal.? Phil.?)
     II Cor., Rom.

End of third missionary journey and arrest,
A.D. 56. End of Caesarea imprisonment,
A.D. 58. To Rome, A.D. 59
60
End of first Rome imprisonment, A.D. 61   (Phil.?), Eph., Col., Philem.
Further journeys   I Tim., Mark, Titus, II Tim., Heb.
End of second Rome imprisonment and
death, A.D. 64
Jewish revolt, A.D. 66

70 Fall of Jerusalem
Fall of Masada, A.D. 73   Matt.? Luke-Acts?

80 Josephus, *History of Jewish War*

90 Josephus, *Jewish Antiquities*

     Rev., II and III John?
     John, I John
100

BIBLIOGRAPHY

The Bibliography which has been collected in the following pages is at best a selection of useful books now available for study. The complete list is, of course, very extensive. For the most part the present suggestions include only books in English, although a few in French and German have been included where they are thought to have special value. Articles from journals have not in general been included here, although in the case of specially significant ones they have been listed in the appropriate chapter. The footnotes in the body of the present book will direct the reader's attention to many more valuable articles in scholarly archaeological journals.

GENERAL BIBLIOGRAPHY

BIBLICAL GEOGRAPHY AND TOPOGRAPHY

Baly, D., *The Geography of the Bible*, 1957 (Harper, New York)
du Buit, M., *Géographie de la Terre Sainte*, 1958 (Les Éditions du Cerf, Paris)
Grollenberg, L. H., *Atlas of the Bible*, E. T. 1956 (Nelson, New York)
———, *Shorter Atlas of the Bible*, 1959 (Nelson, New York)
Kitchen, J. H., *Holy Fields*, 1956 (Eerdmans, Grand Rapids)
Kraeling, E. G. (ed.), *Rand McNally Historical Atlas of the Holy Land*, 1959, (Rand McNally, Chicago)
Rowley, H. H., *The Teach Yourself Bible Atlas*, 1960 (English Universities Press London)
Smith, G. Adam, *The Historical Geography of the Holy Land*, 25th ed., 1931 (Hodder & Stoughton, London)
Van der Meer, F. and Mohrman, C., *Atlas of the Early Christian World*, E. T. 1958 (Nelson, New York)
Wright, G. E. and Filson, F. V., *The Westminster Historical Atlas to the Bible*, rev. ed. 1958 (Westminster, Philadelphia)

Bibliography

OLD TESTAMENT HISTORY

Albright, W. F., *The Biblical Period*, 1950 (Blackwell, Oxford)
————, *From the Stone Age to Christianity*, 2nd ed., 1957 (Johns Hopkins University Press, Baltimore)
Bright, J., *A History of Israel*, 1961 (Abingdon, New York)
Gordon, C. H., *The World of the Old Testament*, 1960 (Phoenix House, London)
Harrison, R. K., *A History of Old Testament Times*, 1957 (Zondervan, Grand Rapids)
Noth, M., *The History of Israel*, E. T., 2nd ed., 1960 (Harper, New York)
Orlinsky, H., *Ancient Israel*, 1960, 2nd ed. (Cornell University Press, New York)

TRANSLATIONS OF ANCIENT RECORDS

Breasted, J. H., *Ancient Records of Egypt*, 1906 (Chicago University Press, Chicago)
Budge, E. A. and King, L. W., *The Annals of the Kings of Assyria*, Vol. I, 1902, (British Museum, London)
Luckenbill, D. D., *Historical Records of Assyria*, 1926-1927 (Chicago University Press, Chicago)
Pritchard, J. B., *Ancient Near Eastern Texts*, 1955 (Princeton University Press, Princeton)
————, *The Ancient Near East*, 1958 (Princeton University Press, Princeton)
Thomas, D. Winton, *Documents from Old Testament Times*, 1958 (Nelson, New York)

Chapter I: BIBLICAL ARCHAEOLOGY TODAY

Albright, W. F., *The Archaeology of Palestine*, rev. ed. 1956 (Pelican, London)
————, *Archaeology and the Religion of Israel*, rev. ed. (Johns Hopkins University Press, Baltimore)
————, *The Bible After Twenty Years of Archaeology* (1932-1952), 1954 (Funk and Wagnalls, New York)
Burrows, Millar, *What Mean These Stones?*, 1941 (American Schools of Oriental Research, Baltimore)
Chiera, E., *They Wrote on Clay*, 1956 (Chicago University Press, Chicago)
Finegan, J., *Light from the Ancient Past*, 1960, 2nd ed. (Princeton University Press, Princeton)
Free, J. P., *Archaeology and Bible History*, 1950 (Scripture Press, Wheaton, Ill.)
Kenyon, K. M., *Beginning in Archaeology*, 1952 (Phoenix House, London)
————, *Archaeology in the Holy Land*, 1960 (Ernest Benn, London)
Owen, G. F., *Archaeology and the Bible*, 1960, (Revell, Westwood)
Parrot, A., *Discovering Buried Worlds*, E. T. 1955 (SCM, London)
Pritchard, J. B., *Archaeology and the Old Testament*, 1959 (Princeton University Press, Princeton)
Unger, M. F., *Archaeology and the Old Testament*, 1954 (Zondervan, Grand Rapids)
Wiseman, D. J., *Illustrations in Biblical Archaeology*, 1958 (Eerdmans, Grand Rapids)
Woolley, C. L., *Digging Up the Past*, 1937 (Pelican, London)

Wright, G. E., *Biblical Archaeology*, 1957 (Westminster, Philadelphia)
————, *An Introduction to Biblical Archaeology*, 1960 (Westminster, Philadelphia)
Wright, G. E., and Freedman, D. N. (eds.), *The Bibical Archaeologist Reader*, 1961 (Doubleday, Garden City)

Chapter II: ABRAHAM THE MIGRANT

de Vaux, R., "Les Patriarches Hebreux et les découvertes modernes," *RB*, 1946 1948, 1949
Glueck, N., *Rivers in the Desert*, 1959 (Weidenfeld, London)
Gordon, C. H., "Bible Customs and the Nuzi Tablets," in *BA*, Feb., 1960
Gurney, O. R., *The Hittites*, 1955 (Pelican, London)
Heidel, A., *The Babylonian Genesis*, 2nd ed. 1951 (Chicago University Press, Chicago)
————, *The Gilgamesh Epic and Old Testament Parallels*, 2nd ed., 1949 (Chicago University Press, Chicago)
Parrot, A., *The Flood and Noah's Ark*, E. T. 1955 (SCM, London)
————, *The Tower of Babel*, E. T. 1955 (SCM, London)
Pfeiffer, C. F., *The Patriarchal Age*, 1961 (Baker, Grand Rapids)
Rowley, H. H., "Recent Discovery and the Patriarchal Age," *BJRL*, Sept., 1949
Woolley, C. L., *Ur of the Chaldees*, 1940 (Pelican, London)
————, *Excavations at Ur*, 1954 (Barnes & Noble, New York)

Chapter III: IN THE LAND OF THE PHARAOHS

Alt, A., *Die Herkunft der Hyksos in neuer Sicht*, 1954 (published in *Kleine Schriften* by C. H. Beck'sche, Munich)
Cottrell, L., *Life Under the Pharaohs*, 1956 (Evans, London)
————, *The Lost Pharaohs*, 1955 (Evans, London)
Engberg, R. M., *The Hyksos Reconsidered*, 1939 (Chicago University Press, Chicago)
Vergote, J., *Joseph en Egypte — Genèse chap.* 37-50 *à la lumière des études égyptologique récentes*, 1959 (Publications Universitaires, Louvain)
Wilson, J. A., *The Burden of Egypt*, 1951 (Chicago University Press, Chicago)
Yahuda, A. S., *The Accuracy of the Bible*, 1934 (Heinemann, London)
————, *The Language of the Pentateuch in Its Relation to Egyptian*, 1933 (Oxford University Press, London).

Chapter IV: FROM EGYPT TO CANAAN

De Wit, C., *The Date and Route of the Exodus*, 1960 (Tyndale Press, London)
Garstang, J. and J. B. E., *The Story of Jericho*, 1940 (Marshall, Morgan & Scott, London)
Glueck, N., *The Other Side of Jordan*, 1940 (American Schools of Oriental Research, New Haven)
————, *The River Jordan*, 1946 (Westminster, Philadelphia)
Kenyon, K., *Digging Up Jericho*, 1957 (Ernest Benn, London)
Montet, P., *L' Egypte et la Bible*, 1959 (Delachaux et Niestlé, Neuchatel)
————, *Le drame d'Avaris*, 1941 (Paris)
Rowley, H. H., *From Joseph to Joshua*, 1950 (Oxford University Press, London)
Van Zyl, A. M., *The Moabites*, 1960 (Brill, Leiden)

Bibliography

Chapter V: SETTLING INTO THE LAND

Albright, W. F., "The Rôle of the Canaanites in the History of Civilisation," 1960 (in *The Bible and the Ancient Near East*, ed. G. E. Wright, Routledge, Kegan, Paul, London)

Driver, G. R., *Canaanite Myths and Legends*, 1956 (T & T. Clark, Edinburgh)

Garstang, J., *Joshua-Judges*, 1931 (Constable, London)

Jacob, E., *Ras Shamra et l'Ancien Testament*, 1960 (Delachaux et Niestlé, Neuchatel)

Kenyon, K., *Digging Up Jericho*, 1957 (Ernest Benn, London)

Macalister, R.A.C., *The Philistines, Their History and Civilisation*, 1913 (Oxford University Press, London)

Chapter VI: ONE NATION – ONE KING

Glueck, N., *The River Jordan*, 1946 (Westminster, Philadelphia)

Parrot, A., *The Temple of Jerusalem*, E.T., 1957 (SCM, London)

Phillips, W., *Qataban and Sheba*, 1955 (Harcourt Brace, World, New York)

Simons, J., *Jerusalem in the Old Testament*, 1952 (Brill, Leiden)

Unger, M. F., *Israel and the Arameans of Damascus*, 1957 (James Clark, London)

Vincent, L. H. and Steve, A. M., *Jérusalem de l'Ancien Testament*, 1954, 1956 (Librairie Le Coffre, Paris)

Yadin, Y., "New Light on Solomon's Megiddo," *BA*, 1960

Chapter VII: THE KINGS OF ISRAEL

Caiger, S. L., *Bible and Spade*, 1936 (Oxford University Press, London)

Contenau, G., *Everyday Life in Babylon and Assyria*, 1954 (Arnold, London)

Crowfoot, J. W., and others, *Early Ivories from Samaria*, 1938 (Palestine Exploration Fund, London)

————, *The Buildings of Samaria*, 1942, (Palestine Exploration Fund, London)

Dupont-Sommer, A., *Les Araméens*, 1949 (A. Maisonneuve, Paris)

Luckenbill, D. D., *Historical Records of Assyria*, Vols. I, II, 1926, 1927 (Chicago University Press, Chicago)

Olmstead, A. T., *History of Assyria*, 1923 (Scribner's, New York)

Parrot, A., *Nineveh in the Old Testament*, E. T., 1955 (SCM, London)

————, *Samaria*, E. T., 1955 (S.C.M., London)

Thiele, R., *The Mysterious Numbers of the Hebrew Kings*, 1958 (Chicago University Press, Chicago)

Unger, M. F., *Israel and the Arameans of Damascus*, 1959 (James Clark, London)

Chapter VIII: THE KINGS OF JUDAH

Caiger, S. L., *Bible and Spade*, 1936 (Oxford University Press, London)

Parrot, A., *Nineveh and the Old Testament*, E. T., 1955 (SCM, London)

Thiele, E. R., *The Mysterious Numbers of the Hebrew Kings*, 1958 (Chicago University Press, Chicago)

Bibliography

Thomas, D. Winton, *The Prophet in the Lachish Ostraca*, 1946 (Tyndale Press, London)
Torczyner, H., *The Lachish Letters*, 1938 (in *Lachish* I, ed. H. Torczyner, London)
Wiseman, D. J., *Chronicles of the Chaldean Kings*, 1956 (British Museum, London)

Chapter IX: DAYS OF EXILE

Conteneau, G., *Everyday Life in Babylon and Assyria*, 1954 (Arnold, London)
Dougherty, R. P., *Nabonidus and Belshazzar*, 1929 (Yale University Press, New Haven)
Howie, C. C., *The Date and Composition of Ezekiel*, 1950 (*Journal of Biblical Literature* Monograph Series IV)
Janssen, E., *Juda in der Exilzeit*, 1956 (Vandenhoeck und Ruprecht, Göttingen)
Koldewey, R., *The Excavations at Babylon*, 1914 (Macmillan, London)
Lane, W. H., *Babylonian Problems*, 1923 (John Murray, London)
Parrot, A., *Niniveh and Babylon*, 1961 (Thames & Hudson, London)
Wiseman, D. J., *Chronciles of the Chaldean Kings*, 1956 (British Museum, London)

Chapter X: THE RETURN OF THE JEWS FROM EXILE

de Vaux, R., *Les décrets de Cyrus et de Darius sur la reconstruction du Temple*, 1937 (*Revue Biblique*, Paris)
Olmstead, A. T., *The History of the Persian Empire*, 1948 (Chicago University Press, Chicago)
Whitcomb, J. C., *Darius the Mede*, 1959 (Eerdmans, Grand Rapids)

Chapter XI: THE PERSIAN PERIOD IN PALESTINE FROM 500 B.C. TO 330 B.C.

Banks, F. A., *Coins of Bible Days*, 1955 (New York)
Ghirshman, R., *Iran*, 1954 (Penguin, London)
Olmstead, A. T., *The History of the Persian Empire*, 1948 (Chicago University Press, Chicago)
Simons, J., *Jerusalem in the Old Testament*, 1952, (Brill, Leiden)
Wright, J. Stafford, *The Building of the Second Temple*, 1958 (Tyndale Press, London)
————, *The Date of Ezra's Coming to Jerusalem*, 1958, 2nd ed. (Tyndale Press, London)

Chapter XII: THE JEWS OUTSIDE PALESTINE IN THE FIFTH CENTURY B.C.

Cowley, A., *Aramaic Papyri of the Fifth Century B.C.*, 1923 (Oxford University Press, London)
Driver, G. R., *Aramaic Documents of the Fifth Century B.C.*, 1957 (Oxford University Press, London)
Dupont-Sommer, A., *Les Araméens*, 1949 (Maisonneuve, Paris)
Kraeling, E. G., *The Brooklyn Aramaic Papyri*, 1953 (Yale University Press, New Haven)

Bibliography

Chapter XIII: THE COMING OF THE GREEKS

Bevan, E. R., *Jerusalem Under the High Priests*, 1904 (Arnold, London)
Farmer, W. R., *Maccabees, Zealots and Josephus*, 1956 (Columbia University Press, New York)
Pfeiffer, C. F., *Between the Testaments*, 1959 (Baker, Grand Rapids)
Russell, D. S., *Between the Testaments*, 1960 (John Knox, Richmond)

Chapter XIV: THE RELIGIOUS COMMUNITY OF QUMRAN

Allegro, J. M., *The Dead Sea Scrolls*, 1957 (Pelican, London)
Black, M., *The Scrolls and Christian Origins*, 1961 (Nelson, London)
Bruce, F. F., *Second Thoughts on the Dead Sea Scrolls*, 1956 (Eerdmans, Grand Rapids)
Burrows, M., *The Dead Sea Scrolls of St. Mark's Monastery*, Vol. I, 1950 (American Schools of Oriental Research, New Haven)
———, *The Dead Sea Scrolls*, 1956 (Secker & Warburg, London)
———, *More Light on the Dead Sea Scrolls*, 1958 (Secker & Warburg, London)
Cross, F. M., *The Ancient Library of Qumran and Modern Biblical Studies*, 1958 (Duckworth, London)
de Vaux, R., *Archaeology and the Dead Sea Scrolls*, 1961 (Oxford University Press, London)
Dupont-Sommer, A., *The Essene Writings from Qumran*, 1961, transl. G. Vermes (Blackwell, Oxford)
Fritsch, C. T., *The Qumran Community*, 1956 (Macmillan, New York)
Gaster, T. H., *The Scriptures of the Dead Sea Sect*, 1956 (Doubleday, New York)
Greystone, G., *The Dead Sea Scrolls and the Originality of Christ*, 1955
La Sor, W. S., *Amazing Dead Sea Scrolls and the Christian Faith*, 1956 (Moody Press, Chicago)
Milik, J. T., *Ten Years of Discovery in the Wilderness of Judaea*, 1959 (SCM London)
Stendahl, K. (ed.), *The Scrolls and the New Testament*, 1958 (SCM, London)
Sutcliffe, E. F., *The Monks of Qumran*, 1960 (Burns & Oates, London)
Van der Ploeg, J., *The Excavations at Qumran*, 1958 (Longmans, London)
Yadin, Y., *The Message of the Scrolls*, 1957 (London)

Chapter XV: THE DAYS OF HEROD THE GREAT

Jones, A. H. M., *The Herods of Judaea*, 1938 (Oxford University Press, London)
Perowne, S., *The Life and Times of Herod the Great*, 1956 (Hodder & Stoughton, London)

Chapter XVI: HISTORY OF NEW TESTAMENT TIMES

Barret, C. K., *The New Testament Background: Selected Documents*, 1957 (SPCK, London)
Blaiklock, E. M., *Rome in the New Testament*, 1959 (IVF, London)
———, *The Christian in Pagan Society*, 1956 (IVF, London)

Bibliography

Bouquet, A. C., *Everyday Life in New Testament Times*, 1953 (Batsford, London)
Jones, A. H. M., *The Herods of Judaea*, 1938 (Oxford University Press, London)
Josephus, Flavius, *Antiquities of the Jews* (Loeb Classical Library, transl. H. St. J. Thackeray and R. Marcus)
―――, *The Jewish Wars* (Pelican, London, transl. G. A. Williamson
Judge, E. A., *The Social Pattern of the Christian Groups in the First Century*, 1958 (Tyndale Press, London)
Perowne, S., *The Later Herods, the Political Background of the New Testament*, 1958 (Hodder & Stoughton, London)
Ridderbos, H. N., *When the Time Had Fully Come*, 1957 (Eerdmans, Grand Rapids)

Chapter XVII: ARCHAEOLOGY AND THE ROMAN OCCUPATION OF PALESTINE

Albright, W. F., *The Archaeology of Palestine*, 1960 (Pelican, London), pp. 146-176, 238-249
Banks, F. A., *Coins of Bible Days*, 1955 (New York)
Blaiklock, E. M., *Out of the Earth*, rev. ed., 1961 (Eerdmans, Grand Rapids)
Bouquet, A. C., *Everyday Life in New Testament Times*, 1953 (Batsford, London)
Bruce, F. F., *The New Testament Documents: Are They Reliable?* 5th ed., 1960 (Eerdmans, Grand Rapids)
Cobern, C. M., *The New Archaeological Discoveries and Their Bearing on the New Testament*, 1922 (Funk & Wagnalls, London)
Dalman, G. H., *Sacred Sites and Ways*, 1935 (SPCK, London)
Parrot, A., *Golgotha and the Church of the Holy Sepulchre*, E. T. 1957 (SCM, London)
Unger, M. F., *Archaeology and the New Testament*, 1962 (Zondervan, Grand Rapids)

Chapter XVIII: THE JERUSALEM THAT JESUS KNEW

Dalman, G. H., *Sacred Sites and Ways*, 1935 (SPCK, London)
Levertoff, B. A., *Jerusalem in the Time of Christ* (SPCK, London)
Parrot, A., *The Temple of Jerusalem*, E. T. 1957 (SCM, London)
―――, *Golgotha and the Church of the Holy Sepulchre*, E. T. 1957 (SCM, London)

Chapter XIX: FIRST-CENTURY TOWNS IN PALESTINE AND SYRIA

Caiger, S. L., *Archaeology and the New Testament*, 1948 (Cassell, London)
Cobern, C. M., *The New Archaeological Discoveries and Their Bearing Upon the New Testament*, 9th ed., 1929 (Funk & Wagnalls, New York)
Hamilton, R. W., *A Guide to Bethlehem*, 1939 (Jerusalem)

Chapter XX: LUKE THE HISTORIAN

Bruce, F. F., *The New Testament Documents: Are They Reliable?* 5th ed. 1960 (Eerdmans, Grand Rapids)
―――, *The Book of Acts*, 1952 (Eerdmans, Grand Rapids)

Metzger, H., *St. Paul's Journeys in the Greek Orient,* 1956 (SCM, London)

Ramsay, W. M., *The Bearing of Recent Discovery on the Trustworthiness of the New Testament,* 1914 (Hodder & Stoughton, London)

————, *The Cities of St. Paul,* reprint 1960 (Baker, Grand Rapids)

————, *St. Paul the Traveller and the Roman Citizen,* reprint 1960 (Baker, Grand Rapids)

————, *Was Christ Born in Bethlehem?,* 1898 (Hodder & Stoughton, London)

Robertson, A. T., *Luke the Historian in the Light of Research,* 1920 (T. & T. Clark, Edinburgh)

Chapter XXI: ARCHAEOLOGY, JOHN'S GOSPEL, AND THE BOOK OF REVELATION

Albright, W. F., "Recent Discoveries in Palestine and the Gospel of St. John," in *The Background of the New Testament and Its Eschatology,* 1956, (Cambridge University Press, Cambridge)

Barclay, W., *Letters to the Seven Churches,* 1957 (Westminster, Philadelphia)

Cadoux, C. J., *Ancient Smyrna,* 1938 (Blackwell, Oxford)

Gold, V. R., "The Gnostic Literature of Chenoboskion," *BA,* Dec., 1952

Morris, L. L., *The Dead Sea Scrolls and St. John's Gospel,* 1960 (Westminster Chapel Bookroom, London)

Ramsay, W. M., *Letters to the Seven Churches,* 1908 (Hodder & Stoughton, London)

Roberts, C. H., *An Unpublished Fragment of the Fourth Gospel,* 1935 (Manchester)

Chapter XXII: THE NEW TESTAMENT AND THE PAPYRI

Deissmann, G. A., *Light from the Ancient East,* 3rd, ed., 1927 (Hodder & Stoughton, London)

————, *The New Testament in the Light of Modern Research,* 1929 (Hodder & Stoughton, London)

Finegan, J., *Light from the Ancient East,* 1946, 2nd ed. (Princeton University Press, Princeton)

Kenyon, F., *Our Bible and the Ancient Manuscripts,* 1958 (Harper, New York)

Milligan G., *Here and There Among the Papyri,* 1923, (Hodder & Stoughton, London)

————, *The New Testament Documents, Their Origin and Early History,* 1913 Macmillan, New York)

Moulton, J. H., and Milligan, G., *The Vocabulary of the Greek New Testament* (Eerdmans, Grand Rapids)

INDEX OF SUBJECTS, PERSONS, AND PLACES

Subjects, Persons, and Places

INDEX OF AUTHORS

461

Authors

Goodenough, E. R., 410
Gordon, C. H., 34, 98, 170
Grenfell, B. P., 422, 437
Greystone, G., 268
Gurney, O. R., 20, 119
Gustafsson, B., 321
Guy, P. L. O., 103

Hall, H. R., 165
Hallo, W. L., 110, 131
Hamburger, H., 362
Hamilton, R. W., 364
Hanfman, G. M. A., 419
Hayes, W. C., 45
Heidel, A., 14
Heinrich, E., 177
Herodotus, 160, 184, 189, 194f., 215
Hogarth, D. G., 422
Howie, C. C., 163
Hunter, A. M., 397

Iliffe, J. H., 315

Johns, C. N., 278, 333
Josephus, 124, 199, 227, 233, 241, 266,
    282, 293f., 298, 326, 328, 334f., 336f.,
    346f., 360, 377ff., 389, 402

Kadman, L., 247, 314
Keller, W., 46
Kelso, J. L., 324
Kenyon, F., 423
Kenyon, K., 9, 60f., 200
Kindler, A., 247, 304, 311
King, L. W., 118
Kitchen, K. A., 45
Kohl, 356
Koldewey, R., 9, 149, 157, 160
Kraeling, E. G., 171, 186f., 199, 211,
    218, 221f., 226, 341, 346, 348, 353f.,
    356, 358, 360, 364, 366
Kraemer, H., 14

Lamon, R. S., 102f.
Lane, W. H., 160
Layard, H., 9, 128
Lightfoot, R. H., 426

Macalister, R. A. S., 244
Maclean, A. J., 376
Maisler, B., 187
Malamat, A., 88, 147
Mallowan, M. E. L., 127

Mayani, M. Z., 50
Mazar, B., 118
McCowan, C. C., 205, 235, 241, 425
McDonald, W. A., 385f., 390, 392f., 397
Meander, 124
Meek, T. J., 14
Milik, J. T., 256
Milligan, G., 426f., 429, 432f., 434, 436
Montet, P., 58
Morris, L. L., 437
Morton, W. H., 233
Moulton, J. H., 426f., 433f.
Mowry, L., 364

North, R., 265
Noth, M., 70

Oesterley, W. O. E., 174
Oliphant, L., 282
Olmstead, A. T., 184, 189, 192, 194,
    201, 215f.

Parrot, A., 314f., 320f., 335f., 348
Parvis, M., 400, 402
Paton, L. B., 195
Pausanias, 389f.
Perowne, S., 273, 282
Peters, J. P., 236
Petrie, F., 85, 422
Phillips, W., 107
Philostratus, 390
Pliny, 265f., 424
Plummer, A., 378, 434
Pritchard, J. B., 14, 24, 30, 38, 47, 62,
    69, 72, 100, 107, 113, 123, 125, 127,
    133ff., 143, 149f., 165, 168, 175, 177,
    184, 186, 197, 218, 222, 224, 312, 342,
    424

Rabinowitz, I., 202
Ramsay, W. M., 373f., 375f., 377f., 379,
    381f., 384, 389f., 394f., 400, 413f., 418,
    420, 429
Rassam, H., 9
Reifenberg, A., 326, 361
Renov, I., 358
Roberts, C. H., 437
Robertson, A. T., 341, 373, 376f.
Robins, F. W., 323
Robinson, E., 277
Robinson, T. H., 174
Rousée, P., 341
Rowe, A., 95
Rowley, H. H., 22, 34f., 170

462

INDEX OF BIBLE REFERENCES

12:21-23 — 294
13 — 379
13:7 — 381
13:9 — 381
13:14 — 382
13:49 — 382
14:6 — 382
15:22 — 322
15:36-40 — 384
15:41 — 384
16:2 — 382, 384
16:6 — 384, 386
16:7 — 384
16:12 — 384
16:12-20 — 384
16:14 — 418
16:16 — 395
17:1-9 — 386
17:13 — 385
17:17 — 388
17:22-31 — 389
18:1-17 — 390
18:2 — 295
18:4 — 392f.
18:5 — 387, 393
18:12 — 394
18:17 — 395
18:18 — 395
18:21f. — 395
18:22f. — 395
18:28 — 396
19 — 414
19:18 — 397

19:19 — 397
19:22 — 397
19:23-41 — 398
19:24 — 398
19:24, 26 — 398
19:27 — 400
19:29 — 400
19:31 — 402
19:35 — 400
20:8 — 323
20:17-38 — 402
21:7 — 352
21:27-40 — 335
21:27-24:27 — 296
21:34 — 402
25:1-12 — 296
25:13-26:32 — 296
28:7 — 402

Romans
2:8 — 431
8:23 — 433
15:28 — 436
16:23 — 397

I Corinthians
1:4 — 431
10:25 — 395
16:19 — 431

II Corinthians
1:22 — 434
3:1 — 429

3:3 — 424
5:5 — 434
11:32 — 234, 370

Galatians
2:1f. — 379
2:10 — 379
3:24 — 433

Ephesians
1:14 — 434

Philippians
1:3 — 431
4:18 — 436

Colossians
1:3 — 431

I Thessalonians
1:2 — 431
4:1 — 434

II Thessalonians
1:3 — 431
3:11 — 436

II Timothy
4:13 — 424
4:20 — 397

Titus
1:11-15 — 437

2:4-8 — 437

Philemon
Verse 15 — 436

Hebrews
11:8 — 20

II Peter
1:19 — 323

II John
Verse 12 — 424

III John
Verse 2 — 431
Verse 13 — 424

Revelation
2:10 — 414
2:13 — 416
2:14f. — 416
2:18 — 418
2, 3 — 413
3:1-6 — 419
3:8 — 419
3:14-22 — 419
4:5 — 323
5:1 — 423
8:10 — 323
21:23 — 323

Aerial view of Jerusalem